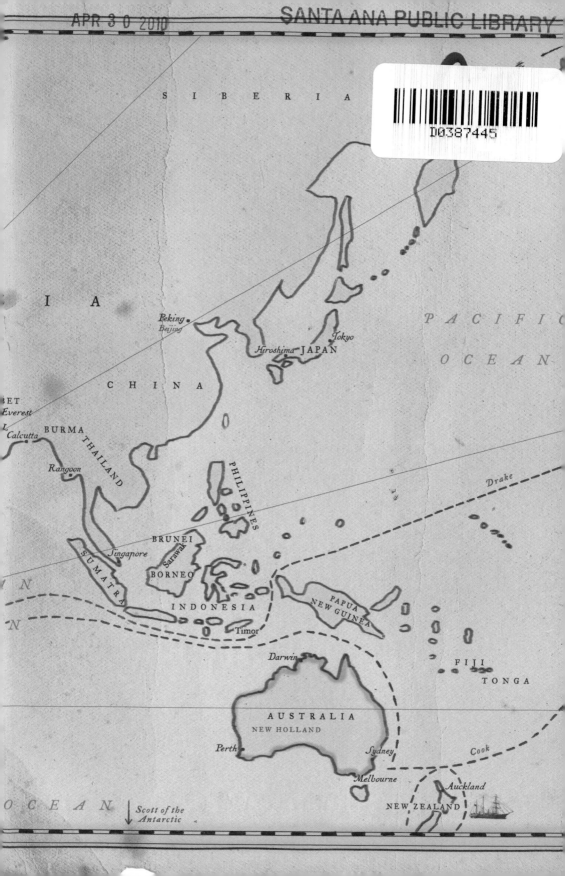

SIBERIA

PACIFIC

OCEAN

Peking
Beijing

Tokyo

Hiroshima JAPAN

I A

CHINA

BET

Everest

Calcutta

BURMA

Rangoon

THAILAND

PHILIPPINES

Drake

BRUNEI

Singapore

SUMATRA

Sarawak

BORNEO

INDONESIA

Timor

PAPUA
NEW GUINEA

FIJI

TONGA

Darwin

AUSTRALIA

NEW HOLLAND

Perth

Sydney

Cook

Melbourne

Auckland

NEW ZEALAND

OCEAN

Scott of the
Antarctic

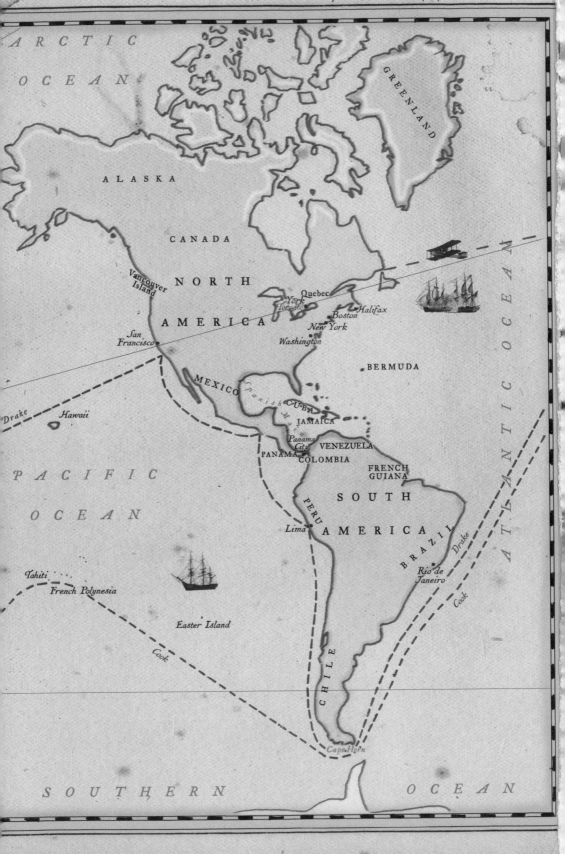

About the Authors

Born in London, **Conn Iggulden** studied English at London University and worked as a teacher for seven years before becoming a full-time writer. He is the author of the bestselling Emperor series and the Conqueror series, and is the coauthor of the *New York Times* bestseller *The Dangerous Book for Boys.* He lives with his wife and two children in Hertfordshire, England. **David Iggulden** served as a deck officer in the Merchant Navy and a private in the Army Reserves before studying journalism and English at Charles Sturt University, Australia. He has since worked as a journalist, press officer, and projects manager, and published several nonfiction books. He has been part of many international adventures, including In the Footsteps of Scott Expedition, the First Fleet Reenactment, and the 2000 Olympic Games. He lives in the Blue Mountains, Australia.

The Dangerous Book of

HEROES

Conn Iggulden & David Iggulden

WM

WILLIAM MORROW
An Imprint of HarperCollins*Publishers*

Library of Congress Cataloging-in-Publication Data

Iggulden, Conn.
  The dangerous book of heroes / Conn Iggulden and David Iggulden. — 1st US ed.
    p. cm.
  Includes bibliographical references and index.
  ISBN 978-0-06-192824-6
  1. Heroes—Biography.   2. Courage—Case studies.   3. Self-confidence—Case
studies.   4. Perseverance (Ethics)—Case studies.   I. Iggulden, David, 1949–
II. Title.
  CT105.I35 2009
  920.02—dc22

2009040140

  10   11   12   13   14   WBG/RRD   10   9   8   7   6   5   4   3   2   1

In memory of John Hall and John Hunt,
who in their different ways lived life to the full

PEOPLE WHO LOSE THEIR HISTORY, LOSE THEIR SOUL.
—AUSTRALIAN ABORIGINAL SAYING

Contents

Introduction

There is a moment in some lives when the world grows still and a decision must be made. Colonel Travis knew it when he drew a line in the dust at the Alamo. George Washington knew it when he marched against Cornwallis at Yorktown. At such moments, *there is no one to save you*. The decision is yours alone.

The heroes in this book are from a variety of centuries. Mainly, they are taken from that common history of Britain and America, as well as Australia, Canada, and New Zealand. That constriction was no hardship, as it left a gold-bearing seam of hundreds of wonderful, inspiring lives.

We have not gone too far back into history, so no Boadicea, though the Magna Carta barons are in. We've avoided the stories of monarchs, sportsmen, saints, and scientists. Once started, those would easily fill a book to the exclusion of all else. Politicians, too, have not made the cut, with the exception of men like Washington and Winston Churchill, who deserve their places for other reasons. No collection of heroes can be utterly definitive, and there will always be too little space for every great tale. Courage is perhaps the first requirement for inclusion here. Courage, determination, and some dash.

Some of the heroes in this book are more rogue than angel—and one or two are absolute devils. Yet in their brief existence they showed what can be *done* with a life, one single span of decades in the light. We have not judged them by modern standards. They would have scorned such judgment.

When you tire of humanity's flaws, perhaps you will read a few chapters and be reminded that we can also be inspiring. Fortune played its part, of course, but there was always that moment when the world fell still and the searchlights of Colditz Castle drifted silently across the yard. They did not falter then—and their lives should be known to all.

—Conn and David Iggulden

And I tell you, if you have the desire for knowledge and the power to give it physical expression, go out and explore. If you are a brave man you will do nothing: if you are fearful you may do much, for none but cowards have need to prove their bravery. Some will tell you that you are mad, and nearly all will say, "What is the use?" For we are a nation of shopkeepers, and no shopkeeper will look at research which does not promise him a financial return within a year. And so you will sledge nearly alone, but those with whom you sledge will not be shopkeepers: that is worth a good deal.

Apsley Cherry-Garrard,
The Worst Journey in the World

George Washington

George Washington was not a great soldier. He was not even a great farmer, yet he was in the right place, at the right time, several vital times. His greatness was thrust upon him, so now it appears that, of all men, George Washington alone was destined to be the founding father of the United States of America.

His family traces its roots to Northamptonshire in England and a land grant by Henry VIII. Colonel John Washington sailed to the Virginia colony in 1657 to farm. The links with Britain were maintained, however, and George's father, Augustine, was educated there. He briefly went to sea before returning to Virginia, where he farmed, built mills, was involved in iron-ore mining, acquired more land, and married twice. George was the eldest of Augustine's second wife, Mary's, six children. He was born at Popes Creek on February 22, 1732.

Three years later Augustine moved his family farther up the Potomac River to his land at Little Hunting Creek, and three years after that to Ferry Farm plantation on the Rappahannock River. It's there that red-haired George Washington was brought up, haphazardly educated at home and at the small local school. There are many tales of his childhood—the chopping of the cherry tree, throwing a silver dollar across the mile-wide Potomac—and all are myths. He was a Virginia farmer's boy with an inclination to arithmetic, measurement, and trigonometry.

His father died when George was eleven, and his eldest half-brother, Lawrence, became a surrogate father to the boy. Lawrence suggested in 1746 that George enlist in the Royal Navy as midshipman. The navy then was becoming fashionable. All Britain, the colonies, and Europe were talking about the recent four-year voyage around the world by Commodore Anson, a voyage from which he returned to

Portsmouth laden with fabulous treasure. George's aptitude for mathematics might have made him a natural navigator, but his mother vetoed that career.

A nearby British landowner, Lord Fairfax, instead offered young George an assistant's position in a survey he was financing. At sixteen years of age George trekked through the wilderness to the Shenandoah Valley, where he helped survey and plot some of Fairfax's five million acres.

His diary of the 1748 journey records the experience of sleeping under a "thread Bear blanket with double its Weight of Vermin such as Lice Fleas & c." Along the way they met a Native American war party bearing someone's scalp. George Washington's dislike of Native Americans surfaces early in his derogatory comment about central European immigrants: "As ignorant a set of people as the Indians they would never speak English but when spoken to they speak all Dutch."

Washington made an impression in the Shenandoah survey. The next year he helped plan the town of Belhaven (Alexandria) and Lord Fairfax sponsored him to become surveyor of Culpeper County. For two years he traveled and camped through Culpeper and other Virginian counties, surveying and mapping the wilderness. It was during this time that Washington's lifelong interest in western land development began. He saved money and purchased "unclaimed" Virginian land.

However, his surveying career ended abruptly in 1851 when Lawrence sailed to the colony of Barbados in a desperate attempt to treat his tuberculosis. George went with his half-brother, but it did neither any physical good. Lawrence died the following year, while George contracted smallpox, which left him with facial scars. Lawrence's daughter died within two months of her father, leaving George to inherit the Little Hunting Creek (Mount Vernon) plantation on the Potomac River.

At twenty, an established and capable surveyor, Washington instead became farmer of a tobacco plantation of two thousand acres with eighteen slaves. The boy had become a large man, six feet two inches tall, with a large nose, big hands, wide hips, and narrow shoulders. His height gave him a commanding presence, made more impressive when his red hair was powdered fashionably white. He never wore a wig.

Washington also applied for Lawrence's vacant commission in the Virginia militia, despite a complete lack of military training and experience, and was appointed major. He concentrated on farming Mount Vernon, gradually purchasing more land and attempting to increase the quality and quantity of his tobacco. In the free London market, Mount Vernon leaf was marked as mediocre.

West of the Appalachians, meanwhile, trouble was brewing. In defiance of the 1713 Peace of Utrecht, French soldiers and settlers had moved back into the Hudson Bay area in the far north and into the Ohio Valley in the west. Successive timber forts marked the French expansion south to the Forks of the Ohio (then Virginia), a strategic gateway into the Ohio Valley. In December 1754, Virginia lieutenant governor Robert Dinwiddie asked Major Washington to deliver an official letter to the French demanding that they leave the area and return north.

Washington recruited a friend of the family who spoke French, Jacob Van Braam, and with a guide and four backwoodsmen set off for Fort Le Boeuf (Beef Fort, now Waterford, Pennsylvania). With Mingo chief Tanaghrisson and three warriors, the small party arrived at the French fort in a heavy snowstorm and Washington delivered the diplomatic letter.

Dinwiddie concluded his letter: "It becomes my duty to require your peaceable departure; and that you would forbear prosecuting a purpose so interruptive of the harmony and good understanding, which his Majesty [George II] is desirous to continue and cultivate with the most Christian King [Louis XV]." Such was the courtesy of the era, when both war and diplomacy were considered two of the gentlemanly arts. The reply, rejecting any withdrawal and in fact announcing further advances, was almost as polite.

It took a month for Washington to return to Williamsburg in Virginia, a harsh, urgent journey through heavy snow and icy rivers. Dinwiddie immediately brought forward the planned construction of Fort Prince George at the Forks of the Ohio. The basic structure was almost completed by April 1755, when a large French military force arrived. The forty British volunteers and carpenters, faced by five hundred French soldiers and eighteen cannons, were threatened with death or withdrawal. They withdrew. The French destroyed the fort and built their own Fort Duquesne.

Washington was promoted lieutenant colonel, commissioned to recruit and train two hundred men and reinforce Fort Prince George. The Virginia colonists were not enthusiastic, so with only 160 men half-trained in the use of their Brown Bess muskets, Washington again crossed into the Ohio Valley in late April. Because of what happened, Dinwiddie's orders to Washington are important. He wrote: "You are to act on the Difensive, but in Case any Attempts are made to obstruct the Works or interrupt our Settlemts by any Persons whatsoever, You are to restrain all such Offenders, & in Case of resistance to make Prisoners of or kill & destroy them." Washington learned of the destruction of Fort Pitt during his march and decided to continue.

As Washington's force advanced toward the Forks of the Ohio, the French commander of Fort Duquesne sent a scouting and emissary party of thirty-five men under the command of Ensign de Jumonville. Jumonville carried an emissary summons written in French. Chief Tanaghrisson and several Mingo warriors intercepted Washington's force at Great Meadows with the news of the French party.

At dawn on May 28, Tanaghrisson, Washington, and forty-seven of his militia reached the hollow where Jumonville had camped. Washington and Tanaghrisson conferred. According to Washington, they "concluded that we should fall on them together" and surrounded the hollow. As the first light filtered through the tangled trees, the French soldiers awoke.

Who fired first is not certain. Washington's report accuses the French; several militia reports and that of a Mingo who deserted to the French agree. An escaped French soldier accused the Virginians. In two volleys from the colonials several French soldiers were killed and eleven wounded. In the exchange of fire a militiaman was killed before an injured Jumonville surrendered to Washington. Jumonville handed Washington the summons, but Washington had little success in his attempt to translate it. French-speaking Van Braam was not with him that morning.

In the smoky hollow, Chief Tanaghrisson slipped up to Jumonville. Saying in French, "Thou art not yet dead, my father," he smashed in his head with a tomahawk. He then dipped in his hands and drew out Jumonville's brains. A third of the body's blood supply is in the head; the scene must have been horrific for the un-bloodied Washington and the Virginians. The other Mingo warriors fell upon the wounded French prisoners. Eleven were murdered and scalped before Washington could bring order to the scene and protect the twenty-two surviving soldiers with his militia. One of the French soldiers was decapitated and his head impaled upon a stake.

The French claimed that the British had intentionally massacred a peaceful emissary, strictly contrary to the rules of war, but there is no possibility that Washington could have known that Jumonville was an emissary. The earlier French action against Fort Prince George had been aggressive, yet nevertheless Washington had exceeded his orders. He might easily have sent a militiaman to Jumonville bearing a white flag.

Instead began the French and Indian War of North America, which escalated into the Seven Years' War—the first true world war. Fighting spread to Europe, the Philippines, Africa, India, the Caribbean, South America, the Mediterranean, and all the seas between. Horace Walpole, MP, son of Britain's first prime minister, remarked: "The volley fired by a young Virginian in the back woods of America set the world on fire."

Washington returned to Great Meadows, where he built a circular, wooden palisade defense he named Fort Necessity. There, no doubt, he also reflected upon his first military action. He thought Fort Necessity could withstand "the attack of 500 men," but it was poorly sited, overlooked from sixty yards, enfiladed on three sides, and lay in a waterlogged creek. Following an aborted advance toward Fort Duquesne and a nightmare return, Washington's four hundred men at Necessity were surrounded by the French that July.

After a day's siege in pouring rain, where the militiamen protected themselves in overflowing trenches, Washington had lost a quarter of his troops, killed or wounded. The position was already desperate when his men broke into the rum supply; soon half were drunk. The French offered a parley at 8 P.M.

Washington accepted an offer of withdrawal rather than certain defeat and imprisonment and signed a document written in French. In it he committed Virginia to withdrawal from the Ohio Valley and to not build any more forts for a year. Further, despite Van Braam being present to translate, Washington admitted to the murder of Ensign Jumonville, although he claimed the word had been explained as "death" rather than "murder." Washington and his men were disarmed and allowed to return to eastern Virginia, where the majority deserted.

The French published the Jumonville admission in Europe, while Washington further remarked in a letter to his brother: "I heard the bullets whistle and, believe me, there is something charming in the sound."

Back in Williamsburg the twenty-two-year-old George Washington resigned his commission, then returned to Mount Vernon. To say he went home to lick his wounds may be strong, but he must surely have reflected upon his first military experiences with dismay. He'd not been able to prevent a massacre of wounded French surrendered to his care; he'd suffered humiliating defeat and desertion by his men; and he'd signed an incriminating document.

Major General Edward Braddock and two regiments of foot were sent from Britain to defeat the French in the Ohio. The initial campaign was supported by all the colonies and might have succeeded, for the colonialists had no desire for French rule. George Washington and Benjamin Franklin introduced themselves to Braddock near

Frederick Town (Maryland) in April 1755 and volunteered their services. For his local knowledge Braddock invited Washington to serve as aide-de-camp, while Franklin acted as Braddock's commissariat, ably and quickly securing wagons, draft horses, and packhorses.

Following the London plans, Braddock advanced 110 miles toward Fort Duquesne along Washington's earlier road. Only it wasn't a road, as believed in London, merely a trail. From a single-file footpath the soldiers and militiamen had to hack out a road so that the supply wagons could pass. It was slow going. Washington, who knew the track and the terrain, proposed splitting the army into two: sending the Virginian militia and half the British soldiers forward quickly and leaving the remaining half with the supply wagons to prepare the road. Braddock agreed.

By July 9, the forward half was only ten miles from Duquesne, but it was sixty miles ahead of its supplies and the rear half. Splitting an advancing army's force is always risky, and as the commanding officer, Braddock must accept that responsibility. The question remains why Washington suggested it at all. Perhaps his dislike of the Native Americans with the French made him regard them as poor fighters. Frontiersman Daniel Boone, driving one of the supply wagons, could have told him otherwise. Braddock, of course, had no experience of the special effectiveness of Native American warriors and their tactics in American terrain. He relied upon Washington for such local knowledge.

By the Monongahela River, Braddock and the forward half of the army were ambushed and routed by a combined Native American and French army. Braddock's bravery is under no question; he had five horses shot beneath him before he was mortally wounded. Washington lost two horses, while forced to ride with a pillow on his saddle because he was suffering from dysentery. The Virginian militia fled back across the river, while the British soldiers made a stand.

It was not French soldiers but the Native Americans shooting from behind trees, logs, and rocks that defeated them. "If we saw of them five or six at one time [it] was a great sight," one British soldier wryly commented. Some two-thirds of those soldiers were killed or wounded before Braddock was shot. The remainder then retreated and reassembled at the wagons.

Washington expressed no criticism of Braddock, saying, "How little does the World consider the Circumstances, and how apt are mankind to level their vindictive Censures against the unfortunate Chief, who perhaps merited least of the blame." He was perhaps criticizing the Virginians; they were the men best suited to combat the Native American style of attack. Yet they had retreated while the British soldiers stood and fought a battle for which they had not been trained. Perhaps he was also acknowledging that his proposal to split the army was wrong.

The western frontiers of the colonies were now exposed to increasing Native American attacks. The Virginia assembly restored Washington his commission and placed him in overall command of the colony's militia. He was charged with training men to defend the western frontier. With a minimal volunteer force, minimal financial support, and equally minimal supplies, he parried the enemies' incursions for the next three years. There were desertions and insubordination, which he punished by hanging and flogging, but Washington was learning the soldier's art.

The world war continued. General Wolfe's victory at Quebec, the capture of Montreal, and victories by the Royal Navy as far away as Quiberon Bay and Lagos turned the tide for eventual defeat of the French.

In the French and Indian War, the British—and especially Braddock's replacement, Brigadier General John Forbes—understood that Native American friendship and alliances were necessary for a speedy victory. More important, their friendship and alliances were vital to win the peace for the colonies afterward. One after the other, most of the Native American nations turned to support Britain. The basis of negotiation was what they'd desired at the beginning of the war— that the British would trade with them but would not invade and settle their territories west of the Appalachian Mountains.

In November, just before winter, General Forbes made a forty-mile advance to the Forks of the Ohio in a surprise campaign. On the fifteenth, using Colonel Washington's Virginians and militia from the Carolinas, Delaware, and Maryland, Forbes marched his small force west from Loyalhanna, Pennsylvania. Washington wanted to use the old trail once more, but Forbes blazed a new road, which could be used again to resupply the Ohio country. Forbes himself was actually dying and was carried by litter.

The force was ten miles from Fort Duquesne when the French abandoned and destroyed it. Forbes quickly built a new fort, Fort Pitt (Pittsburgh), garrisoned it with Pennsylvanian militia for the winter, and secured peace with the local Delaware chiefs. He was carried back to Philadelphia but died six weeks later. The other militia dispersed, their terms of service expired, while Washington resigned again with the honorary rank of brigadier general.

He returned to Mount Vernon in early 1759, dissatisfied that he had not secured a permanent commission in the British army. Whether he was qualified to become a regular soldier is one matter. The more important matter is that from his experience with the British, in particular serving under General Forbes, he had absorbed *the* vital fact about how to conduct and win a war in the terrain of North America.

He wrote at the time: "Suppose the Enemy gives us a meeting in the Field and we put them to the Rout. What do we gain by it? perhaps triple their loss of Men in the first place, tho our numbers may be greatly superior (and If I may be allowd to judge from what I have seen of late, we shall not highten much that good opinion they seem to have of our skill in woods fighting)—therefore to risk an Engagement when so much depends upon it, without having accomplishment of the main point of view, appears in my Eye, to be a little Imprudent."

In other words, winning battles in a wilderness war does not win the war if the enemy disperses, regroups, and returns to strike back elsewhere. British commanders soon forgot this tactic, for they were not required to use it again. The British army considered the North American campaign of the Seven Years' War a unique experience it would never meet again. After all, the Canadian colonies and the American colonies were British.

In January 1759, George Washington married Martha Custis, a widow he had met the year before. She brought to the marriage two children, seventeen thousand acres, twenty-three thousand pounds, and some fifty slaves. Although the war continued until eventual British victory in 1763, Washington remained at Mount Vernon to farm and manage his wife's estates. For his war services he was granted land in present-day West Virginia.

Unlike the Native Americans in the south, the nations in the north and in Canada had continued to support the French until defeat in 1763. Led by Chief Pontiac of the Ottawa and others, these nations rebelled in a further combined effort to prevent the loss of any more of their land. From this conflict comes the story that General Amherst gave blankets used by smallpox patients as gifts to Native Americans, in a deliberate attempt to infect them. However, smallpox was then endemic in North America, as it was in Europe and Britain, and the cause and transmission of the disease was not known.

In a response to Pontiac's rebellion and the southern negotiations, the Royal Proclamation of October 1763 banned further British settlement or purchase of Native American territory, effectively the land west of the Appalachian Mountains. Many colonialists were unhappy with these terms.

George Washington, meanwhile, lived the life of an English gentleman farmer, which was exactly what he was. He rode to hounds, watched cockfights, bred horses and livestock, took snuff, smoked a pipe, drank punch and Madeira wine, played billiards, and gambled at cards. He patronized the theater, concerts, and balls when in town, ordered his clothes from London, and hosted house parties, picnics, and barbecues at an extended Mount Vernon. In turn, he and Martha were invited to visit other influential Virginian plantations. He bought more and yet more land and employed thirteen house servants to look after his mansion.

To pay for it all, he exported tobacco to the free-market London tobacco exchange. His leaf, though, was still only mediocre. Like many others living an expansive lifestyle, he found himself accruing debt as tobacco prices fell in the postwar economic depression. Thomas Jefferson was another of the plantation owners who indebted themselves, from the falling value of their crop and by living beyond their means. Washington decided to diversify.

He replaced much of his tobacco with wheat and, by using and letting his own mill, smithy, kilns, and cider presses, tried to make the combined estates self-sufficient. His overseers were instructed to "buy nothing you can make yourselves." He even expanded into coastal fishing, salting the catch for sale and for food for his slaves. Despite all this, it was only the inheritance from his stepdaughter's death in 1773 that allowed him to clear his debts.

By 1775 he had doubled the size of Mount Vernon to sixty-five hundred acres and had more than a hundred slaves. Yet Washington still coveted the Native American territories west of the Appalachians, the lands he had visited and admired as a surveyor and soldier. Like many colonials he resented the 1763 proclamation, despite the 1768 and 1771 modifications in which Native American chiefs conceded settlement along the Ohio Valley from Fort Pitt to the Kentucky River.

Washington confided to a business associate: "I can never look upon that Proclamation in any other light (but I say this between ourselves) than as a temporary expedient to quiet the minds of the Indians." He was a member of both the Ohio and the Mississippi Companies investing in this territory. More land meant more wealth through crops, speculation, mortgages, and credit.

As a result of the Seven Years' War the British government had the largest national debt in its history, £146 million. It had secured North America and the Caribbean from French control, as well as a lasting peace with Native Americans. That three-year conflict had been fought from Niagara to Virginia solely by the British army, with only four of the thirteen colonies assisting in a minor way. Parliament thought that the colonies should pay a share of the cost of these wars, which, after all, had been started by the massacre at Jumonville's Glen. At the time, those in Britain liable to taxation were levied an average of eighteen pounds a year, those in the colonies, eighteen shillings a year.

Acts authorizing taxes such as the stamp tax, the quartering tax, and tea tax were introduced. Some were repealed after protest, but all led to discontent. "No taxation without representation" was the catchphrase. It's true that there was little direct representation in Parliament, but each colony had had its own legislature and elections for more than 100 years—some for more than 150 years—and conducted its own affairs.

Despite the protests and anger, it wasn't taxation that led to war. That was an argument put forward afterward by France. If that had been the cause, the Canadian colonies with their stronger French background would also have joined the thirteen colonies' move for independence. As the radical Thomas Paine explained, taxation was merely the spark that ignited the fire.

The root cause of the Revolutionary War was land. After the French had been kicked out, there was no threat at all to the American colonies. Therefore, the colonialists argued, there was no need for a British garrison. Without a British garrison, the colonialists would be free to expand westward across the Appalachians, across the 1763 proclamation border, into Native American territory.

Western expansion had never been a goal of the British government—it had enough empire elsewhere—but it had become of major importance to the colonial governments. During the 175 years of British settlement the concept had entered the psyche of the thirteen colonies. It remained so for a further hundred years, until all the western American nations had been conquered.

If the British parliament would not support or allow the colonies' expansion, the colonies would go it alone. In fact, their militias could handle resistance by Native American warriors better than the British regulars. And triggered by the Age of Enlightenment, English-speaking peoples everywhere were demanding more independence.

George Washington and Ben Franklin were pro-British, against independence, and hoped that war with Britain—civil war—would not happen. Yet if it did, both saw their allegiance being to the colonies and acted accordingly. Franklin, in fact, had earlier proposed a federated government of the mainland American colonies, responsible for local defense, frontiers, and Indian affairs, under British rule. Parliament had not been hostile to the idea, but none of the colonial governments had shown any interest whatsoever and it had lapsed. So, as in most wars, step by small step the factions differed, separated, and became opposed to the point of confrontation.

In December 1773, consignments of East India Company tea were thrown overboard from ships in Boston Harbor; in 1774 Britain temporarily closed the port. A meeting of the colonies was called, the First Continental Congress, and trade sanctions were imposed against British goods. On April 19, 1775, Massachusetts minutemen made a surprise attack on small British garrisons at Lexington and Concord. Rebellion was spoken of openly.

At the Second Continental Congress held that May, Washington was elected, although not unanimously, to command the combined militia of the colonies. He was reluctant, had himself recommended General Lewis for the command, and said: "I beg it may be remembered that I . . . do not think myself equal to the command I am honored with." Yet he was seen as the man, perhaps the only man, who could unite the patriots throughout the thirteen colonies. He took command of the forces outside Boston and, that June, defeated Britain at the battle of Bunker Hill.

It was an extraordinarily dangerous appointment for Washington to accept. Looking back, with the outcome known, we see it as just another step in history. Yet at the time, like Oliver Cromwell 136 years earlier, Washington made a decision that was literally traitorous. He was leading an armed insurrection against the democratically elected parliament and its king; there would be a rope around his neck if he was captured. Further, the elected legislatures of the thirteen colonies were divided about a rebellion; there was no consensus. About half the colonialists were ambivalently neutral, with the remainder equally split between Loyalists and patriots. Even Parliament was divided, as were families in both America and Britain. So began the American Revolutionary War.

Elsewhere, it's more accurately called the American War of Independence, for this was no revolution. It was a straight fight for independence from a controlling power. The eventual federal government, with its two houses of Congress and an elected president, was very similar to the British constitutional government, with its two houses of Parliament and elected prime minister. In January 1776, Thomas Paine published his influential propaganda pamphlet *Common Sense*. A phenomenal 120,000 copies were distributed throughout the colonies and Britain.

In Charlestown, meanwhile, General Howe's winter quarters were an indefensible position. As soon as Washington placed cannon on Dorchester Heights in March, Howe was forced to leave by sea. Washington then hurried overland to invade and fortify New York, while in July the colonies made the Declaration of Independence at Philadelphia. In August, Howe's army arrived at New York by sea and, in a succession of clever land and sea maneuvers, defeated Washington's army. Howe pursued it south through New Jersey. By winter, he had forced Washington across the Delaware River into Pennsylvania. Nearly ten thousand patriots were wounded, killed, or captured, while many more men deserted.

It was then that Washington recalled the lessons learned in the earlier French and Indian War. His patriot army could never meet and ultimately defeat British armies on a traditional battlefield. Instead, it had to fight as the British and the militia had fought against the French: a small victory here, a small victory there, even a small defeat, then withdrawal to regroup and attack again elsewhere. In that way, he would wear down Britain's resolve, politically and militarily. This is exactly what Washington ordered for most of the next six years, beginning that Christmas night.

Conducting a standard war, Howe had gone into winter quarters, leaving two outposts near the Delaware at Trenton and Burlington. Washington and his men crossed the icy river in darkness and attacked the mercenary Hessian regiment at Trenton, forcing its surrender. In response, General Cornwallis quickly advanced to trap Washington at Trenton and retake the post. The wind shifted into the north, the impassable bog roads around Trenton froze, and Washington was able to escape by night. He marched around to attack the Princeton garrison, putting the British detachment there to flight before withdrawing again, to New Jersey.

He had found the way to win the war. He wrote to Congress: "We should on all Occasions avoid a general Action, or put anything to the Risque, unless compelled by a necessity, into which we ought never to be drawn." Not everyone agreed and Washington was persuaded at times to return to more traditional tactics.

A patriot army invaded Canada in late 1776 in an attempt to destabilize the loyal colonies. It was defeated by General Carleton near Quebec on the last day of the year. Although outnumbered, General Burgoyne advanced south into New York Colony in 1777, hoping to take the patriots by surprise. However, he lost minor actions at Freeman's Farm and Bemis Heights, to surrender to General Gates at the battle of Saratoga. Farther south in Pennsylvania, Washington was defeated later that year by Howe at Brandywine Creek and Germantown, with the subsequent loss of Philadelphia.

Behind the scenes, Washington's command was also threatened. A congressional plot to dismiss him, led by an Irish adventurer named Conway, was defeated. At his Valley Forge winter quarters in Pennsylvania, Washington lost a *quarter* of his ten thousand men to disease and starvation. A doctor recorded in his diary: "Poor food, hard lodging, cold weather, fatigue, nasty clothes, nasty cookery, vomit half my time, smoked out of my senses, the devil's in it, I can't endure it."

Benjamin Franklin, meanwhile, had lobbied France to enter this civil war in support of the patriots. That a decadent monarchy should send arms, ammunition, soldiers, and ships to support a republican rebellion, while viciously suppressing its own republicans and liberty at home, has its own irony. Such was France's enmity toward Britain. A French rear admiral who fought with the loyalists was guillotined in Paris during the later Reign of Terror.

General Sir Henry Clinton replaced Howe and changed Britain's strategy. He saw that holding patriot centers such as Philadelphia was not effective; Congress simply left to reassemble elsewhere. Somehow General Washington's forces had to be defeated in the field. So Clinton left Philadelphia, made a single British stronghold of New York, and sent General Cornwallis to recapture the southern colonies lost by an earlier tactic. Although slavery had been constitutionally illegal in Great Britain since the 1580s, it was not in its colonies. So when Governor Murray had offered freedom to any slave—black or white—who fought for Britain, he had pushed the lukewarm southern Loyalists into the patriot camp.

Yet Clinton's new tactics were really an admission of defeat. For as long as Washington refused any pitched battle, it was a war Britain couldn't win. A patriot army merely had to exist, somewhere, for ultimate victory. Supported by a French army in 1780, Washington had positioned himself at Brunswick so that Clinton's army could not move from New York without his knowledge or hindrance.

Cornwallis, meanwhile, campaigned through Georgia and North and South Carolina, winning engagements at Savannah, Charleston, and Camden before entering Virginia in 1781. Yet he had no more control over those colonies than he had had two years before; the patriot forces had simply withdrawn to reappear elsewhere. By then, the passions of the war had increased. The Loyalist colonials were desperate in their desire to engage the patriots in the open, while the patriot colonials were vindictive in their raids on Loyalist settlements. For every Loyalist Guilford Courthouse bloodletting there was a vicious patriot Kings Mountain.

In addition—for Britain but not the patriots—this 1755–83 American war had also spread overseas. Britain found itself fighting, sometimes separately and sometimes together, the Dutch, French, and

Spanish, and an armed neutrality of Russia, Denmark, and Sweden. As far afield as the North Atlantic, the Caribbean, India, and the Mediterranean, British territories were attacked as its European enemies attempted to take advantage of the American rebellion. Included in this conflict was a four-year siege of Gibraltar, from 1779 to 1783.

It's no wonder the British resolve to fight other Britons, never strong, had wavered significantly. By the beginning of 1781, the American war was incredibly unpopular in Britain. Washington had hung on to his ragged and underpaid army in an uneasy alliance with the French. He believed that just one significant victory or British surrender would win him the war—not in the field but in Parliament itself.

Most Native American nations had remained Loyalist, although there was no specific coordination with the British army. Constant colonial breaches of the 1763 proclamation and various colonial attacks and massacres had made them firmly opposed to the patriots. The worst of the massacres was by the Paxton Boys in, of all colonies, Pennsylvania. Irish-Scots frontiersmen from Paxton had murdered twenty Christian Native Americans at Conestoga village. They then broke into Lancaster jail, butchered 14 in protective custody, threatened 140 more sheltering on Province Island, and finally marched on Philadelphia to murder the "Indian-lover" Quakers. Ben Franklin negotiated their dispersal, but none was prosecuted.

The Delaware nation was one of the few to sign a treaty of military support with Washington. At Fort Pitt in 1778 the Delaware were given the right to send representatives to Congress, although Congress never honored the terms. In retaliation to Iroquois attacks against the patriots, however, Washington ordered that they be not "merely overrun but destroyed." In late 1779, General Sullivan carried out a scorched-earth policy in present-day Upstate New York. His men cut down crops and orchards, destroyed more than forty towns, and burned five hundred dwellings and a million bushels of corn. Colonel Brodhead murdered many women and children. As a result the Iroquois called Washington *conotocarius*— "town destroyer"—still their name for the president today.

In Virginia in 1781, faced by two armies trained by Prussian general Baron von Steuben, Cornwallis withdrew his seven thousand men to the deepwater port of Yorktown. He expected supplies and support by sea from General Clinton in New York, and hoped then to draw the patriot forces into battle. On the peninsula before the city, the Chesapeake Bay on two sides preventing escape, he would defeat them in a traditional battle.

With the main Royal Navy fleet in New York and other vessels farther north, there was only one frigate, one sloop, and some transports stationed at Yorktown. French admiral Comte Grasse therefore risked sailing north in support. Washington saw a chance and marched his army south from Brunswick, not to do battle with Cornwallis but to besiege him. Steuben and Lafayette blocked the neck of the peninsula with local militia while Grasse ferried Washington's army across Chesapeake Bay. With his twenty-four ships of the line he then blockaded the bay, where he was joined by a second French squadron and more French soldiers. At that crucial moment in history, the Royal Navy had temporarily lost control of Chesapeake Bay, while the main British army remained in New York.

Cornwallis was in dire trouble. Even then, with prompt action that September, he could have attacked and defeated Lafayette's six thousand French soldiers and then advanced out of the peninsula, but he hesitated. In New York, Clinton believed Washington's march south was a feint in order to take New York, and he also delayed. It was poor leadership.

Isolated, fever-stricken, running out of food, and by then vastly outnumbered, Cornwallis surrendered his small army to George Washington on October 19, 1781. That same day, Clinton finally ordered the main army and navy to move south to support Cornwallis. It was too late. There were further skirmishes in 1782, but the war was effectively over that spring when the British government withdrew its support and funding for the war. As Washington had told Congress, he would win the war not on the battlefield but in Parliament. There never was any fundamental British interest in fighting the war; there was not even a coordinated military strategy.

The French army, the force against which the British army might have fought a regular battle, was never once engaged.

In France, meanwhile, plans had been hatched by the French and Spanish monarchies—yet again—to invade democratic Britain. Two French divisions totaling forty thousand soldiers and sixty-six French and Spanish ships had gathered to cross the English Channel, with possible American support negotiated by Benjamin Franklin. Opposing them were thirty-eight vessels of the Royal Navy's Channel Fleet. It would have been a close battle, but poor weather and sickness delayed the invasion attempt. By then, the navy had returned from North America and the opportunity had gone.

Separate peace with Britain was signed on November 30, 1782. The international treaty—recognizing the independent nation of the United States of America, the boundaries of the thirteen states, British Canada, and access to the Grand Banks fishing grounds—was completed in September 1783.

Many of the former slaves who'd fought for Britain fled to the Canadian colonies of Nova Scotia and Newfoundland and to Britain. Eleven hundred of these black Nova Scotians later helped establish Freetown in Sierra Leone. Those who couldn't escape the new United States were returned to slavery.

The majority of Loyalists were dispossessed of their property. Some of the eighty thousand who left the United States found various positions and opportunities in Britain or in other British colonies, particularly Canada. One such Loyalist was James Matra of New York. He had sailed as midshipman with Captain James Cook in his first great voyage of discovery. After American independence, he became an enthusiastic supporter of the eventual British settlement of Australia in 1788. A suburb of Sydney, Australia, is named for him.

Another was Ben Franklin's son William, the last governor of New Jersey Colony. He remained steadfastly loyal to Britain, and his father cut him from his will and his life. William, too, left the United States. Civil wars are the bitterest of all.

During the long war, Washington had managed to keep the fragile colonial alliances together and maintain the Continental army in the field. In March 1783 there was mutiny. Claims for large arrears of pay—supported by Washington—and arguments about the future leadership of the federated thirteen states led to the Newburgh mutiny. Some wanted Washington to be crowned king. During his rejection speech, Washington stopped to put on spectacles. He glanced at the assembled officers and said: "Gentlemen, I have grown gray in your service, and now I am going blind." It was the end of the mutiny. The Continental army was disbanded in November, leaving a small standing force of artillery, while the last British forces left New York in December. Washington resigned his commission at Annapolis and returned to Mount Vernon.

Except for the one brief visit it was the first time he'd been home since 1775. He'd taken this step before, of course, after his first unsuccessful military endeavors and after his successful defense of Virginia Colony. At fifty-one years of age, he was tired, but it was also a canny political move. There were the usual complaints, jealousies, rivalries, retributions, and vendettas that follow every civil war. There was a postwar economic depression, and the new federation of states was bankrupt, with no way to collect revenue to pay its debts. The loose union created by Franklin's Articles of Confederation gradually began to break apart.

At Mount Vernon, Washington was well out of such petty politics. He was also in debt again. For three years he reorganized Mount Vernon and its crops. He made only the one trip away, to view his western lands and the new land near the Ohio River given him by Congress for his services.

By 1787, however, the states had decided an actual constitution was necessary to replace the defunct federation. The Virginia assembly unanimously elected Washington to lead its delegation, and at Philadelphia he was unanimously elected by the delegates to chair the Constitutional Convention itself. It lasted four months. The resulting constitution leaned heavily upon the Magna Carta of 1215, Britain's Declaration of Rights of 1689, and John Locke's *Two Treatises on Government* of 1690.

Washington actually made few contributions in the debating chamber, reputedly breaking silence only once. Yet by the time the Constitution was ratified by each state assembly in 1788, he had become the automatic choice for first president. Of his popularity, he said: "I feel very much like a man who is condemned to death does, when the time of his execution draws near."

Ratification itself was not easy: in Washington's state of Virginia it passed by just ten votes. It's argued that the seeds for the next civil war of 1861 were actually sown in the Constitution, in its contradictions between ideals and application. Despite every person being a "freeman," slavery was accepted, although the words *slave* and *slavery* were carefully not used. Further, although no slave had a vote, each slave counted as three-fifths toward another vote for their freeman "owner."

It was Washington who summed up the realities facing the states. He wrote that the Constitution "or dis-union, is before us to chuse from." Without its unifying force, the thirteen states would have parted company and France, for one, would have stepped in and snapped up some of them. As it is, there was a threatened French invasion in 1798.

Although there were other choices for the first president, including John Adams and Thomas Jefferson, once again it seemed inevitable that Washington would be chosen. In the first presidential election—by an electoral college, not the people—Washington received every primary vote. He took office on April 30, 1789, his wife joining him in New York.

That first presidency concentrated on internal affairs. Washington was determined to bind the states together, to create a stable mechanism of government and establish future presidential and congressional practices. He set the precedents for the presidency and government that exist today. Washington also visited every state, traveling in a white coach-and-four, with footmen in attendance and his stallion trotting behind.

During the first presidency there were no political parties at all, only men with different opinions. Of no political faction himself, Washington attempted to keep it that way. He selected a balanced, nonpartisan cabinet: Alexander Hamilton was appointed secretary of the treasury, Thomas Jefferson secretary of state, Henry Knox secretary of war, and Edmund Randolph attorney general.

Hamilton, a pragmatist from the West Indian colonies, introduced several controversial monetary policies. In particular, the federal assumption of state debts, the creation of the Bank of the United States, and, ironically, excise taxes, the spark that had set off the revolution. There were demonstrations and riots against the new taxes, too, and Washington was forced to call on the state militias to calm parts of the country. Hamilton and Jefferson were often in opposition, with the president smoothing the crises.

Washington's second presidential term was dominated by foreign affairs. Despite his publicly stated intention to retire to Mount Vernon, he was unanimously reelected in 1792.

The bloody excesses of the French Revolution, begun in 1789, had horrified Washington. Only days after his second inauguration, without provocation, revolutionary France had declared war on Britain and a host of European countries. The treaty made between monarchist France and America during the Revolutionary War still existed, but Washington had no intention of aligning the United States with this new France and its horrors. The Federalist Hamilton supported the president, but Jefferson was strongly pro-France—or rather, anti-British—and his democrats wanted the United States to support France militarily.

Meanwhile, the French revolutionary ambassador, Edmond Genet, traveled the country to establish French fund-raising societies. He whipped up support for the United States to declare war on Britain, recruited American volunteers to fight for France, and issued French letters of marque for armed American ships to attack other countries' cargo vessels. He received no support from the neutral George Washington and so threatened to "appeal from the president to the people." This amounted to foreign interference in American domestic politics.

When Genet overruled the president's order that a French-financed private warship remain in Philadelphia, Washington demanded his recall. In reality, the president kicked the French ambassador out of America. Suddenly, Genet changed his tune and begged to be allowed to stay. Yet another revolutionary mob had assumed power in France, and Genet himself was now in danger of the guillotine. He sought, and was given, the first political asylum in the United States.

Washington wrote: "I want an *American* character, that the powers of Europe may be convinced that we act for *ourselves,* and not for others." He adopted a policy of strict neutrality in regard to the new French wars, alienating Jefferson in the process. Jefferson resigned at the end of 1793 and formed the Democratic-Republican Party.

The first invasion and war with Native American nations also began in Washington's second presidency. The 1785 and 1786 treaties forced on the northwest Native Americans by the federation of states had caused huge resentment; three thousand people died in the subsequent fighting. After a major U.S. defeat in present-day Ohio, the decisive 1794 battle at Fallen Timbers (near Toledo) imposed temporary peace along the border.

In order to promote trade, finalize borders, and conclude various outstanding matters, the president sent Chief Justice John Jay to Britain to negotiate a treaty of commerce. It was the first major U.S. international trade negotiation. The Jay Treaty was signed in 1794 but provoked bitter criticism from pro-French congressmen. Washington was accused of negotiating an abject surrender, and Congress demanded the details. In fact, the treaty was a major success.

Through the Jay Treaty, Britain withdrew its trading posts from the Ohio country, the U.S.-British northern borders were confirmed mostly in U.S. favor, prewar debts were written off, trade was established between the United States and British West Indian colonies, the United States was given a "most favored nation" status in British trade, and the exports of both countries increased. What Britain would not agree to was a demand for compensation for freeing the slaves of its former colonies, withdrawing the right to impose a military trade embargo against its enemies (at that time France, in two later world wars Germany), and stopping impressment of seamen into the Royal Navy.

Britain was leading a twenty-two-year world war against militarist France and refused to have its hands tied in such a way. By 1796, it was the French who harassed U.S. ships and threatened sanctions. Eventually gunfire was exchanged, and in 1798 there was almost war. As a result, Washington realized that the United States needed her own warships and commissioned the first. One of them, USS *Constitution,* was built from captured British frigate plans.

Following the success of the Jay Treaty, Washington sent his ambassadors to Spain to negotiate another treaty. The Treaty of San Lorenzo gained U.S. access to Spanish Mississippi and to the Spanish port of New Orleans. Yet the political maneuverings of Congress, the virulent attacks by Jefferson's supporters, and the public criticism of the excise tax had exhausted Washington. His sight and hearing had deteriorated further, and he refused to run for a third presidential term.

The farewell address he gave on September 19, 1796, is reread every year in the Senate. In three specifics Washington spoke against "the baneful effects of the Spirit of [political] Party," endorsed a foreign policy of independence but not isolation, and proposed that "the very idea of the power and the right of the people to establish government pre-supposes the duty of every individual to obey the established government."

Once more, George Washington returned to Mount Vernon and

farming. Apart from a brief period in 1798, when he was commissioned commander in chief of a new army raised to resist the potential French invasion, he remained at home until his death.

In the winter of 1799, he came down with a fever and throat infection after riding. He died on the evening of December 14, in some pain. He said, "I die hard but I am not afraid to go." He is buried at Mount Vernon.

George Washington was born to an era of great and visionary men—Cook, Franklin, Burke, Nelson, Wilberforce, Jefferson, Wellington—but he stands with them equally. When the news of his death reached Britain, his former protagonist, the Royal Navy, fired a salute to him of twenty guns—just one less than for the monarch.

At the time of his death, Americans considered George Washington cold and indomitable, a steadfast man of war rather than of peace. Yet the modern republic he helped found, in those first precarious and unstable years of peace, has lasted longer than any other republic in the world. The shadow of his spirit crosses the centuries to the present day.

In the 1920s, Calvin Coolidge once swung around in his chair and looked through the windows of the Oval Office at the Washington Monument. "He's still there," that president commented. So he is, another hundred years later.

Recommended
Patriarch: George Washington and the New American Nation by Richard Smith
Crucible of War: The Seven Years' War and the Fate of Empire in British North America, 1754-1766 by Fred Anderson
The Life of George Washington by Jared Sparks et al.
USS *Constitution*, Naval Shipyard, Boston, Massachusetts
Mount Vernon Estate, Virginia
Sulgrave Manor, Sulgrave, Northamptonshire, U.K.

Sir Ranulph Fiennes

Through obsession, daring and sheer talent, the men and women in this book often achieved extraordinary things. They saved India, escaped from Colditz, climbed Everest, and even defeated Napoléon. There is a reason for including such lives that goes beyond a collection of "ripping yarns from history." In this day and age, it is all too easy to become mired in paying the mortgage, getting promoted, filling the hours with hobbies and anything else we can find. There is a place for such things, of course—we cannot all climb Everest.

When disaster strikes, each of us is capable of courage and quiet dignity. Yet somehow, it is harder without these stories and others like them. Men and women alike take strength from the courage of Edith Cavell or the insane recklessness of Teddy Roosevelt or, indeed, Ranulph Fiennes. Put simply, their lives help us to endure the hard times. As Prince Charles once said: "My admiration for Ranulph Fiennes is unbounded and thank God he exists. The world would be a far duller place without him."

Ranulph Twisleton-Wykeham-Fiennes was born in Windsor on March 7, 1944. His father commanded the Royal Scots Greys Regiment in World War II and died without seeing his son. In fact, Ranulph Fiennes's first claim to fame was being the youngest posthumous baronet in existence.

His first years were spent in South Africa, in idyllic surroundings. He ran around with a gang of local lads, sometimes carrying bamboo spears. They took turns throwing them at one another, protected by a trash-can lid.

In 1952, Ranulph was sent as a boarder to Western Province Preparatory School. When he won the divinity prize, he was so pleased he decided briefly to become a priest. That dream fell to pieces when he was taken to see a film on the ascent of Mount Everest in 1953. Given the man he became, it is not fanciful to suggest that the film shaped his life.

The following year his mother took the family home to England, drab and gray to a boy who had known the sun of South Africa. She rented a small cottage, and he was sent to board at Sandroyd School near Salisbury. After a miserable start, he grew to love his time there, though mathematics was always a particular challenge. He found that his classmates would listen to stories based in South Africa, and he charged them squares of chocolate to hear them. He formed a gang named the Acnuleps (Latin for *cave* spelled backward), who signed their rules in blood, as boys tend to do. They went on to fight another gang, which led to the leaders being caned and the gangs disbanded.

After prep school, Ranulph went to Eton, where he was bullied and made thoroughly miserable. It is interesting to consider the old myth that the British Empire was won on the playing fields of Eton. The implication is of fair play and teamwork, but there may be another truth underlying the idea. Boys' private schools can be hellish places, but those who survive them are rarely worried by any other difficulty in later life.

At Eton, he made the boxing team and learned to love history. He was thrilled at news of Edmund Hillary's expedition to the South Pole. At sixteen, he was diagnosed with rheumatic fever and told to rest for six months. He spent part of that golden spring and summer learning to make explosives in a gardener's shed at home.

Back at school, he moved up to light-heavyweight boxing and he and a friend began to climb the school buildings at night, despite the threat of expulsion for anyone caught. One night they successfully left a toilet seat and a trash-can lid on the summit of the school hall, but on another occasion they were discovered sitting on a roof. Ranulph got away without being caught, but his friend was found and questioned by the headmaster. As it turned out, the head had been a keen climber in his youth and was more interested in their methods than in punishment.

After Eton, Ranulph joined the Royal Scots Greys tank regiment in 1963. He trained in Germany on seventy-ton Centurions. At six feet two, he had grown to the point where he could box in the heavyweight division. He also joined the cross-country running team and the ski team and formed a canoe club. Under his supervision, the men would regularly paddle a hundred miles a day. To Scots, his name was pronounced "Feens," and they described it as "Mr. Feens's Concentration Camp."

From the Scots Greys, he applied to join the Special Air Service. To prepare, he trained alone in the Brecon Beacons and took a parachuting course. The highest peak in the Brecons is Pen-y-Fan, and one part of the training was to run up and down it three times in eight hours. Another unusual part of SAS training was planning and carrying out a bank raid in Hereford. To his great embarrassment, he managed to leave the plans in an Italian restaurant. They were handed to the police and the plans reported in newspapers around the country. Despite that incident, Fiennes passed the famously harsh training and specialized in demolitions.

His career with the SAS came to an abrupt end in 1966. A friend of his told him about a film set in Castle Combe, Wiltshire. Twentieth Century-Fox was about to begin shooting *Doctor Dolittle* and had built sets and a twenty-foot-high concrete dam in the area, ruining the peace of an ancient English village. Fiennes agreed to help destroy the dam and also to tip off an ex-SAS man named Gareth Jones, who had become a journalist. Instead, Gareth Jones told the *Daily Mirror,* and they called the police. With explosives and detonators, Fiennes went in darkness to Castle Combe, unaware that police cars were waiting for him. His own car was an ancient and unreliable Jaguar, which he parked nearby and then walked in across the fields.

Unseen, he and two friends laid explosive charges as well as gasoline flares on timers to lure away the film company's security men. As they lit the fuses, the night was shattered by police with dogs. The dam was destroyed in the explosion that followed, but the trap had been sprung.

Interestingly, Fiennes had been trained to avoid exactly this sort of capture. He submerged himself in the river and made his way in darkness back to his waiting car. However, it wouldn't start so he was stuck. Things were not looking good for the escape when a police car came up and parked next to it. Trying to brazen it out, Fiennes asked the policemen if they would help him start his car. He was arrested.

For his efforts that night, Fiennes was expelled from the SAS and demoted from captain to second lieutenant. He rejoined the Scots Greys and became engaged to his childhood sweetheart, Virginia "Ginny" Pepper, before traveling with his regiment to Oman in Arabia. He took part in active fighting there and won the Sultan's Medal for bravery. At the same time, he was looking ahead to a life after the army, hoping to make his later career with exploration and record breaking. On leave, he made preparations for an expedition to follow the Nile from the mouth, near Alexandria, to the source, two thousand miles south. He assembled a group of like-minded adventurers and used Land Rovers and hovercrafts to reach the source successfully, following in the footsteps of earlier adventurers such as Richard Francis Burton. The Nile trip would be the first of many such expeditions.

After his tour in the army ended, he needed to earn money, and a chance came with an advance to write a book on the Nile expedition. Fiennes wrote it in six weeks, while his fiancée researched the history. It was his first experience of publishing. His plan was to make a living through expeditions and writing about them. However, his drive to travel and explore meant that he and Ginny separated for a time, as he did not seem ready to marry.

Alone again, Fiennes joined the R Squadron of the Territorial Army, who acted as reinforcements for the SAS in time of war. The physical tests were the same as for the SAS, and he passed the grueling ordeal. At the same time, he set about assembling a team for an expedition to Norway. The plan was to free-fall and parachute from a small Cessna plane onto Europe's highest glacier. The *Sunday Times* referred to it as "the World's Toughest Jump" and paid to cover the event.

Fiennes was first out of the plane and quickly reached terminal velocity of 120 miles per hour before pulling his rip cord and making a safe landing in the drop zone. The rest of the team came down in two runs, and from a safe base they began to climb and survey the area. A storm came in and almost killed them, but they survived to get down. His career as a renowned explorer had begun in earnest. Ten days after his return to England, he married Ginny.

In the early 1970s he was asked to audition for the part of James Bond. Producer Cubby Broccoli said Fiennes had a face and hands like a farmer and chose Roger Moore instead. It's interesting to speculate how different the films would have been with Fiennes as the hero. Instead, he took part in unmapped river expeditions across British Columbia, where he survived rapids and moose stew. The BBC accompanied him to make a documentary, and although this meant he didn't have to find sponsors, he was unhappy with the final programs, as they portrayed him as both cruel and incompetent. Yet the audiences were eight million for each episode, and he actually found sponsors easier to find afterward.

To supplement his income, Fiennes began to give lectures. He wrote about the Canadian experience and for years planned what would become one of his most famous exploits, the attempt to circumnavigate the world around both poles. The Transglobe Expedition of 52,000 miles would last from 1979 to 1982 and lead to Fiennes and Charlie Burton being the first men to reach both poles overland.

In most lives, that single achievement would have been enough to make him what *Guinness World Records* once called "the greatest living explorer." Yet other, more astonishing events were still to come. Fiennes continued to write, uniquely qualified to produce a book about Robert Falcon Scott's tragic race to the South Pole. His life had brought him fame, and he traveled around the world to give lectures. He took a job for a time with Occidental Petroleum, but it was always with an eye to planning the next great expedition.

In 1992 he discovered the lost city of Ubar in Oman, previously

believed to be a myth. He went on to make the first unsupported crossing of the Antarctic continent on foot. He endured heat and cold and continued to demonstrate what a human being can do in extreme conditions.

In 2000 he was involved in a solo, unsupported attempt to walk to the North Pole. Disaster struck when his sledge fell through the ice and he suffered frostbite in his fingers trying to pull it out. He had known this danger before and found that windmilling his arms restored circulation, but on that occasion it didn't work. His fingertips had frozen solid. The attempt had to be abandoned, and by the time he came home, the first joints of all the fingers on his left hand had died. Amputation was the only answer, but his surgeon wanted to wait for five months to allow as much skin as possible to recover. Fiennes found the pain of jarring the fingertips excruciating and decided to cut them off in his toolshed. His first attempt, with a hacksaw, was too slow and agonizing, so he used a Black & Decker fretsaw. Strangely enough, Black & Decker have yet to use this in their advertising. He also lost a toe to frostbite; it came off in the bath and he put it on the side and forgot about it until his wife found it lying there.

In 2003, Fiennes had a heart attack and endured a double bypass operation. Months later, he wanted to raise money for the British Heart Foundation and planned a series of seven marathons in seven days on seven continents. At the time, he asked his doctors whether such activity would put too much strain on his heart. They replied that they had no idea—no one had ever tried such a thing before. In November of that year he completed all seven with his running partner, Mike Stroud.

In 2005 he came to within a thousand feet of the peak of Everest. He tried again in 2008, at age sixty-four, but bad weather and exhaustion overcame him.

One of the strangest things about him is that despite the similarities to other heroes in this book, Fiennes is always understated, softly spoken, and modest about his achievements. He is certainly a man driven to push himself to extraordinary lengths, to such a degree that he becomes not so much an inspiration as a force of nature. His attitudes to trials and hardship are a pleasant antidote to some of the touchy-feely aspects of modern society. In short, he is not the sort of man to whom the "compensation culture" caters. We do need such men, if only to highlight the silliness of some of the other sort.

Recommended
Living Dangerously and Mad, Bad and Dangerous to Know
by Ranulph Fiennes

Captain Sir Richard Francis Burton

Richard Francis Burton was born in Devon, England, in 1821. Victoria came to the British throne in 1837, when he was just sixteen, so he was in some ways the archetypal Victorian scholar-adventurer. In his life, he was a soldier, a spy, a tinker, a surveyor, a doctor, an explorer, a naturalist, and a superb fencer. As an undercover agent, he was instrumental in provinces of India coming under British control, playing what Kipling called "the Great Game" with skill and ruthlessness. In recent times, Burton was one of the inspirations for Harry Flashman in the books by George MacDonald Fraser.

Burton spoke at least twenty-five languages, some of them with such fluency that he could pass as a native, as when he disguised himself as an Afghan and traveled to see Mecca. He spent his life in search of mystic and secret truths, at one point claiming with great pride that he had broken all Ten Commandments. In that at least, he was not the classic Victorian adventurer at all. Burton always went his own way. When he was asked by a preacher how he felt when he killed a man, he replied: "Quite jolly, how about you?"

At various points in his life, he investigated Catholicism, Tantrism, a Hindu snake cult, Jewish Kabbalah, astrology, Sikhism, and Islamic Sufism. He was convinced that women enjoy sexual activity as much as men, a very unfashionable idea in Victorian England. He enjoyed port, opium, cannabis, and khat, which has a priapic effect. He was six feet tall, very dark, and devilishly handsome, with a scar from a Somali spear wound on his cheek that seemed only to add to his allure. In short, he was a romantic and a devil, a dangerous man in every sense.

After Richard was born, his parents moved to France in an attempt to ease his father's asthma. Two more children were born to them there: Maria and Edward. Richard showed a remarkable facility for languages from an early age, beginning Latin at the age of three and Greek the following year.

The two boys were also taught arms as soon as they could hold a sword. They thrived on rough play and, at around the age of five, knocked their nurse down and trampled her with their boots. They fought with French boys and were constantly beaten by their father, but to little effect. Their tutor took all three children to see the execution by guillotine of a young Frenchwoman. This did not produce nightmares, however, and the children later acted out the scene with relish.

At the age of nine, Richard used his father's gun to shoot out the windows of the local church. He lied, stole from shops, and made obscene remarks to French girls. His appalled father realized that France was not producing the young gentlemen he had wanted, so he packed up and took the family back to England.

At home, Richard made new enemies at school, until at one point he had thirty-two fights to complete. In frustration, the senior Burton decided to take his family back to France. They settled at Blois, where the children were taught by a Mr. Du Pré and a small staff. They learned French, Latin, Greek, dancing—and, best of all, fencing. Both boys excelled with foils and swords.

It was perhaps their father's restless spirit that would infect Richard with the desire for constant movement. From Blois they went to Italy, where Richard learned the violin until his master said that while the other pupils were beasts, Richard was an "archbeast." In reply, Richard broke the instrument over the master's head.

The family moved on to Siena, then Naples, where the boys learned pistol shooting, cockfighting, and heavy drinking. Cholera swept Naples, and out of ghoulish curiosity, Richard and Edward dressed as locals and helped to remove the dead to the plague pits outside the city. They also discovered prostitutes and spent all their pocket money on them.

From a young age, the brothers were determined to enter the military. Their father was equally determined that they become clergymen.

To that end, he sent Richard to Oxford University and Edward to Cambridge, splitting them up for their own safety. Other tutors were engaged, and it was then that Richard met Dr. William Greenhill, who spoke not only Latin and Greek fluently but Arabic as well.

Despite his delight in languages, Burton disliked Oxford intensely. He attempted to arrange a duel on his first day, only to be ignored. He said later that he felt he had fallen among grocers. He hated the food, the beer, and the monotony. Annoyed by the hostility toward his dark and foreign appearance, he kept his door open but left a red-hot poker in the fireplace to repel unwanted visitors. He became determined to have himself expelled and broke every rule he could find, but at first the university ignored his excesses. Over the winter holidays in London, Richard and Edward met the sons of a Colonel White, from whom they heard tales of service in India and Afghanistan, where British forces had recently been defeated with great losses. Burton redoubled his efforts to be thrown out of Oxford, going to a horse race after being forbidden to attend. Called before the university authorities, Burton launched into a long speech about morality and trust and showed no remorse. He was expelled at last and left Oxford riding on a tandem-driven dog cart, blowing a coaching horn.

Burton's father was appalled and furious but, recognizing the inevitable, allowed both his sons to join the East India Company army. Edward was posted to Ceylon, now known as Sri Lanka, while Burton was posted to the subcontinent itself.

Warned of the heat in India, Burton shaved his head and bought a wig as well as learning Hindustani. During the voyage, he boxed, fenced, and practiced his language skills. By the time he landed in India, he was almost completely fluent. He did not know it then, but he was about to begin a relationship with the subcontinent that would provide a driving force to his previously aimless life.

It did not begin well. Burton fell ill with diarrhea and spent time in a sanatorium. He disliked the smell of curry and the lack of privacy in the company rooms. He began to learn Gujerati and Persian, ignoring the distressing presence of a crematorium next door, of which he said, "The smell of roast Hindu was most unpleasant." He found the tiny society of five hundred Europeans stifling, though he enjoyed the brothels and bazaars. For almost two months he endured, then he was sent at last to his first posting, at Baroda. He took a horse, servants, a supply of port, and a bull terrier with him. He was slowly falling in love with India, in all its endless variety.

Baroda was a baking-hot maze of alleys and exotic sights, with summer temperatures up to 120° F. The lives of the inhabitants were brutal, with appalling punishments for misdeeds, such as placing a criminal's head beneath an elephant's foot to be crushed. Burton loved it, from the strange smells of incense, hashish, and opium to the courtesans, shrines, alien flowers, and colorful mosques. Of the white officers, he said: "There was not a subaltern in the 18th Regiment who did not consider himself capable of governing a million Hindus." He took a temporary native wife, whom he described as his "walking dictionary," and found the courtesans more playful and less inhibited than their frosty counterparts in England. He threw himself into an exploration of sexual matters that would inform his writings many years later. Hunting and hawking kept him busy for a while, but he quickly lost the taste for it. He kept a company of monkeys, who ate at the table with him. He won the regimental horse race, learned the Indian style of wrestling, and taught his troops gymnastics to keep them agile.

In 1843, Burton took government examinations in Hindustani and made first in his class. He so successfully immersed himself in a Hindu snake cult that he was given the *janeo,* the three-ply cotton cord that showed he was a Brahmin, the highest caste. This was a unique event, unheard of before or since. In all other cases, a Hindu had to be born into that religion and only attained the highest caste after millennia of reincarnation. This honor came despite the fact that he remained a meat eater and is the more astonishing for it. He went on to discover Tantrism, with its philosophy, as he wrote, "not to indulge shame or adversion to anything . . . but freely to enjoy all the pleasures of the senses."

He attended Catholic chapel, then later converted to Islam and then Sikhism, in love with the mysticism of all faiths and throwing himself into one until he found himself drawn to the next. He was not a dilettante, however. In each case, he searched and learned all he could and completed every ritual with steadfast determination and belief, yet somehow his soul wandered as much as his feet and there were always new towns to see.

In 1843, Burton became the regimental interpreter for the Eighteenth Bombay Native Infantry and moved to Bombay (now Mumbai), bound for Karachi to join General Charles Napier and the British forces fighting in Sindh. Napier recognized Burton's abilities and used him in a variety of diplomatic missions through 1844 and 1845. Many of the details have been lost, but Burton became indispensable, a man who could fight or talk his way out of anything. He became used to traveling in disguise, and his contemporaries whispered that he had "gone native." In 1845, when Burton was just twenty-four, Napier sent him to infiltrate and report on a male brothel. Burton wrote of what he saw in such grisly detail that his many enemies suggested he had taken part in the activities he witnessed. There is, however, no evidence for this, and in fact Burton was always scathing about "le Vice," as he called it. Napier had the brothel destroyed after reading the reports, and it is worth pointing out that the famously straitlaced general lost no confidence in his agent as a result of this mission.

Away from the society of Britons in India, Burton became more and more of an outsider. He wore native clothing constantly, complete with turban and loose cotton robes. His experience of different faiths meant that he could work as a spy among Muslims or Hindus with equal invisibility. He also had himself circumcised so that his disguise would be foolproof even while bathing. In the Indus Valley, he found remnants of Alexander the Great's forts, as well as far more ancient ruins. He soaked it all up into his prodigious memory and delighted in fables and stories wherever he traveled for Napier. His reports were often inflammatory, and he complained constantly that the English did not understand the natives. Napier, for example, tried to make punishments humane, and thus they lost their effect on a people used to brutal rulers. Instead of cutting off a hand for stealing, the English merely imprisoned a man, who then thought them effete. Napier also issued a proclamation that he would hang anyone who killed a woman on suspicion of unfaithfulness, as was common in Sindh at that time. Burton may have had a personal reason to resent this practice, as his own affair with a high-born Persian woman came to an abrupt and possibly violent end, though details are sketchy.

When Burton was not working, he endured the hottest months, took notes, and drew everything he saw. He was always prolific and either wrote or translated more than fifty books in his time, on subjects ranging from the history of sword making to the strange places and people he saw. He was the first white man to publish details of the Islamic Sufi sect, which he threw himself into with his usual ferocious enthusiasm.

In 1845, suspecting that the British were about to annex the Punjab, a Sikh army crossed into British-held territory. It was a short war but hard fought, and by 1846, the Sikhs were brought to the negotiating table. The Punjab came under British rule. Around this time, Burton became ill with cholera and recovered very slowly. During his sick leave, he explored the Portuguese colony at Goa. He left his regular mistress behind in Sindh and spent some time trying to get a nun out of a local convent to be his next one. In one attempt, he visited the wrong room in the night and found himself being chased by an elderly nun. He pushed her into a river as he made his escape.

In the company of Englishwomen, he found himself a man apart, almost unable to communicate or remember the strict rules of contact and flirtation. In the end, he managed to find another "temporary wife." By this time, Burton dressed and acted as a man of the East rather than the West and had been made very dark by the constant sun. He continued to study Sufism but around 1847–8 also had himself inducted into Sikhism, a "conversion" that was never likely to last long with this firebrand of a man.

In 1848 war with the Sikhs broke out again. Burton was passed over for duties as an interpreter, a decision he later claimed was due to his report on the brothel. Ill and thin, he decided to return to Europe in 1849 after seven years in India. He made a partial recovery on the voyage, but poor health continued to plague him. He traveled to Italy and settled for a time in France, where he began further study of sword work, becoming a renowned master of the blade. In one exhibition he disarmed a French master seven times in a row.

In the relative peace of France, Burton completed many of the manuscripts that survive today, such as *Falconry in the Valley of the Indus* and *A Complete System of Bayonet Exercise*. In Boulogne he met the woman who would become his wife, Isabel Arundell. She was beautiful, of an ancient English family, and nineteen years old. Perhaps surprisingly, he would remain faithful to her always. She wrote in her diary: "Where are the men who inspired the 'grandes passions' of bygone days? Is the race extinct? Is Richard the last of them?" Burton adored her, but at the same time, the world of France and England was too small for him. He was given a year's leave from the East India Company for a journey to Arabia, where he would need all the skill and knowledge he had won in India to survive. The Royal Geographical Society backed him, and he set off in 1853. Once again he fell into the role of a Muslim, even working under the guise as a doctor in Alexandria for a month. He traveled from Cairo to Suez, the number of his companions growing to a large party as he met others making journeys to Medina, where the tomb of Muhammad lies. Burton was not impressed by the place, finding it "mean and tawdry" after great expectations. He took notes on everything he saw and learned, from folklore and the prices of slaves to the practice of female circumcision. The discovery of such notes would have meant his death, and he kept them in numbered squares that only he could reassemble.

From Medina he traveled to Mecca itself. Burton saw the fabled black stone there, deciding to his own satisfaction that it was a meteorite. He completed the tour of the pilgrim sites and got out alive. He was due back in Bombay by 1854 and was not able to return to London in time, though he would have been lionized there for his achievement.

After Mecca, Burton became famous and his exploits were widely reported. He had a free hand in choosing other expeditions. With company approval, he visited the fabled Ethiopian city of Harar, where he was held prisoner for ten days. Around that time, in 1855, his brother was badly wounded by natives in Ceylon. Though Edward recovered for a time, he lost his health and sanity and spent his last forty years in a sanatorium in Surrey, a sad end for the less turbulent Burton brother.

Meanwhile, Richard Burton went from triumph to triumph. At that time, Africa was truly "the Dark Continent," a place of mystery, strange animals, and vast unknown lands. With John Speke, Burton attempted a trip into the continental interior, known as the "Mountains of the Moon," but was badly wounded by a Somali spear. Speke was wounded in eleven places, and they were lucky to survive. However, Burton was still the man of choice when the Royal Geographical Society wanted to organize an expedition to find the fabled "inner sea" of Africa and the source of the Nile in 1856. He became secretly engaged to Isabel before he and Speke became the first white men to see Lake Tanganyika. Speke went on to find what is now known as Lake Victoria, though the journey almost killed both men. It was Burton's most celebrated exploration, though he fell out publicly with Speke afterward. On their return to London, Burton and Speke wrote viciously about each other, each one claiming the glory for himself and ignoring the other's contribution.

In 1861, Burton married Isabel at last in a Catholic ceremony, though with his history, it is likely to have been merely expedient. He continued to explore West Africa after his marriage and became consul in Damascus for a time. He also continued to write and in 1863 founded the Anthropological Society of London. By then an establishment figure, he was knighted by Queen Victoria in 1886.

He is perhaps best known for his translation into English of the *Kama Sutra*, an Indian sexual manual, as well as *Arabian Nights*, *The Perfumed Garden*, and *Vikram and the Vampire*, a collection of Hindu stories. He died in 1890 of a heart attack, and his wife had the Catholic last rites performed for him. Sadly, she then burned all his surviving notes and manuscripts, just as Byron's were burned before him. It was a truly great loss to both literature and culture. There are some men who rise above the period of their lives and the cultures in which they are born. Burton was a man of insatiable curiosity and endless wonder. His example has inspired many explorers after him, both of the world and the spirit. He and his wife are buried together in a tomb shaped like a Bedouin tent in Mortlake, near Richmond in London.

Recommended
Captain Sir Richard Francis Burton: A Biography by Edward Rice
A Rage to Live: A Biography of Richard and Isabel Burton by Mary S. Lovell

Daniel Boone

I can't say as ever I was lost, but I was bewildered once for three days.
—Daniel Boone

Daniel Boone is *the* iconic backwoods frontiersman. A mixture of fact, legend, and mythology, the story of this colonial adventurer and explorer who blazed trails from the coastal plains into the interior makes him the first folk hero of modern America. The popular images of the real-life Davy Crockett and the fictional Hawkeye—their exploits, their fame, even their clothes—are based upon Daniel Boone.

Boone's family was from Devonshire, in the southwest of England. Daniel's father, Squire, and grandfather George were among those who took that adventurous step to start a new life in the colonies. Squire arrived in Philadelphia in early 1713, followed by George in 1717. The family worshipped with the Society of Friends, so it was natural for them to settle in Pennsylvania as did many other Quakers. Thomas Paine was another, sixty years later.

Quaker William Penn had founded Pennsylvania in 1681. Using a land grant from Charles II, he established a colony where all religions could worship freely. Very few people then imagined what might be the future of the many British colonies in America, but Penn got it right when he predicted: "Colonies . . . are the seedlings of nations."

Squire Boone married a Welsh Quaker, Sarah Morgan, in 1720 and ten years later bought 158 acres near Reading in Berks County. In the sparsely populated Oley Valley he felled trees and built a simple log cabin—just one room above a cellar and spring. The two-story stone addition with a front porch that remains today was built later. In the original cabin, the sixth of their eleven children was born in 1734. They named him Daniel for the biblical hero. According to the family Bible, when grandparents George and Mary died, they left seventy descendants: eight children, fifty-two grandchildren, and ten great-grandchildren. There are now many Boones across the United States.

Daniel and his siblings spoke with the broad, soft Devonshire accent of their father, overlaid by their mother's Welsh lilt. Their childhood in and around the Oley Valley was peaceful, for the Quakers had a treaty of friendship with the Delaware and Susquehannock nations that lasted into the 1760s. Daniel helped his father with the farming, fished, trapped, and hunted with a crude spear for food. He received his first squirrel gun when he was twelve. He learned his reading and writing skills from his family and his woodcraft and hunting skills from Native Americans.

One early story tells of Daniel and other boys hunting in the wilderness when they were attacked by a puma. All the boys except Daniel scattered. He stood his ground, cocked his gun, and, as the puma leaped toward him, shot it through the heart.

In 1750, Squire Boone sold his land to relative William Maugridge and moved south. His eldest son, Israel, had married a "worldling," a non-Quaker, and as a result had been "read out" of the local meeting. By refusing to criticize his son's conduct Squire was also read out. So the family made the long trek down the Owatin Creek, through Maryland and Virginia. Plodding oxen hauled the wooden wagons for more than a year until they reached North Carolina. The Boone family built their new homes in the Yadkin Valley, a few miles west of Mocksville.

Back in the Oley Valley, Maugridge moved on to the first Boone farm but soon landed in debt. He was forced to mortgage the property for two hundred pounds to an insurance friend in Philadelphia—Benjamin Franklin.

Adventure in the shape of the French and Indian War (internationally, the Seven Years' War) beckoned the young Daniel Boone, and he left home in early 1755 at age twenty. He became a wagon driver in Major General Braddock's unsuccessful campaign to clear the French from the Ohio country. It was here that he first met volunteer Colonel George Washington of the Virginia militia. Having returned home, Boone married neighbor Rebecca Bryan a year later. On his father's farm, like his father before him, they built a log cabin for their home.

Victories at Quebec and Montreal in 1759 turned the war in Britain's favor. However, a pointless conflict arose in the Carolinas between settlers and their Cherokee allies. When Cherokee warriors raided Yadkin Valley in 1759—in retaliation for British executions—the Boone family and others moved north to Culpeper County in Virginia. Boone remained to serve with the North Carolina militia, for which he traveled west across the Appalachian Mountains into Tanasi (Tennessee) country. This journey set the pattern for the rest of his life.

Through the passes of the Alleghenies, the Cumberlands, and the Shenandoah Valley lay a great unspoiled wilderness of woods and forests, hills and plains, clear streams and broad rivers. In Britain and Europe no one had been able to step through such a door for centuries. It offered both a geographic and a spiritual freedom, though a freedom with its own particular dangers and its own requirements for survival. Boone was enchanted. Still in Tennessee today is a tree bearing the deeply carved inscription: D. BOON CILLED A. BAR ON TREE IN THE YEAR 1760. He didn't return home for two years.

A truce and peace was arranged between the Cherokee and the colonies in 1762; three Cherokee chiefs visited Britain, and the Boones returned to their Carolina homes. The following year, the Peace of Paris saw the end of the French and Indian War, the French being forced to withdraw from most of North America so that Canada, the American colonies, and Florida were all British.

The Carolinas were peaceful, but a northern alliance of Native Americans led by Ottawa chief Pontiac successfully rebelled against further white settlement westward. The British government saw their argument, and George III's 1763 Royal Proclamation banned colonization west of the Appalachian Mountains. This proclamation remains today the legal baseline for Native American claims in Canada and the United States.

Daniel Boone continued commercial hunting and trapping to feed a family that eventually numbered ten children. In winter he'd travel for many months along the riverbanks, trapping beaver and otter, then returning in the spring with packhorses laden with furs. In summer he'd farm maize and, with a single-shot musket, hunt deer for their meat and skins. The buckskins, simply called bucks, were bartered and sold for cash, so that the question was asked, "How many bucks for a pound?" *Buck* became slang for the pound and later the dollar. Boone and the other frontiersmen were known as Long Knives and Long Hunters.

During these trips from home, Boone repaired and made his own clothes from what was available to him. Sewn moccasins replaced his English leather boots, buckskin leggings replaced threadbare breeches, and a fringed hide top replaced his torn woolen shirts. Although only the head of Chester Harding's full-length portrait of Boone survives, an engraving of the original painting shows Boone in these distinctive hunting clothes. He didn't wear a coonskin cap; he wore a beaver hat, as did Davy Crockett later.

Boone's father died in 1765, and Daniel traveled south to investigate the new colony of Florida as a future home. Florida was rejected, so Daniel and Rebecca moved farther up the remote Yadkin Valley. Historical interpretations of him always seeking a life far from villages and towns annoyed him. Years later he said: "Nothing embitters my old age as much as the circulation of absurd stories that I retire as civilization advances." In his saddlebags he usually packed his Bible and *Gulliver's Travels,* and at night he often read to other frontiersmen by the light of the campfire.

Boone and his brother Squire explored farther west into the Appalachians, into the borders of the Kentucke country (Kentucky and West Virginia). The land then was abundant with wild game, but preserving the meat was the key to survival. Daniel fortunately had a knack for finding salt pans and brine creeks wherever he hunted—it was said he could smell salt from thirty miles—so that in the winter of 1767 the brothers camped at Salt Springs. Around the fire they talked about the Kentucke country west of the mountains, where the Iroquois and Shawnee hunted.

By the 1768 treaty of Fort Stanwix, the Iroquois allowed British settlers to hunt in Kentucke. Very soon the trader John Findley visited Boone's home. He was arranging a hunting and trading expedition across the Appalachians and asked Boone to join. On May 1, 1769, a five-man expedition left for the Appalachians, intending to explore and hunt for two years. Passing through the 1,665-foot-high Cumberland Gap and into Kentucke proper, they found wild turkey, deer, buffalo, and green pastures ideal for farming. Yet it was also Shawnee land, and their chiefs had not signed the Fort Stanwix treaty.

Boone and another man were captured by Shawnee in December. Their furs were confiscated and they were ordered to leave. Boone, however, doubled back to remain until 1771, exploring and hunting as far west as the Forks of the Ohio (Louisville). Under a ledge in the Great Smoky Mountains there is still a tiny backwoods hut, only four feet high, in which Boone spent one winter. He was so impressed with the Kentucke country that he returned again in 1772. He was thinking of settlement.

He sold his idea to settlers in the Carolinas, and in September 1773, he led his family and fifty others westward in the first attempt at settlement of Kentucke. The Shawnee, Delaware, and Cherokee met them in October in the Cumberland Gap. One of Boone's sons and another settler's son were captured and tortured to death. The expedition turned back.

Early the following spring, surveyors who were unaware of the attack entered Kentucke. Boone and a companion traveled some eight hundred miles that summer to warn them of their danger. A brief local war developed during which Boone helped defend settlements in Virginia. He was made a captain in the militia. His fame was spreading with colonists as well as with Native Americans, and developer Richard Henderson hired him to travel to the Cherokee villages to arrange a trade meeting. In 1775 Henderson bought from the Cherokee much of modern Kentucky for ten thousand pounds' worth of goods. He then hired Boone to blaze a road for settlers.

Boone and thirty woodsmen marked and built a trail through the Cumberland Gap and onward to the Kentucky River, deep into the heart of Kentucke. It is the famous Wilderness Road, nearly three hundred miles long. By the end of the century, some two hundred thousand settlers had traveled on it across the mountains. On the Kentucky River, Boone established the settlement he named Boonesborough and moved his family there that September.

This movement of settlers west of the Appalachians was in complete breach of the 1763 proclamation. Native Americans were not pleased about it. Neither was the British government, but short of garrisoning the long border with soldiers, there was little it could do. The independent-minded colonists simply ignored the law; in those days London was several months away.

Discontent had thus been simmering for several years. Many settlers saw the proclamation as an unjustifiable interference in their travel, trade, and search for wealth. In addition, it was argued that if British soldiers garrisoned in North America were not going to protect the settlers in their move westward, there was no point in having them.

In Massachusetts, open rebellion broke out at Lexington and Concord on April 19, 1775, with a surprise attack on the British garrisons there. A second attack on Boston in June was defeated at Bunker Hill, and the American Revolutionary War was begun.

Named the American War of Independence on the other side of the Atlantic, in fact it was a civil war—Britons fighting Britons, colonists fighting colonists. All civil wars create more than usually strong passions, and between 1775 and 1782, each side vented its frustrations and anger. Daniel Boone's personal experience is typical of these divisions: he was charged with collaborating with the enemy.

His first daughter, Jemima, and two other teenage girls were captured by Shawnee outside Boonesborough, ten days after the 1776 Declaration of Independence. Like the majority of Native Americans, the Shawnee supported Britain. Boone and two other men set off in pursuit. For two days he tracked the Shawnee warriors westward through the wilderness, until he caught up to them, ambushed them, rescued the girls, and returned safely to Boonesborough. James Fenimore Cooper fictionalized the event in *The Last of the Mohicans*, Hawkeye taking the part of Daniel Boone.

The next year Boone was shot in the ankle during a Shawnee attack on Boonesborough. For almost a year the settlement was under attack and the settlers' crops and cattle destroyed. In February 1778, Boone led out a party of thirty men for desperately needed fresh food and salt. While the others collected salt, Boone was hunting for game when he was sighted by some Shawnee. He ran, but he was now forty-five years old, and he was caught by fleet-footed warriors half his age.

The Shawnee chief, Blackfish, was about to fall on the rest of Boone's party and then assault Boonesborough. Boone persuaded Blackfish not to kill the salt collectors if they surrendered without fighting. They were all escorted to the Shawnee village of Chillicothe. Boone further persuaded Blackfish that Boonesborough was too heavily defended for an assault to succeed. The party was kept prisoner by the Shawnee for many months.

During his imprisonment, Boone was forced to "run the gauntlet"— to run between two lines of warriors facing inward and armed with tomahawks and knives. He ducked, sidestepped, and twisted through the slashing tomahawks in the first half of the gauntlet, handed off the next few warriors, and simply sprinted past the last to survive. Blackfish adopted him into his tribe, giving him the name Sheltowee, "Big Turtle." Yet he still turned him and his party over to the British at Fort Detroit as prisoners.

In mid-June, Boone discovered that the Shawnee were planning a major attack against Boonesborough. He escaped from Detroit and in five days made the 160-mile journey to the settlement by horse and foot to alert the settlers. The fortifications of the wooden village were quickly improved. In September, Shawnee surrounded Boonesborough, but Boone again delayed the assault by arranging a parley with Blackfish. During the negotiations in a meadow, fighting broke out. Boone and the settlers retreated inside, and the siege of Boonesborough began. It lasted ten days before the Shawnee withdrew, a siege not being their type of warfare.

Daniel Boone was charged by two officers of the patriot Kentucke militia of collaborating with the Loyalist Shawnee during his time with them. He was court-martialed in Boonesborough itself.

It is possible Boone collaborated with the British—although all his other actions belie it and there is no British record of it—but almost certainly he was trying to stop needless bloodshed at Boonesborough. He was brought up with Native Americans, he liked them, and in their turn they admired him. A Shawnee victory over Boonesborough was not going to decide the outcome of the war.

Boone was acquitted and promoted to major, but he left to gather his family in North Carolina and never returned to Boonesborough. Instead, he established a new settlement, called Boone's Station, nearby. His court-martial had left a bitter taste, and he rarely spoke of it.

He joined General Clark's 1780 invasion of the Ohio country as its guide, taking part in the fighting at Pickaway (Piqua). In the division of the Kentucke territory that November, he was made lieutenant colonel in the Fayette militia and the following year was elected representative to the Virginia assembly. On his way to attend the assembly, he was captured by British dragoons near Charlottesville. Assumed to be a civilian legislator, he was given parole after only a few days.

If Boone had been a Loyalist, he would by then have been known as a traitor to Britain. For he'd left Fort Detroit to warn Boonesborough of a Loyalist attack, campaigned with Clark, and fought at Pickaway. It's very unlikely he would have been released from Charlottesville.

In 1782 he fought the Shawnee in almost the last skirmish of the war, the battle of Blue Licks, where his son Israel was killed. He served once again as guide to Clark's second expedition into the Ohio country at the end of the year. By September 1783, when the United States of America was formally recognized as an independent nation, Daniel Boone was already a famous American.

The following year, at age fifty, he became a legend with the publication of *The Discovery, Settlement and Present State of Kentucke* by John Filson. This history includes a large appendix titled "The Adventures of Colonel Daniel Boone." It sold successfully on both sides of the Atlantic, so that Boone became famous in the land of his father as well as his own. Filson interviewed Boone for the facts of his life but invented most of his speech. Filson, like later Hollywood portrayers of Boone, did not let truth stop him from embellishing a good story. He also omitted Boone's court-martial.

In 1785 a condensed version of Filson's account, *The Adventures of Colonel Boone*, was published. That, too, sold well. Through no desire of his own, Daniel Boone had become the world's archetypal frontiersman. He was the backwoodsman able to survive in the wilderness, living in harmony with nature and with the mutual respect of Native Americans.

After the Revolutionary War, Boone resettled his family at the river port of Limestone (Maysville) while he worked as a surveyor along the Ohio River. He bought a tavern, speculated unsuccessfully in land, and was again elected to the Virginia state assembly. In the northwest, though, war continued as Native American nations fought on until 1794 against U.S. expansion across the proclamation border.

Boone took part in one 1786 expedition, his last military action. After it he negotiated a Shawnee-American prisoner exchange.

He moved farther upriver to Point Pleasant in 1788, opened a trading post, and returned to hunting and trapping. After being appointed lieutenant colonel of the Kanawha militia, he was elected for a third time to the Virginia assembly in 1791. Still he couldn't settle, and he moved his large family back to son Daniel's land in Kentucke.

By then, his small wealth had disappeared, for he'd lost the colonial lands he'd cleared and claimed from lack of title in the new United States. In 1798 a warrant was issued for his arrest when he

forgot, or ignored, a summons in a court case. Yet his fame had not died. The newly created state of Kentucky named Boone County for him the same year. Fittingly, the county contained a very large salt lake.

However, it seems the new nation was not for him. Perhaps the continuing war against Native Americans, increasing federal interference in the states, new taxes, and escalating violence and riots persuaded him to move on. He was also in debt. In 1799 he left the United States.

The silver-haired Daniel Boone led his family on an amazing journey, downriver along more than a thousand miles of the Ohio and the broad Mississippi all the way to Saint Louis—by canoe. He hunted and trapped along the riverbank while the family paddled slowly downstream. In the afternoon they'd choose a site for their camp, light a fire, and prepare for the evening meal. It was idyllic. Legend says that on the wooden landing stage at Cincinnati somebody asked him why he was leaving. "I want more elbow room," Boone replied laconically.

Louisiana was then a large Spanish colony, its borders spreading indeterminately north toward Canada. Within a year of his arrival in the Femme Osage district (Saint Charles County) of what is now Missouri, Boone was appointed syndic, a Spanish type of magistrate. He received land for his services and later was made military commandant of the district by the Spanish governor. He continued to hunt and trap for food—a lot of families in the world did in those days—and had one brief skirmish with the Osage tribe in the spring hunt of 1802. He discovered some Shawnee who had also escaped from Kentucky to Saint Louis, and they became friends.

In 1803 the U.S. government purchased Louisiana—although purchasing foreign territory contravened the new Constitution. However, under military threat from Napoléon Bonaparte in Europe, Spain had transferred her Louisiana colony to France and the transfer immediately rang loud alarm bells in Washington. The last thing English-speaking North America wanted was a return of French militarism.

President Jefferson wrote: "The day that France takes possession of New Orleans, we must marry ourselves to the British fleet and nation." Bonaparte, despite his looting of various European nations, was short of currency with which to pay for his wars. For fifteen million dollars cash down he sold Louisiana—and Daniel Boone once again lived in the United States.

Almost immediately the new Louisiana Territory confiscated Boone's land, and he and Rebecca were forced to move to son Nathan's farm. After he petitioned Congress, his land was finally returned in 1814. He sold most of it to clear his outstanding Kentucky debts.

Rebecca, his wife of fifty-seven years, died in March 1813. She was buried near daughter Jemima's home on Tuque Creek. That same year, the third account of Daniel Boone was published, a long poem by Rebecca's nephew Daniel Bryan. It was called *The Mountain Muse,* and Boone considered it embarrassingly inaccurate. He said: "Many heroic actions and chivalrous adventures are related of me which exist only in the regions of fancy." It sold well, nevertheless.

Boone remained on his son's land and continued to hunt and trap into old age. It's probable he made one last, long hunt up the Missouri to the Yellowstone River around 1815, a remarkable journey for a man aged eighty-one. He died on September 26, 1820, and was buried beside Rebecca. Although the man was dead, the legend continued, and increased, with various colorful accounts over the years.

Strangest of all, Daniel Boone features in the classic poem *Don Juan* by Lord Byron. In the epic satire composed from 1819 to 1824, Byron wrote seven stanzas about "natural man" living simply in the wilderness:

> *Of the great names which in our faces stare,*
> *The General Boone, back-woodsman of Kentucky,*
> *Was happiest amongst mortals anywhere;*
> *For killing nothing but a bear or buck, he*
> *Enjoyed the lonely, vigorous, harmless days*
> *Of his old age in wilds of deepest maze.*

James Fenimore Cooper published the first Hawkeye tales in 1823, and a romantic account of Boone's life by Timothy Flint, *Biographical Memoir of Daniel Boone, the First Settler of Kentucky,* was released in 1833. Many more fiction and factual accounts followed, while Theodore Roosevelt founded the conservationist Boone and Crockett Club in 1887. A half-dollar coin was minted in 1934 to commemorate the bicentenary of his birth.

The remains of Daniel and Rebecca Boone were moved from Tuque Creek, Missouri, to Frankfort Cemetery, Kentucky, in 1845.

This has caused some resentment in Missouri, giving rise to another story—that the wrong bodies were removed, a mistake caused by the graves being left unmarked for some fifteen years. Daniel Boone's own words make a suitable comment: "With me the world has taken great liberties, and yet I have been but a common man."

Recommended
The Discovery, Settlement and Present State of Kentucke
by John Filson
The Life and Legend of an American Pioneer by John Faragher
Daniel Boone Homestead, Reading, Pennsylvania

The Few
The Royal Air Force Fighter Command in the Battle of Britain

There were: 2,340 British, 32 Australians, 112 Canadians, 1 Jamaican, 127 New Zealanders, 3 Rhodesians, and 25 South Africans. In addition, there were 9 Americans, 28 Belgians, 89 Czechoslovakians, 13 French, 145 Polish, and 10 from the Republic of Ireland. They were the men and women of Royal Air Force Fighter Command, and they fought the most famous air battle of them all—the battle of Britain.

By the end of June 1940, the United Kingdom stood alone against Nazi Germany, Austria, Czechoslovakia, and France. The Czechs were conscripted into Nazi forces, while Vichy French forces fought with Germany until 1943 against Britain in the Middle East and North and West Africa. French spies around the world reported to Germany and Japan until they were captured, while in Southeast Asia the French agreed to Japan taking control of French Indochina (Vietnam, Cambodia, and Laos).

From Norway to the Pyrenees, all of western and central Europe was Nazi-controlled, with enemy radio interception and spy networks operating in neutral Spain and Ireland. In the north, Sweden supplied the Nazis with steel and other metals. In the east, Russia, Hungary, Romania, and the Balkans supplied oil, coal, and food. In the south, Fascist Italy joined Germany and opened two more fronts against Britain in North and East Africa. At sea, German submarines and surface raiders attacked unprotected British convoys, the escorts having been withdrawn to defend Britain against invasion.

The German victory in Europe had been so fast that no plans had been prepared for an invasion of Britain. In July that was remedied with Hitler's War Directive 16, which stated: "As England, in spite of her hopeless military situation, still shows no signs of willingness to come to terms, I have decided to prepare, and if necessary to carry out, a landing operation against her. The aim of this operation is to eliminate the English Motherland."

For a German invasion to be possible, the Royal Navy had to be pushed out of the eastern English Channel, at least temporarily. To do that, Germany needed command of the air so that its formidable and experienced bomber and dive-bomber squadrons could knock out the navy. For command of the air, Royal Air Force Fighter Command first had to be destroyed.

To defeat Britain in 1940, German forces had only to take London, just fifty to sixty miles from the Kent and Sussex coasts. As with the Norman invasion of 1066, the remainder of the country could be overrun later. There would have been resistance, of course, far stiffer than they had encountered on the Continent, but an invasion was on. After all, the 1915 Gallipoli landings in the Mediterranean had been carried out successfully from ships' boats in the face of machine guns, artillery fire, and barbed-wire defenses, and without tanks. The Gallipoli campaign failed only because it was fought on a narrow peninsula and uphill against cliffs. No such problems would confront German troops on the broad and level battlefront of southeast England.

With German control of the air, there would have been no insurmountable problems for an invasion fleet to cross the channel, supported by glider troops and parachutists. The Royal

Navy stated that it could not prevent an invasion, because it wouldn't know the landing ports and beaches, but it would be able to stop support and supplies by sea to that invasion—as long as the RAF maintained control of the air.

The German Sixteenth and Ninth armies rehearsed for landings at ports and beaches between Folkestone and Brighton, while the Sixth Army practiced for landings between Weymouth and Lyme Regis. Panzer tanks were made watertight and fitted with snorkels, and rehearsed offloading some distance from a beach to proceed along the seabed and then ashore. The German navy scoured western Europe for suitable ships, barges, craft, and tugs—some 2,500—and moved them to the ports of Holland, Belgium, and France. Meanwhile, under Reichsmarschall Hermann Göring, the Luftwaffe prepared for "Eagle Attack."

The amphibious invasion, known as Operation Sea Lion, was scheduled for the week of September 19–26, 1940, the date by which an invasion fleet could be assembled and when the tides were

favorable for a dawn landing on the Kent and Sussex beaches. Göring promised Hitler that by then Germany would command the air over the channel and southeast England. On August 1, Hitler signed War Directive 17 for the destruction of RAF Fighter Command, and so began the battle of Britain. It was to be a busy three months.

RAF Fighter Command was then led by air chief marshal Sir Hugh Dowding, a brilliant, determined, but reserved man who knew more about aerial warfare than anyone else in Britain. It was Dowding who had changed the peacetime RAF from wooden biplanes to metal monoplanes. As a result, the first Hawker Hurricane flew in 1935 and the first Vickers Supermarine Spitfire in 1936. It was Dowding who arranged the first demonstration of Watson-Watt's new radar, who created the radar air-defense network, and who developed airborne radar for night fighters. In 1936 he was appointed commander-in-chief of the newly formed Fighter Command.

His senior officer was Air Commodore Keith Park, a New Zealand air ace who had twenty-four victories in World War I and who was the RAF's fighter expert. Together, they reorganized Fighter Command and the fighter defenses of Britain for war. An Observer Corps was formed of volunteers who reported from the ground all aircraft movements over Britain. Operation rooms were created for all levels of command, from airfields like RAF Duxford to Group Operations Headquarters at RAF Uxbridge. The airfields were converted to all-weather facilities—with concrete runways as opposed to grass.

Dowding and Park also realized that, although the theorists correctly anticipated attack by large bomber squadrons, they were incorrect when they said there was no defense except attack by opposing bomber squadrons. There was a defense: fighter squadrons. Fortunately, they were supported in this belief by the new minister of defense, Sir Thomas Inskip. Dowding increased the number of fighter squadrons, airfields, and pilot-training units and created the vital centralized command linked to the new radar network. He pressed and argued for even more pilots and ever more aircraft, although one type, the Defiant, turned out to be a turkey.

However, Dowding was not popular in the Air Ministry. He was usually right and ruffled too many feathers. He was "retired" in 1938 but immediately reinstated, a sequence that would happen four times. He sent a requisition to the Air Ministry for bulletproof glass for Hurricane and Spitfire cockpits; the politicians laughed at him. He told them: "If Chicago gangsters can have bulletproof glass in their cars, I can't see any reason why my pilots cannot have the same." He got the glass. How out of touch many politicians were with the reality of modern warfare and the role of the RAF is difficult to appreciate many years later.

During the collapse of France, despite Dowding's advice, squadron after squadron of Hurricane fighters was deployed to France and destroyed. However, Dowding refused to commit Spitfire squadrons and, eventually, any more squadrons at all. Of 261 Hurricanes sent to France only 66 returned, a destruction rate of 75 percent. As a result, Fighter Command was reduced to almost half its strength, the loss of experienced pilots more critical than the loss of airplanes. If more squadrons had been sent to France, the battle of Britain would have been lost and Britain invaded.

Behind the scenes, Prime Minister Churchill appointed Canadian Lord Beaverbrook as minister of Aircraft Production, an inspired choice. Beaverbrook bypassed the Air Ministry, took over factories, and stopped production of bombers to increase production of Spitfire and Hurricane fighters. He had them delivered directly from the factories to the squadrons, created a "while-you-wait" repair service to which pilots flew their damaged fighters, and arranged the ferrying of aircraft across the Atlantic from Canada, which the Air Ministry had said was impossible. When the pro-Nazi American Henry Ford refused to support Britain by building Rolls-Royce Merlin engines under license, Beaverbrook paid the rival Packard company to do so. Later in the war, this led to the building of the brilliant British-designed and -engined P-51 Mustang fighter for the U.S. Army Air Force.

Dowding said later: "The country owes as much to Beaverbrook for the Battle of Britain as it does to me. Without his drive behind me I could not have carried on during the Battle."

In the spring of 1940, Dowding appointed Keith Park as commander of 11 Group, the squadrons defending the vital southeast of England. Trafford Leigh-Mallory already commanded 12 Group, defending central England and Wales. Richard Saul commanded 13 Group, defending Scotland and northern England, while Quintin Brand commanded 10 Group, defending the west and southwest England.

So Dowding and a depleted Fighter Command entered the battle of Britain, facing a Luftwaffe that had flown and fought successfully in Spain, Poland, and western Europe. Göring's strategy was to bomb the fighter airfields out of action, destroy fighter aircraft on the ground by bombing and strafing, and destroy them in the air with his fighters. It was the same tactic used successfully against the Polish, Norwegian, French, Dutch, and Belgian air forces.

For the attack on Britain, the Luftwaffe had operational along the channel coast 656 single-seat single-engine Messerschmitt 109 fighters, 168 two-seat two-engine Messerschmitt 110 fighters, 248 two-seat single-engine Junkers Stuka dive-bombers, and 769 twin-engine bombers. Also on squadron strength but not operational were 153 Messerschmitt 109 fighters, 78 Messerschmitt 110 fighters, 68 dive-bombers, and 362 bombers.

In Denmark and Norway they had a further 34 Messerschmitt 110 fighters, 129 bombers to attack northern Britain, and 84 Messerschmitt 109 fighters (out of range of England but which could be brought south within range). In all, there were 2,749 aircraft. Additionally there were 244 reconnaissance and coastal aircraft for mine laying and pilot recovery.

On July 20, Fighter Command had operational 504 single-seat single-engine fighters, Hurricanes and Spitfires in a ratio of approximately four to one. Also on squadron strength but not operational were 78 Hurricanes or Spitfires for a total of 582 aircraft.

There were also 27 Boulton Paul two-seat single-engine Defiant fighters. The only time these were sent into action, July 19, they lost two-thirds of their number without a single loss to the enemy. They were not used again. The RAF also had Bomber Command and Coastal Command, but those aircraft could not be involved in the battle of Britain; they were not suitable.

In all aircraft, Fighter Command was outnumbered by four to one. In fighters, it was outnumbered by two to one.

Radar detection gave Fighter Command the time to deploy its squadrons to the right place at close to the right time, but rarely to the right height. The Nazi fighters invariably had the great advantage of height. Radar was vital to the battle, giving Fighter Command's fewer aircraft more time in the air, and to a certain extent redressing the imbalance of numbers, but this became a double-edged sword for the RAF pilots. It meant that they flew many more hours than the German pilots, an average of six sorties or more each day. In addition, Luftwaffe aircrew knew the time they were to fly every day, whereas RAF pilots were on standby to "scramble" from dawn to dusk (woken at about 3:30 A.M., stood down at about 8:30 P.M.). As a result, the British pilots eventually became exhausted, and exhausted pilots make fatal mistakes.

Fighter Command did have the advantage of fighting over home territory, so that most of the pilots who survived a destroyed aircraft were returned to their squadron, whereas most Luftwaffe pilots who survived became prisoners of war. However, in war-experienced pilots as well as reserve pilots, Fighter Command was vastly outnumbered by the Luftwaffe. It was this lack of pilots and experience that brought it closest to defeat.

In early July the Luftwaffe attacked shipping and convoys in the English Channel and North Sea, made fighter sweeps across Kent and Sussex, and probed and tempted Fighter Command in order to assess its response times and the standard of the opposition. Dowding was careful not to commit his men and airplanes at the beginning of the battle, so Park and Leigh-Mallory made only limited responses to the attacks on shipping. The fighter sweeps were ignored. Even so, air activity was increasing. As early as July 10, Fighter Command flew more than six hundred sorties.

By the seventeenth, there were daylight bombing raids on factories in England and Scotland and on southern coastal towns, ports, and radar stations, as well as night bomber training flights. On the twenty-fifth—a rare sunny day in an overcast and wet July—several engagements took place protecting a convoy in the Dover Strait. Fighter Command lost 7 fighters against 16 German aircraft shot down, the heaviest casualties to that point. It was during that month that Park developed the tactic of sending Hurricanes to attack enemy bombers while Spitfires attacked the protecting fighters above. By the end of the month, however, neither air force was clear about how much damage had been done to the other.

For the benefit of the German public and the occupied countries, Luftwaffe propaganda announced only half its losses and higher RAF losses than even its pilots claimed. Fighter Command on the other hand announced its true losses, which the Luftwaffe assumed were false figures like its own. This resulted in the Luftwaffe believing it was doing better than it was. For the British public, Fighter Command accepted its pilots' high claims of enemy aircraft destroyed, claims that were naturally error-prone from emotion, from two or more pilots claiming the same aircraft, and from the fact that everything happened in three dimensions at 300 miles per hour.

Fighter Command lost 145 aircraft in July, the majority of which had been replaced by Beaverbrook's supply chain, but it was the loss of pilots that was the major concern. Of all aircrew lost in July, eighty were experienced flight and squadron commanders of the Fighter Command, irreplaceable and vital men.

On August 8 another convoy battle took place in the channel, over which several hundred aircraft fought. The Germans had 31 aircraft destroyed for the loss of 19 British fighters.

Still Dowding held Fighter Command back, so that the intercepting fighters were heavily outnumbered by both German fighters and bombers. This caused some questioning, even by the pilots themselves.

It must also have reduced the chances of destroying German aircraft and increased the chances of losing more British aircraft, but Dowding knew that the crisis was yet to come. It began on August 12, coincidentally the opening of the grouse-shooting season.

Radar stations along the southeast coast were bombed, Portsmouth was hit by 150 bombers, and airfields of 11 Group were bombed, while hundreds of Luftwaffe 109 and 110 fighters protected their bombers. RAF Biggin Hill in Kent was in the thick of it, and its close-of-day intelligence report was typical for 11 Group: "Operational sorties: 36. Enemy casualties: 5 confirmed, 16 unconfirmed, 4 probables and damaged. All pilots safe. 1 in hospital." The average age of the fighter pilots at Biggin Hill was several months under twenty-one. A headline in the following day's newspapers read: "The Battle of Britain Is On."

August 13 was Göring's "Eagle Attack" day. The Luftwaffe flew 1,485 sorties and night-bombed cities in all four countries of the kingdom, including two aircraft factories in Belfast and Birmingham. The RAF responded with 700 sorties, shooting down 46 enemy aircraft for the loss of 13 fighters but losing a further 47 assorted aircraft on the ground. Overall it was the Luftwaffe's day. On the fourteenth more airfields, radar stations, and factories were bombed.

The fifteenth saw the largest attack of the battle, with more than 1,800 German aircraft launched in five massive assaults. It included all German aircraft stationed in Norway, Denmark, Holland, Belgium, and France in an all-out attempt to smash Fighter Command and bring the RAF to its knees. Hurricane and Spitfire pilots shot down 75 aircraft for the loss of 34 fighters shot down and 16 destroyed on the ground. That was the RAF's day. The Luftwaffe called it "Black Thursday," yet the following day it continued the onslaught, flying another 1,700 sorties against Britain.

By mid-August, the Luftwaffe had lost a total of 363 aircraft as well as most of their pilots and crews. The RAF had lost 181 fighters shot down and 30 destroyed on the ground, a total of 211, but Fighter Command also had lost 154 pilots, of which only 63 could be replaced. In addition, a further 80 percent of squadron commanders had been lost to death, injury, or exhaustion, so that by then, inexperienced commanders were leading inexperienced pilots into battle. Fighter Command was wavering.

The smiling young pilots in their white silk scarves, leather-and-sheepskin flying jackets, blue uniforms, and shaggy flying boots were becoming drawn and exhausted. During standby, they lounged in the mess or sprawled outside in deck chairs and on the grass, reading, smoking, chatting, drinking tea or coffee, waiting for the inevitable telephone call from Control to scramble once again. Some dozed under the wings of their airplanes; one squadron's pilots remained in their cockpits. In the few hours off-duty, they slept, socialized at the local pub, scrawling their names on the ceilings and walls, went to the movies, fell in love, or made the occasional trip to London on a twenty-four-hour pass.

The ground crews, too, suffered heavy casualties and were tired, working throughout the day and night repairing, servicing, re-arming, and refueling the planes, then repairing the airfields. The effectiveness of the Hurricanes and Spitfires depended as much on the ground crews as on the pilots. Dowding rotated his squadrons—pilots and ground crews—whenever possible; during the three months of the battle of Britain, six different squadrons flew from Biggin Hill.

Yet there were simply not enough replacement pilots, and at the end of each day even more were required. From the Fleet Air Arm, 58 pilots were transferred to Fighter Command, a few suitable bomber pilots were retrained as fighter pilots, and RAF technicians who at least knew about fighters were sent to flying school.

On the other side of the channel, Göring was fuming

at his Luftwaffe's inability to destroy the RAF. His pilots, too, were frustrated. Every time they attacked, there were the Hurricanes and Spitfires, always waiting, no matter how many they shot down.

At a meeting on August 19, Göring asked his two most experienced and successful fighter pilots what they required to defeat the RAF. Major Moëlders asked for a more powerful engine for the Messerschmitt 109 to counter the Rolls-Royce Merlins, while Major Galland famously asked for an "outfit of Spitfires for my Group."

Göring changed tactics to twenty-four-hour attack. He relocated most of his fighters to airfields around Calais to provide even closer support for his bombers and concentrated the assault on fighter airfields. He was forced to withdraw the Stuka dive-bomber because of its high casualty rate. Dowding and Park countered by ordering their pilots to concentrate on the bombers, to leave the fighters alone whenever possible and not to pursue over the English Channel. The bombers were the priority. The battle of Britain now entered its critical period.

On the night of the twenty-fourth, during a 170-bomber raid against the Thames Haven oil tanks, a German aircraft dropped its bombs on the center of London, apparently because of a navigational error. Already bombs had been dropped around the capital and in the suburbs as well as other British cities and ports, but never before on the center of London. Similarly, no raids had been made against Berlin by Bomber Command, which itself was beginning strategic night-bombing.

Churchill naturally assumed it was intentional and, as in May when Rotterdam was blitzed by the Luftwaffe, ordered a retaliatory raid. The target was Berlin, which Göring had boasted would never be bombed.

On the very next night, August 25, Bomber Command sent 81 twin-engine bombers to Berlin. Of those, 29 reached the target and dropped their bombs on the city. Enraged, Hitler pledged to annihilate London. He ordered Göring to commence the wholesale bombing of London and other British cities by day and night, a destruction he hoped would bring Britain to demoralized defeat. So began "the Blitz," which Hitler called "terror raids." The first city to catch it badly was Liverpool, bombed four nights in succession.

On August 30 a feint by the Luftwaffe to the Thames estuary was followed by repeated and heavy raids on airfields. Fighter Command destroyed 49 German aircraft for the loss of 25 fighters and 10 pilots, but its southeastern airfields were a mess. A shop in the village became the operation room for Biggin Hill, yet Fighter Command still flew 1,000 sorties for the first time.

The next day the Luftwaffe struck again, bombing airfields and radar stations. It lost 39 aircraft, but Fighter Command also lost 39 fighters and 13 pilots. Several squadrons were forced to relocate to the grass fields of private flying clubs. Dowding told Churchill: "We are fighting for survival, and we are losing."

To a major extent, both air forces were boxing blind, not knowing how much damage they were inflicting on the other. Fighter Command had destroyed 800 Luftwaffe aircraft but thought that they'd destroyed more. The error didn't matter, for while the Luftwaffe continued its assaults across the channel, they had to be countered. On the other side of the coin, between August 24 and September 5 the Luftwaffe destroyed 466 RAF fighters, killed 231 pilots, damaged several radar stations, and put 6 fighter airfields out of action. German intelligence reported that Fighter Command was on its knees. Yet somehow Hurricanes and Spitfires rose from the green fields to meet every attack.

Dowding could no longer rotate his squadrons—there weren't enough left—so resorted to A, B, and C designations. A squadrons were in the southeast front line commanded by Keith Park, B squadrons were in the center and west of Britain commanded by Leigh-Mallory, and C were as far from the fighting as possible, training new pilots. In those appalling two weeks to September 5 Dowding lost a quarter of his remaining fighter pilots. With the best will in the world, their replacements were rookies with only a few flying hours—often as little as ten—in their logbooks and under two weeks' squadron experience. Their survival in battle was numbered in just days.

There were instances of Luftwaffe pilots machine-gunning RAF pilots in parachutes. There were also isolated incidents of the machine-gunning of British civilians, as earlier machine-gunning of civilians on the Continent had been common. Göring was a fighter ace from World War I, but he was also the creator of the German secret police, the Gestapo.

In September 1940, Göring announced on radio: "I myself have taken command of the Luftwaffe's battle for Britain." The two air forces were now trading punches, losing as many of their own aircraft as they destroyed of the other, the Luftwaffe flying about 770 sorties a day and Fighter Command just under 1,000. On one horrific day, for the first time, Fighter Command lost more aircraft—and pilots—than it shot down.

September 7 began as usual with Luftwaffe attacks on airfields, but on this occasion it was a feint for the first mass attacks on London. In the afternoon, 1,000 aircraft crossed the English Channel from France in a formation two miles high, flying over Cape Blanc-Nez and a watching Göring below. No intelligence reports suggested such a raid was planned. The controllers expected further attacks upon their airfields and so delayed the fighters from taking off until the last moment, too late for London.

There had never been an attack on a city on that scale before, anywhere in the world. The bombings of Guernica, Warsaw, and Rotterdam paled into insignificance. From 16,000 to 20,000 feet, new high-explosive bombs and incendiaries hammered the London docks and homes. There were more raids in the evening, and raids throughout the night until dawn on the eighth. At night the bombers followed radio beams to London, although little navigation was required: the East End was burning and the glow of its fires could be seen ninety miles away. That was a day for the Luftwaffe.

They bombed London again on the night of the eighth, and a second massive daylight attack was launched on the ninth, again with almost 1,000 enemy aircraft, in two formations crossing the coast above Dover and Beachy Head. Park's A Group squadrons scrambled to meet them in the air south of London. So fiercely did the Hurricane and Spitfire pilots fight that they literally forced back the first formation above Canterbury—upon which the Luftwaffe dropped their bombs as they retreated—and scattered the second formation away from the docks into the south and west of London. There, Leigh-Mallory's B Group met them. Bombs were jettisoned anywhere as the Luftwaffe retreated. That was the RAF's day.

At the end of that momentous week, Fighter Command's airplane reserves reached their lowest—just 80 Hurricanes and 47 Spitfires.

September 15 saw the climax of the struggle. It was also the day Prime Minister Churchill chose to visit A Group Operations Headquarters, the underground command center at Uxbridge in Middlesex.

That day the German attacks on Britain came in two waves at very high altitude, 20,000 feet and higher, above radar. However, British intelligence had monitored the increased radio traffic, giving Park time to move his squadrons forward. They fought the 500 enemy aircraft all the way to London and all the way back. RAF ground crews refueled and re-armed aircraft in a frenzy of servicing whenever and at whatever airfield the pilots landed, so that from the ground it seemed as if the skies were permanently full of aircraft. Vapor trails and smoke trails scrawled the signature of battle across the summer sky.

While the fighters of A Group fought above Kent, Sussex, and the coast, that was the day that Londoners—and the Luftwaffe pilots—saw 200 Hurricanes and Spitfires together above the city, Leigh-Mallory's "big-wing" from B Group. All squadrons and reserves of A and all squadrons of B were scrambled that day.

Fighter Command shot down and destroyed 60 Nazi aircraft. It lost 26 fighters and 13 pilots. Two days later Hitler postponed indefinitely the invasion of Britain. Later he canceled it completely. Since the end of the 1939–45 war, that September 15 is celebrated every year. It is the Royal Air Force's Battle of Britain Day.

Yet the battle of Britain did not end then. It continued for the rest of the month and into October, gradually reducing in intensity as the Luftwaffe ran out of steam. Bletchley Park had decoded Hitler's Enigma signal of the seventeenth, postponing the invasion, as well as further military signals authorizing the dismantling of invasion air-transport units.

From September 7 to 30, Fighter Command destroyed 380 German aircraft for the loss of 178 fighters. The Luftwaffe's brief aura of invincibility was destroyed forever. By the end of October, Göring was forced to reduce daylight attacks to mere harassing sorties and to direct his bombers to night raids against Britain. There is a limit to the losses any military force can withstand, and the Luftwaffe had reached its own. The battle of Britain was won.

RAF Fighter Command lost 544 killed. The Luftwaffe lost 2,877: 1,176 bomber crew, 171 fighter pilots, 85 dive-bomber crew, and 1,445 missing in action, assumed killed.

In that autumn of 1940, London was bombed fifty-seven nights in succession, still a record for sustained bombing. Buckingham Palace and the Houses of Parliament were hit. The Blitz continued into 1941, culminating in a 550-bomber raid on May 10. Fighter Command had few effective night fighters at that stage of the war—no air force did, although Dowding's developments were soon to reap benefits with airborne intercept radar in the Bristol Beaufighter. The defense of London and other cities, meanwhile, was maintained by antiaircraft batteries.

The United Kingdom was bombed north, south, east, and west by the Luftwaffe. In particular Bath, Belfast, Birkenhead, Birmingham, Bristol, Cardiff, Clydeside, Coventry, Exeter, Glasgow, Hull, Ipswich, Liverpool, London, Manchester, Middlesbrough, Norwich, Plymouth, Portsmouth, Sheffield, Southampton, Sunderland, Swansea, and Wolverhampton suffered heavy damage from indiscriminate night-bombing.

Winston Churchill crystallized the importance of victory in the battle of Britain in seventeen words: "Never in the field of human conflict was so much owed by so many to so few."

About 75 percent of Fighter Command pilots were commissioned officers and 25 percent were noncommissioned sergeants, although their ranks don't matter: they flew identical airplanes against an enemy who operated a similar system in its air force. Some of their names are legend—Ginger Lacey, Peter Townsend, Josef Frantisek, Al Deere, Douglas Bader, Richard Hillary, Stanford Tuck, Johnnie Johnson, Pat Hughes, Sammy Allard, Adolph "Sailor" Malan, John Kent, J. C. Mungo-Park, "Kill 'em" Gillam, Michael Crossley—while others are proud names on a stone memorial or a part of family history. More than 500 RAF fighter pilots were killed in their tubes of aluminium, but many more were wounded, some crippled, some disfigured terribly from burns. Those who survived continued flying, through a further four and a half years of world war. There were 791 fewer at the end of that.

The successful and the unsuccessful, the brave and the fearful, Dowding and Park, the pilots, the ground crews, the radar plotters and the observers, the controllers, Beaverbrook, those who flew all the sorties and those who flew only one: they all played their part in the victory over evil.

For if the battle of Britain had been lost and the United Kingdom invaded, Europe would not have been liberated from Nazism. The German death camps would have multiplied, Russia would have been defeated, Japan would have conquered Asia and India, and all the commonwealth and empire countries would have fallen to the Nazis and Japan. As Churchill warned in 1940, a new dark age would have fallen upon the world.

Bless 'em all.

Recommended
The Last Enemy by Richard Hillary
Leader of the Few: The Authorised Biography of Air Chief Marshal the Lord Dowding by Basil Collier
Dowding and the Battle of Britain by Robert Wright
Duel of Eagles: The Struggle for the Skies from the First World War to the Battle of Britain by Peter Townsend
One of the Few by John Kent
Film: *Battle of Britain*
The Royal Air Force Church, Saint Clement Danes, the Strand, London
The Battle of Britain Memorial, Runnymede, River Thames, U.K.
The Royal Air Force Museum, Hendon, Middlesex, U.K.
The surviving inns and pubs in Kent, Sussex, and Essex with pilots' signatures and messages preserved on their ceilings and walls

The Magna Carta Barons

No free man shall be seized or imprisoned, or stripped of his rights or possessions, or outlawed or exiled, or deprived of his standing in any other way, nor will we proceed with force against him, or send others to do so, except by the lawful judgement of his peers or by the law of the land.

—Article 39

Two of the sons of Henry II would become king after him. Richard I was the older brother. He was a famous warrior and is better known as "the Lion-Hearted." He fought constantly to retake Jerusalem for Christianity and after becoming king in 1189 spent only seven months of his ten-year rule at home. In his absence, his younger brother, John, ruled as regent. When Richard was captured by the Holy Roman Emperor, John wrote a letter offering to pay £60,000 to have Richard quietly disappear. Instead, the emperor ransomed Richard back to England for £100,000—at that time, more than twice the annual income of the country. Their mother organized the ransom. Churches were ransacked for silver and gold, and rich and poor were taxed for a quarter of everything they owned. When Richard returned home, John begged him for mercy and Richard forgave him, where any other king would have had him beheaded for treason. Richard had unfinished battles in Jerusalem, and he knew there was a good chance he would die there.

In 1199, when the news came that Richard the Lion-Hearted had been killed in a siege, John had himself crowned king of England. The one danger to his new position was the line of his older brother Geoffrey. Though Geoffrey had died, his young son, Arthur, had a strong claim to the throne. The boy was in France when John became king and was barely twelve years old, but John feared he would one day become a threat. Worse news came when the French king, Philip, decided to support Arthur and made him Duke of Normandy and Aquitaine. Those titles were John's, as they had been his father's before him. In fury, John ordered every shipyard in England to create at least one ship for a fleet. By the end of 1204, he had forty-five heavy galleys, and he is sometimes credited with beginning the domination of the seas that would be the hallmark of British history for the next seven centuries.

As soon as he had the ships, John embarked an army and sailed for France. His one ally was his mother, Eleanor. She doted on John and, when he was forced to return to England for a time, even organized the battles without him. She was outmatched by the French forces and found herself besieged in a castle by Philip's army and the boy Arthur.

John returned to France at great speed when he heard the news. He landed in secret and force-marched an army to save his mother. The sudden appearance of his soldiers surprised the French, and they were routed. Arthur became John's prisoner, completely at his mercy. At first John merely demanded that Arthur renounce his claim on the English throne. Arthur refused. We do not know if John killed his nephew personally or merely gave the order, but Arthur was never seen again. There are various records from the period that suggest the boy was either blinded, castrated, or had his throat cut. John was already known as treacherous, cruel, and spoiled. He was ever after known as a murderer.

While in France, John met a beautiful young noblewoman named Isabella. Lusting after her, he sent armed men to carry her off. He then arranged a divorce from his wife to marry the woman he had kidnapped. The French king demanded that John appear before him to answer for his crimes, but John decided it was too dangerous and stayed at home. As a result, King Philip of France declared the French possessions of the English Crown forfeit. John did not have the army to resist the decision, and all the gains of his father were lost.

In 1205, John quarreled with the pope in Rome. At that time, England was Catholic, but John refused to acknowledge the pope's authority in appointing archbishops. Instead, he sent armed men to drive the priests out of the country. In response, the pope placed England under an interdict in 1208: all religious services were forbidden and all churches closed. Church bells could not be rung, and there were no marriages, christenings, or funerals. The bishops left England together, only one staying. John himself was excommunicated in 1209, which, for the Christian ruler of a Christian country, had serious implications.

Day by day, John made enemies and lost loyal supporters. When one of his lords fled the country, John had the man's wife and children imprisoned and starved to death. The king of France was building an army to invade and remove him, and John had no allies to resist them. He wrote to an Islamic ruler in Spain, offering to become a Muslim and pay annual tribute if the man lent his soldiers. The emir of Cordova refused, saying to the ambassador from John: "Your king is unworthy to be a vassal. He is a coward and a weakling and his infamy stinks in my nostrils." The fortunes of the English Crown had never been so low.

With an invasion expected at any moment, John decided to grovel to the pope and allow his choice as Archbishop of Canterbury. He hoped this would mean the French king canceled his invasion. Unable to trust even his own men, John sealed himself in Nottingham Castle and waited for the papal legate to arrive. In 1213 he traveled to Dover to meet the legate and heard alarming descriptions from him of the French army massing across the channel.

In terror, John promised to abide by anything the pope wanted and even handed his crown to the papal legate, who handed it back as a master to a servant. John also gave the legate a bag of gold coins as tribute, but the man showed his contempt by scattering the coins with his foot. In all of England's extraordinary history, there has never been such a moment of humiliation as the one John brought about.

News of his appalling actions spread to nobles and commoners alike. Wherever John went in England, he was greeted by hostile crowds, furious with what he had done. Taxes remained cruelly high, and poverty and starvation were widespread. Having lost his French possessions, the king was known as John Lackland, John Softsword, or sometimes simply John the Bastard.

John had one success when one of his lords, the Earl of Salisbury, took the English fleet and destroyed French ships waiting to carry the invasion army. The king of France could not cross without them, and John was safe for a time.

However, he made the situation worse at home when he hired foreign soldiers to take revenge on his enemies in the north of England. They burned and slaughtered freely, and John merely cheered them on. The Archbishop of Canterbury came north to see the king and, in an act of great courage, rebuked John for his actions, reminding him of his coronation oath, when he had sworn to protect his people. John raged at him, telling him to mind his church while leaving the king to mind the country. The archbishop faced him again and threatened to excommunicate him once more. The threat was a potent one, as it had once almost led to his destruction. Reluctantly, John agreed to take council with his barons.

The barons of England did not trust him. They were led by Stephen Langton, a name once famous in British history as a founder of freedom. Rather than accept his promises and see them broken, they began to consider drawing up a charter of rights that they could make him seal in front of witnesses. His great-grandfather, King Henry I, had once created such a document. From it, they would write a great charter—in Latin, a *magna carta*.

In 1214 the barons met in secret at Bury Saint Edmunds. At the altar of the church, as the freezing air made plumes of their breath, they swore a holy oath to force the king to accept the charter or begin bloody civil war. There was no mention of a parliament in the document, as the idea did not yet exist, but these men were the first parliament of England. Kings had always had councillors and advisers, but before that date, these aides had no real authority.

That winter was bitterly cold and the country suffered. At Christmas, John met the Council of Barons in Worcester. Despite the driving rain and wind, men gathered around the country, ready to go to war if John refused. Even then John tried to delay the process by offering to let the pope decide the dispute, but the barons knew the cunning king too well. They presented the Magna Carta. He could not read so had a scribe explain the details. As he understood the contents, he raged at them, shouting: "You wish to take away my crown and make a slave of me!" His temper left them unmoved. One by one, the barons walked out and left him to his choice.

The barons had demanded he meet them to seal the document at Runnymede, near Windsor, the date set for June 15, 1215. As the spring turned to summer, his remaining knights left him, until in the whole of his kingdom, he commanded only seven men. His choice was stark: accept the new order, or lose his life and his kingdom.

As the fifteenth dawned, King John came to the meadow by the Thames, where he was met by 25 armed nobles and a much larger number of witnesses and retainers. Those 25 would offer their personal surety that the charter would be observed, but in addition, more than 140 noblemen had taken up arms and declared against the king, Fulk Fitzwarin of the Robin Hood legends among them. They had chosen a place where John could not launch a surprise attack, even if he had been able to find supporters. He was completely in their power, and all his treachery and cunning had brought him to that chill morning, with the cold and misty river running past.

John took his seat by a tented pavilion, with the flags of the barons fluttering around him. The archbishop handed him the Magna Carta, but even then John did not act. He argued long and passionately, and the barons waited as the evening came, ignoring all his protests. Those twenty-five noblemen had the support of both Prince Llywe-lyn of Wales and Alexander II of Scotland, as well as eleven bishops, twenty abbots, and the arch-bishops of Canterbury and Dub-lin. Almost without exception, every man of power in Britain supported the attempt to limit John's powers. The only commoner to offer surety with the barons was William Hardel, the lord mayor of London.

As servants lit the lamps, John gave up and pressed his royal seal to the charter. In one stroke, he had given away power to elect a council of twenty-five barons. Though neither he nor they were aware of all the implications, they were laying the foundations of con-stitutional government, an independent judiciary, and trial by jury.

There are sixty-three parts to the astonishingly varied document.

For example, it states that a widow must receive her husband's goods without delay, that only competent men can be appointed as justices and constables, and that a case cannot be brought to court on the word of a single accuser. Also "that men in our kingdom shall have and keep these liberties, rights and concessions . . . for them and for their heirs, in all things and in all places for ever."

John went on to break his oath and all the promises he had made. With another mercenary army, he laid waste to the lands of the barons, even burning down the house where he stayed each night in his royal fury. Thousands were killed by his foreign soldiers, and some of the barons sent an appeal to the king of France to enter the country. The French dauphin moved quickly and entered London just a few days after landing. It would fall to John's son Henry III to make peace with the French.

For a time after 1215, it seemed that all the work that had gone into the creation of the Great Charter had been in vain. Although it was confirmed and reissued over the following decade, it would not be until the seventeenth century that it was recognized as the foundation stone of democracy and constitutional liberty.

One famous incident remains of John's ill-favored reign. He retreated north when he heard of the French threat, and on crossing the Wash, where Norfolk meets Lincolnshire, his baggage carts were caught by a rising tide and he lost the crown jewels as well as the money to pay his men. In 1216 he rode on to Newark without them and died probably from dysentery, alone, despised, and unmissed. He is buried in Worcester Cathedral. His oldest son went on to be King Henry III, and from him the Plantagenet, Tudor, and Stuart dynasties arose, including such famous monarchs as Edward I, Henry V, Henry VIII, and Elizabeth I.

There are four copies of the Magna Carta still in existence, all in Latin. Two are in the British Library and the others in the cathedrals of Lincoln and Salisbury. The Great Charter was designed to protect the rights of nobles and commoners against the king. There were earlier charters, but this was the first to grant liberties to "all the free men of our kingdom." It also bore witness to the king being bound by the law, rather than above it. That is what is meant by the phrase "the rule of law"—that all authority comes from the law itself.

From 1215 onward, rights existed in England that would travel to Ireland, Wales, Scotland, America, and much of the English-speaking world. The Magna Carta provided the foundation of Parliament and English law, which would influence the world through the British Empire. It was also the first step in creating an independent judiciary, as it allowed cases to be heard away from the king's presence. Those judges became the Common Bench, while the judges who followed the king were called the King's Bench. They too would eventually become separate from the royal court.

The original charter was confirmed more than fifty times by kings from Henry III to Henry V. Though it was largely overlooked between the thirteenth and seventeenth centuries, it became prominent in the Puritan parliament after the civil war as a bulwark of democracy against dictatorship. As such, it was the basis of written law in the country and remained on the statute book until the nineteenth century, with some clauses surviving until the 1950s before being superseded by other laws. It is at least as important as the English Declaration of Rights of 1689, which allowed freedom of speech and was the condition by Parliament of the Prince of Orange taking the throne.

The ideals of the Magna Carta form the basis of legal systems around the world, from Australia and New Zealand to America, India, and Canada. In the U.S. Declaration of Independence and its Constitution, the words of Clause 39 appear twice in direct quotation. In Europe, the system of law has its origins in ancient Rome. One stark difference between the systems remains today. Under British law, that which is not forbidden is allowed. On the Continent, only that which is granted is allowed. It is a subtle but crucial distinction.

Clause 39, as quoted at the beginning of this chapter, created "habeas corpus"—literally "thou shalt have the body"—which is fundamental to good governance. No man can be taken from his home and imprisoned without charge in England—until very recently, with the introduction of anti-terror legislation. Although defeated in the British House of Lords, the notion that the House of Commons could vote to imprison a subject for forty-two days without charge is a step backward to John's times, when the monarch or nobles could take whatever they wanted and common men had no recourse to law.

In recognition of England's common heritage with America, Queen Elizabeth II gave an acre at Runnymede to the United States on May 14, 1965. Apart from the American embassy, it is the only piece of U.S. soil in England. A memorial garden to John F. Kennedy is there, with views across the river to where King John sealed the Magna Carta. As Winston Churchill once said: "When the long tally is added, it will be seen that the British nation and the English-speaking world owe far more to the vices of John than to the labours of virtuous sovereigns."

Recommended
History of England by G. M. Trevelyan
Magna Carta and Its Influence in the World Today
by Sir Ivor Jennings
The Magna Charta Barons and Their American Descendants
by Charles Browning

Oliver Cromwell

Oliver Cromwell remains one of the most controversial figures in history—and indeed in this book. He is a hero to few, but it is no exaggeration to say that he changed his country forever and ushered in the modern age. Cometh the hour, cometh the man. He fought a civil war and executed a king—and by doing so saved a nation from tyranny. He had no appreciable charm or desire to flatter, yet he could inspire intense loyalty. He was certainly a man of heroic imagination, able to encompass a future without slavish obedience to inherited nobility.

In Cromwell's time, kings such as James I and Charles I believed that they ruled by divine right, that they had been appointed by God. No royal decision could ever be questioned and no injustice challenged. The man who reversed this style of government was a fanatic both for Protestantism and for England. His life would make him the champion of the common man, and his efforts were the crucible out of which parliamentary democracy arose. As Churchill would say in 1947: "Democracy is the worst form of government except all those other forms that have been tried from time to time."

Very little is known about Cromwell's first forty years. He was born in 1599, at the end of the Elizabethan age. Though the great storms of Elizabeth and Mary had passed, it remained an age of fervent religious belief, with Catholics and Protestants often in brutal conflict.

Cromwell went to Cambridge University in 1616 and left a year later when his father died. His mother was alone with seven unmarried daughters, and it is likely that Cromwell returned home to Cambridgeshire to protect them. He married Elizabeth Bourchier, from a wealthy Essex family, in 1620. The marriage seems to have been a happy one and produced nine children: five boys and four girls.

When James I died in 1625, his son ascended the throne as Charles I. From the first, Charles ruled as an autocrat, utterly disdaining the power of Parliament. He married a French Catholic and had obvious sympathies with Catholic countries such as Ireland and France. He created new taxes and made sweeping decisions on commercial policy. Lacking his father's intelligence and political sense, he simply could not see that the age had changed and men like Cromwell were on the rise.

In 1628, Cromwell stood for Parliament and in the same year was treated for *"valde melancholicus"*—depression. His health was poor, and it was around this time that he experienced the conversion to Puritan Protestantism that would dominate his personal and political life. In a letter, he wrote: "If I may serve my God either by my doing or my suffering, I shall be most glad."

Charles I resorted to "forced loans" from his subjects to support himself and imprisoned those who refused to pay. Puritans like Cromwell held up the king's lavish lifestyle as an example of everything they despised. In 1628, Cromwell took his seat in Parliament as they declared such taxation illegal. It was Parliament that voted the king's funds, so to maintain control, they attempted to make sure he could not find money anywhere else. The battle lines had been drawn.

In 1629, Charles dissolved Parliament and attempted to rule without them. Until he called them back to Westminster, they could not legally meet. He did not call them for eleven years. During that time he raised taxes directly from the population, which caused great resentment. Many Puritans left for America, to find new lives. The famous *Mayflower* had sailed in 1620, and there were many others in the years that followed.

In addition to Charles's English troubles, his attempt to reform the Scottish Church led to war. Desperate for money, the king could not raise funds on his own and was forced to return to Parliament, Cromwell among them. Instead of arranging the king's money, the MPs discussed the legality of his taxes. The "Short Parliament" lasted for only three weeks before Charles dissolved it in disgust.

By August 1640, the Scots had brought an army to Newcastle. Reluctantly, Charles was forced to recall Parliament once more. This is known as the "Long Parliament," and once again Cromwell was present. They brokered the Treaty of London with the Scots in 1641, and one of Charles's problems ended. However, on that occasion the members of Parliament became determined to curtail the king's power over them, even if it meant civil war.

The mood of the country was with Parliament, in part because there was still a great fear of "popish" Catholic plots. Money and faith were the main issues that brought about the civil war.

In 1642, Charles wrote to Cambridge University for a loan that would have made him temporarily immune to parliamentary control. Cromwell himself went north on the orders of Parliament. With two hundred men, he blocked the road so that the silver could not be moved south, then took command of Cambridge Castle.

It was the last straw for the king, and in August he raised his banner in Nottingham. His loyal supporters, known as Royalists or Cavaliers, began to flock to him, while an army of Parliamentarians assembled under the Earl of Essex, Cromwell with them. They were commonly known as Roundheads, after the shape of their helmets.

The armies met first at Edgehill in October, a few miles from Banbury. In numbers they were roughly equal, and the battle ended in stalemate. The king was unable to return to London and withdrew first to Reading and then to Oxford.

It is difficult now to imagine the shock wave that went through England at the outbreak of civil war. To attack the king himself was considered close to blasphemy in some quarters. Men like Cromwell had a sense of purpose, of right, of God-given destiny, that held the doubters together. He rose quickly in the ranks and in 1643 was effectively in sole command of forces in Essex, Hertfordshire, Cambridgeshire, Huntingdonshire, Suffolk, and Norfolk.

His military ability has led some biographers to speculate that he must have been a soldier on the Continent for some of those mysterious early years. He was certainly a man who handled authority as if he had been born to it. As Cromwell wrote in a letter to subordinates: "Service must be done. Command you and be obeyed!" He regarded the battles as a test of Puritanism, but he was also a pragmatist. Famously, he warned his men: "Put your trust in God, but mind to keep your powder dry."

The Royalists won a victory at Roundaway Down in 1643, while other battles ended in stalemate. No one could have predicted the outcome of the war as the year ended, but the most important battles were still to come.

Cromwell was more than just a brave and quick-thinking military officer. He was also an able politician and, as the war went on, played a key role in parliamentary discussion. He proposed reform of the churches and the power of the bishops. He opposed the enclosure and sale of common land that was often the only means of support for the poorest families.

In February 1644, Cromwell was promoted to lieutenant general. Conscription was introduced around that time, in part to counter Highland Scottish forces coming south to support the king. The parliamentary force became known as "the New Model Army."

On July 2, 1644, Cromwell commanded the left cavalry wing at Marston Moor, one of the most important battles of the English civil war. Parliamentary forces outnumbered the Royalists, and for the first time a Royalist cavalry charge was broken in the field. The king's infantry was then slaughtered. Cromwell later denied his own part in it, giving the honor to God, who may or may not have been there. It was at Marston Moor that Prince Rupert, a grandson of James I, nicknamed Cromwell "Ironside" for his stern demeanor.

The battle of Naseby in 1645 was Cromwell's greatest military triumph. He commanded the cavalry at the town near Oxford and faced a roughly equal force of Royalist horse under Prince Rupert. King Charles I commanded a small reserve of infantry. Though the battle took place in June, the ground was sodden and soft in places, hampering maneuvers. As the forces came into range of each other, Cromwell saw that a line of trees and hedges provided perfect cover for a flank attack. He sent a message to his commanding officer asking him to withdraw, and, as he had hoped, the Royalist forces came forward in response. Cromwell sent a detachment of cavalry under cover of the hedges to pour musket fire into the Royalist flank. Like Marlborough and Wellington, he was a man able to read a battlefield and position his forces for maximum effect, remaining calm even under heavy fire.

The Royalist cavalry responded to the flanking attack with a sudden charge, routing some of the parliamentary forces against them and almost carrying the day. In one of those strange events that can decide battles and even the fate of nations, the pursuing Royalists came across the enemy baggage train and stopped to loot it. For a short time the Royalist infantry was left with just one cavalry wing. Nonetheless, they pushed the parliamentary forces back in brutal hand-to-hand fighting and with musket fire. From a hill, Cromwell watched coldly as men struggled and died in the mud. He held his own riders back, waiting for the remaining Royalist cavalry to charge. At the height of the battle, he saw them move.

He spurred his horse and the two forces galloped together in a great crash. The air filled with bitter musket smoke and the screams of the dying. It was a brief and bloody fight. The Royalists were quickly routed, and by the time Prince Rupert brought his cavalry back, the day had been lost.

Over the following year, Cromwell commanded at many different sieges. In 1646 his army moved through Devon and Cornwall, rooting out the king's supporters. He accepted surrender whenever he could, more interested in winning quickly than in crushing the enemy. The first major conflict of the civil war ended in 1646.

Parliament was triumphant, the king had survived, and some regiments of the New Model Army were disbanded. For a time it looked as if Charles I might accept the limited power of a constitutional monarchy. He was held in various country houses in East Anglia and Hertfordshire and finally at Hampton Court. There Cromwell met the king and presented parliamentary bills that would severely limit the monarch's powers. Charles prevaricated and delayed, then escaped from custody in 1647, fleeing to the Isle of Wight.

The king still had many supporters in Ireland, Scotland, Wales, and the south of England. In 1648 revolts against the New Model Army broke out and the Scots gathered an army of invasion to relieve Charles.

Once more, Cromwell joined his army. He took back Chepstow and Tenby, then starved Pembroke Castle in Wales into surrender. After that, he marched north against the Scottish army and defeated them at the battle of Preston, in Lancashire. Denied support, the king was taken into custody once more.

Parliament tried to open negotiations with Charles I. At first Cromwell supported the king abdicating in exchange for his life, but Charles

scorned the offer. He was then sent for trial in London. At an early session the king said: "I would know by what power I am called hither. I would know by what authority, I mean lawful authority." He was found guilty of high treason, and Cromwell was one of those who signed his death warrant.

King Charles I was executed in London on January 30, 1649. When his head was cut off, the crowd was allowed to dip their handkerchiefs in royal blood as a souvenir. Cromwell looked down on the body and murmured: "Cruel necessity."

England was without a king for the first time in more than a thousand years, and there were many who feared the void in power.

Cromwell's immediate purpose was to prevent the new regime from collapsing after the traumatic event. Ripples of shock spread through society, and there was even a threat of foreign invasion from Scotland, France, Ireland, or Spain. Not many in Parliament had thought beyond the death of the king. Mutinies occurred around England and had to be put down with force. The country was in danger of flaring up into a bloody revolution, and Parliament was hard-pressed to keep the peace.

In Ireland and Scotland, support was staunch for King Charles's eldest son, also named Charles. His father had been king of England, Scotland, and Ireland, and Royalists now supported the son's claim.

He was proclaimed king of Scotland after his father's death in 1649, though not crowned at Scone until 1651.

With the New Model Army, Cromwell was dispatched by Parliament to Ireland to crush Royalist support. In doing so, he earned a reputation for ruthlessness that survives him today. For forty weeks, between August 1649 and May 1650, Ireland ran with blood. The slaughter at Drogheda is the most infamous, when Cromwell's army killed around three thousand Royalist troops, then rampaged through the town, butchering clergy, women, and children. Those who surrendered were executed. Cromwell followed Drogheda with an attack on Wexford, where another two thousand were killed. In less than a year, he assaulted twenty-five fortified towns and killed or routed Royalist garrisons. He saw Ireland as the central stronghold of Royalist Catholicism, and his aim was the utter destruction of all forces loyal to Charles II. He used his army as an instrument of terror, so that Catholics would never again dare to rise against his Puritan new order. In his religious fanaticism, Cromwell allowed no mercy, and his name is forever blackened by that year.

He returned to England in 1650 to lead the army against Royalists in Scotland. It would prove a harder task than the fighting in Ireland. He could not bring the Scots to battle at first. Disease and desertion reduced his fighting strength to eleven thousand, while the Scots had twenty-two thousand. It should have been the end for Cromwell, and before the battle, he bit his own lips until they bled, almost insane with fervor. Near Dunbar, he broke the Scottish right wing, then crumpled the lines into the center and finally the left wing. Cromwell said of the battle: "By the Lord of Hosts, they were made as stubble to our swords."

It was an astonishing victory against such odds, and Cromwell laughed when it was over, convinced that God had shown his hand to support him.

Throughout 1651, Cromwell's army feinted with still-rebellious Scottish lords, tempting them to come south against London. They took the bait and Cromwell crushed a second army led by Charles II at Worcester, finally ending the battles of the civil war. Charles escaped from the battlefield and, over six weeks, made his way to France. Famously, he had to spend one night in an oak tree in Shropshire to avoid detection. Ever since, there have been both pubs and ships named the Royal Oak. Charles was aided by Catholics and would eventually become one himself on his deathbed. Meanwhile, Cromwell returned in triumph to London and was received as the savior of a nation.

His first task was to get rid of the "Rump Parliament" that had held power without elections for more than a decade. They delayed, as men in power often will, and Cromwell lost patience and declared Parliament dissolved. He had the army, and his word carried weight. He refused to become king, but the country needed a ruler and flailed without one. Cromwell allowed the term "Lord Protector" and assumed the role as head of state in a new Parliament in 1653. His health was poor and it is doubtful that he wanted the role, but he saw it as vital to establish England as a stable republic and to tide her over the storms that had raged since the death of Charles I. Cromwell had taken part in most of them, after all.

He lived less than five years after taking up this last great office. During that time he hammered out a constitution, rejecting the crown and title of king more than once. He did not have dictatorial powers and in fact was often overborne by the councillors and parliaments. He saw himself as a warden of the peace. His health worsened daily, and he was never sure he had done enough to prevent England from descending into anarchy on his death. In 1656 he wrote that he wanted to see an end to the persecution of Catholics and hoped that England would be populated by "Godly men." He also sought greater equity for the poor in the law. In some ways he was successful, as only six thousand men were needed to keep the peace in England, while forty thousand had to remain in Scotland and Ireland.

Cromwell died of pneumonia in 1658. His body was buried and his effigy carried through almost empty streets to Westminster Abbey. His son Richard tried to rule after him but lacked the strength and authority of his father. Instead, Parliament asked Charles II to return to the throne in 1661. From then on, the seat of power was with Parliament, not the monarch. The man who had done more than any other to bring about such a change became the focus for poisonous hatred.

Just a few weeks after Charles II became king, Cromwell's body was exhumed. The green and moldering corpse was given a trial, hanged as a traitor, decapitated, quartered, and buried in secret locations around England. It may have looked as if the monarchy was back in all its power, but a bloody lesson had been learned and the people had been heard. Never again would a king or queen rule in tyranny, unfettered by the will of the country.

In the centuries after his death, Cromwell has had his supporters and detractors by the thousand. For a long time he was a heroic figure in England. He was certainly a man of enormous personal strength, who managed to overturn an entire society and leave it forever changed. He was unflinchingly brave in battle and an inspiring leader to his men. He remains difficult to like, but he was revered by many. Yet any tale of his life must reflect the words he famously uttered to his portrait painter and be "warts and all."

Recommended
God's Englishman: Oliver Cromwell and the English Revolution
by Christopher Hill
Oliver Cromwell by John Morrill
Cromwell by Barry Coward
Film: *Cromwell,* directed by Ken Hughes

Helen Keller

Everyone who wishes to gain true knowledge must climb Hill Difficulty alone, and since there is no royal road to the summit, I must zigzag it in my own way. . . . Every struggle is a victory. One more effort and I reach the luminous cloud, the blue depths of the sky, the uplands of my desire.

—Helen Keller

Helen Keller was born in 1880 in Tuscumbia, Alabama. Her father was a captain in the Confederate army during the Civil War, and her grandmother was second cousin to General Robert E. Lee.

When the war ended, the Keller family moved to Tennessee, where her father became a newspaper editor. Baby Helen was bright and alert, learning her first words and delighting her parents. At the age of nineteen months she was struck by an illness described by her doctors as "a congestion of the stomach and brain." It could have been scarlet fever or a strain of meningitis.

The disease left her both blind and deaf. In just a short time, all light, color, and sound had been stolen away from her. At first it seemed as if there was no way she could ever learn to speak. A deaf person learns sign language by sight. A blind one learns by hearing. Denied both those senses, Helen was unable to communicate at all. Instead, she would seek out flowers in the garden, feeling her way in darkness and silence to enjoy the scent of blossoms in summer.

As Helen grew, she began to make signs to her mother. They developed a simple language together, beginning when Helen understood by touch that a shaking head meant no and a nodding one meant yes. When she wanted ice cream, she would mime opening the freezer and shivering.

At the age of five, she was able to help her mother around the house, folding clothes and recognizing her own by touch alone. She spent a great deal of time with Martha Washington, the daughter of her mother's cook. Between them, Helen made more signs, such as placing her hands on the ground when she wanted to look for bird eggs in the long grass outside.

She already knew that the adults in the house had another world. She would sometimes reach out and feel that their lips were moving. Yet when she moved her own, no one understood. In frustration, she would throw wild tantrums, kicking and screaming without words. She felt no guilt or regret afterward, though she hurt those around her and broke toys in her rage.

There was no question then as to whether she would ever be able to leave that home for the wider and more dangerous world. On one occasion she set her clothes alight trying to dry a wet apron on a fire. Her nurse smothered the flames, but for a little girl who could neither see nor hear, the world would always be perilous.

Helen Keller was not the first to be both deaf and blind, nor even the first to overcome such a start in life. In Charles Dickens's *American Notes,* her mother read of Laura Bridgman, both blind and deaf, who had nevertheless been educated by a Dr. Gridley Howe. Howe was long dead, but it raised a hope in her mother's heart that something could be done with her bright and endlessly frustrated daughter.

When Helen was six, her parents took her to an eye specialist in Baltimore, believing that something could be done for her. The specialist saw no hope for her eyes, but for her deafness, he recommended Dr. Alexander Graham Bell in Washington, D.C. Bell's mother and wife were deaf, and he was famous chiefly for his work with deaf people. That he was the first to take out a U.S. patent on a telephone sprang from his research into hearing.

Helen was induced to sit on Bell's knee, and to her pleasure, he understood her rudimentary signs. Through Bell's recommendation, the Keller family was able to find a teacher for their daughter, a young woman who would change her life forever: Miss Anne Mansfield Sullivan.

In March 1887, Anne Sullivan arrived to live with the family in Tennessee, just before Helen turned seven. She gave Helen a doll that had been dressed by Laura Bridgman herself. As Helen played with it, Anne spelled the letters *d-o-l-l* onto the palm of Helen's open hand.

It was not long before Helen could proudly copy the action onto her mother's hand, though she did not know what letters were. In the same way, she learned simple words for things she encountered and even a few verbs, but there was still a huge gulf in her understanding. Anne Sullivan was endlessly patient and showed her that *d-o-l-l* could be used for other toys, as well as the first. Things had names!

After one frustrating morning, when she could not be made to understand the difference between *mug* and *water,* Helen smashed the doll on the floor. She felt no regret or sorrow. Without the accompanying concepts, she may not even have been capable of such emotions. Patiently, her new teacher took her outside. Sullivan knew she needed some way to make the words less abstract, to make them real for a little girl who had no frame of reference, no key to the lock of the world.

Sullivan walked with Helen to the pump outside and placed Helen's hand under the cold water as it gushed out. At the same time, she spelled *w-a-t-e-r* on Helen's palm.

It was an awakening. In moments, Helen understood and there was a true chink of light in her darkness. It was not long before she patted Sullivan's arm and was rewarded with the word *T-e-a-c-h-e-r* spelled into her hand. After that, the little girl went very still. Nervously, her hand crept up to her own head and she tapped herself. Slowly, Sullivan spelled out *H-e-l-e-n*.

When they returned to the house, Helen touched the pieces of the broken doll and was suddenly crying. She said later that it was the first time she had ever experienced repentance and sorrow.

That same day, inspired by her sudden link to the world, she learned *mother, father, sister, teacher,* and many other words and concepts. Anne Sullivan had broken through.

That summer of 1887, Helen spent every day with her teacher, learning new words. Each one would bring sudden understanding, and Helen delighted in her widening perception.

On one occasion, Helen and Sullivan climbed a tree, then her teacher left her to fetch a picnic from the house. While Helen was alone there, more alone than many of us can imagine, a summer storm came. The wind howled around the branches where Helen clung, terrified. Sullivan came running back to get her down, but Helen had survived the tempest and the tree had not fallen. Later, she grew to love the flowering mimosa trees and climbed to the very tops of them, sitting in the swaying branches for hours at a time with the wind on her face.

Concepts other children took for granted had to be learned slowly. At first Helen wondered if love was the sweetness of flowers or the warmth of the sun. Yet she made progress and her teacher became devoted to her. As the years passed, Helen and Sullivan could hold more and more complex conversations, spelling words into each other's palms in perfect silence. Even so, there were mountains still to climb.

To teach Helen to read, Sullivan gave her pieces of card with the letters raised so she could trace them out with her fingers. It was not long before Helen could pin *girl* to herself and hide in the wardrobe, leaving the words *is, in,* and *wardrobe* on the shelf where Sullivan could find them. All learning was a game between teacher and student, and Helen took enormous pleasure in every new thing. She learned simple sums by counting beads; she even learned geography, as Sullivan taught her to make landscapes from clay, so that the course of rivers could be traced with her hands.

Endlessly inventive, Sullivan also made a model of the earth from circles of twine and a stick, to teach Helen about the poles and zones of the planet. They grew flowers on a windowsill, raised tadpoles, and examined shells and fossils until Helen dreamed of strange creatures from the dawn of time. One of her tadpoles leaped out of the jar and Helen rescued it, pleased that it had the courage to see more of the world around it, just as she had.

By 1888, the darkness of Helen Keller's childhood had been eased enough for her to travel to Boston and the Perkins School for the Blind, where Laura Bridgman had been taught. Anne Sullivan herself had been a pupil there, when a childhood illness damaged her sight. Though Anne had recovered almost completely, she had learned manual signing from Laura Bridgman, then the first deaf-blind American to be educated.

For the first time, Helen met other blind children and was thrilled to discover that they too had been taught the manual alphabet. Her horizons opened further with visits to the sea, to Bunker Hill, and to Plymouth, where the Pilgrims had landed. Later in life she would call Boston "the City of Kind Hearts."

She was breathing in education in great gulps by then, and at home she rode a pony she called Black Beauty, having read the book in Braille lettering. It is difficult to comprehend the courage it took for a deaf and blind girl to ride, swim in the sea, and even go tobogganing on a snowy Boston day, yet she did those things. Anne Sullivan was with her at all times, talking and teaching her constantly. Even so, they were nearly caught by a train as they crossed a trestle and had to climb down to the cross braces of the bridge as it puffed by.

When she was ten, Helen went to see another teacher who would make a crucial change in her life. Miss Sarah Fuller let Helen touch her mouth as she spoke slowly and clearly. It was incredibly hard for Helen to produce sounds from the memory of her fingers, but she never gave up. She would tell herself over and over, "I am not dumb now," and she promised herself that her little sister would one day understand her. With her first spoken sentence, "It is warm," she had opened another door in her life. From then on she worked night and day to improve the sounds she could make, constantly corrected by Miss Fuller and aided by Anne Sullivan.

After an intensive period of study, Helen traveled home with Sullivan by train. Her entire family came to meet her at the station. They waited in fearful anticipation for her to speak, and when she greeted them aloud, her mother wept in joy and her sister, Mildred, kissed her hand.

The following year was a difficult one for Helen. She wrote her first story, "The Frost King," and sent it to Mr. Anagnos of the Perkins School for the Blind. He was impressed enough to publish it in the school's report, and then it came out that Helen had somehow repeated most of a story she had heard, called "The Frost Fairies."

It was no small matter. She had no memory of the original story, but the similarities were too obvious to ignore. Mr. Anagnos felt he had been deceived and shamed, and at the school, Helen was summoned before a formal gathering to be questioned. Sullivan was not allowed to remain at her side, and Helen, a girl of twelve, suffered terribly. Marked by her grief, she never wrote fiction again, for fear that her mind would betray her into reproducing something she had once read or heard. In all her later writing, even letters to her mother, she was tortured by the idea that a sentence might not be her own and read each one over and over again to be sure.

Her next attempt at writing came the following year—a brief account of her life for a periodical, written on a Braille typewriter. Around that time she also traveled to Niagara Falls and the World's Fair, where she was allowed to touch the exhibits and sculptures. Alexander Graham Bell accompanied her and took pleasure in explaining the sights and inventions—from his own telephone to Egyptian mummies. Helen's mind was flowering with Braille French and Latin as well as Greek, Roman, and American histories. In addition, she practiced and polished her speech constantly, hoping always to one day be understood even by strangers. Progress was very slow. How could she be corrected when the sound she made was not quite right? It was a hard, frustrating process, but she worked at it night and day.

Her world was a small one, because only those who knew the manual alphabet or the techniques of getting a blind girl to read their lips by touch could speak to her. Even so, she went on to a school for the deaf in New York, where, among other things, she studied Latin, algebra, Greek, and geography for two years. She became almost fluent in German at that time and could read Braille in four languages.

In 1896 she entered the Cambridge School for Young Ladies—the only deaf and blind pupil there. Sullivan was allowed to go with her and interpret when she could not read the teachers' lips by touch. She could not make notes in class so had to retain all that she needed and then copy it out each evening on a typewriter.

When it came to her exams, she sat in a room with a typewriter and the principal, Mr. Gilman, who had taken the time to learn the manual alphabet. She passed them all and achieved honors in English and German. Her teachers had assumed it would take five years for her to prepare for college but revised the estimate down to three. Helen worked herself into illness, and her mother withdrew her from the school and sent her to a tutor.

In 1899, Keller, age twenty, took her final exams, reading them in American Braille. She qualified to go to Radcliffe College in Cambridge, Massachusetts, in 1900. She was the first deaf and blind person to attend an institute of higher education and the first one to graduate with a Bachelor of Arts degree. She said later that she had felt compelled to try her strength against the standards of those who could see and hear.

At the age of twenty-two, Keller wrote the details of her extraordinary life to that point. *The Story of My Life* was published and became a sensation; it was translated into more than fifty languages. It remains in print today, and from the first page, the vivid quality of the writing is astonishing when you consider that the author wrote without sound or color or light, on a Braille typewriter.

Keller's friendship with Sullivan continued, even through Sullivan's marriage to John Macy in 1905. The three of them lived together for a time, and Macy introduced Keller to socialism.

She became a fiery defender of the rights of the downtrodden and wrote numerous articles for magazines and journals on subjects such as the rights of women, deafness, blindness, and social inequality. Through her writing, she became known to a much wider audience. She and Sullivan toured the country, with Sullivan translating questions and answers between Keller and the public. Keller rarely trusted her speaking voice in public. She had no way of being certain that it was making the right sounds—for a mind with no concept of sound can only ever approximate. Sadly, she never became as fluent in speech to convey the words that flooded her mind, full of color and life.

Her achievements inspired others, and she became a fund-raiser for the American Foundation for the Blind and sat on the first board of directors for the American Braille Press. She and Sullivan had to take on a secretary, Polly Thomson, to handle the correspondence. Her lectures and writing were vital work. At that time, many blind people were treated as helpless invalids. Some were even kept in asylums, with no attempt made to communicate with them. Helen Keller showed that the blind and the deaf were valuable. She spoke for those who had no voice when she said: "The public must learn that the blind man is neither a genius nor a freak nor an idiot. He has a mind that can be educated, a hand which can be trained, ambitions which it is right for him to strive to realize, and it is the duty of the public to help him make the best of himself, so that he can win light through work."

Keller's mother died in 1921, and Anne Sullivan Macy fell ill with bronchitis around the same time. For a while she could no longer translate for Keller at lectures and Polly Thomson took over the role, having worked closely with Keller for years. Sullivan died in 1936. The wonderful, dedicated woman who had given life and light to one of the great souls of the twentieth century had gone.

Keller began writing a book about their relationship, but the first draft was destroyed in a fire while she was away on a fund-raising tour. She traveled by ship to Japan, Australia, Europe, and South America. She met many heads of state, and it was said that all ranks of people felt their troubles melt away when they met her. No matter what problems other people faced, she had walked over a higher hill and come down the other side. Mark Twain said: "The two most interesting people of the nineteenth century were Napoléon and Helen Keller."

Keller and Polly Thomson toured constantly, raising fortunes for the care of the blind around the world. Polly was not a young woman, and the workload was grueling. She suffered a stroke while they were in Japan, though she later recovered.

Keller rewrote her book *Teacher: Anne Sullivan Macy*, and it was published at last in 1955 to add to her other books and a host of articles. It is a poignant record of a life, written in a more mature style that is both extraordinarily vivid and learned.

Helen Keller tried to use every day she had. She would not allow herself to rest, and the demanding workload wore her out as well as those around her. Thomson died after a stroke in 1960. Thomson's nurse, Winnie Corbally, would care for Keller in her final years.

By the 1960s, films and books had made Helen Keller the most famous deaf-blind woman in the world. Never again would a child like her be left to the terrors of darkness and silence. Her example shone further than she knew and remains compelling today.

Her work and achievements were recognized while she was still alive. As well as countless awards and honors on her travels, she was awarded the Presidential Medal of Freedom in 1964 and elected to the Women's Hall of Fame at the World's Fair.

In 1968, Helen Keller died in her sleep at the age of eighty-eight. She was cremated and her ashes were placed next to those of Anne Sullivan Macy and Polly Thomson at the National Cathedral in Washington, D.C. There is a Braille plaque there that reads: HELEN KELLER AND HER BELOVED COMPANION ANNE SULLIVAN MACY ARE INTERRED IN THE COLUMBARIUM BEHIND THIS CHAPEL. The raised dots of the Braille letters have been worn down by so many gentle hands that the plaque has to be replaced regularly.

Helen Keller inspired millions of those who had to struggle with blindness, deafness, or both. She inspired millions more who never did.

Recommended
The Story of My Life by Helen Keller
Teacher: Anne Sullivan Macy by Helen Keller

James Cook

On a Sunday morning in Kealakekua Bay in the Sandwich Islands (Hawaii) an islander struck a naval officer on the back of the head with a club. The officer staggered and fell onto one knee. Before he could rise, a dagger was thrust into the back of his neck. He tumbled into the knee-deep sea, and a crowd of islanders rushed to hold him underwater. He struggled, raising his great head toward his boat for help. He was pushed under, hit again on the head, then beaten with stones, knives, and clubs. The tropical water grew red before his body was dragged onto the beach and torn apart.

That was the tragic end of the extraordinary life of James Cook, RN, on February 14, 1779—the death of the greatest explorer, navigator, discoverer, surveyor, seaman, cartographer, and ethnographer the world has ever seen.

His ships' names—*Endeavour, Resolution, Adventure, Discovery*—are still famous and have been used for research and exploration vessels ever since. Today they are also used in the exploration of space. How did the son of an obscure Yorkshire laborer come to die in the far Pacific, honored and revered by geographers and scientists throughout the world?

Recognizing his intelligence his father sent the young James to the village school so that he knew the three Rs of reading, writing, and 'rithmetic. With education he hoped James might become manager—perhaps even owner—of a grocer's or draper's shop. However, during his apprenticeship to a shopkeeper in a town on the northeast coast, young James saw the masts and sails of North Sea colliers in Whitby Harbor, and that was the end of potatoes, groceries, and linen for him.

At the age of seventeen, Cook was apprenticed to the collier *Free-love,* carrying coal from northeast ports to London and sometimes to Scandinavia and the Baltic. It was an exacting trade sailing through the shoals, sandbanks, estuaries, fogs, wild weather, and lee shores of the North Sea. Good seamanship was vital there, and Cook learned and excelled in his new career.

Cook was twenty-six and first mate when he entered the Wapping naval depot to join the Royal Navy. He was posted able seaman to the fifty-eight-gun HMS *Eagle,* going from second in command of a merchant ship to nobody; from a small cabin of his own to four-teen inches in which to swing his hammock. Cook took a romantic gamble with fate, or perhaps he recognized destiny.

In a few weeks he was promoted to master's mate, a lowly petty officer, while a new captain took command. Hugh Palliser immedi-ately noticed the tall, big-boned Yorkshireman who knew his way about the ship as if he'd been there for years. Very shortly, Cook was made boatswain and given command of the *Eagle's* forty-foot sloop, patrolling the English Channel and the Western Approaches. The Seven Years' War, fought by Britain and Prussia against Austria, France, Russia, and Spain, began in 1756, and Cook saw his first ac-tion.

The *Eagle* captured two French ships and Cook was made prize master of the larger to sail her to London. He was paid off when the *Eagle* was refitted, but with the recommendations of both Captain Palliser and the MP for Whitby, he was made master. Such a promo-tion was more usual after some six years in the navy; James Cook had served just two. Palliser, who went on to become Lord of the Admiralty, knew a good seaman when he saw one.

Cook was appointed master to the sixty-gun *Pembroke* and in 1758 made his first ocean voyage, escorting the fleet from Plymouth to Nova Scotia for the Canadian campaign. It was a horrendous passage, the weather dead foul, and it took an amazing three months. The French, however, knew of British plans to capture Quebec and had made preparations. The city seemed impregnable, and all the naviga-tion marks and buoys in the Saint Lawrence River had been removed.

Cook was ordered to survey, chart, and buoy the rock-strewn and shoaling Saint Lawrence so that the navy could sail soldiers upriver to attack Quebec. He borrowed masters from other ships and completed the task in one week—at night. They were seen by native Canadians supporting the French, and in one attack, as natives clambered over the stern of a launch, Cook left rapidly by the bow. During daylight Cook drew a chart of the Saint Lawrence that was so accurate it remained in use for more than a century.

On a September night, the ships sailed up Cook's channel to reach the Heights of Abraham. Not one vessel went aground or was damaged, and General Wolfe went on to defeat General Montcalm on the Plains of Abraham to take Quebec.

In 1763, James Cook was given his first command, becoming master and commander of the schooner *Grenville*. He was known as "Mr. Cook, Engineer, Surveyor of Newfoundland and Labrador." For five years, from spring to autumn, he surveyed and charted the east coasts of Canada, while in winter in Britain he drew his charts, wrote sailing directions for other mariners, and studied spherical trigonometry and astronomy. In 1766 there was an eclipse of the sun. Cook took many observations and measurements and presented a scientific paper to the Royal Society in London, the first of several to the world's premier scientific organization. Yet the navy had other extraordinary plans for this farm laborer's son.

The Pacific Ocean was then a mostly unknown region where there might be—some geographers said *must* be—a continent known as Terra Australis Nondum Cognita, the "southern land not yet known." The Pacific was greater in area than all the lands of the earth added together, but it was the Enlightenment, and high time for Great Britain to find out whether what is now known as Antarctica existed or not. The Royal Society and the Royal Navy raised an expedition.

It was not by any means the first venture into the Pacific. The Spanish had discovered the Philippines, the Dutch western "New Holland" (Australia) and Van Diemen's Land (Tasmania), while the British had touched Japan and discovered western North America, the Tuamotus, Otaheite (Tahiti), the Gilberts (Kiribati), New Britain,

New Ireland, the Carolines, and other islands. Yet all had sailed through the middle and the north of the Pacific. None had sailed south, where Terra Australis was expected to be. The Royal Society also wanted observations of the forthcoming transit of Venus across the sun, in order to calculate exactly the distance from the earth to the sun. Captain Wallis, returned from discovering Otaheite, recommended that island as an observatory because of its friendly people, ample food, and fresh water and because its exact position was known.

The Royal Society wanted the expedition to be commanded by Alexander Dalrymple, the world's expert on Terra Australis, but he was a difficult man and refused to sail under naval authority. Someone in the Admiralty—perhaps Palliser—proposed James Cook. It was pointed out that he wasn't a commissioned officer, so he was commissioned for the task.

On April 1, the Admiralty announced that the Whitby collier *Earl of Pembroke* had been purchased for the expedition and renamed *Endeavour*. She cost £2,307 5s. 6d., and a further £2,500 was spent fitting her out to carry people, equipment, stores, and food for more than two years. The new Lieutenant Cook hoisted his commissioning pennant and took command of His Majesty's Bark *Endeavour* on May 27, at Deptford on the River Thames.

The Royal Society accepted that Cook qualified as one astronomer and sent Charles Green of the Royal Observatory as another. Also sailing were botanists Joseph Banks and Daniel Solander, completing a ship's company of ninety-four, including a dozen marines. Also joining the crew was a previous circumnavigator—the *Dolphin*'s goat, a good milker and not prone to seasickness.

Cook sailed first to Plymouth, which took three weeks. The *Endeavour* was a sturdy, safe, but not fast vessel; her maximum speed was no more than eight knots in ideal conditions. She was a three-masted bark, 110 feet long with a 29¼-foot beam. At 2 P.M. on August 26, 1768, the *Endeavour* and Cook departed Plymouth for the South Seas, the first of the three greatest voyages of exploration, discovery, and mapping ever made.

The *Endeavour* was not equipped with one of Harrison's new chronometers, vital for the most accurate measurement of longitude. Instead, Cook and Green used the complicated lunar observations invented by Sir Isaac Newton, although Cook did have a copy of the very first *Nautical Almanac* (1767), containing the most up-to-date lunar tables.

He also took it upon himself to be ship's purser, so that the type of food served was under his control. He was determined that there would be no deaths from scurvy—a lack of vitamin C then guaranteed in long voyages. To this end, he packed the holds with barrels of pickled cabbage, tubs of orange and lemon juice, hogsheads of malt, portable soup (solid blocks of meat extract), wort (infusions of malt), and saloups (a drink made from sassafras).

Down the length of the North and South Atlantic oceans sailed the little ship to reach the southernmost tip of South America by Christmas. Cook rounded Cape Horn in remarkably good weather and, taking the opportunity, sailed farther southwest searching for land. He reached 60° south, the farthest south ever recorded, to find only the fetch of the sea: deep, long swells from the west indicating no land for perhaps a thousand miles. There might be land or ice to the south—Cook suspected there was—but nothing in the immediate west. In a good wind, he turned northwest for Otaheite, again sailing seas never crossed before. He found no Terra Australis and reached Matavai Bay in April 1769.

For three months the *Endeavour* remained at the exotic green island of Otaheite. Cook and Green observed the transit of Venus. Several seamen were flogged for harshness to the Tahitians and ignoring Cook's rules of fair barter. Cook explored and charted the beautiful island; two marines deserted and took to the hills with their Tahitian "wives," and draftsman Buchan died of a fit. The two marines were returned by Tahitians and put in irons, and it was discovered that there was now venereal disease in paradise. King Tynah of Otaheite said it had arrived with French sailors under Bougainville.

There were tears when the *Endeavour* departed in July, for many friendships had been formed, not least between Tynah and Cook. Many islanders offered to sail with their British friends, but Cook was bound for the cold south in search of Terra Australis; it would be very unpleasant for a Tahitian, and how were they to return? A priest and navigator named Tupaia pleaded to join, and Cook relented.

Cook first sailed west, charting the Society Islands he named after the Royal Society. Tupaia was a great help, for he knew those waters well. At exotic Tetiaroa, Huahine, Raiatea, Tahaa, and Bora-Bora there was a welcome for them all. There was no continent, so Cook took the *Endeavour* into latitudes 40° south and then to the northwest, southwest, and west, searching for Terra Australis. There might have been land, rocks, or reefs at any moment, but they encountered nothing but ocean until October, when a tall headland was sighted. Might this be the fabled Terra Australis?

Cook navigated twenty-five hundred nautical miles around the coasts of this land and proved them to be two long islands—New Zealand—sighted once before, in 1642. He surveyed and charted the coasts, met the Maori peoples with whom Tupaia shared a Polynesian language, and carried out necessary work to the ship in Queen Charlotte Sound. Cook's surveys became the basis for New Zealand charts for the next two hundred years. The *Endeavour*'s artist sketched a mountain with snow on its peak and gave it the title "Mount Egmont, New Zealand, Australia," the first definite written reference to an "Australia."

It took six months to chart New Zealand, half a year in which

Cook became a legend and entered Maori folklore. Fifty years later a Maori chief recalled meeting Cook as a child: "We knew that he was chief of the whole by his perfect, gentlemanly and noble demeanour. He seldom spoke . . . he came to us and patted our cheeks and gently touched our heads. . . . My companions said: 'A noble man cannot be lost in a crowd.' "

However, New Zealand was not Terra Australis. By then the *Endeavour* and her crew had been at sea for twenty months, so Cook called a conference of senior men to discuss their voyage home. There were two known routes: east to Cape Horn or north around New Guinea to the Dutch settlement of Batavia (Jakarta) and then Cape Town. Typically, Cook agreed to a third unknown route—west to find the coast of New Holland (Australia), the continent discovered by Englishman William Dampier in 1688, to chart it north and west to Batavia.

Cook steered for Van Diemen's Land but was blown by a storm until he was north *and* east of its position. Sunrise on April 20, 1770, revealed the southeast corner of New Holland, a cape he named Point Hicks, and so began the famous voyage along the immense east coast of what is now known as Australia, surveying, charting, and naming as he went. On the twenty-ninth, he sailed into a bay to anchor "under the South shore about 2 mile within the entrance in 6 fathoms of water."

A boat was lowered, and Cook, Banks, Solander, and Tupaia rowed for the beach, where there were several Aborigines, similar to those Dampier had encountered in the far northwest. Tupaia couldn't communicate with them, and they weren't interested in trade. They were primarily defensive of their primitive canoes.

As in New Zealand, Cook raised the flag and claimed the land for Britain, while Banks and Solander collected every example of the unknown flora and fauna they could find. Cook named the bay Botany Bay and the land New South Wales because it reminded him of Wales along the Bristol Channel. They buried seaman Sutherland, who had died of tuberculosis, and continued north.

Cook was disappointed that he'd made no meaningful contact with the Aborigines as he had with other Pacific peoples, but he was no fool. He knew that contact meant change at the hands of the stronger—whether the explorers were Phoenician, Greek, Roman, or British.

Cook navigated two thousand miles northward into the southern tropics until he was sailing between continuous reefs to the east (the Great Barrier Reef) and the mainland to the west, in a gradually narrowing seaway. Inside eighty thousand square miles of the largest reef in the world, Cook conned the *Endeavour,* turning and twisting through narrow passages, around dangerous coral, and past uninhabited islands. Inevitably, the *Endeavour* ran onto a submerged reef. Seventeen fathoms had been the last sounding of the lead line in the June moonlight; suddenly the ship was aground.

After jettisoning cannon, transferring stores into the boats, and floating the topmasts overboard, Cook managed to haul off. The sinking ship limped to a nearby river for careening on the beach. The choice of a sturdy, broad-bottomed Whitby collier was justified. By August, after weeks of repairs, the *Endeavour* put to sea once more.

Sailing north, Cook reached and named Cape York, the northern tip of New Holland. From there he turned westward to Batavia, proving that New Guinea was not joined to New Holland. He named the channel Endeavour Strait. A battered and worn *Endeavour* reached Batavia on October 10.

Since departing Plymouth, Cook had lost three men by drowning, two from exposure, one each to drink, epilepsy, and tuberculosis, but none to scurvy. Repairs to the *Endeavour* took three months at Batavia, where every man contracted fever. Thirty-one, including astronomer Green and Tupaia of Otaheite, died of Batavia fever before the ship reached Britain. The last was Lieutenant Hicks in the North Atlantic.

On July 13, 1771, one month shy of a three-year voyage, the *Endeavour* anchored off Deal in Kent. Of her original crew of ninety-four, fifty-six survived, and the goat from the *Dolphin* had completed her second circumnavigation.

In Britain it had been thought that the *Endeavour* was lost. Botanist Joseph Banks was lionized as a great scientist and knighted; Cook, who'd made the decisions and done the work, was promoted to commander. Yet Alexander Dalrymple was angry that Cook had discovered no new continent other than the Pacific coast of New Holland; what we now call Australia was not the unknown southern land. However, there was still a small chance that such a continent might exist, and Cook proposed a circumnavigation around the Antarctic to settle the matter.

Meanwhile, Cook returned home to find two of his four children dead, one of whom had died without him ever seeing him. It was not an uncommon story for an eighteenth-century seaman.

After the success of the *Endeavour,* the Admiralty purchased another two Whitby colliers and named them *Resolution* and *Adventure.* One year to the day after Cook had come ashore he was away again. What Mrs. Cook thought is not recorded. The *Resolution* and the *Adventure* sailed from Plymouth on July 13, 1772, bound almost everywhere in the southern hemisphere. Lieutenant Tobias Furneaux commanded the *Adventure,* while twenty *Endeavour* men rejoined Cook in the *Resolution.* Somehow, Cook had managed to persuade the Navy Board to pay the *Endeavour*'s crew their arrears of three years' pay, with an advance of two months for those who rejoined— one of his lesser-known accomplishments. He also shipped two Whitby men with Arctic ice experience.

The second expedition was even more remarkable and successful than the first. This time, Cook was entrusted with the K1 chronometer, a copy of John Harrison's prize-winning and more famous H4, so that longitudes could be calculated more exactly than ever before. They sailed to Cape Town and, after reprovisioning the two vessels, headed due south. It was November, the southern summer, and Cook ventured far beyond 60° south.

Christmas was spent deep in the Southern Ocean. On January 17, 1773, Cook crossed the Antarctic Circle, 66° 32.5′ south, to be the first to enter the Antarctic. The *Resolution* and the *Adventure* sailed through seas littered with icebergs before their way was barred by pack ice. From the masthead they saw only ice, for their circle of vision was no more than twelve miles. Yet they were only seventy-five miles from the ice-covered continent of Antarctica. The Whitby ice experts expressed their concerns as Cook maneuvered between icebergs, ice floes, and pack ice, but there was no passage south.

He turned northeast toward the Kerguelen Islands, to investigate French claims of Terra Australis. There was no land. In appalling weather, the *Adventure* and the *Resolution* were separated, but Cook had given orders for just such an eventuality and the ships continued their explorations independently. The *Adventure* explored north of due east to a rendezvous in New Zealand, while the *Resolution* searched south of due east following the ice edge. After eleven thousand miles and 117 days from Cape Town, with no new land sighted, the *Resolution* reached the south of New Zealand. Numerous pods of whales were recorded, an observation Cook knew spelled doom for the mammals even as he recorded it. In mid-May he reached the Queen Charlotte Sound rendezvous to find the *Adventure* waiting.

Furneaux, too, had discovered no land but had found a good anchorage in Van Diemen's Land that he'd named Adventure Bay.

The ships were repaired and fresh food and water taken on board in exchange with the Maoris for hogs, goats, and vegetable seeds. By mid-June, Cook was off into the Pacific, searching again for Terra Australis. A circular exploration took them in mid-August to Otaheite, where they replenished their stores. "And how is the great King George?" asked King Tynah, delighted to see them.

Cook strove for friendly relations wherever he went, but Otaheite and the Society Islands were particular successes. Yet with the exception of the Maoris, Polynesians everywhere stole prodigiously. To counter this, Cook secured their chiefs as willing hostages until the important items were returned. This system was accepted by all with smiles and laughter until it became almost a game.

On departure from Matavai Bay there were more tears. Sailing west, Cook discovered, surveyed, and charted the Friendly Islands (Tonga), where again the ships and crews were welcomed. In October 1773 Cook turned his ships south for a brief stop at Queen Charlotte Sound for provisions and water. The *Adventure* became separated again and reached Queen Charlotte Sound after the *Resolution* had left.

While the *Adventure* was reprovisioning, Maoris attacked one of the boats, killing and eating the crew of ten.

After the shock of the attack, following Cook's orders, the *Adventure* searched the Southern Ocean eastward through latitudes 60° south, passed far south of Cape Horn and on to Cape Town, and then headed home—yet another British circumnavigation in the eighteenth century. Spain had long considered the Pacific her waters. Already it was British and, very soon, international under the freedom of the Royal Navy.

On the *Resolution,* Cook ventured far south to the Antarctic ice and then east. December 25 was spent at 67° south, the first Antarctic Christmas. Gifts were extra tots of rum and brandy with "wind northerly a strong gale with a thick fog sleet and snow which froze to the rigging as it fell and decorated the whole with icicles." Cook sailed north to investigate another blank in the map, then south again to cross the Antarctic Circle for the third time.

He recorded that the ice "extended east and west far beyond the reach of our sight, while the Southern half of the Horizon was illuminated by rays of light which were Reflected from the ice to a considerable height. . . . It was indeed my opinion that this ice extends quite to the Pole, or perhaps joins to some Land to which it has been fixed since Creation." The *Resolution* was stopped by the ice on January 30, 1774, at 71° 10′ south, the farthest south then recorded. Cook reached the ice edge all the way around Antarctica, saw lines of icebergs broken out from the continent, but never saw the ice-covered land itself.

In a very rare personal comment, he wrote: "I who had Ambition not only to go Farther than any one had done before, but as far as it was possible for man to go, was not sorry at meeting with this interruption as it in some measure relieved us, at least shortened the dangers and hardships inseparable with the navigation of the Southern Polar Rigions." The hardships were many. The *Resolution* was, literally, freezing cold and wet, the hammocks and bunks permanently damp. Most work had to be done without gloves, and there was then no effective cold-weather clothing. The rope rigging froze solid, the canvas sails turned into stiff boards that ripped out fingernails, and metal parts froze and stripped the skin. Cook himself suffered from colic, which nearly killed him. Perhaps there is no finer testament to James Cook's seamanship, navigation, and care for his men than this: in a vessel completely unsuited for the conditions, he was the first to chart the limits of Antarctica and did not lose one man.

In February, approaching Cape Horn, Cook turned north to explore the last unknown area of the Pacific where there *might* have been land. There had been a possible sighting there in the late 1500s, which Alexander Dalrymple thought might be the edge of a continent. After 103 days at sea since Queen Charlotte Sound, Cook discovered Easter Island. He charted the island, met the welcoming Polynesians, and learned that they also didn't know who had carved the amazing stone statues. They were there when *they'd* arrived.

In the rejuvenating warmth of the tropics, Cook sailed farther northwest to discover the beautiful Marquesas Islands, sighted once in 1595 and since lost. Again he was welcomed by Polynesians as he surveyed and charted their islands and took on fresh food. There was still no scurvy on the *Resolution*. He then sailed west for repairs and rest once more at Otaheite, to its green hills, its tang of wood smoke, and, for the crew, other delights. Despite many offerings by chiefs of Polynesia, Cook remained celibate. He focused on learning the language.

From Otaheite, Cook navigated west through the Friendly Islands, then northwest. Missing the Fiji Islands, Cook discovered and named most of the New Hebrides (Vanuatu), landing despite the cannibalism of those Melanesian islanders. Turning south again, he discovered, named, and charted the New Caledonia islands and, on October 10, the uninhabited Norfolk Island. He brought the *Resolution* back to provision at Queen Charlotte Sound in November 1774.

Cook made a final sweep eastward across the Pacific Ocean through latitudes 50° south, to the dangerous coast of Tierra del Fuego. He surveyed Cape Horn over Christmas and in the new year turned southeast once more toward Antarctica. Geographers had identified "land" there, but there was only the wild Southern Ocean. In 1775 he discovered uninhabited South Georgia Island and Clerke Rocks. He recorded in his journal the almost unbelievable number of whales, seals, and birds, commenting again that these discoveries would only bring men to plunder another region of the world.

In a last dig southeast he discovered and named Sandwich Land (South Sandwich Islands), which he thought might be off a southern promontory. He was right—the Antarctic Peninsula is not far away. Cook turned the *Resolution* to the east once more, crossed his track of 1772, and completed the first circumnavigation of Antarctica. Finally, he turned north and in March reached Cape Town, where he was told that the *Adventure* had passed safely a year before.

James Cook returned to England in July 1775, to complete an incredible exploration of three years and eighteen days. He lost just four men: three drowned, one of natural causes, none to disease. In the *Resolution* and the *Endeavour* he'd sailed 120,000 nautical miles, twice around the world and many times around the Pacific. At forty-six years of age, he was truly the greatest explorer, discoverer, navigator, surveyor, cartographer, and seaman of his age.

Cook was made captain and presented again to King George III. He prepared and delivered his scientific papers to the Royal Society, which awarded him its gold medal and elected him Fellow for his geographic and scientific achievements. Not bad for a man whose only formal education was a village school in Yorkshire.

Of Terra Australis, he concluded: "I had now made the circuit of the Southern Ocean in a high Latitude and traversed it in such a manner as to leave not the least room for the Possibility of there being a continent, unless near the Pole and out of the reach of Navigation . . . thus I flatter my self that the intention of the Voyage has in every respect been fully Answered, the Southern Hemisphere sufficiently explored and a final end put to searching after a Southern Continent. . . . That there may be a Continent or large tract of land near the Pole I will not deny. On the contrary I am of opinion there is, and it is probable that we have seen a part of it." Captain Cook, the first Antarctic explorer, was absolutely right.

The Admiralty also made Cook captain of the Royal Naval Hospital at Greenwich, a sinecure that he accepted with the condition that he could leave should he be required elsewhere. For already the Admiralty was arranging a third great exploration into the Pacific and the *Resolution* was refitted for further duty. This time the destination was north, to explore Sir Francis Drake's "New Albion" west coast of North America. From there, to sail along the last unknown coastline in the world in search of a sea passage around the top of Canada, the fabled Northwest Passage, and a sea passage around the top of Russia, the Northeast Passage. Neither could be located from the Atlantic. If anyone could find the Pacific entrances, it was James Cook.

Having sent the *Adventure* elsewhere, the Admiralty purchased another Whitby collier to accompany the *Resolution* and named her *Discovery*. She was commanded by Lieutenant Charles Clerke, ex-*Endeavour* and ex-*Resolution*. Joining Cook as master of the *Resolution* was the talented William Bligh; rejoining as first lieutenant was John Gore, while many more officers and seamen also rejoined. As well as taking home Omai, a Tahitian brought to Britain in the *Adventure*, further gifts for the South Seas' kings were taken on board including, for the first time, horses. With goats, sheep, chickens, pigs, and horses, the *Resolution*'s decks looked and smelled like a farmyard when she left Plymouth on July 12, 1776. Cook had been home for less than a year, which may have been the secret of his long and happy marriage.

As soon as the *Resolution* put to sea, Cook found she leaked like a sieve; her refit was appalling. Throughout this expedition Cook and his crew suffered from this negligence, and ultimately, it was to be fatal. At Cape Town, Cook had almost every seam recaulked as well as replacing some masts.

The *Resolution* and the *Discovery* departed Cape Town in November 1776, sailing southeast to explore, survey, and chart the subantarctic Marion, Crozet, and Kerguelen Islands. There were further problems with the *Resolution*'s masts, and Cook anchored at Adventure Bay in Van Diemen's Land for repairs. He met the Australian Aborigines a second time but made little progress with them. When he stopped at Queen Charlotte Sound for yet more repairs, the Maoris were surprised to find that the great Cook intended no punishment for the murder and eating of the *Adventure*'s boat crew three years before. Cook understood that it was a collision of cultures and that retribution would gain nothing. Instead, he tried to explain the concept of mercy and forgiveness. The Maoris were puzzled and Omai was scornful.

Cook sailed the *Resolution* and the *Discovery* on a new route to the northeast, another of his Pacific wanderings in which he was destined to discover unknown islands and peoples, including another Polynesian community in what he named the Hervey Islands (Cook Islands). The two vessels nudged the occasional unknown reef and sandbank—immediately charted—then sailed west to the Friendly Islands. Cook and Bligh landed on Tofua, and King George's gifts—sheep, goats, pigs, and rabbits—were distributed to the island chiefs, while one of the horses was presented to the Tongan king. Cook sailed through the Society Islands to Otaheite, his Pacific home, and returned Omai to his people after several years away. He presented the remaining gifts: two horses, sheep, cattle, geese, a cock, and a hen. Two *Discovery* crew deserted—desertions occurred on every visit—but the Tahitians located the sailors on another island and returned them to be flogged.

It was during this visit that Cook's rheumatism, the sailor's curse, was relieved with massage by a dozen strong women using the a'pi plant. After two treatments, it never returned. One of the Tahitians massaging Captain James Cook was Isabella, who later married a master's mate named Fletcher Christian, the notorious *Bounty* mutineer.

In November 1777 the two ships departed Otaheite and Cook directed them north. On Christmas Eve he made yet another discovery, at the equator. He named them the Line Islands and the first land sighted Christmas Island (Kiritimati). Sixteen days later Cook discovered the last great island group of the Pacific Ocean, the Sandwich Islands (Hawaii), first reaching Atui (Kauai) Island. There were more Polynesians, and Cook wondered again at these island seamen who had sailed the Pacific in their simple outrigger canoes, from Hawaii to New Zealand, from Easter Island to the Friendly Islands.

When Cook landed on Atui on January 20, 1778, the islanders lay flat on their faces. This had never happened before, and, embarrassed,

Cook waved them up. It was explained that this was how these Polynesians greeted their chiefs. It was actually how they greeted their gods, but Cook was not told this. He made friends with the Polynesians in his usual way, bartering for fresh vegetables, meat, and water before setting off to the east.

The *Resolution* and the *Discovery* sailed to a February landfall in North America at Drake's New Albion, north of San Francisco. The weather was cold and the seas lively, but Cook wanted to be far north by the beginning of summer for his exploration into the Arctic. The two Whitby colliers coasted northward along what are now the states of Oregon and Washington, passing Drake's farthest point north, charting and naming as they went. Vancouver Island was named after the *Resolution*'s midshipman, Cape Suckling after Nelson's uncle, Bligh Island after the *Resolution*'s master, and so on. Cook anchored for further repairs to the *Resolution* at Prince William Sound, where the *Discovery*'s crew beat off an attack by knife-wielding Eskimos. Cook ordered the men not to use firearms.

The ships were forced south again by the long Alaska Peninsula. Cook Inlet was thought to be a possible passage east or north, but when Bligh explored he found it to be only a river mouth. The two ships reached the bottom of the peninsula at Ounalashka (Unalaska), where they passed between the Aleutian Islands and sailed northward again through the cold Bering Sea. Cook noted the estuary of the great Yukon River and, finally, passed between the continents of America and Asia to enter the Arctic.

In the charts drawn in the great cabin of the *Resolution*, Captain James Cook had mapped the last, major unknown coastline of the world. The *Resolution* and Cook also became the first ship and man to cross both polar circles, 66° 33.5' south and north of the equator— and thus the first to reach both the Antarctic and the Arctic.

Northward, Cook navigated the little ships into the bitter polar weather. Once again, ice coated the *Resolution*'s rigging until the latitude measured was almost 71° north, as before it measured 71° south. Once again, it was ice that stopped Cook, sea ice piled twelve feet high and impassable. Cook had indeed reached the Pacific end of the elusive Northwest Passage, only to find it choked with ice. He tacked and wore his ships along the edge of the frozen sea, searching for a channel through, but there was none. He turned west for the Northeast Passage.

He beat along the edge of the ice from 164° west across the international date line to 176° east. The pack ice was solid from the North Pole to the coast of Siberia. Cook had reached the Pacific end of the Northeast Passage, and it, too, was choked with ice. It was evident that both passages were unsuitable for commercial navigation.

By then it was September and the pack ice was beginning to reform. Cook turned his ships back along the Siberian coast—he was charting the coast of Siberia in two Whitby colliers!—and south into the Bering Sea. The *Resolution* was in a poor state once more and needed rerigging. Cook required a warm winter anchorage, and he chose the Sandwich Islands, where they'd been welcomed earlier.

For two months Cook searched the islands for a suitable anchorage, surveying and charting as he went. On January 17, 1779, he found Karakakooa (Kealakekua) Bay on the west coast of Owhyhee (Hawaii) itself, the largest island. He sent William Bligh in a boat to sound the bay. The bay was open only to the southwest, and the holding ground was good. It would do.

His reception was overwhelming. Thousands of islanders canoed or swam out to the ships, climbing aboard in their feathers and flowers even while the sailors were anchoring. When Cook stepped ashore with gifts of pigs, goats, and iron tools, the islanders again prostrated themselves before him. Elaborate ceremonies were performed and he was accompanied by priests wherever he went. In awe, the Polynesian king Kalaniopu'u visited Cook's ships. They called Cook "Orono," "Lono" or "Rono." No one aboard the two ships understood what was happening. It wasn't until many years later, after interviews with the islanders involved, that the truth was uncovered.

Orono was a Hawaiian god who'd been exiled. The legend was that one day he would return, bearing gifts of swine and dogs. Who else but Orono could the tall, noble Captain Cook be?

Cook stayed only three weeks. With the *Resolution*'s rigging repaired and the ships provisioned and watered, he set sail to complete his survey of the Sandwich Islands, explore the northwest Pacific, and return to the Arctic. He wrote that Owhyhee had "enriched our voyage with a discovery which, though the last, seemed in many respects to be the most important that had hitherto been made throughout the extent of the Pacific Ocean." Those were the final words in his journal. That he wrote "the last" discovery is intriguing.

The *Resolution*'s log records that a strong blow caught the ship and the morning inspection revealed severe damage to the foremast and fore-topmast, one more relic of the poor refit. Repairs required a safe anchorage, for the masts had to be removed. Cook did not want to return to Owhyhee, but there was nowhere else. He put about and anchored again in Karakakooa Bay on February 10.

This time, the welcome for "Orono" was somewhat thin. Cook went ashore to explain to King Kalaniopu'u and his chiefs the reason for his return—only to repair the masts. He believed they'd understood him, but what the priests said when he'd gone was another matter. Working as quickly as they could, the British seamen "fished" the masts and floated them ashore for repair. It was complicated, skilled work. As it progressed, stones were thrown at them and there were minor assaults. Thefts increased dramatically until the islanders actually swam under the ships to pull out the nails holding the copper sheathing to the hulls. Cook had an islander flogged as a deterrent.

On the night of the thirteenth, the *Discovery*'s cutter was stolen from her mooring. This was extremely serious. In the morning Cook went ashore in the *Resolution*'s pinnace with ten marines in the launch to carry out his usual bloodless punishment. He would take a chief hostage until the cutter was returned. It had always worked before. Four more boats cordoned the bay to stop islanders from rowing their canoes or the cutter away. Cook's reluctant orders were to fire if necessary and unusually, he carried a shotgun himself.

Cook reported the theft to Kalaniopu'u, who agreed to go with him to the *Resolution* until the cutter was returned. The king's young sons asked to go as well and, with their father's agreement, ran ahead. On the beach they heard gunfire along the bay. Cook's men had fired to stop a canoe from leaving.

One of the king's wives wailed and begged him not to go. Two young chiefs took hold of the king's arms and sat him on the beach, while other islanders collected stones, spears, and clubs. The lieutenant of marines lined his men along the water's edge, their muskets loaded and ready. From the crowd someone cried that a chief had been killed in the firing along the bay. Cook understood what had been said and left the king sitting on the beach. He ordered the marines to return to the ships to avoid bloodshed and walked down the beach.

A warrior rushed at him wielding a stone and a dagger. Cook turned and in Polynesian ordered: "Put those things down!" but the man drew back his arm to throw the stone.

Cook fired his shotgun, using the barrel containing round shot, which would sting but not kill. The shot hit the warrior's coconut breastplate. He laughed and came on with his dagger raised. Cook fired the second barrel, containing ball, and the warrior fell to the beach.

There was a roar and the islanders attacked with stones and spears. The marines fired. Undeterred, the islanders killed four marines before they could reload. The seamen in the boat came in to help, telling the king's sons to run for it before they were hurt. The boys ran away through the shallows.

Cook stood at the water's edge, a tall, commanding figure in navy-blue tailcoat and white breeches, facing the islanders. They paused. He turned to his seamen and marines with his hand held palm up to command a ceasefire. It was then, with his back to the islanders, that he was clubbed, stabbed, and killed. The marines and seamen fired their muskets into the mob and retreated to the boat. From the *Discovery,* the watching Clerke fired two ship's cannon overhead into the trees. Cook's body and the bodies of the four marines were torn apart as the boats rowed into deep water. It was over.

The next day, parts of Cook's body were returned to the *Resolution* by a sorrowful chief. Those remnants—missing his head—were given a naval funeral to a captain's salute of ten guns.

Lieutenant Clerke took command of the *Resolution* and promoted Gore to command of the *Discovery.* The masts were repaired, and on a gray February day the two ships departed Owhyhee. Clerke continued as Cook had planned, exploring northwestward across the Pacific, but discovered nothing. The two ships sailed the cold northern sea into the Arctic, where Clerke found the ice farther south than the year before. There was no way through. Neither the Northwest nor the Northeast were viable passages. They are not still.

In the Arctic, Clerke died of tuberculosis. It was the worst weather for him, but he'd insisted on completing Cook's plans. Gore took command and turned south for the small Russian port of Petropavlovsk. There, Clerke was buried. The *Resolution* and the *Discovery* were repaired and departed for Britain. The passage home took a year. They arrived at London in October 1780, completing a voyage of four and a quarter years. Not one man in either ship had died of disease.

The chronometer in the *Resolution* was removed and supplied later to another ship bound for the South Seas named *Bounty.* It was removed from the *Bounty* at Pitcairn Island and is now in the National Maritime Museum at Greenwich.

Mrs. Cook received a royal pension from King George, her

husband's share of the royalties of his published journals, and a specially struck gold medal from the Royal Society. She lived mostly alone until she died at age ninety-three. All six of their children died without heirs, the two eldest sons in service with the navy.

In Australia, Canada, New Zealand, the United States, and throughout the Pacific Islands there are memorials to Captain James Cook. In the United Kingdom there is a statue in the Mall near the Admiralty and one on the cliffs near Whitby. It's late, but not too late, for a significant memorial in London's Westminster Abbey or Saint Paul's to the greatest cartographer, surveyor, seaman, and navigator in history.

Recommended
Captain Cook: The Seaman's Seaman by Alan Villiers
The Journals of Captain Cook, edited by J. C. Beaglehole
The Life of Captain James Cook by J. C. Beaglehole
The Royal Naval Museum, Portsmouth, Hampshire, U.K.
The National Maritime Museum, Greenwich, London
The Whitby Museum, Whitby, Yorkshire, U.K.
The Mitchell Library, Sydney, Australia
Endeavour replica, Whitby, Yorkshire, U.K.
Endeavour replica, Sydney, Australia
Captain Cook's Cottage, Melbourne, Australia

Edmund Hillary and Tenzing Norgay

If you cannot understand that there is something in man which responds to the challenge of this mountain and goes out to meet it, that the struggle is the struggle of life itself, upward and forever upward, then you won't see why we go. What we get from this adventure is just sheer joy.   —George Mallory

We look up. For weeks, for months, that is all we have done. Look up. And there it is—the top of Everest. Only it is different now: so near, so close, only a little more than a thousand feet above us. It is no longer just a dream, a high dream in the sky, but a real and solid thing, a thing of rock and snow, that men can climb. We make ready. We will climb it. This time, with God's help, we will climb on to the end.

—Tenzing Norgay

Less than sixty years ago, no one in the history of the world had conquered Everest. It is possible that George Mallory and Andrew Irvine made it in 1924, but they died in the attempt and there is no way to know if they were still climbing or coming down. Mallory's body was not even found until 1999.

The highest mountain in the world is still incredibly dangerous, and climbers die in the attempt every year. More than forty bodies remain frozen on the north side of the mountain, and others have been lost in avalanches, their whereabouts unknown.

Everest is part of the Himalayan range, on the border between Tibet and Nepal. In Tibet it is known as Chomolungma, or "Saint Mother," while the Nepalese call it Sagarmatha, meaning "Goddess of the Sky." Everest is named after George Everest, a British surveyor in nineteenth-century India. Before World War II, ascents began in Tibet, but when China occupied and closed that country to foreigners, future attempts had to come from the Nepalese side.

Everest stands 29,035 feet high—a fraction under five and a half *miles* from sea level. For those who are interested in such things, the highest mountain from foot to tip is actually a Hawaiian island, though obviously, almost all of that is underwater.

Above 27,000 feet, the air is too thin to breathe without severe training and months of acclimatization. Edmund Hillary and Tenzing Norgay used bottled oxygen to make their ascent. Bad weather can make climbing impossible, which leaves only a small window each year when summit attempts can take place.

The British Everest expedition of 1953 came after years of expeditions to survey the approaches from Nepal. In 1951 a potential route to the top was noted, and in 1952 two Swiss attempts on the summit were made. The British team was in the Himalayas, training at high altitude and ready to climb if the Swiss failed. A French team was ready to go after them. At that time, nine of the eleven major attempts on the mountain had been British-sponsored. Such energy and risk is either impossible to explain or very simple. As George Mallory said when he was asked why he wanted to climb Everest: "Because it's there."

The 1953 British expedition was led by John Hunt. It was a massive undertaking just to reach the area. More than three hundred porters were employed to bring ten thousand pounds of supplies and equipment. Twenty native Nepalese guides were engaged for the task, some of whom, like Tenzing Norgay, had climbed to 28,000 feet with the Swiss the previous year. As the expedition unpacked on the lawns of the British High Commission in Kathmandu, they discovered that they had forgotten the British flag to fly on the summit of Everest. Rather than go without it, the high commissioner gave them one from his official Rolls-Royce.

More than one climb had come within a thousand feet of the

summit but then been overwhelmed by exhaustion or blizzards. At that height, the mountain has already taken a fierce toll. All equipment, including oxygen bottles, has to be carried up, and progress is bitterly slow as the last reserves of strength and fitness dwindle away. As with breaking the four-minute mile, that last stretch seemed an impossible obstacle.

By May 1953, the British team had crossed crevasses and climbed sheer ice and rock to set up Advance Base Camp at 21,000 feet. The region above that height is known as the "death zone," as climbers can endure only a few days in some of the most hostile conditions on earth.

Two-men summit teams were considered to have the best chance. The first assault on the summit was by Charles Evans and Tom Bourdillon. They made it to within a few hundred feet of the top when their oxygen failed. Without warning, they were suddenly strangling in air too thin to breathe, and they had to return to the lower camp.

On May 28, an advance party went up to carry equipment to the highest camp possible. In that way, they could prepare the path for Hillary and Tenzing, who were the least exhausted pair. Hillary and Tenzing carried some fifty-six pounds of supplies up to what would be called Camp IX—about halfway between Advance Base Camp and the summit. With three other men— Alfred Gregory, George Lowe, and Sherpa Ang Nyima—they rested as best they could. In a cramped tent, they slept for four hours and woke at dawn to find that the weather had cleared. The temperature was around −13°F (−25°C), which made windchill of the utmost importance. Winds on Everest regularly gusted up to eighty miles per hour and were a constant, deadly threat.

Both Hillary and Tenzing carried cylinders of oxygen and other equipment: fifty to sixty-three pounds for each man. The plan was for Gregory, Lowe, and Ang Nyima to go first and cut ice steps as high as they could, allowing Tenzing and Hillary to make a fast ascent and perhaps push on to the very top.

Hillary and Tenzing climbed quickly, joining the first party on a ridge at 27,900 feet. There they found the tattered remnant of the Swiss tent from where Tenzing himself had tried for the peak the year before. That experience would prove vital, as he was able to guide the team to the best route.

Their trail-breaking work done, Lowe, Gregory, and Ang turned back. After cutting steps in ice all day, they were exhausted, but they had given Hillary and Tenzing a chance to make the summit.

To preserve oxygen for the attempt, the two remaining men put away their breathing apparatus, gasping without it, to make a camp for the night. They pitched a tent, using only their weight to hold it in place. Tenzing made soup while Hillary checked the oxygen supplies. He had less than the ideal amount, but the first attempt by Bourdillon and Evans had abandoned oxygen cylinders even higher, and they hoped to find those and use them to get back down alive. Before they slept, Hillary and Tenzing ate sardines, tinned apricots, biscuits, honey, and jam, as well as drinking hot water with lemon crystals and sugar to ward off dehydration. Hillary found that his boots had frozen solid and had to cook them on a Primus stove to soften them.

In the morning they hoisted the heavy oxygen tubes onto their shoulders. The day was bright and still, and they could see the South Summit ahead of them. Making good speed, they climbed a ridge toward it, locating the abandoned oxygen cylinders on the way. They passed the cut steps and reached the South Summit by 9 A.M. on the twenty-ninth. A virgin ridge led onward, with a ten-thousand-foot drop along one edge. Hillary began to cut new steps in the snow, ascending in forty-foot stages. Eight thousand feet below them, they could see the Advance Base Camp as they climbed. At one point, Tenzing's oxygen tubes froze solid and Hillary freed them when he saw the Sherpa growing weak. There was no margin for error of any kind.

They had to halt at a smooth forty-foot cliff of rock, still known today as the Hillary Step. Hillary said afterward that it would have been an interesting challenge to a group of expert climbers in England's Lake District, but at that height it seemed impassable. He found a place where he could wedge his body into a crack between the rock and solid snow and heaved himself up and onto a ledge at the top. Tenzing followed on the rope and began to cut steps once more as the ridge went on.

They pushed themselves to the limit of endurance and thought they had reached the top time and time again, only to find more to do. The "false summits" were heartbreaking. Slowly and painfully, they cut steps and trudged upward. At 11:30 A.M. they stood on top of the world, the first men ever to stand on that spot. They thumped each other on the back and grinned.

Tenzing did not know how to work the camera, so Hillary took three pictures of him standing on the summit. He held an ice ax aloft, with the flags of the United Nations, Britain, Nepal, and India fluttering from it. Tenzing made an offering to the gods of the summit, burying a bar of chocolate and some biscuits. John Hunt had given Hillary a small crucifix to take to the top, and he placed it beside the other offerings. They also looked for traces of Mallory or Irving, as the bodies were still missing at that time, but saw no sign of them.

Exhausted as they were, they could not tarry for long, even for the best view on earth. They remained on the peak for just fifteen minutes before beginning the descent, moving as quickly as possible to reach the oxygen dump before their own supply ran out.

Hillary and Tenzing made it back to a lower camp and were greeted by George Lowe, carrying emergency oxygen and a hot lemon drink. They were too exhausted to say much, though Hillary managed: "Well, George, we knocked the bastard off." The following day they climbed down to the Advance Base Camp and the rest of the team came out to see if they had been successful. George Lowe gave them the thumbs-up and waved his ice ax at the summit. The highest mountain on earth had been conquered at last. The job was done and Edmund Hillary and Tenzing Norgay became famous around the world. The French team next in line to make the attempt were, frankly, gutted.

News reached England in time for the coronation of Queen Elizabeth II in June 1953. Her husband, the Duke of Edinburgh, had been the patron of the expedition, and the queen took a personal interest. Hillary was made a Knight Commander of the British Empire (KBE). In his twilight years, he was also made a member of the Order of the Garter, an honor completely in the queen's discretion. Only the reigning monarch, the Prince of Wales, and twenty-four "companions" hold the honor at any one time. Hillary returned to England on many occasions to attend the annual service in Saint George's Chapel, Windsor.

Tenzing Norgay was given the George Medal by Queen Elizabeth. He was honored by both India and Nepal and became director of the Himalayan Mountaineering Institute in Darjeeling. He lived until 1986, dying at the age of seventy-one. His son climbed Everest in 1996.

Edmund Hillary was just thirty-three when he stood on the peak of Everest. Though only two men made the summit, he always praised the teamwork that had made that final push possible. He also never revealed whether he or Tenzing had stepped onto the peak first. As far as Hillary was concerned, it just didn't matter. He went on to climb ten other peaks in the Himalayas and made a successful journey to the South Pole. Much of his later life he spent creating and working with the Himalayan Trust in Nepal. Nepalese people form the Gurkha regiments that have been Britain's allies for almost two hundred years, and Hillary's trust built bridges, hospitals, airstrips, and almost thirty schools there.

He died on January 11, 2008, aged eighty-eight. In April of that year, Queen Elizabeth held a final service for him in Saint George's Chapel. Outside, Gurkha soldiers stood guard for the last time as the great man was honored and remembered.

Recommended
The Ascent of Everest by John Hunt; includes the chapter "The Summit" by Edmund Hillary

The Abolition of Slavery in the British Empire
Sharp, Clarkson, Wilberforce, and Buxton

There is today a vast amount of misinformation and misunderstanding about the history and origins of slavery. Slavery is, unfortunately, as old as mankind itself. The oldest oral histories, cave drawings, and written histories of every race include slavery—in Africa; throughout Asia and Asia Minor; Europe; North, Central, and South America; India; and Oceania. It's been practiced everywhere from the beginnings of history, when the British Isles were uninhabited marshes and mountains.

The great Indian civilizations of 5000 B.C. traded slaves. All the Middle Eastern and Mediterranean states had slaves. Classical Greek civilization—the so-called "Cradle of Democracy"—was based upon slavery. While Plato and Aristotle debated democracy, less than 1 percent of people had any say in that society, and 50 percent were slaves. Plato's ideal republic contained slavery, while Aristotle suggested that some peoples were naturally slaves.

The Roman Empire was built on slavery. In every land they conquered, the Romans created slaves, from civilians as well as defeated armies, enslaving Britons in the north, Carthaginians and Egyptians in the south. For a one-hundred-year period B.C., slaves outnumbered freemen by three to one, with almost 21 million slaves.

Meanwhile, in Africa, slavery was already practiced, both locally and in the form of exports to the Middle East. As in every continent, the nations and tribes of Africa waged war among themselves for thousands of years before the Europeans arrived. The defeated of those wars became slaves to their victors and were either worked locally, sold on to other tribes, or used to pay debts and penalties. With the sweeping spread of Islam after A.D. 650, a huge slave trade in Africans was created, trading from sub-Sahara to Muslim North Africa and to the Muslim Middle East. Black slaves were sold by black Africans to Muslim traders for transportation by caravan across the deserts, by boat down the Nile River, and by sea from centers such as Zanzibar to the Arabian Gulf, the Red Sea, and Indian slave ports. In the late 800s, Arab geographer al-Ya'qubi recorded: "I am informed that the kings of the blacks sell their own people without justification or in consequence of war."

No figures exist for the number of Africans enslaved this way, but for thirteen hundred years of Islamic slavery, the caravan routes, Nile River, and jungle paths were littered with the bones of dead slaves. During the 1800s, missionary and abolitionist Dr. David Livingstone put the figure at 500,000 dead each year. That trade continues today.

Arab slavers also made raids by sea, to the Canary Islands, Madeira, Malta, Sicily, Spain, Portugal—and the British Isles. Villagers from southern England, Wales, and Ireland were snatched from their homes and sold in markets on the Barbary Coast of North Africa. In the Middle East, Muslim armies raided eastern Europe for Christian slaves, and in Russia they bought slaves captured by the conquering Vikings. Into the 1800s, Turkey, France, Venice, Genoa, Spain, and Morocco sentenced convicts of any nationality to be galley slaves.

Elsewhere, the various civilizations of Central and South America—particularly Aztec, Mayan, and Incan—rose on the backs of slaves. North American tribes were enslaved by their captors, especially the Haida. The Middle Kingdom of China and other Asian nations were slave societies, as were the Hindu and Muslim states of the Indian Subcontinent. Even in Oceania, the fabled South Sea paradise, slavery was practiced, as well as infanticide and cannibalism.

The Atlantic slave trade was begun by Portugal in 1444, when 225 slaves were captured from West Africa and sold in the market at the town of Lagos, on the Portuguese coast. Papal decrees permitted the

Portuguese to enslave all unbelievers, and by 1450, 1,000 Africans had been enslaved in Portugal. By 1650, Portugal had enslaved 1.3 million from Angola alone. Meanwhile, Spain introduced African slaves to the Canary and Balearic Islands.

After the discovery of the Americas, Portugal and Spain decided to transport African slaves to their colonies for the new sugarcane plantations. Within a hundred years, the Dutch joined the trade, transporting slaves from West Africa for sale in Brazil, the Caribbean, and its North American colony of New Amsterdam (New York). They were quickly followed by the Danes, French, Prussians, and Swedes.

The first Africans were brought to the English colonies by the Dutch in 1619. They were given the same status as white indentured servants, so that, after ten years, English colonies had black and white freemen as well as black and white slaves. Black freemen also bought slaves; there are records in the U.K. National Archives at Kew of the purchase of white and black slaves in the colonies. Later, African slaves were preferred because three Africans could be purchased for the same price as one white slave. White slaves were more expensive because they could talk, read, and, sometimes, write English. It was simple economics that favored African slaves.

British merchants joined the Atlantic slave trade in earnest in 1663, purchasing African slaves as cheap labor for sugar and tobacco plantations in the West Indian and American colonies. At the same time, Britain also traded white slaves for labor in the colonies.

The white slaves' sea passage—in conditions similar to those en-

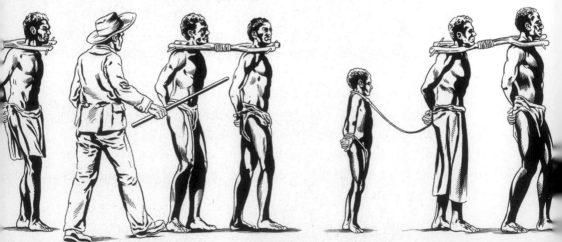

dured by their cousins from Africa—were paid for by the plantation owner. The term of labor was for three, five, or ten years, after which they were supposed to be freed with a small grant of land, although this rarely happened. In Britain a profitable kidnapping trade developed to supply white slaves, and ports became dangerous areas for men, women, and children. Many thousands of British convicts and political prisoners were also transported to the West Indian and American colonies as slaves.

The infamous "triangle" shipping route developed in the eighteenth century and was used by all Atlantic slaving nations. From Europe, ships sailed with tools, hardware, weapons, beads, cloth, salt, rum, and tobacco, which were traded in West Africa for gold, ivory, and slaves—all delivered to the trading forts by Africans from inland as well as the coast. The ships then sailed the "Middle Passage" across the Atlantic to South, Central, and North America and the Caribbean, where the slaves were sold or bartered at auction. The third leg took the ships back to Europe with sugar, rum, tobacco, and cotton. The American slavers began their triangle with cotton, tobacco, and other American products for Europe.

The slave trade was horrific everywhere in the world, particularly from our standpoint of the twenty-first century. Yet the only true judgment that can be made of any event in history is by the standards of those days. Was slavery considered evil in the seventeenth and eighteenth centuries? The answer is no. Slavery was an accepted practice the world over and had been since records began.

The treatment of slaves was also horrific but, in truth, was little

different from the treatment of other people in those days. Sir Hans Sloane, the great doctor of the Enlightenment, recorded in 1686 that for severe crimes some slaves in Jamaica had been burned to death. This is almost beyond belief, but death by burning was the statutory punishment for many crimes in Britain and European countries until it was replaced by hanging, garroting, boiling, or guillotining. In Spain and Portugal, Catholic priests burned non-Catholics; suspected witches were burned or drowned everywhere, while the Salem witch executions of Massachusetts are still famous today.

Slaves were placed in wooden stocks for various misdemeanors; so in every town in England there were stocks for punishing miscreants. Slaves were flogged and, sometimes, flogged to death in punishment for crimes; so, too, were soldiers in the army, sailors in the navy, and even the seamen of slave ships. Another punishment was to place slaves upon a treadmill; Oscar Wilde was punished on the treadmill of Reading Jail—in 1895. Slaves were hanged for minor offenses; so, too, were the English, Irish, Scots, and Welsh. The expression "You may as well be hanged for a sheep as a lamb" originated in 1700s Britain when stealing livestock was a capital offense. Many British felons were hanged by chains on gibbets at crossroads, their bodies tarred and left to rot as a warning to others.

Slaves were packed into the cargo spaces of ships during the Middle Passage, averaging about nineteen inches of space each in decks only five feet high; in the Royal Navy each seaman had twenty-two inches of space to sling his hammock but in two layers, one above the other, in decks five feet high. The death rate was higher among the crews of British slave ships than among the slaves. The simple reason is that the slaves were the profitable cargo of the voyage—the more who survived, the greater the profit—while the crew were the loss-making part of the voyage: they had to be paid.

This description is typical:

During the voyage there is on board these ships terrible misery, stench, fumes, horror, vomiting, many kinds of sea-sickness, fever, flux [dysentery], headaches, heat, constipation, boils, scurvy, cancer, mouth-rot, and the like. Add to this want of provisions, hunger, thirst, frost, heat, dampness, anxiety, afflictions and lamentations, together with other trouble, as the lice abound so frightfully, especially on sick people, that they can be scraped off the body. . . . The water which is served out on the ships is often very black, thick and full of worms, so that one cannot drink it without loathing, even with the greatest thirst. When the ships have landed after their long voyage no one is permitted to leave . . . they must remain on board the ships until they are purchased. The healthy are naturally preferred first, and so the sick and wretched must often remain on board in front of the city for two or three weeks, and frequently die.

The voyage described was in 1750 from Britain to Pennsylvania—carrying white slaves and fare-paying emigrants. Those were brutal days.

So how was the acceptance and business of slavery brought to an end? Who were the heroes who made that amazing leap of moral judgment to declare—after seven thousand years—that slavery was wrong and that the slave trade must be abolished?

The 1600s and 1700s were the Age of Enlightenment in Europe, particularly in England and Scotland. Scientists, philosophers, doctors, writers, and radicals such as Sir Isaac Newton, Robert Boyle, Thomas Hobbes, David Home, Sir Hans Sloane, John Locke, Thomas Paine, Joseph Priestley, and many more questioned, challenged, and changed the accepted order of science, society, government, and liberty. The *Rights of Man*, equality, and modern democracy were created in Great Britain, so it's no surprise that the first abolitionists were also British.

Those radicals also questioned the role of religion. Yet it was Christianity, in the form of enlightened Quakers, Anglicans, and Nonconformists, that was the catalyst for abolishing the slave trade and slavery.

Quaker doctrine in England and the colonies gradually became opposed to the slave trade and slavery. Anglican philosopher John Locke described slavery as a "vile and miserable estate." In 1688, Aphra Behn wrote the first novel with a slave as its hero: *Oroonoko: Or, The Royal Slave*. Methodist John Wesley called the trade "the execrable sum of human villainy," and poet and satirist Alexander Pope condemned it outright.

By the 1770s, there were about fifteen thousand black Africans living in England and Wales and several thousand more in Scotland. Slavery was not allowed in Britain, but was there a specific law prohibiting it? Generally in Britain, where there is no constitution, if there is no law prohibiting an act, then it's not illegal; it is the most liberal of all systems. Constitutions actually restrict liberty. So a test case was required to confirm whether or not slavery was illegal in Britain.

In 1765, a clerk in the civil service, Granville Sharp, became the first practical slave abolitionist in the world when he issued a writ of assault against a slave "owner" for beating black slave Jonathan Strong. Sharp secured Strong's release from prison; his "owner" responded with a counter-writ accusing Sharp of robbing him of his property. The grounds for a test case were established. Public outrage about the "owner's" counter-writ was so immense—showing that the public did indeed consider slavery illegal in Britain—that he withdrew his writ. There was no case. Sharp tried again with fugitive black slave Thomas Lewis, but the jury decided that Lewis's master had not established his case as "owner" and so Lewis was a free man anyway.

Sharp was able to pursue a case to its conclusion with another African fugitive, James Somersett. In 1771, Somersett escaped his Boston master while the two were visiting London, then was recaptured in 1772 and imprisoned on a ship about to sail for Jamaica. Under the Act of 1679, Sharp applied for and was granted a writ of habeas corpus. This prevented Somersett from being removed from England, on the grounds that he was wrongfully imprisoned because there was no such legal status as slavery.

Sharp's lawyer quoted as precedent a trial two hundred years earlier in Elizabeth I's reign, where the verdict determined "that England was too pure an air for slaves to breathe in." He argued further that a law of another country, even a British colony, had no jurisdiction in England and Wales.

Judge Lord Mansfield applied the impartial law of England and agreed: "The power claimed [of ownership] never was in use here nor acknowledged by the law. The state of Slavery is of such a nature that it is incapable of being introduced on any reasons, moral or political, but only by positive law. . . . It is so odious that nothing can be sufficient to support it but positive law. Whatever inconveniences, therefore, may follow from this decision, I cannot say this case is allowed or approved by the law of England, and therefore the black must be discharged."

Judge Mansfield had confirmed the Elizabethan verdict that slavery was illegal. This judgment was the beginning of the end of slavery throughout the world. In practical terms, it meant that any slave setting foot in England or Wales was immediately a free man. There was jubilation, with Africans dancing outside the court. Scottish law followed suit, when the courts there prohibited the forced return of former slaves to Jamaica. Great Britain was the first country in the world where slavery was actually written into the statute books as illegal. Escaped slaves fled to Britain from Europe and its colonies.

With the leadership of Granville Sharp, the scattered sentiments against slavery coalesced into the abolition movement. Sharp wrote an incredible sixty-one treatises condemning slavery. The next step was to abolish the slave trade itself.

In 1776, abolition received unexpected support with the publication of economist Adam Smith's classic work *The Wealth of Nations.* Smith demonstrated that slave labor was not as profitable as free labor: over time slaves were more expensive than freemen. Further, the land suffered from lack of care when worked by slaves, whereas freemen cared for the land because they had a vested interest.

Recent examinations of the contribution of slave labor to the British Empire and the Industrial Revolution have revealed a far smaller impact than previously thought. For example, the port of Liverpool's profit from the slave trade in the heyday of 1750–1800 was only 7.5

percent of its total profit, while the overall profits from slave industries for Britain amounted to only 1.5 percent of the national investment. It was not slavery but the East India Company—which at its peak controlled more than half the world's trade—upon which the British Empire was built. Adam Smith's arguments against slavery were economic rather than moral, but they were important because slavers and their supporters claimed that abolition would ruin Britain economically. Smith showed that argument to be false.

The Society for the Abolition of the Slave Trade was formed in London in 1787. The chairman was Granville Sharp, and its founding members—all of whom should be remembered for what they achieved—were William Dillwyn, Samuel Hoare, George Harrison, John Lloyd, Joseph Woods, Richard Phillips, John Barton, Joseph Hooper, James Phillips, Philip Sansom, and twenty-seven-year-old Thomas Clarkson. Sharp, Sansom, and Clarkson were Anglicans; the rest were Quakers. Potter Josiah Wedgwood devised the society's seal, a manacled slave with the legend AM I NOT A MAN AND A BROTHER?

Cambridge graduate Thomas Clarkson trained as a deacon but never practiced. Instead, he devoted his working life to the abolition of slavery. He traveled Britain campaigning for the society, formed antislavery branches in boroughs, towns, and cities, and collected damning information about the trade. In seven years he rode 35,000 miles. To find one witness, he traveled to five ports and visited fifty-seven vessels.

He sailed to France to persuade the revolutionaries of 1789 to include abolition within their charter of liberties. Despite six months of meetings and submissions, he was unsuccessful. In 1791–92 he took a petition around Britain, gathering 390,000 signatures before presenting it to Parliament. In 1794 his health collapsed and he had to rest from the campaign.

Clarkson's most important single act was to recruit to the society the similarly youthful MP for Yorkshire, William Wilberforce. Wilberforce became the abolitionists' brilliant advocate in Parliament, Clarkson their passionate voice in the country, and Sharp their writer and tactician behind the scenes. It was a formidable trinity.

Wilberforce's conversion to abolition took place in stages. The first was meeting former slave captain John Newton, who had undergone a spiritual conversion and been ordained in the Church of England. He knew the slave trade and supplied details and inside information about the business to Clarkson and Wilberforce. The hymn "Amazing Grace" was written by Newton about his redemption:

Amazing Grace, how sweet the sound,
that saved a wretch like me.
I once was lost but now am found,
was blind but now I see.

At his wedding, Wilberforce sang the hymn with pride.

The second stage for Wilberforce was recruitment by Clarkson to the society. The third was a conversation with close friend and visionary, the twenty-four-year-old prime minister William Pitt the Younger. Pitt urged Wilberforce to make abolition his special political cause and promised him his support. Pitt and Wilberforce were the young shooting stars of Parliament.

Pitt ordered inquiries into the slave trade and forced through an act restricting it and improving standards. The inquiries reported in 1789, and after a Wilberforce speech of three and a half hours, it was agreed that a select committee would report to Parliament with details. A general election interrupted the committee, but it presented its

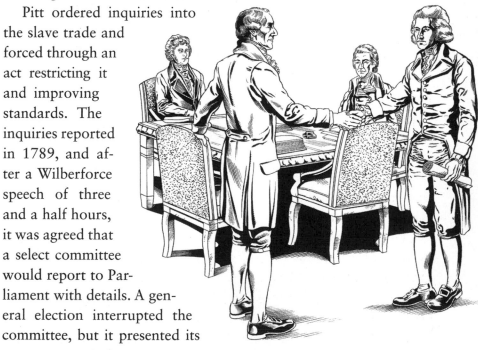

report supporting abolition in 1791. The dying Methodist John Wesley sent his last letter to Wilberforce, urging him to continue the campaign.

After a four-hour speech by Wilberforce, two evenings of impassioned debate, and support from Pitt and the king, the bill to abolish the slave trade was still defeated, although by only seventy-five votes. It was apparent it was going to be a tough campaign. However, the abolitionists had gained the support of another liberal from the opposition party, the hell-raising drinker Charles Fox.

Pitt and Wilberforce persisted and in 1792 Wilberforce again presented a bill for the abolition of the slave trade. The Commons debate lasted throughout the night, with Pitt speaking so eloquently that for "the last twenty minutes he seemed to be really inspired." With an amendment to "gradual abolition," the motion was passed by an incredible 145 votes. Two weeks later, a date for the beginning of abolition was approved: January 1, 1796.

A bill for the abolition of the slave trade in the British Empire—in effect, the world—had been passed by the House of Commons. It was surely only a matter of time before it was approved by the House of Lords and became law. The opponents of abolition were reduced to delaying tactics, which they began immediately. In the House of Lords they moved a postponement to the next parliamentary session and then to the following year; both succeeded.

Meanwhile, supported by Clarkson and Wilberforce, Granville Sharp established a "province of freedom" in West Africa, a settlement for free Africans living in Britain who wished to return. Black colonial Loyalists who had fought with Britain during the American War of Independence also applied to go to the Freetown settlement. Several thousand had escaped from the United States and were living in Nova Scotia Colony. In 1792, Clarkson's brother led a fleet of fifteen ships carrying 1,196 free black settlers from Halifax to Freetown.

After France declared war on Britain in 1793, the threat of French invasion concentrated Parliament's energies on survival. The date for commencement of abolition came and went against a background of war and elections. Wilberforce submitted motions for a new bill annually, but all were defeated. However, as the Royal Navy began to dominate the seas and as British forces defeated French, Dutch, and Spanish armies outside Europe, confidence returned.

Following Pitt's victory in the general election of 1804, Wilberforce presented a new bill for the abolition of the slave trade; it was passed by the Commons but too late for presentation to the Lords. He reintroduced it in 1805, but it was defeated in its second reading. Such frustration took its toll on Wilberforce, who suffered from severe colitis. Opium was then the only pain relief, and he was almost addicted, so great was his pain.

Wilberforce persuaded Pitt to use an Order in Council to ban all slave trading to the captured Dutch colony of Guiana. After the battle of Trafalgar, with the threat of French invasion virtually gone, the government had time to address issues other than war. With abolition regaining momentum, Clarkson returned to the battle and experienced lawyer James Stephen joined the cause.

At the age of only forty-six, worn out from orchestrating the defense against France, Pitt died in the new year. A coalition with Lord Grenville as prime minister and Charles Fox as foreign minister succeeded him. In a new tactic devised by James Stephen, Wilberforce

reintroduced the Foreign Slave Trade Bill. It banned all Britons from slave trading outside the empire and was passed by both Houses of Parliament. Grenville and Fox had shown their colors; the coalition leaders were in favor of abolition.

In an agreement with Wilberforce, Fox himself moved a resolution in the Commons in June that "all manner of dealing and trading in slaves" should be "utterly abolished, prohibited and declared to be unlawful." It was passed by 101 votes. Then Fox died and Lord Grenville was forced into a general election. He was returned and introduced Fox's abolition bill to the Lords in January. For the first time, the Lords passed the bill and returned it to the Commons.

On February 23, 1807, the bill's second reading in the House of Commons took place, the final reading if passed. The vote was a landslide, 283–16—in favor. At last the bill was passed. Wilberforce was applauded by Commons. Overcome with emotion, he wept at his bench.

The king signed the royal assent on March 25. Immediately Sharp, Clarkson, Wilberforce, and others formed the African Institution, to promote the application of the act and to campaign for abolition of the slave trades of other countries. Ironically, because of the French wars and delays orchestrated by its opponents since 1792 when the bill was first passed, Britain was not the first country to abolish the slave trade. Denmark had abolished it in 1803. Yet—with all respect to Denmark—in global terms that abolition was irrelevant. It was what Great Britain decided that would dictate to the world the future of the slave trade. The navy began policing the ban.

With continental Europe liberated from France in 1815, Wilberforce led a campaign—including petitions of one million signatures gathered around Britain—to include in the Vienna peace treaty an anti-slave-trade clause. Foreign Minister Castlereagh responded: "The nation is bent upon this object. I believe there is hardly a village that has not met and petitioned upon it. Ministers must make it the basis of their policy." It was also at Vienna that Britain stopped European nations from dismembering France into small states and principalities as punishment for its twenty-two years of war.

Defeated France and the Netherlands had no choice but to abolish their slave trades, but allies Spain and Portugal refused. Britain stepped forward and paid them to reduce and to end their slave trades. Despite this, all those countries continued trading slaves illegally. Between 1811 and 1870, some two million more African slaves were shipped across the Atlantic, mostly to the United States, Cuba, and Brazil.

It wasn't easy for the Royal Navy to police the Atlantic in the days of sailing ships. Between 1808 and 1845 it lost 1,338 men off the West African coast alone, mostly to disease. Agreements were negotiated with many other countries, giving the navy the right to board and search their ships for slaves; the United States notably refused. From 1825 to 1865, the United States imported a further million slaves.

The abolitionists genuinely thought that stopping the slave trade would lead the British plantations to free their slaves and employ them, as economist Adam Smith had earlier promoted. The majority of transported slaves had been male. With no more arriving—ever—it was in the planters' best interests to promote free families for future labor. Through the fears and stupidity of the plantation owners, this didn't happen.

Rising again to the challenge, the abolitionists mounted another social and political campaign. Granville Sharp, however, had died in 1813, while Wilberforce was then sixty-seven, with failing health, and Clarkson was sixty-six and going blind from cataracts. Thomas Buxton, a young Anglican MP, led the new campaign under the banner of the Anti-Slavery Society. On May 15, 1823, Buxton moved a resolution in the Commons to abolish all slavery in the British Empire. He saw freedom in the empire as the major step in the wider battle for freedom throughout the world, although he was realist enough not "to suppose that we can at once, by a single effort, solve the problem which lies before us."

That year, in the new colony of Guiana (formerly Dutch Guiana), there was an uprising by thirteen thousand slaves in which two overseers were murdered. The Dutch colonists proclaimed martial law, hanged forty-seven slaves, and sentenced to death English missionary and abolitionist John Smith for complicity in the uprising. He was imprisoned and died in jail. Smith's death, the first abolitionist martyrdom, became a catalyst for the new cause.

Buxton forced through sweeping reforms for the West Indian and Guiana colonies. They included automatic freedom for all female children born after 1823, abolition of flogging, holidays for religious instruction, a nine-hour working day, savings banks for slaves, and admission of evidence by slaves in court. In 1828 the landmark British ruling was made that "free people of colour in the colonies" have legal equality with their fellow citizens. The planters were not pleased.

Government in the British Empire was complicated by the fact that each colony had its own separate government. This allowed local representation and administration but also created policy differences with Parliament in London. In 1832, Jamaican colonists threatened to secede and join the United States. Slave conditions in the United States were then horrific, and this threat prompted an uprising by fifty thousand Jamaican slaves. The Jamaican administration was severe, executing one hundred slaves after peace was restored. Upon a wave of revulsion in Britain, Buxton again moved a motion in the Commons for the abolition of slavery in the empire.

On July 26, 1833, the final reading of this bill was passed by the Commons; it became law on August 29. At a stroke, some 800,000 people were freed.

In a clever move, Parliament compensated the planters for half of each slave's market value. On the one hand it pacified the planters; on the other the money enabled them to continue the plantations and other industries and provide employment and apprenticeships for the freed slaves.

William Wilberforce died on the morning of July 29 at his home in Chelsea, aware that the abolition of slavery had been secured. He is buried alongside William Pitt in Westminster Abbey. Thomas Clarkson lived until September 26, 1846, age eighty-seven, and was buried at home near Ipswich. His last public appearance was to address the World Anti-Slavery Convention in London in 1840.

Successive British governments in the 1800s sent the navy and the army around the world to stop slavery, particularly in Africa. Anti-slavery squadrons patrolled the African coasts, and expeditions blazed paths inland, destroying slave markets and liberating slaves at source.

The British and Foreign Anti-Slavery Society and the British Aborigines Protection Society campaigned throughout the world, while Anglican and Methodist antislavery missionaries such as David Livingstone worked at private expense. One missionary, Arthur West, bought the entire slave market of Zanzibar and freed the slaves. Arab sheiks, African chieftains, Turkish emirs, Egyptian pashas, Persian princes, and Sudanese khedives were all coerced by the British to join foreign governments in signing slavery-suppression and abolition treaties. When Zanzibar became British in 1890, the slave market and stockades were blown up and the Muslim slave trade by sea almost totally stopped.

Throughout the 1800s, abolition of slave trades and slavery spread from Britain across the world, but the going was hard. The interests and moralities of African, Arab, and other slavers were far more difficult to change than the opinions of members of Parliament. Slavery ceased officially in the greatest slave nation of all, the United States, in 1865 and in the second-greatest slave nation, Brazil, in 1888.

Astonishingly, some modern revisionist historians criticize the abolitionists. One found it "reprehensible" that abolition of slavery was not the abolitionists' avowed aim until 1823. Yet the British abolitionists made slave trading illegal throughout the empire, believing that without resupply, slavery itself must stop. It didn't, so they then made slavery illegal.

Abolitionists were also accused of being blind to slavery in other parts of the world, in particular the colonies of Portuguese Brazil, Spanish Cuba, and the United States. Yet Clarkson attempted to gain French cooperation, Sharp created the Africa Institution, and Wilberforce forced anti-slave-trade clauses into the Vienna peace treaty. In addition, the British government paid Portugal and Spain to end their slave trades, the navy stopped the trade at sea, and the government negotiated international boarding rights with every country it could. Short of going to war—and after twenty-two years of world war that was not an option—there's a limit to what can be achieved in a very short time. When you're first, you're breaking new ground.

As it was, the Atlantic slave trade had been stopped after a 420-year history. The abolitionists and British governments campaigned for and abolished slavery throughout most of the world.

The simple truth is that seven thousand years of slavery was turned on its head in just fifty-five years by the British abolitionists. Such was their fervor that they changed public and government endorsement of an economic practice into a perception of a monstrous evil. They changed the world. An amazing grace indeed.

Recommended
A Sailor Boy's Experience Aboard a Slave Ship by Samuel Robinson
The British Anti-Slavery Movement by Sir Reginald Coupland
William Wilberforce by Robin Furneaux
The Rise and Fall of Black Slavery by C. Duncan Rice
History of Slavery by Susanne Everett
Gottlieb Mittelberger's Journey to Pennsylvania in the Year 1750 and Return to Germany in the Year 1754 by Gottlieb Mittelberger

Tatanka Iyotake—
Sitting Bull

He put in your heart certain wishes and plans,
and in my heart he put other and different desires.
It is not necessary for eagles to be crows.

—Tatanka Iyotake (Sitting Bull)

Tatanka Iyotake, or Sitting Bull, is the most famous Native American in the world. There are others whose names are widely known—Geronimo, Crazy Horse, Cochise, Hiawatha, and Pocahontas, who lies buried in England—but Tatanka Iyotake is preeminent among them all. He has come to represent the defense and resistance of all Native American nations to invasion and eventual dominance by the United States.

A child of the Hunkpapa band of the Sioux nation, Sitting Bull was nicknamed "Hunkeshnee"—in English, "slow." Slightly bowlegged, he was not one of the fast, loping Native Americans who could run all day long. But he was brave, he was strong, and even as a child he knew that his spiritual destiny was to be a holy man. Hunkeshnee earned his proper name in traditional Sioux fashion—through an exploit or event.

After a Hunkpapa buffalo hunt, the children were reenacting the day's hunting with some of the captured calves when Hunkeshnee was thrown by his pony. A large, angry bull calf turned upon the boy. Defying his nickname, Hunkeshnee quickly turned on the calf and took it by the ears. In a struggle of strength and balance, Hunkeshnee pushed the calf backward until it was forced to sit down on its haunches. His friends shouted, "He has subdued the bull calf! He's made it sit down!" He had earned his man's name.

The Sioux nation comprises seven distinct tribes in three geographical divisions—from east to west across the Great Plains, the Dakota, Lakota, and Nakota. Each tribe is further divided into bands. Thus Sitting Bull was of the Hunkpapa band, in the Teton tribe, of the Lakota Sioux. Yet Sioux itself is not a Native American name; it is an English corruption of "Nadowesiwug," "little snakes."

A British officer in the mid-1700s, Lieutenant Gorrell, judged the Sioux to be "certainly the greatest nation of Indians yet found. . . . They can shoot [with bows and arrows] the wildest and largest beasts in the woods at 70 or 100 yds distance. They are remarkable for their dancing; the other nations take their fashion from them." The living and hunting lands of the Sioux nation then stretched roughly twenty-five hundred miles north to south and six hundred miles east to west—the Great Plains of North America.

When Sitting Bull was born in present-day South Dakota in 1831, the borders of Sioux and U.S. government territory had been agreed upon in a treaty of 1816. Sioux territory included most of present-day North and South Dakota, much of Minnesota, and large parts of Nebraska, Wisconsin, Iowa, Missouri, and Wyoming, as well as lands north into Canada. The U.S. government had promised no further incursions into the Great Plains.

However, subsequent treaties were forced upon the Sioux, treaties in which they were persuaded under great pressure to sell their land to the government for practically nothing. Today it would be called compulsory purchase at well below market value. In 1837 all land east of the Mississippi was sold, and in the 1851 Fort Laramie treaty the majority of Minnesota went the same way. Even so, white settlers and miners broke the new treaty and encroached upon more Sioux land. Although Sitting Bull was brought up along the busy Willow Creek and Grand River, at that time he had little conflict with the settlers.

During his childhood and youth his skirmishes were with the traditional enemy, the Crow, another Plains nation. He first fought when he was fourteen. In a raid upon the Crow he killed his first man, to return with a scalp about the size of a silver dollar hanging from his belt.

By Sitting Bull's time the traditional dog-and-travois days of the Plains tribes were gone. Sitting Bull rode small horses, descendants of the first horses brought to the continent by the Spanish, British, and French. He rode the broad prairie as well as the uplands and pine forests of the sacred Paha-Sapa, the Black Hills of South Dakota. There he communed with his ancestors and the Great Spirit. Gradually, he became known as much for his spiritual as for his battle leadership, conducting songs and performing rituals such as the Sun Dance. Yet he also became a leader of the Strong Heart warrior society, uniting young warriors from the Lakota and Dakota bands. He was both warrior and holy man.

Sitting Bull's first dispute with the United States did not come until 1863. The Santee Sioux of Minnesota had "rebelled" and killed settlers after the government broke the 1851 Fort Laramie treaty. The U.S. Army conducted a general campaign against all Dakota Sioux, and Sitting Bull became involved. The Santee were defeated, their remaining Minnesota lands seized, and the thirteen hundred survivors transported to a reservation on the Missouri River. The water there was unfit for drinking, rainfall was low, the earth barren, and game scarce. In the first year more than a quarter of them died.

Among the visitors to that reservation was Sitting Bull. It was there that he realized that, despite treaties, he would have to fight to preserve Sioux territory and its peoples. He said of the United States: "This nation is like a spring freshet; it overruns its banks and destroys all who are in its path." This was true, but it's true of all invaders, and at some time every country in the world has been invaded by another. The British Isles, for example, have been invaded and settled by Britons, Celts, Romans, Angles, Saxons, Jutes, and Vikings. In turn, Britain invaded and settled other lands, such as Australia and North America.

Sitting Bull fought his first skirmish against U.S. soldiers in 1864 at Killdeer Mountain. The following year, in a major escalation, four columns of white men illegally invaded the Powder River country of the Sioux. One was an armed wagon train of prospectors heading for the Montana goldfields. It was allowed through. Under the 1851 treaty, wagon trains of emigrants bound for the west coast were permitted to pass through Sioux territory and usually managed the journey without incident. Despite the Wild West mythology, more than 250,000 pioneers traveled through Native American territory from 1851 to 1871, and fewer than 400 were killed, mostly in the far west.

Following the trail of two military columns, Sitting Bull and four hundred warriors came upon two thousand soldiers camped on the Powder River. A truce party approached the bluecoats but was shot at without warning. Sitting Bull then engaged the enemy, but fighting mainly with bows and old muskets against rifles and howitzers, he was forced to conduct harrying attacks. However, the soldiers had to kill their starving horses and retreat on foot along the river. The fourth army column arrived to escort the soldiers to Fort Reno, where they were besieged by Sioux throughout the winter. Sitting Bull, meanwhile, led another siege, of Fort Rice in North Dakota.

The 1865 Harney-Sanborn treaty guaranteed to the Sioux, Arapaho, and Cheyenne nations the vital Powder River country. That area, lying between the Black Hills and the Rocky Mountains, was those nations' traditional source of food and clothing, and the best buffalo country in the Plains.

Yet the following year more negotiators arrived from Washington. Because gold had been discovered in present-day Montana, the government wanted a new treaty to allow the building of the Bozeman Trail and a chain of army forts through the Powder River country. It was a direct contravention of the treaty only just signed. At those negotiations, which took place at Fort Laramie in Wyoming, the Sioux discovered from the U.S. Army that the road was to go ahead with or without their approval. Chiefs Red Cloud and Spotted Tail withdrew.

There followed two years of intermittent warfare, in which Crazy Horse of the Oglala band of the Lakota achieved military fame. In 1868 the road and forts were abandoned and a new Fort Laramie treaty was signed by Sioux chiefs and the government. The same year, Sitting Bull was elected a principal chief of the entire Sioux nation.

One of the terms of the 1868 treaty stated: "No white person or persons shall be permitted to settle upon or occupy any portion of the territory, or without the consent of the Indians to pass through the same." Another stated that the territory, including the Black Hills and Powder River country, would remain Sioux forever. Chief Sitting Bull joined Red Cloud and Spotted Tail in their second visit to Washington and met President Grant, "the Great Father." There they discovered that other terms of the treaty—written in English—were not what had been translated to them by Indian agents before they signed.

In the hundred years after 1778—the very first treaty between Native Americans and a U.S. authority—some 370 treaties were negotiated. Like that first treaty, promising the Delaware nation representation in Congress, almost every one was broken or revised by the government. Whenever the government wanted to change the terms, Native American nations were threatened, or attacked, and made to sign a new treaty.

Sitting Bull said of the 1868 treaty: "You are fools to make yourselves slaves to a piece of some fat bacon, some hard tack and a little sugar and coffee." He did not sign. He and Crazy Horse refused to live in the reservations. On their return home, they took their respective bands northwest into Montana. They lived in the so-called Badlands area of the Bighorn River.

Farther south that September, the flamboyant Civil War soldier George Custer, lieutenant colonel to the Seventh Cavalry at Fort Dodge,

Kansas, had winter orders to campaign against villages in the independent Indian Territory (Oklahoma), in retaliation for raids into Kansas. At first light on November 27, in heavy snow, he attacked a Cheyenne encampment at Washita with four columns of cavalry. He captured fifty-one lodges and nearly nine hundred ponies and killed more than a hundred men, women, and children. Unable to take the booty away, he burned the canvas teepees and shot the ponies. So "Long Hair" Custer became known to the Plains nations.

Farther north, relative peace was maintained in Sioux territory with all signatories keeping fairly close to the terms of the treaty—until 1872. Prospectors had passed through the Black Hills, the sacred Paha Sapa, illegally and reported gold deposits. Despite the treaty, a small gold rush began and the Lakota Sioux defended their land, killing some prospectors and chasing others away.

President Grant promised "to prevent all invasion of this country by intruders so long as by law and treaty it is secured to the Indians." Yet the prospectors and mining lobbies in Washington, D.C., demanded other action from the government.

An army expedition, one thousand of the Seventh Cavalry under the command of General Custer, illegally entered Sioux territory and camped in the Black Hills. Custer wrote that there was gold "from the grass roots down" as well as rich farming and timber land—and gave his report to the newspapers. The gold rush escalated, with hundreds of miners traveling to the Black Hills by the Missouri River and the Thieves' Road.

Another Civil War general, Crook, made a second trip to the Black Hills in 1875 and found more than a thousand miners prospecting for gold. He told them they were in violation of the treaty and ordered them to leave. No action was taken.

Red Cloud and Spotted Tail protested to Washington. The U.S. government responded by sending a commission "to treat with the Sioux Indians for the relinquishment of the Black Hills."

Chief Sitting Bull and Crazy Horse were invited to meet the commission. Sitting Bull responded, "I do not want to sell any land to the government." He took a pinch of dust from the earth, saying, "Not even as much as this." He added: "We want no white man here. If the whites try to take them [the Black Hills], I will fight." Crazy Horse also refused to attend.

The commission offered to purchase the Black Hills or purchase the mineral rights, and further requested that the Sioux hand over the Powder River country, their vital buffalo lands. Fully within the terms of the 1868 treaty, all offers were rejected; the Paha Sapa was not for sale or lease. Returned to Washington, the commission recommended that Congress appropriate a sum of a "fair equivalent of the value" and force purchase the Black Hills. In other words, break the treaty.

This Congress did, and some fifteen thousand miners flooded into the Black Hills. By February 1876, Generals Crook and Terry had been ordered to prepare military incursions into the headwaters of the Powder, Rosebud, Tongue, and Bighorn rivers in the northern Sioux territory. The first action was by Crook's forces on March 17. Attacking a village of reservation and non-reservation Sioux and Cheyenne, the cavalry rode in without warning at dawn, firing indiscriminately. The survivors fled northeast to Crazy Horse's camp. In turn, Crazy Horse moved everyone north to join Chief Sitting Bull.

In spring, those several thousand assorted Sioux and some Cheyenne moved farther north to the Rosebud River in Montana. It was the annual hunt for food and skins to supply them for the coming year. Forty-five-year-old Sitting Bull led them in a major Sun Dance.

For three days at the huge camp the

warriors danced, shuffling the earth into dust clouds among the tee-pees. Chief Sitting Bull danced around the Sun Pole for eighteen hours continuously, bled himself with fifty cuts to each arm, and stared into the sun until, in an exhausted trance, a vision came to him. A voice called: "I give you these because they have no ears." When he looked into the sky he saw bluecoat soldiers falling like grasshoppers, headfirst, into the Sioux camp. Because the white men had no ears and would not listen, the Great Spirit was giving these soldiers to the Sioux to be killed.

Three days later an approaching column of twelve hundred men under General Crook was sighted by Sioux scouts, thirty miles down the Rosebud Valley. Sitting Bull and Crazy Horse, thinking these would become the falling soldiers of the vision, gathered half their warriors and rode overnight to meet them. Sitting Bull sent a warning to Crook that if he crossed the river, he would be attacked. On the morning of June 17, Crook crossed the river.

The Sioux were heavily outgunned by the rifle-carrying bluecoats. The battle, one of charges, feints, skirmishes, advances, retreats, and counterattacks, went on for nine hours before they disengaged.

The next day at first light, Sioux and Cheyenne scouts approached to find that the bluecoats had recrossed the river and were retreating southward. Crook's men had fired twenty-five thousand rounds of ammunition and lost about twenty-eight killed and fifty-six wounded (numbers vary). Later they were awarded three Congressional Medals of Honor, but they didn't fight again. The battle of the Rosebud was a strategic and tactical victory for the Sioux, but Sitting Bull decided it was not the victory of his vision. He had lost some thirty-eight men.

With reports of good grass and plentiful antelope to the west, Sitting Bull moved camp to the valley of the Greasy Grass—the Little Bighorn River. The new camp sprawled over three miles along the west bank. There were now about ten thousand Sioux, Cheyenne, and other Native Americans there, of whom two to three thousand were warriors. Black Elk, a thirteen-year-old Oglala Sioux, was one of them.

On June 24, scouts rode in to report to Sitting Bull that a second group of bluecoats was advancing up the Rosebud Valley. It was Long Hair Custer and six hundred cavalry. After resting his men and horses that evening, Custer marched a further five hours overnight to reach the Sioux camp the next day.

On Sunday the twenty-fifth, Custer and one Seventh Cavalry column crossed the ridge separating the Rosebud and the Little Bighorn valleys and advanced on the Sioux. Not seen by the Sioux scouts was a second column led by Major Reno, riding to attack the southern end of the camp, or a third column under Captain Benteen, circling farther south to block any escape.

Chief Red Horse recalled the urgency at midday: "We came out of the council lodge and talked in all directions. The Sioux mount horses, take guns, and go fight the soldiers. Women and children mount horses and go, meaning to get out of the way." Not all of them could.

Major Reno's surprise attack across the river caught women and children in the open. Almost all the family of Sitting Bull's adopted brother, Gall, was killed. "After that, I killed all my enemies with the hatchet," Gall reported. In the south of the camp where Reno's cavalry attacked were the Hunkpapa with Sitting Bull; in the center were the Oglala with Crazy Horse.

"Sitting Bull was big medicine," said Gall. "The women and children were hastily moved downstream. . . . [T]he women and children caught the horses for the bucks to mount them; the bucks mounted and charged back to Reno and checked him, and drove him into the timber."

For whatever reason, Reno had stopped and dismounted when he might have charged further. Gall's counterattack turned his flank and forced the bluecoats into the trees, where horses could not operate freely. "They were brave men," Sitting Bull said of the cavalry, "but they were too tired. When they rode up, their horses were tired and they were tired." Reno retreated farther, back across the Little Bighorn. The retreat turned into a rout, and his column was isolated.

In the center of the Sioux camp Crazy Horse held his warriors back, waiting for Custer to make his move on the opposite bank of the river. Custer continued riding northward and sent an order to Benteen to rejoin him. Crazy Horse gathered his warriors and rode through the camp *away* from Custer in order to outflank him. Gall, meanwhile, gathered his men in the south and crossed the river behind Custer. Other Sioux and Cheyenne splashed across the river opposite Custer's column.

Custer probably realized by then that he was cut off, if not already surrounded, and ordered his cavalry to the small hill at the northern end of the river bluff. His two hundred men with carbine rifles would establish and hold a defensive perimeter until Benteen, Reno, or other cavalry reached him. As his stretched-out column approached the brow of the rocky hill, fighting a rear guard against Gall's warriors, Crazy Horse suddenly appeared above them. He had reached the top first, from the other side.

There was a moment's pause as Crazy Horse appreciated the situation. Then he led his charging warriors down the slope and fell onto Custer and his 208 men.

Chief Kill Eagle said the Sioux were "like bees swarming out of a hive." Watching from across the river, young Black Elk saw a big dust swirl on the hillside from which horses galloped out with empty saddles. *This* was the battle of Sitting Bull's vision. No quarter was given.

Although not at Custer Hill, Sitting Bull gave this account of Custer's death only a year later, derived from Crazy Horse and others. "Up there where the last fight took place, where the last stand was made, the Long Hair stood like a sheaf of corn with all the ears fallen around him. . . . He killed a man when he fell. He laughed. . . . He had fired his last shot." Dead alongside Custer was his brother, Tom, twice awarded the Medal of Honor in the Civil War.

Benteen, meanwhile, had ridden back to the river as ordered to find Reno holding a static position. They joined forces in a successful defense. In total, fifty of Reno's men were killed and forty-four wounded; thirteen Medals of Honor were awarded. The following afternoon, Sitting Bull moved south to the Bighorn Mountains and the Sioux bands dispersed. There would be little hunting that year.

On July 5, 1876, the river steamer *Far West* berthed at Bismarck

Landing in South Dakota. A telegram was sent to Washington, beginning: GENERAL CUSTER ATTACKED THE INDIANS JUNE 25, AND HE, WITH EVERY OFFICER AND MAN IN FIVE COMPANIES, WERE KILLED. It was the centenary of U.S. independence.

That August, Congress enacted a law providing that "until the Sioux relinquished all claim to the Powder River country and the Black Hills, no subsistence would be furnished them." Which is ironic, for it was the government that broke the treaty, the government that sent in the army to attack the Sioux, while the Sioux never wanted subsistence, only their traditional hunting lands.

Two thousand five hundred more cavalry were sent to the Plains, so that Sitting Bull, Crazy Horse, and other chiefs were harried and hunted throughout their lands. Many chiefs surrendered, and by November, the first Sioux had fled to Canada. In January 1877 the two great warriors met for the last time at Tongue River village. Sitting Bull announced his intention to escape across the border to the land of "the Great Mother," the Canada of Queen Victoria. Crazy Horse spoke of surrender, to which Sitting Bull replied, "I do not want to die yet."

Sitting Bull gathered about three thousand of his people and, in May 1877, led them across the border to Wood Mountain. He advised the Royal Canadian Mounted Police of his arrival and requested a meeting. In the interview with the "redcoats" he produced a gold medal. "My grandfather received this medal in recognition of his battle for King George III during the [American] revolution," he said. "Now, in this odd time, I direct my people here to reclaim a sanctuary of my grandfather. I have come to remain with the White Mother's children." The RCMP explained that Canada must not to be used as a base for raids into the United States, that he must obey the laws of Her Majesty, and that he and his tribe were welcome in Canada as a free people but, like free people, must fend for themselves.

Also in May, Crazy Horse with some two hundred Oglala lodges surrendered to the U.S. Army. In September he was murdered by guards at Fort Robinson in Nebraska.

Chief Sitting Bull and his people lived in Canada for four years, but the buffalo there were few, mere remnants of the millions wiped out by the skin traders and settlers in the United States. His people began to starve. In July 1881, responding to repeated U.S. government offers of food, reservation life, and a "pardon," the tired chief returned to the United States. He left his famous head-dress in Canada.

Sitting Bull allowed his young son to hand over his rifle to the commanding officer at Fort Buford in Montana, to teach the boy "that he has become a friend of the Americans." Sitting Bull was the last chief of the free Sioux to surrender his weapons.

Despite the offered "pardon," for two years he was held prisoner at Fort Randall, south on the Missouri River. In 1883 he was allowed finally to rejoin his Lakota at Standing Rock Reservation in North Dakota. There he became a revered member of the Silent Eaters, a select group concerned with the welfare of the surviving Sioux nation. There also began a strange interlude in Sitting Bull's life. Despite his publicly and outspoken antipathy to the U.S. government, it arranged a Sitting Bull speaking tour of fifteen cities. He was a sensation. Buffalo Bill Cody visited him and invited him to join his Wild West Show.

The Wild West Show was unique. Touring the United States and Canada, it eulogized the myths and modern legends of the American West even as they were being created. Among those who appeared with Buffalo Bill were Geronimo, Annie Oakley, Rain-in-the-Face (who perhaps killed General Custer), Wild Bill Hickock, and, most famous, Chief Sitting Bull. One of the most popular events recreated was the battle of the Little Bighorn. Sitting Bull gave most of his wages to poor white urchins, who flocked to him wherever he went.

In 1885 Sitting Bull had another mystical vision. He saw a meadow lark alight on a hillock beside where he was sitting, and the bird said to him, "Your own people—Lakotas—will kill you."

Buffalo Bill asked Sitting Bull to tour with the show to Great Britain, where in 1887 it played before Queen Victoria in London. Sitting Bull declined, for the government was beginning moves to take yet more land from the Sioux. He returned to Standing Rock Reservation. It was Black Elk, by then a holy man like Sitting Bull, who sailed with Buffalo Bill to Britain. There, a British soldier joined the show. He was Private William Jones, one of the defenders of Rorke's Drift in the Anglo-Zulu wars and recipient of the Victoria Cross.

Despite Sitting Bull's political resistance, more land was taken from his people. By 1890 the Sioux had only islands of reservations surrounded by white settlers, less than sixteen thousand square miles. No Sioux lived freely in their own lands. Then, in early 1889, began the phenomenon of the Ghost Dance.

A new religion swept the Plains nations. Its prophet, Wovoka, predicted the coming of a "messiah" who would end the white man's domination, return to the Plains the slaughtered buffalo and antelope, and resurrect the men, women, and children slain by the bluecoats. Native Americans who danced the Ghost Dance, for five days every six weeks, would enjoy this new future. The dance was adopted throughout the Great Plains, especially by the Sioux, for Chief Sitting Bull refused to condemn the movement.

At Standing Rock, Sitting Bull still lived the Sioux way, although he sent his children to a Christian school so that they could read and write English. The Ghost Dance contained no incitement to violence, and no government official or journalist ever interviewed Wovoka about it, yet it was portrayed as a demonic war dance inciting armed rebellion. About three thousand warriors did gather in the Badlands that winter, but all they did was dance in the snow.

In December the government asked Buffalo Bill Cody to visit Sitting Bull to persuade him to travel to Chicago for a conference. The Standing Rock Reservation agent, James McLaughlin, had always disliked and belittled Sitting Bull, and refused to let Cody and Sitting Bull meet. Cody's authority was rescinded and he left.

Just before daylight on December 15, forty-three Indian police surrounded Sitting Bull's log cabin. They were supported by a squadron of cavalry. McLaughlin had given orders: "You must not let him escape under any circumstances."

Two policemen entered the cabin and woke Sitting Bull. "You are my prisoner," one of them told him. "You must go to the agency." The fifty-nine-year-old Sitting Bull dressed and quietly went outside to find himself surrounded by forty armed Indian police.

Sioux from nearby cabins came out and surrounded the police. There was argument, shouting. A fracas developed; someone fired a gun; and Sitting Bull was shot in the back and in the head by the Indian police. The shot in the back may have been accidental; the bullet in the head, which murdered him, was intentional. It was fired by Red Tomahawk, a Lakota Sioux. Sitting Bull died immediately, his last vision come true.

With the death of the spiritual leader of the Sioux nation, Big Foot became the prominent chief. His arrest was ordered as well, but he was already moving his band—120 men, 230 women and children—to the Pine Ridge Reservation. With him was Black Elk. On December 28 a unit of the Seventh Cavalry intercepted Big Foot's band in heavy snow. He immediately flew a white flag and surrendered to the smaller force.

They were escorted to Wounded Knee Creek in South Dakota, Big Foot riding in an army ambulance wagon because he was suffering from pneumonia. When the Sioux awoke the next day, they found their teepees surrounded by 470 cavalry soldiers, with four Hotchkiss revolving cannons on slopes aimed into the camp.

After breakfast, Colonel Forsyth ordered the Sioux to surrender all their weapons. A few guns were handed over but Forsyth was not satisfied. He sent bluecoats into the teepees; they hauled possessions out into the snow and removed hatchets and knives. Two more rifles were uncovered, one in the possession of Black Coyote, a deaf warrior. Accidentally or on purpose, whether by Black Coyote or someone else, while the warrior was being manhandled by two soldiers, a rifle was fired.

The surrounding Seventh Cavalry immediately fired their carbines into the camp. Big Foot was one of the first killed. Then the four cannons opened fire, sending in two-pound explosive shrapnel shells. When the shooting stopped, between two and three hundred Sioux were lying dead in the snow, with fifty-one wounded. The cavalry lost twenty-five dead and thirty-nine wounded, most from their own shrapnel and bullets.

Black Elk, witness to both the battle of Little Bighorn and Wounded Knee, recalled years later: "I can still see the butchered women and children lying heaped and scattered all along the crooked gulch as plain as when I saw them with eyes still young. . . . A people's dream died there."

Chief Sitting Bull's body was moved from Standing Rock Reservation in 1953 to Mobridge, South Dakota, the land of his birth. A granite shaft now marks his grave. Described in his own words, the creed of his life is a suitable epitaph for the last great Native American chief: *oyate ptayela*—"taking care of the nation."

Recommended
Bury My Heart at Wounded Knee: An Indian History of the Amerian West by Dee Brown

The Plains Indians by Colin Taylor
American Indians in American History, edited by Sterling Evans
For Valour: Victoria Cross and Medal of Honor Battles by Bryan
Perrett
The Royal Ontario Museum, Ontario, Canada

Edith Cavell

To be a nurse is not easy, but it is worth the sacrifice.
                                                        —Edith Cavell

One of the reasons for writing this book is to breathe new life into the extraordinary stories of heroes and heroines who were once known to all. Time and changes in education have meant that sometimes stories are forgotten where they should be remembered.

The life of Edith Cavell is one such tale. In 1915 her death rocked the world and helped bring America into the First World War. Queen Alexandra attended her funeral, the same lady who visited Robert Scott on his ship before he set off to the South Pole. Such was the outcry at her death that the German kaiser insisted no other woman would be executed unless he had reviewed the case and given his personal order. Edith Cavell's statue stands at Saint Martin's Place near Trafalgar Square in London. Very few of the thousands who pass it each day know how courageous she was, or of the lives she saved at the expense of her own.

Her father was a vicar in the village of Swardeston in Norfolk. He was sometimes known as "the One-Sermon Vicar," as he repeated the same one every Sunday for nearly forty-six years. Edith Louisa Cavell was born on December 4, 1865. It was a devout and stern upbringing. As there was no village school, the vicar taught Edith himself with her two sisters and a brother.

Cavell discovered a talent for languages at a young age. She was engaged as a children's governess for some years, then traveled to Brussels in 1890, where she taught for five years before returning home to nurse her father through a long illness. That experience would give her life direction as she began formal training as a nurse in 1896, at the London Hospital on Whitechapel Road. In 1903 she was promoted to assistant matron at Shoreditch Infirmary. Her efficiency and powers of organization were said to be outstanding, and she was asked by an eminent surgeon, Antoine Depage, to start the first school for training nurses in Belgium. She opened the school in 1907.

Cavell was a serious woman who rarely smiled but had the respect of all those with whom she dealt. She trained the nurses with stern discipline, coupled with a deep well of personal kindness. When she discovered that one of her patients had become a drug addict, she kept the fact from the authorities until she had helped the girl break the habit. She also refused to expel one probationer nurse who had become a stripper, worrying what would become of the girl if she was turned away. In fact, the nurse gave up her second career and eventually became the supervisor of another European hospital.

As the "directrice" of the clinic, Cavell taught anatomy, cleanliness, and the importance of hard work to the trainee nurses, sometimes using Florence Nightingale as an example. On one summer day she refused to let them kill a wasp that had gotten in, saying: "Turn it free. A nurse gives life; she does not take it."

When war broke out in 1914, Cavell was at home on holiday in Norfolk. In June of that year, Archduke Franz Ferdinand was assassinated in Serbia, and one by one, the great nations were dragged into the conflict. Despite the entreaties of her mother, sisters, and brother, Cavell knew her duty was with the nurses and patients in Brussels and returned immediately. On August 20, German soldiers marched into the city.

As a noncombatant, Cavell was offered safe passage to Holland, but she refused. Battle casualties were coming into the clinic every day, and she stayed to tend them. Even then, she could have lived out the war in perfect safety if she had not felt so strongly that she must also do something for the Allies. When two British soldiers on the run asked for shelter at her clinic, she hid them in the cellar. As far as possible, Cavell took on this secret part of her work herself, keeping her nurses away from the hunted men so they could not be implicated. Despite the danger, she had them smuggled out to Holland, and the clinic quickly became known as part of the Belgian Underground and a safe place to hide.

Cavell was aware of the danger in her activities. She kept her diary hidden, sewn into a cushion in case the clinic was ever searched. There was little money and not much to eat, but Edith and her nurses shared what they had with those who came to them, while always expecting the knock on the door that would mean they had been discovered.

She was eventually betrayed by a German spy named George Quien. He had discovered some details of the underground work going on at the clinic. He appeared one day, pretending to be a Paris doctor with a minor complaint that required him to remain in the clinic for some weeks. There he took note of the clandestine activities and asked innocent-sounding questions of the nurses. When he disappeared without warning in early 1915, one of Cavell's contacts was arrested shortly afterward. She said to another nurse: "I suppose it won't be long before they come for us." Even then, under terrible strain, she continued helping Allied soldiers find their way home, passing two hundred of them back to safety. Her work was too important to give up, no matter what storm clouds were on the horizon.

In August 1915, three Germans demanded entrance to the clinic. Once inside, they produced a pistol and had the nurses line up against the wall. Edith was summoned, and she came down to them in her nurse's uniform, carrying a small traveling case and gloves. They took her to the Saint-Gilles prison, where she was charged with aiding the enemy. She remained there for two months. In her absence, one of the nurses, Sister Wilkins, sought out the American ambassador. He tried desperately to contact the German governor of Brussels, but to no avail. The nurses sent her roses, and she kept them in her cell.

Sister Wilkins was allowed to visit Edith in prison and found her worn out and thin but still determined to keep her dignity.

"I have done what was my duty," Cavell said. "They must do with me what they will." Her faith was a comfort to her, and she wrote to the nurses: "Remember that it is not enough to be good nurses; you should also be good Christian women."

At her trial, Edith Cavell would not lie. She admitted in court that she had cared for two hundred British, French, and Belgian soldiers, helping many of them to escape. The sentence was death. On October 12, 1915, a chaplain was allowed to visit her in her cell. Before she was taken out to be executed, she said to him: "Standing as I do in the view of God and Eternity, I realize that patriotism is not enough. I must have no hatred or bitterness toward anyone." Deeply moved by her courage, he said later: "I came to comfort her and she has given me comfort."

At 7 A.M., Cavell was made to stand against a wall and a firing squad assembled. Some of the men fired deliberately wide, and it is said that one refused to shoot. He was also killed and buried in a shallow grave beside her.

A few days later, her personal effects were returned to the clinic, with a final letter to the nurses. In it, she wrote:

I hope you will not forget the little talks we had each evening. I told you that voluntary sacrifices will make you happy; that the idea of duty before God and yourselves will give you support in the sad moments of life and in the face of death. I know I have sometimes been harsh, but never have I been voluntarily unjust. I loved all of you more than you will ever know.

When the war ended, Cavell's body was returned to England. An impressive ceremony was held at Westminster Abbey. From there the coffin was taken home to Norfolk and she was laid to rest outside Norwich Cathedral. Every second year since, in Swardeston, a flower festival is held around October 12 in her memory. Her courage, her sense of duty, her example, are as valuable today as they have ever been.

Recommended
Edith Cavell by A. A. Hoehling
Oxford Dictionary of National Biography

Thomas Paine
and *Rights of Man*

*If liberty means anything, it means the right to tell people
what they do not want to hear.* —George Orwell

The United Kingdom is the originator of modern democracy. Not
for nothing is Westminster called "the Mother of Parliaments."
English common law, dating back to Alfred the Great (871–99), is
the basis of many countries' legal systems as well as Britain's. In the
United States, created almost a millennium after Alfred united England, its law refers back through British law to this common origin.

Like much progress, the spread of British democracy around the
world has always been a case of "two steps forward one step back."
The governing of Ireland should have been better, while the independence of the Australian colonies in 1901 is an example of good intentions misused. The earlier British act of 1828 decreed "free people of
color in the colonies" had legal equality with their fellow citizens, yet
two of the first acts of the independent Australian government classified Aborigines as "subhuman" and removed their right to vote. These
acts have since been overturned, yet they demonstrate the constant
threat to our freedoms and "rights," even from ourselves.

The greatest backward step for Britain was the imposition of the
European feudal system upon the English freeman system. Most of
the freedoms developed from Alfred's reign were lost in 1066 when
William defeated King Harold at the battle of Hastings. Feudalism
created peasantry, serfdom or slavery, a class-divided society, and the
divine right of kings—dictatorship. It took four hundred years to
overturn all these, through the Magna Carta and the 1381 Peasants'
Revolt, to the civil war and Cromwell's commonwealth of 1649.

Our freedoms, liberties, and civil rights come at a price—human life. It's the greatest argument of all for never losing them.

Radical thinkers such as Thomas Hobbes, David Home, John Locke, and Thomas Paine devised the principles of our modern democratic society in seventeenth- and eighteenth-century Britain. They attacked authoritarian government, oppression, censorship, and religious dogma. As a result, equality before the law, votes for everyone, freedom of speech, and secret ballots are British concepts, while the first Declaration of Rights was passed into law in Westminster in 1689. Even the concept and term "rights of man" was created in Britain. The later U.S. and French constitutions are based upon Locke's revolutionary *Two Treatises of Government* of 1690.

Yet in practical terms, no one in the world has a "right" to anything, not even life itself. When a person is drowning, the sea does not recognize any right to survival. All our "rights" are man-made, and while armies and navies are necessary to protect them, the first step is their creation. The man who brought all these diverse rights and concepts together—who sent shock waves through governments, churches, through society itself—was Thomas Paine, son of a humble corset maker from Thetford in Norfolk.

Born on January 29, 1737, Thomas Paine was brought up a Quaker and attended the local Thetford school. When he was twelve years old he was apprenticed to his father. He lasted four years before running away from corsetry to the sea. He served as a seaman in the British privateers *Terrible*—commanded by a Captain Death and Lieutenant Devil—and the *King of Prussia,* preying on enemy shipping during the Seven Years' War.

After his first wife and baby died in childbirth, Paine became a customs officer in Kent and then Sussex, the county of Quaker William Penn. With the separation from his second wife, Elizabeth, in 1774 came the first indication of Thomas Paine's ideals of personal freedom. Despite the patriarchal laws of the time and although poor himself, he signed his ownership to Elizabeth's inherited property back to her, permitted her to carry out business and trade with the rights of a single woman, and split the proceeds from the sale of their house and goods.

Dismissed from the customs office the same year because of his labor agitation and pamphleteering, he wrote the fiery *Case of the Officers of Excise,* and in London he met the British colonial freethinker Benjamin Franklin. With Franklin's letter of introduction, Paine sailed to the Quaker colony of Pennsylvania.

In Philadelphia he was appointed editor of the *Pennsylvania Magazine*—just in time to campaign for the American colonies' independence from Britain. Paine had discovered his life's purpose: the campaign for individual freedom.

The background to the American War of Independence is unique. On the one hand was Great Britain, then the most democratic and liberal nation in the world; on the other were thirteen of Britain's American colonies, each with its own independent assembly and its people also British. In each land, sometimes in the same family, there was support for the other. It was almost a civil war.

Paine's magazine contributions included several essays condemning slavery, but it was his pamphlet *Common Sense,* written and published in 1776, that made his name. It was the most widely read pamphlet of the war, both in Britain and America, and in addition was translated and read widely in monarchist Europe. In *Common Sense* Paine made his arguments for independence, crystallizing the vague views of radicals in Britain as well as the British colonists. He sketched a system for a united self-government, although as he asserted in another essay, his "principle is universal. My attachment is to all the world, and not to any particular part."

When Paine was appointed secretary to an American committee for foreign affairs, he uncovered the French supply of free arms and munitions to the colonials. He was a man of great personal integrity, and despite the adverse effect it would have on the cause for independence, Paine exposed this foreign interference. Politically embarrassed, France denied the arms supply and demanded Paine's dismissal. When the American colonial congress refused to support Paine, he resigned.

Bizarrely, the French then offered Paine seven hundred pounds to write articles supporting France and an alliance with the colonists against Britain. He refused. In 1782 he published *Letter to the Abbe Raynal,* a refutation of the French version of the War of Independence. He destroyed the argument—still promoted—that the war arose mainly from dispute over taxation. Paine recognized that the colonists' desire for independence was self-driven, a part of the progressive enlightenment within the English-speaking world, like an adolescent breaking free of its mother. Taxation was merely the spark that ignited the flame.

This Anglo-American revolution was only the beginning for Thomas Paine. Although given a farm at New Rochelle by the state of New York for services to liberty, he returned home in 1787 to campaign for political and social change in Britain and Ireland. In July 1789, the Paris mob stormed the Bastille. The first French revolution had begun, and Paine was again in the right place at the right time. Although a symbol of the revolution, the sacking and destruction of the Bastille was not by the bourgeois revolutionaries and was not to release political prisoners; there were just seven common criminals inside. It was merely a mob looting the citadel for weapons and money.

In Britain there was sympathy and support for this revolution at first. The excesses and tyrannies of King Louis XVI were well known, and British radicals such as Edmund Burke looked on with approval. At last the French were resisting their own feudal system. When ideals degenerated into civil war, and civil war into war on neighboring countries, most British radicals withdrew their support. Paine, however, took this opportunity to reaffirm his support for the original ideals. He used the publicity to write and publish in 1791 his watershed *Rights of Man*. That same year the first biography of Thomas Paine, encouraged by the government to be critical of him, was also published.

So radical were Paine's proposals, the first publisher withdrew for fear of prosecution, yet *Rights of Man* became so popular that a second publisher was forced into further printings. After only two months, fifty thousand copies were in circulation, an immense number in those days of smaller populations.

Paine completed a second part to *Rights of Man* in 1792, and soon sixpenny joint editions and translations abroad circulated widely. In his introduction to Part 2 he declared: "If universal peace, civilisation and commerce are ever to be the happy lot of man, it cannot be accomplished but by a revolution in the system of governments."

In *Rights of Man*, Paine advocated in Great Britain and Ireland a major redistribution of wealth, a progressive taxation system to finance poverty relief, child benefits, pensions at sixty, maternity grants, free education for all, accommodation for the homeless, and compensation for discharged soldiers and sailors. Internationally, he proposed treaties limiting armaments and the formation of a league of nations to prevent wars. It was 1792, the same year that a bill for the abolition of the slave trade was first passed by the House of Commons. They were heady days of ideas and social change.

Argued singly, each of Paine's proposals could be accepted as a reasonable step for the improvement of society. Brought together in one document, they were dynamite. *Rights of Man* was read aloud in coffeehouses and inns throughout the land. Paine's arguments commanded people to listen and to think; his proposals were debated and argued from government chambers to cottage kitchens.

However, after two overseas revolutions in thirteen years, the British government was nervous. While the United States was small, weak, and nine thousand miles away, France was large, powerful, and only twenty-two miles away. Under attack, Parliament introduced a law prohibiting seditious libel and publication. The publisher of *Rights of Man* was quickly charged. Despite Paine's pleas to him to make it a test case, the publisher pleaded guilty and paid the fine. A further Royal Proclamation instructed magistrates to seek out authors and printers of seditious writings; some were charged but all were acquitted.

That June, Paine himself was charged with seditious libel, yet he refused to be cowed. He published letters criticizing the repressive law, including *Letter Addressed to the Addressers on the Late Proclamation.* (While his arguments were incisive, Paine's titles sometimes were not.) That letter was effectively Part 3 of *Rights of Man,* in which he argued that true representative government must rely upon votes for all. A government's power must rest upon the sovereignty of its people, not upon itself.

Paine's prosecution was delayed until December, yet the pressure on him remained intense. Modernist societies applauded and debated his arguments, while for traditionalists it was too much, too soon. He was arrested for a business partner's debt, a charge instigated by the government. The debt was paid by Dr. Johnson, creator of the famous dictionary. Paine had influential friends as well as enemies, but in September he fled to France, where he had been given honorary citizenship.

In France, he was actually appointed deputy to the French National Convention, but already the revolution was unraveling. The revolutionaries declared war on Prussia, and in November they offered military aid to all "oppressed peoples" of other countries—an excuse to invade. In an open letter to his British prosecutor, Paine unwisely supported revolution in Britain. He was outlawed.

In the new year the French king was executed. By February 1793, France had invaded or declared war on most western European countries, including Britain. In September began the bloody Reign of Terror and the revolution was destroyed.

The uprising had gotten rid of the antique French monarchy and feudalism only to replace it with a republican dictatorship. That was soon followed by a military dictatorship and twenty-two years of world war. In the long term little was gained at a huge cost in lives and liberty. English radical philosopher William Blake estimated that resisting and defeating the French dictatorships set back democratic

reform in Britain by more than fifty years. It was this parallel struggle for survival that made life so difficult for British radicals; the abolition of slavery was delayed, Blake charged with sedition, scientist
Joseph Priestley's house set on fire, and radical William Cobbett imprisoned. Survival takes priority over freedom.

Against this background of chaos and bloodshed, Thomas Paine
began his second great work, *The Age of Reason*. In December 1793,
Paine himself was arrested for his opposition to the French king's execution. He was imprisoned in Paris, sentenced to death, and had his
honorary citizenship revoked. The translated manuscript of Part 1
was already with French publishers, and the original English text was
immediately smuggled to Britain.

Paine's health deteriorated during ten months in Luxembourg
Prison, and he was nursed from death by two imprisoned British
doctors. Paine completed Part 2 between bouts of fever and semicon-
sciousness. Part 1 was published in London and Paris at the beginning of 1794, Part 2 in 1795.

In *The Age of Reason* Thomas Paine argued strongly against the
religion of his time. Still a Quaker, he prefaced his work with the
statement: "I believe in one God, and no more; and I hope for happi-
ness beyond this life." He rejected organized religion with the argument "All national institutions of churches, whether Jewish, Christian
or Turkish [Islam], appear to me no other than human inventions, set
up to terrify and enslave mankind, and monopolise power and profit."

He also disavowed religious revelation, stating: "A thing which
everyone is required to believe requires that the proof and evidence of
it should be equal to all, and universal." Like scientist Sir Isaac Newton earlier, Paine found his proof and evidence of God in nature. He
was the first to argue that religious books such as the Bible, Koran,
and Torah were the writings of men, not the holy words of God.

Once again these were groundbreaking—even dangerous—views
to publish in a predominantly Christian Europe, especially in a time
of world war. Understandably, they created great hostility toward
Paine, and he has been much misrepresented ever since. However, in

their separate fields, *Rights of Man* and *The Age of Reason* are watersheds in society as important as Charles Darwin's *On the Origin of Species*. All three are part of the framework of today's Western secular societies.

With a new French regime in place, the American ambassador took up the issue of Paine's imprisonment, claiming that he was American as well as British. His death sentence was overturned, and Paine was released in November 1794, although his health collapsed again with further fevers. Because of the threat of British imprisonment, he remained in Paris for eight more years. He wrote the important essay for reforming land ownership, *Agrarian Justice*, advocating ownership based not upon a destructive socialist redistribution but upon commercial viability and individual freedom. He also wrote essays about how Bonaparte might invade Britain and America. Paine was still blinded to the realities of dictatorship by the original ideals of that first French revolution.

With gifts from other British radicals, Paine cleared his debts, and during the 1802 Treaty of Amiens, he took ship to America. There he found himself rejected by many former colonial friends because of his writings. Once again he was temporarily arrested for a dubious debt. By that time, the revolution in the United States had also unraveled, the principles of freedom and liberty not applying to slaves and Native Americans. Presidents Washington and Jefferson both were slave owners, and the new republic was on the path to federalism and becoming the greatest slave society of them all.

Paine wrote against this new America in a series of letters, *To the Citizens of the United States*. His books were burned and he was publicly booed and hissed. He was even shot at by his disgruntled farm manager, though, typically, Paine did not prosecute.

In 1809, after further illness, Paine died in New York. His request to be buried in the Quaker cemetery was refused. Ten years later his remains were brought home to Britain, but burial there was also prohibited. His bones have since disappeared, although his skull is claimed to be at Sydney University in Australia.

Thomas Paine did not invent all the radical theories, principles of freedom, and social philosophies he promoted, but in *Rights of Man* he was the first to combine them into a system of government. His ideal was not a leveling of society but one of equal opportunity. Other British radicals campaigned with and after him—Jeremy Bentham, William Godwin, Samuel Whitbread, Richard and John Carlile, Joseph Priestley, Mary Wollstonecraft, Elizabeth Fry, John Wilkes, Emmeline Pankhurst, and many more. While violent, false revolutions failed abroad, a true revolution began to take place quietly and successfully in Britain.

After the defeat of military dictatorship in Europe in 1815, a catalog of democratic, social, and political reforms was enacted in Britain throughout the nineteenth century. This included repealing the law of seditious libel and publication. These principles of human rights, justice for all, and liberty—begun from the first modern document of rights, the Magna Carta of 1215—were sent out into the world and our modern, Western society created.

Further editions of Paine's great works were published. Voting rights for everybody was slow in coming, but in 1856 the colony of Tasmania held the first secret ballot, which became British law in 1872. Women first voted in 1880 in British local elections, while New Zealand introduced the first national women's vote in 1893.

How advanced our now casually accepted rights then were is shown by events outside the English-speaking world. Frenchwomen, for example, did not receive the vote until October 1944, and other countries later still. Thomas Paine was more than a century ahead of his time. His League of Nations was finally created in 1919 and its successor, the United Nations, in 1945.

Yet now Britain is suffering another step back. Many of the liberties and rights hard won by Paine and others are being lost, to British governments and to the laws and directives from the unelected European Union.

In this twenty-first century, the European Court of Justice ruled that E.U. institutions have the right to suppress criticism that damages "the institution's image and reputation," or in other words, any criticism at all. This ruling is identical to the law the British government introduced to muzzle Thomas Paine back in 1792—seditious libel and publication. Paine wrote then that only "when opinions are free, either in matters of government or religion, will truth finally prevail."

Recommended
Thomas Paine by A. J. Ayer
Tom Paine: America's Godfather by W. E. Woodward
The Light's on at Signpost: Memoirs of the Movies Among Other Matters by George MacDonald Fraser

The Women of SOE: Setting Europe Ablaze

In Manchester, northern England, they trained as parachutists. This began with rolling correctly on the ground, then jumping from a truck moving at 30 miles per hour, and ended parachuting from an airplane at five hundred feet with only thirty seconds before landing at 69 miles per hour—at night.

In Inverness, Scotland, they trained in unarmed combat, in silent killing, in sabotage using the new British plastic explosive, in living off the land, in using weapons, including enemy weapons.

In Beaulieu Palace in England's New Forest, they were instructed about coded messages and secret inks, to blow safes, to forge documents, and to live in enemy territory. They were awakened and "interrogated" in the middle of the night.

They became wireless operators, arms instructors, couriers, organizers, liaison officers, decoders, and saboteurs. They learned new identities, code signals, and passwords. They were each given an "L-pill," a lethal capsule of cyanide to use should they be captured. They were parachuted, landed by light airplane, or taken by sea into occupied Europe. After that, they were completely on their own.

They were from different backgrounds and education, from different countries and of different ages, of opposing religions and no religion. Yet they had one thing in common. They were the women of Britain's Special Operations Executive (SOE)—who carried the fight for freedom behind enemy lines in World War II and, according to Winston Churchill, "set Europe ablaze." More than five hundred SOE agents were sent into Nazi Europe to organize resistance; fifty of these were women.

The first woman wireless operator sent into France was Noor-un-nisa Inayat Khan, a Sufi Indian born in the Kremlin of Tsar Nicholas

in 1914. Her father was the head of a Sufi sect, an ascetic Islamic movement that emphasizes a direct, personal experience of God. Her mother was American, a relative of Mary Baker Eddy of Boston, who established the Christian Science sect in 1879.

Khan was the great-great-granddaughter of Tipu Sultan, the man the British came up against during the conquest of Mysore in India. Her family lived in London and Paris, where Khan studied music for six years and played the veena, an Indian stringed instrument, as well as piano and harp. She also studied at Sorbonne in Paris for her degree in child psychology. Before the war, Khan wrote children's stories for French radio, while a book of her children's fairy stories was published in Britain in 1939. She spoke French like a native.

At the fall of France the family escaped to Britain, where Khan's brother, Vilayat, joined the Royal Air Force and she joined the Women's Auxiliary Air Force (WAAF). From there she was recruited by SOE in late 1942 to be trained as a wireless operator. Her code name was Madeleine.

A supporter of Indian independence, Khan had said, "I wish an Indian would win high military distinction in this war. It would help to build a bridge between the British and the Indians." Of the thirty-six thousand Indians who died in World War II, that Indian was to be Khan herself.

Khan landed by Lysander airplane in northern France one night in June 1943 and made her way to Paris. Many SOE wireless operators were tracked when the enemy took cross bearings of their signals and arrested them—it took about twenty minutes to locate them—and by that autumn there was a shortage. Khan was busy throughout the day and night transmitting and receiving messages, decoding and encoding signals, for other networks as well as her own.

Moving from one safe house to another, she remained just one step ahead of the Gestapo. At one address, she transmitted from an apartment block full of German officers. SOE twice offered Khan repatriation to Britain, but she refused and remained working. There were then so few wireless operators that her work was vital.

Although there were several thousand brave men and women in the French Resistance, security was at best basic, at worst nonexistent. Even with the Free French Forces, living in and paid by Britain, security was a joke. Eventually, Churchill was forced to deny them all vital information, while British intelligence fed false information to the Nazis through the Free French—it took only two days for it to reach Berlin.

In October a Frenchwoman betrayed Khan to the Gestapo for 100,000 francs ($12,000). Many SOE captures came about through betrayal. Khan was arrested with some files and taken to the Gestapo's Paris office at 84 Avenue Foch for interrogation. She escaped almost immediately but was recaptured climbing down the outside of the building. She was interrogated, attempted another escape, was recaptured again and tortured. The Gestapo gained no information from her other than the captured files.

German torture of women included, as well as the usual beatings, cutting off breasts, pulling out fingernails and toenails, sleep deprivation, rape, laying red-hot pokers against the spine, near-drowning, and other horrors. The chief of the German police, Heinrich Himmler, ordered: "The agents should die, certainly, but not before torture, indignity and interrogation has drained from them the last shred of evidence that should lead us to others. Then, and only then, should the blessed release of death be granted them."

Giving up on her, the Gestapo sent Khan to the German prison of Pforzheim. Her hands and feet were manacled, the manacles were chained together, and she was kept in solitary confinement for almost a year. Her food was passed through a hatch in the door, the door itself opened only to change her drinking water. In September 1944, Khan was removed to the Dachau concentration camp. On the twelfth she was taken to a bloody yard with three other captured SOE agents,

Elaine Plewman, Madeleine Damerment, and Yolande Beekman. In pairs, kneeling and holding hands, the women were shot in the back of the head.

Noor-un-nisa Inayat (meaning "light of womanhood") Khan was awarded the posthumous George Cross, the highest civilian British award for gallantry, and made MBE, Member of the British Empire.

Violette Szabó was born Violette Bushell, the daughter of a British veteran of World War I, who'd married his mademoiselle from Armentières and taken her to England. Thanks to her mother, Violette spoke excellent French. At the beginning of the war she was working behind a counter at Woolworth's in Brixton, London.

In 1940 she met and married Etienne Szabó of the Foreign Legion, a Hungarian who'd made his way to Britain to continue the fight against the Nazis. Violette joined an antiaircraft battery before having her only child, Tania, born in 1942. Etienne died at the 1942 battle of el-Alamein, never having met his daughter. A few months later Violette was recruited by SOE.

Five feet tall, she turned out to be a crack shot and kept her fellow SOE recruits in cigarettes by winning them at public shooting galleries. She'd cut out the cardboard bull's-eye with just four shots. She passed all the courses, although she damaged her left ankle parachuting, and became a liaison officer code-named Louise. She was commissioned ensign and returned her L-pill, determined that she would never use it.

Landed by Lysander in Normandy one April night in 1944, Szabó began her first mission in and around Rouen: to find out who—if anyone—had survived of a French Resistance group that had been betrayed, and to contact them. At great risk, using the false identity of Corinne Leroy from Le Havre, she located the only four survivors of fifteen and passed on the message from London to blow a vital railway bridge. Szabó was arrested twice by the French police but talked her way out, explaining that she'd come to Rouen to search for missing relatives. The night after the second arrest she left for

Paris. That same night, the railway bridge was destroyed.

In Paris, Szabó met her British field organizer, who arranged her return to Britain for debriefing. Years before in Britain, in another lifetime, she and her husband had vowed that they would buy a dress from Paris for their daughter. This Szabó now did, bringing it back to Britain in her airlift across the English Channel.

Her second mission, after parachuting into Limoges on D-day plus one (June 7, 1944), was to liaise Resistance activity in support of the Allied invasion. She and Resistance leader Jacques Dufour were intercepted by German SS troops. During their flight, Szabó twisted her ankle again. She sent Dufour on to escape while she delayed the SS, firing on them with her Sten machine gun. She received a slight flesh wound and was captured after she'd run out of ammunition.

Imprisoned and interrogated first in Limoges, Szabó was then transferred to Fresnes Prison in Paris. She was interrogated and tortured by the Gestapo at 84 Avenue Foch. As well as the names of other SOE agents, French Resistance fighters, and Resistance circuits, the Germans wanted her "poem"—the key to her personal message code. With that, they would be able to send false messages to London and decode her earlier messages.

Szabó's poem was composed by the head of SOE coding, Leo Marks. It's the most famous of them all and might be the epitaph for all SOE agents:

> *The life that I have is all that I have*
> *And the life that I have is yours.*
>
> *The love that I have of the life that I have*
> *Is yours and yours and yours.*

A sleep I shall have a rest I shall have
Yet death will be but a pause,

For the peace of my years in the long green grass
Will be yours and yours and yours.

Szabó gave the Gestapo no information. She was sent to Ravens-brück, a concentration camp for women. She and two other captured SOE agents made two plans to escape, but each was thwarted. On February 5, 1945, Violette Szabó and her two friends were executed in a dark passage by a single shot into the back of the neck. A Ravensbrück survivor remembered Szabó as "outstanding" among the thousands of women imprisoned there.

On December 17, 1946, wearing the dress her mother had bought her in Paris, four-year-old Tania Szabó was presented with Violette's posthumous George Cross by King George VI at Buckingham Palace. Tania later wrote her mother's story in the book *Young Brave and Beautiful.*

Like Violette Szabó, Lilian Rolfe was born to parents who were British and French. When the war began in 1939, Rolfe was living in Brazil.

She worked for the British embassy, reported shipping movements in Rio de Janeiro, and in 1943 joined the WAAF. Because of her native French she was recruited by SOE and trained alongside Violette Szabó, specializing as a wireless operator. Rolfe's code names were Claudie and Nadine. She was landed in France in April 1944.

She worked preparing for the D-day invasion of June. Arranging vital drops of arms and explosives, she sent sixty-seven messages from a highly active Gestapo region. Her field organizer was arrested, but she continued operating. In July, a month after D-day, Rolfe took part in an engagement against German troops before finally she was captured. She, too, was interrogated and tortured at Avenue Foch, and then sent to the Ravensbrück concentration camp north of Berlin. There she joined Violette Szabó and their friend Denise Bloch.

Rolfe contracted a disease of the lungs from her forced labor and had great difficulty breathing. Toward the end she could barely stand. On February 5, 1945, she had to be carried by stretcher to her execution with Szabó. She was awarded the posthumous MBE.

Denise Bloch was French, a Jewess, and worked with the Resistance from 1942. She escaped to Gibraltar and in Britain was trained by SOE as a wireless operator at the same time as Szabó and Rolfe.

The SOE organized, armed, supplied, trained, and directed the French Resistance; reliable communications both ways were critical. Although all SOE work was dangerous, wireless operators were particularly vulnerable, since dedicated German radio units monitored frequencies to track the operator agents.

With the code name Ambroise, Bloch was returned to France in March 1944 to join the Resistance circuit at Nantes. In the immediate aftermath of D-day, this circuit sabotaged the railway and high-power lines at the Nantes port, disrupting German efforts to send supplies, soldiers, and equipment to the Normandy invasion area.

On June 18, Bloch was captured during a Gestapo raid and taken the usual route to Ravensbrück via Avenue Foch. On February 5, with Violette Szabó and Lilian Rolfe, she was shot in the back of the head. Their bodies were burned in the crematorium along with those of one hundred thousand Gypsies, Russians, Poles, Slavs, Jews, and other "undesirable" women between 1938 and 1945. Bloch was awarded the King's Commendation for Brave Conduct.

Ravensbrück saw many SOE agents. Yvonne Baseden was captured and also met the three friends in the concentration camp. The Gestapo did not realize that Baseden was an SOE agent—they thought she was simply another Resistance worker—and no execution was ordered. She was included in the last Red Cross transport to Sweden and survived the war.

Eileen Nearne, an SOE field agent along with her two older sisters, Jacqueline and Francis, was captured in July 1944 in Paris. She'd just finished transmitting a signal to London when German soldiers broke in. By that time the head of SOE codes, Leo Marks, had introduced the simple but brilliant "one-time pad," a pad of unique codes written on silk. As soon as a code was used, the agent burned that piece of silk. The only copies were in London for decoding, and every agent had a different pad so, if a pad was captured by the Germans, they were unable to retrieve any messages at all. The one-time pad is still used today.

Nearne had burned her pad and dismantled the radio, but the German soldiers found her pistol. She was interrogated and tortured at Avenue Foch and sent to Ravensbrück in September 1944. There she was reunited with Szabó, Rolfe, and Bloch. At first Nearne refused to work, so her head was shaved in preparation for her execution. She changed her mind—a decision that both saved her life and led to her freedom. In December she was sent to a labor camp near Leipzig, but when she was moved to another camp she escaped into a forest. All three Nearne siblings survived the war, and the eldest, Jacqueline, played agent Cat in the film about the SOE, *Now It Can Be Told*.

Of the agents who were captured, most were intercepted in the second half of 1944, after D-day, when they were most active supporting the American, British, and Canadian invasion forces. Odette Hallowes, though, was one like Khan, captured earlier in 1943.

Born as Odette Brailly and brought up in Amiens, France, Brailly married Roy Sansom, son of a British officer billeted with her family during World War I. With Roy she moved to London, had three daughters, and volunteered for SOE service. She trained as a liaison officer. Codenamed Lise, she was lifted into southern France by fishing vessel from Gibraltar in the autumn of 1942. With her field organizer, Peter Churchill, she was captured by a German double agent in 1943 and sent to Fresnes Prison. From there she was taken daily to the Gestapo headquarters on rue de Saussaies and tortured.

All ten toenails were pulled out until her feet were so mutilated she couldn't wear shoes. A red-hot poker was pressed against her spine, and she endured other tortures. She gave no information. She was sent to Ravensbrück and kept in solitary confinement for ten months, fourteen weeks of it in darkness, ten of those days without food.

She hung on to her sanity by designing clothes for her daughters in her imagination, redecorating the houses of her friends room by room, and maintaining a strict regimen of smartness. Every day she rotated her skirt one inch so that it would wear uniformly, while every night, curls being the fashion in the 1940s, she curled her hair using strands from her ruined stockings. She also created the fantasy that her organizer, Peter Churchill, was the nephew of Winston Churchill and that they were married. This she told the commandant of Ravensbrück.

He believed her, and with the Allied armies closing in from north, south, east, and west, he took her with him when he surrendered. She denounced him immediately, and he was tried and executed as a war criminal. Meanwhile, Odette Sansom's real husband had died in Britain, and she and Peter Churchill did marry after the war.

Odette Sansom (later Hallowes) was awarded the George Cross and the MBE and spent the remainder of her life helping ex-SOE agents and keeping the memory of those who died. She wrote that war taught her two great truths: "that suffering is an ineluctable part of the human lot, and that the battle against evil is never over."

American Virginia Hall, Radcliffe College graduate and traveler, was in Paris when war broke out in September 1939. She joined the French army ambulance service as a private and, with many other "neutrals," fled to Britain when France surrendered in June 1940. During the battle of Britain and the Blitz she worked as a code clerk in the U.S. embassy.

As the fighting and bombing raged above, she saw that on the British side of the English Channel were forty million fighting in the cause of freedom, while on the other side were some two hundred million hoping for freedom. She resigned from the embassy in February 1941, stating she was seeking other employment. In fact, she'd been recruited by SOE.

Hall's recruitment by SOE was remarkable because she had a wooden leg. In a 1933 hunting accident in Turkey, her shotgun had discharged into her left foot. By the time she reached the hospital, gangrene had set in, and her leg had to be amputated below the knee. She'd christened the wooden replacement "Cuthbert."

After completing her initial training in April 1941, Hall openly entered collaborating Vichy France that August. Her SOE cover was as a journalist for the *New York Post,* reporting the war to America. Her code name was Germaine, but the people of the Resistance networks she set up nicknamed her "la Dame qui Boit"—the lady who limps.

She was transferred to the Lyons area in early 1942. Hall was forced to work underground when the United States entered the war, using thick French peasant stockings to hide her wooden leg. She helped create and operate escape networks for aircrew and escaped prisoners of war. Through French informers she became known to the French police and the Gestapo. They thought she was Canadian and knew her nickname but not her identity. When Klaus Barbie— "the Butcher of Lyons"—took command of the Gestapo in southern France he launched a wide hunt for her, circulated wanted posters, and offered money for her betrayal. He's reputed to have said: "I would give a lot to lay my hands on that Canadian bitch."

In the winter of 1942, after she'd spent fifteen months in France, SOE withdrew Hall. Her route out of Nazi Europe was over the Pyrenees and via neutral Spain. Her last message to London was "I hope Cuthbert won't be troublesome." SOE responded dryly: "If Cuthbert troublesome eliminate him."

In May 1943, London posted her to Madrid to set up safe houses, her cover this time being a journalist for the *Chicago Times*. After four months she returned to Britain for training as a wireless operator. Hall was awarded the MBE. She didn't want to accept it publicly at the time, so the presentation was postponed.

The following year she transferred to the new U.S. Office of Strategic Services, now working alongside SOE. OSS needed some experienced agents, and Virginia Hall was an obvious choice. Another American agent trained by SOE was William Colby, future director of the CIA.

At her own request Hall returned to France in April 1944; a Royal Navy fast patrol boat landed her in Brittany. From the central Haute-Loire region she reported German troop movements and liaised with Resistance groups in support of the D-day landings. Like Noor Khan earlier, Hall at one period sent and received messages from the attic of the local police chief. After D-day her Resistance networks were involved in blowing bridges, sabotaging communications, and harassing and reporting the German retreat.

She returned to the United States in 1945 and was awarded the Distinguished Service Cross. Once again, she didn't want to accept the award publicly so it was presented privately. After the war she joined the Central Intelligence Group, which President Truman formed after dissolving the OSS and which evolved into the Central Intelligence Agency. She worked for the CIA until her retirement in 1966. She died in 1982 at age seventy-six.

Nancy Wake was also living in France when the war began in 1939. Born in Wellington, New Zealand, and brought up in Sydney, Australia, she was working as a journalist in Paris when she met and married Henri Fiocca and moved to Marseilles.

With the creation of Vichy France in 1940, France extended the war against Britain from its colonies abroad, while at home it began the arrests and deportation to death camps of seventy-five thousand Jews. Nancy and Henri became an integral part of a successful Marseilles escape route out of Vichy France. The route through Spain and Portugal took out Royal Air Force aircrew, escaped prisoners of war, and refugees from the French. The couple was soon high on the police list of suspects. Wake's exploits were attributed to an agent the French police named "the White Mouse"; by 1943 there was a reward of one million francs for her capture. Inevitably, Wake was betrayed, but she fled to Gibraltar using her escape route. Henri continued operating in Marseilles; later he was betrayed, interrogated, tortured, and executed.

In Britain, SOE recruited and trained Wake, commissioned her captain, and gave her the code name Hélène. She was parachuted back into France, to the Auvergne region, in April 1944. There she led the Resistance in months of increasing combat action before and after D-day, action that included sabotage, guerrilla war against German units, and even an attack on a Gestapo center. Wake developed into a ferocious soldier—"like five men," a Frenchman described her.

In 1945 in London, Nancy Wake was awarded the British George Medal and the U.S. Medal of Freedom; later she received many French medals. She is the most decorated servicewoman of World War II. "I hate wars and violence," she said, "but if they come, I don't see why we women should just wave our men a proud goodbye and then knit them balaklavas." France had just granted women suffrage the previous year.

All the women agents of SOE enlisted as volunteers in the FANY (First Aid Nursing Yeomanry), the first-ever women's military force, raised in London in 1907. In consequence, they were not prevented by the Geneva Convention from fighting and they served around the world. Fifty-two FANY were killed during World War II, thirteen in the French section of SOE. They are all our mothers and sisters.

Recommended
Young Brave and Beautiful by Tania Szabó
The Wolves at the Door: The True Story of America's Greatest Female Spy by Judith Pearson
The White Mouse by Nancy Wake
SOE: The Special Operations Executive, 1940–46 by Michael Foot
Sisterhood of Spies: The Women of the OSS by Elizabeth P. McIntosh
FANY Memorial, Saint Paul's Church, Knightsbridge, London

The Siege of the Alamo

Within fifty years of the siege of the Alamo, it had become an emotional—even spiritual—milestone in the creation of the United States of America. The cry "Remember the Alamo!" was heard on many subsequent U.S. battlefields.

Like all good legends, the siege of the Alamo has its dead heroes—Colonel Travis, Jim Bowie, and Davy Crockett; its live heroes—General Houston, Susanna Dickinson, and Joe the slave; and its villains—General Santa Anna and the Mexican army. No true event is ever that simple though. The full details of what happened are still not known, and today, remembering the Alamo is to step back almost two hundred years, to 1835.

North America was then a vastly different continent than it is today. The United States was a fledgling nation of just twenty-six states. In the north, Canada was British. In the northwest, present-day Oregon and Washington were joint U.S.-British colonies, while in the west and south, Mexico was a large, newly independent nation. North of the Rio Grande, Mexico included most of present-day California, Nevada, Utah, Kansas, Arizona, Colorado, New Mexico, Oklahoma—and Texas.

Mexicans had fought for and gained their independence from Spain in 1821 under General Iturbide. In 1823 he was ousted as emperor by General Victoria, who was himself ousted by General Antonio López de Santa Anna in 1824.

The United States wanted to expand its territory, but there were only two alternatives. North lay Canada, which it had invaded twice in the War of 1812 and had there been defeated by Britain. Mexico, on the other hand, was weak from many internal problems. Their common western border had been agreed to in 1819; it lay along the Sabine River, the Red River, the Arkansas River, and north to Oregon. To the east of the border were the U.S. lands of the Louisiana Purchase; to the west were the lands of Mexico. At that time, Mexican land cost one-tenth the cost of land in the United States. Mexico allowed immigration, and so American settlers flocked across the border into Texas. Slavery in Mexico had been abolished in 1824, but as long as the immigrants obeyed the rest of the constitution, the authorities turned a blind eye to the African slaves imported by Americans.

Some Americans, like Moses Austin and his son Stephen, cooperated with the Mexican government, so that by 1830 some five thousand Americans had emigrated peacefully to their Austin settlements. Others were not so cooperative, and there had been several invasions of Texas.

As early as 1812 an American group marched in from Louisiana, captured the town of San Antonio de Béxar (San Antonio), murdered the Spanish governor and his officers after they'd surrendered, and declared what they called the state of Texas. Spanish forces, of which one was Lieutenant Santa Anna's, wiped them out. Bonapartist exiles from France invaded near Corpus Christi in 1818 and declared a republic, and in 1819 more Americans invaded and declared a state. After 1821, independent Mexico reestablished its authority, but those who wished to were allowed to remain in Texas.

Spain attempted to reconquer Mexico but was defeated in 1829 by General Santa Anna. In 1830 Mexico called a halt to immigration, levied customs duties on imports, and organized its province of Texas into three departments, each with its own garrison and forts. One of those forts was the former 1724 Franciscan mission of San Antonio de Valero, on open ground immediately outside San Antonio. Because of the cottonwoods that grew there, it came to be called the Alamo, after the Spanish name for the tree.

At that point, American immigrants and their slaves made up 75 percent of the thirty thousand people of Texas and were becoming dissatisfied with their Mexican government. In 1832, Santa Anna took complete control of the Mexican government and suspended the constitution. From then on, Texas was a powder keg waiting to explode.

Things came to a head in 1835 when American immigrants, calling themselves "Texians," rebelled at Zacatecas. Unrest spread across the province until in October the Texian rebels joined together in an armed insurrection. A rebel Army of the People was raised. One of its generals was immigrant and former governor of Tennessee Sam Houston. The Texas Revolution had begun.

Across Texas, one after the other, the Mexican garrisons were defeated by Texan forces. The Mexican soldiers retreated farther into Mexico, south and west over the Rio Grande. The last garrison to fall was the Alamo, on December 9. Twenty-one Mexican cannons, including one eighteen-pounder, were captured.

The rebels declared their support for the previous constitution. Most of the Texans with property and businesses then returned to their homes. As far as they were concerned, the Mexicans were defeated. The small Texian army was left to the control of a provisional government.

Meanwhile, south of the Rio Grande, President and General Santa Anna had not been asleep. He quickly raised an army of conscripts, raw recruits, and convicts preferring to serve an army than a prison sentence. In response to the armed Americans still flocking into Texas, the Mexican congress passed a resolution: "Foreigners landing on the coast of the Republic or invading its territory by land, armed, and with the intent of attacking our country, will be deemed pirates and dealt with as such, being citizens of no nation presently at war with the Republic and fighting under no recognized flag."

Importers of arms and ammunition were to be similarly treated, and Santa Anna sent a letter to President Andrew Jackson warning that any Americans found fighting in Mexico would be considered pirates. In 1835 pirates caught in the act were immediately executed.

Despite the winter weather, General Santa Anna moved his army northward to Texas in late December, training his men as they marched. Some veterans and volunteers joined along the way until he crossed the Rio Grande on February 16, 1836, with between fifteen hundred and two thousand men. The winter was unusually bitter that year, with snowfalls in Texas of fifteen inches. As well as hypothermia, his army was thinned by dysentery, and by the attacks of Comanche Native Americans—who still considered Texas *their* land.

Santa Anna's determined march through the snow caught the Texans by surprise. The Mexican army reached San Antonio on the afternoon of the twenty-third, three weeks earlier than expected. The Texan garrison withdrew into the Alamo mission, while the residents of San Antonio fled into the surrounding countryside. A further six hundred Mexican troops arrived on February 24, and the mission was surrounded. The second siege of the Alamo had begun.

General Sam Houston, meanwhile, had ordered the small Texian force to demolish the Alamo fortifications. He saw no strategic importance in the location, and he knew the small force there could not fight the Mexican army. He planned to have the Texians retreat, to allow time for reinforcements to join them.

Colonel Neill, in charge at the Alamo, did not want to abandon or destroy the mission. Houston sent adventurer and knife fighter Jim Bowie—a colonel of the volunteer forces of the Texian army—to assist Neill's retreat. They were to remove the cannons and blow up the mission. Yet Bowie and Neill were of like mind. Both detested the idea of giving up land to an enemy. Instead, Bowie wrote directly to the provisional governor Henry Smith. He requested more "men, money, rifles, and cannon powder" to defend the Alamo, finishing with the plea: "Colonel Neill and myself have come to the solemn resolution that we will rather die in these ditches than give it up to the enemy."

Overriding Houston, Governor Smith promised Neill and Bowie his support. He ordered twenty-six-year-old lieutenant colonel

William Travis of the regular army to raise a legion of cavalry to reinforce the Alamo. With the majority of Texians returned home, Travis could gather only twenty-seven men. With these, he rode into San Antonio on February 3 and reported to Colonel Neill. Five days later, more American adventurers arrived. It was a small group of riflemen from Tennessee, led by Davy Crockett.

Crockett, a famous frontiersman, sharpshooter, bear hunter, and congressman from Tennessee, had suffered in the recent elections of 1835. Despite eight years in Congress, he had not had a single bill passed by the House, and his political popularity had waned. When asked what would happen if Tennesseans didn't reelect him, he'd replied famously: "You may all go to hell, and I will go to Texas." They didn't reelect him, he did go to Texas, and by chance he rode into San Antonio on February 8.

With news of a severe illness in his family and due for leave, Neill departed. He placed Travis, the highest-ranking regular officer, in charge and on February 11 rode out. At this time, there was no knowledge of any imminent Mexican attack. Santa Anna's army crossed the Rio Grande five days later.

The experienced but increasingly ill Bowie did not get along with the younger Travis. Colonel Bowie's volunteers would not obey Lieutenant Colonel Travis, and Travis's regulars would not obey Bowie. It was a dangerously divided command. A vote of the men was called, and Bowie won. He got drunk that night, caroused through San Antonio, and released the convicts from the town jail. In remorse, he agreed with Travis that each would command his own men as well as cosign the other's orders until Neill returned.

From a provisional-government convention at Washington-on-the-Brazos, General Houston again sent orders for Travis and Bowie to destroy the Alamo and withdraw. He had no doubt that with cannons, a Mexican army would defeat the outnumbered Texians. The mission was fortified but only against attacks from Native Americans, not from a modern army. It was not a regular fort.

Travis and Bowie disobeyed Houston and prepared to defend the Alamo. The mission had already been strengthened under the direction of engineer Green Jameson. Wooden firing gangways had been erected behind the nine- and twelve-foot-high walls, the captured Mexican cannons strategically positioned, wooden palisades reinforced, and a secondary defense of earthen breastworks dug inside the walls. There was little more they could do.

When Santa Anna arrived on the afternoon of February 23, he sent emissaries under a flag of truce. They and the Texians met on the bridge across the San Antonio River, between the Alamo and the town. The emissaries offered unconditional surrender. Travis replied with a shot from the eighteen-pound cannon. Santa Anna responded by ordering a red flag raised—the signal that no quarter would be given.

Bowie was angry that Travis had acted so defiantly and sent Jameson to meet the Mexican emissaries again. According to the journal of emissary Colonel Almonte, Jameson requested an honorable surrender. Almonte recorded: "I reply to you, according to the order of His Excellency [Santa Anna], that the Mexican army cannot come to terms under any conditions with rebellious foreigners to whom there is no recourse left, if they wish to save their lives, than to place themselves immediately at the disposal of the Supreme Government from whom alone they may expect clemency after some considerations." The Texian reply was a second cannon shot.

The exact number defending the Alamo's rectangular three acres is not known; it lies somewhere between 189 and 257. This total includes Davy Crockett, his Tennessean sharpshooters, and the men who later made their way through the Mexican lines to join those inside. Also in the mission were Susanna and Angelina, wife and daughter of Texian captain Almaron Dickinson, two of Bowie's cousins-in-law, Bowie's young nephew, and some Tejano women from San Antonio. Travis's black slave, Joe, and Bowie's black freedman, Sam, also remained.

James Bowie collapsed from his illness on the twenty-fourth. It's thought that he had pneumonia or tuberculosis, and he was unable to leave his cot for the rest of the siege. William Travis assumed full command of the Alamo.

While Mexican light cannon bombarded the walls from batteries surrounding the mission, Travis inside wrote his famous letter "to the People of Texas & All Americans in the World." He sent it out by courier rider. It was eventually copied across Texas, reprinted throughout the United States, and even carried across the Atlantic to Britain. It was only fifty years since independence, and there were still many close relatives there. Travis concluded the letter: "I call on you in the name of Liberty, of patriotism, and everything dear to the American character, to come to our aid, with all dispatch. . . . I am determined to sustain myself as long as possible & die like a soldier who never forgets what is due to his own honor & that of his country. VICTORY OR DEATH."

The Mexican barrage continued. More than two hundred cannonballs plowed into the Alamo plaza in the first week alone. Each night, the cannons were maneuvered closer to the walls. During the day there were skirmishes for the control of abandoned huts outside the mission walls, which the Texians burned to deny the Mexicans cover. Travis ordered his men to conserve their sparse ammunition but allowed Crockett and his riflemen to shoot at any Mexicans in range.

On March 3 another thousand Mexican soldiers entered San Antonio, marching proudly past in their blue-and-gold full-dress uniforms. From the battered white walls of the Alamo, the defenders rested on their long-barreled muskets and watched. By then, some four thousand soldiers surrounded them.

News also arrived that General Urrea had defeated Colonel Johnson at the battle of San Patricio. Unless a Texian army could reach the Alamo, there would shortly be a second defeat. Travis sent out another urgent request for reinforcements.

Yet for Sam Houston to march his small army to relieve the Alamo is exactly what Santa Anna wanted. Outnumbered by about seven to one, they likely would have been defeated, and Texas secured for Mexico. Houston knew that. He had twice ordered a withdrawal from the mission. There was nothing further he could do.

Inside the Alamo, Travis drew a line in the earth of the compound with his sword. On one side of the line were the assembled defenders; on the other stood Travis. He told his men that there was no escape for them, and asked those who would stand beside him and fight to the death to cross the line. Every man but one stepped across. That man was Louis Rose, who then left the mission and also evaded the Mexicans. He was known forever after as "the yellow Rose of Texas."

That part of the story was not written down until 1873, thirty-seven years later, by which time the story's source—Rose himself—was dead. Survivors Susanna Dickinson and Enrique Esparza both mentioned the incident later, although their details differed. It is now a part of the legend of the Alamo, as is Bowie's role. He asked his men to carry his cot over the line, as he was too weak to walk.

That evening, Travis sent out Davy Crockett and two others to search for the expected reinforcements from Goliad. Crockett found them at midnight, at Cibolo Creek, and led them through the Mexican lines before dawn on the fourth. A second group were driven off, the skirmish recorded in a Mexican journal.

In San Antonio, Santa Anna summoned his senior officers. He proposed ending the siege with a massive assault. Some officers demurred, suggesting he wait until two heavy cannon arrived on the seventh. He postponed his decision. That evening Travis sent out James Allen with personal letters. They were the last messages from the Alamo.

On March 5, 1836, Santa Anna made his decision. The assault would take place in darkness, immediately before dawn, on Sunday the sixth. At 10 P.M. he ordered the cannon to cease firing. For the first time in eleven days there was peace in the Alamo mission and the tired defenders slept well—as Santa Anna had planned.

In the blackness of a cloudy night, Santa Anna deployed some thirteen hundred of his infantry into four separate columns and quietly moved them forward, to about six hundred feet from the mission. The columns were ringed by a screen of cavalry to prevent any Texian escape. Despite the cold, the men were ordered not to wear their greatcoats, which might have impeded easy movement. At 5:30 A.M. the infantry advanced in silence.

The three Texian sentries posted outside the walls had fallen asleep and were killed before they could raise the alarm. With cries

of "Viva Santa Anna!" and "Viva Mexico!" along with stirring bugle calls the Mexican soldiers charged the Alamo from every side—but they had shouted too soon.

The defenders rushed to the walls. Travis called to them: "Come on, boys, the Mexicans are upon us and we'll give them hell!" Crockett found time for a brief prayer in the chapel. Supported by accurate rifle and musket fire, the nineteen cannons preloaded with canister repulsed the attack, with heavy casualties. "More than forty men fell around me in a few moments," a Mexican soldier recorded. "It seemed every cannon ball or pistol shot of the enemy embedded itself in the breast of our men."

Standing behind Travis on the north bastion, slave Joe continually reloaded rifles and passed them forward. The muzzle flashes from the cannons lit the blue coats of the soldiers below the walls.

An immediate second Mexican charge was also repulsed with more heavy casualties, soldiers shot and clubbed down even as they reached the top of the walls on their scaling ladders. Yet the Alamo perimeter was 1,320 feet long—a quarter of a mile—and it could be only a matter of time.

Three of the Mexican columns converged opposite the northern wall. Santa Anna sent in four hundred reserves. Just fifteen minutes after the first charge, a third attack breached the twelve-foot northern wall. It was there that William Travis fell, shot through the forehead. Lieutenant Colonel de la Peña described Travis's death: "He would take a few steps [forward] and stop, turning his proud face toward us to discharge his shots; he fought like a true soldier. Finally he died, but he died after having traded his life very dearly. None of his men died with greater heroism, and they all died."

Following their officers, the Mexican soldiers clambered over the northern wall. General Amador dropped down to open the postern gate below, and infantrymen poured through into the Alamo. The Texians retreated, fighting a rear-guard action across the broad earthen compound to the barracks. Those on the south wall turned their cannons around and fired into the enemy within, but then the south wall was breached behind them.

The east wall was breached next, more infantry surging in through the cattle pen. Some Texians escaped via the horse corral but were hunted down outside by the waiting Mexican cavalry. From the wall above, Almaron Dickinson and his team fired their cannons into the cavalry.

At the west wall another group of perhaps fifty Texians was cut off by the Mexicans inside the compound. These fifty retreated westward toward the San Antonio River, pursued by more cavalry. They made a last stand in a ditch, and died where they stood.

The majority of defenders inside the Alamo retreated from the walls as planned, across the compound to either the long barrack block or the mission chapel. Dickinson survived that dangerous journey and called to his wife in the chapel: "Great God, Sue, the Mexicans are inside our walls! If they spare you, save our child."

Crockett and others fought off the infantry from a low wall in front of the chapel doors until they found themselves the last defenders in the open. When they no longer had time to reload their muzzle-loading rifles, they fought with knives and reversed their guns to use them as clubs. A Mexican musket volley cracked out, and a bayonet charge killed those who still lived.

On the roof five Mexicans soldiers were shot dead while replacing the Texian flag with the Mexican, their bodies silhouetted against the first light of dawn. From the walls Mexican soldiers turned the abandoned cannon onto the barrack block. One after the other the barricaded doors were blown in. A volley was fired into the darkness beyond, and a bayonet charge followed. As promised, there was no quarter given. Lieutenant Colonel José de la Peña recorded: "A horrible carnage took place, and some were trampled to death. The tumult was great, the disorder frightful; it seemed as if the furies had descended upon us."

In one of those barrack rooms lay the sick Jim Bowie. Mexican accounts vary as to whether he had the strength to fight. Legend has it that from his cot he fired his two pistols at the entering soldiers and was bayoneted to death where he lay.

The chapel was defended by a sandbag barricade inside the doors, with two twelve-pound cannons in the apse behind. One shot from the eighteen-pound cannon in the compound destroyed the barricade, and in the gray light the Mexican infantry charged through. Dickinson and his men fired their cannons, while others inside fired their muskets and rifles. Without time to reload, all were shot or bayoneted to death.

Robert Evans, in charge of ordnance, moved to fire the gunpowder magazine but was killed. Sheltering in the sacristy were women, children, and other noncombatants. Among them were Susanna Dickinson and her daughter, Travis's slave, Joe, and Bowie's freedman, Sam. If the magazine had been blown, they all would have died.

It was 6:30 A.M. The sun had risen, the compound was hazy from gunpowder smoke, and the Alamo had fallen. Some four to six hundred soldiers of the Mexican army were killed or wounded, although the exact number is not known. Amazingly, seven defenders still lived. One of them was Davy Crockett.

Lieutenant Colonel Peña's account of the aftermath of the battle, supported by every other Mexican record, was accepted by both Texians and Americans. It contains the following report.

Some seven men survived the general carnage and, under the protection of General Castrillón, they were brought before Santa Anna. Among them . . . was the naturalist David Crockett. . . . Santa Anna answered Castrillón's intervention in Crockett's behalf with a gesture of indignation and, addressing himself to the sappers, the troops closest to him, ordered his execution. The commanders and officers were outraged at this action and did not support the order, hoping that once the fury of the moment had blown over these men would be spared; but several officers . . . thrust themselves forward . . . and with swords in hand, fell upon these unfortunate, defenseless men. . . . Though tortured before they were killed, these unfortunates died without complaining and without humiliating themselves before their torturers.

It is only late-twentieth-century versions of the siege that claim that Crockett died during the battle.

Santa Anna ordered the Mexican dead to be buried and the Texian dead to be burned. An unnamed Mexican soldier wrote: "Poor things—no longer do they live—all of them died, and even now I am watching them burn." The smoke from their bodies drifted above the Alamo to become their funeral pall.

The surviving thirty noncombatants were interviewed by Santa Anna the next day, and all were given their freedom. Also spared was a Mexican deserter who claimed he'd been taken prisoner. Susanna Dickinson saw the mutilated body of Crockett, and Joe the bullet-riddled body of Travis, but not until well after the battle. A former slave serving Santa Anna's army escorted Susanna, her daughter, and Joe through the Mexican lines to Gonzales.

There Susanna broke the news of the fall of the Alamo and delivered a message from Santa Anna: "Fighting is hopeless."

General Houston arrived at Gonzales on March 11. After he'd interviewed Susanna, he advised the settlers to evacuate and ordered the four hundred Texian soldiers there to withdraw eastward.

The fall of the Alamo had the exact opposite effect from the one

Santa Anna had hoped for. Instead of being dispirited, Texians were swept by a flame of indignation and the desire to avenge the Alamo. Whatever borders Mexico might claim, the blood of men such as Travis, Crockett, Bowie, and Dickinson had surely made Texas theirs. Texians left their homes to rejoin Houston's army, but he resisted all entreaties to take up battle immediately. Before the advancing Mexican army he retreated far into eastern Texas, allowing his numbers to increase. The weather also improved.

Along the banks of the San Jacinto River, near Lynchburg Ferry, Houston found the battleground he wanted. On the afternoon of April 21 his scouts reported the Mexican army at siesta. He led his ragtag army through the warm spring grass to catch Santa Anna by surprise.

With the cry "Remember the Alamo!" Houston attacked. His men responded, calling "Remember the Alamo!" again and again. In only eighteen minutes, the battle of San Jacinto was won. The Mexican army was routed, scattered, and sent fleeing by the yelling Texians.

Santa Anna was captured the following day. He said of Sam Houston, "That man may consider himself born to no common destiny who has conquered the Bonaparte of the West." Santa Anna had forgotten that Bonaparte was ultimately defeated by the Duke of Wellington.

Threatened with death, the Mexican general was forced to withdraw his entire army from Texas. As Mexican president, Santa Anna was forced to acknowledge the independence of Texas. It was formalized in the treaty of Velasco on May 14, 1836. The Alamo had been avenged.

Recommended
With Santa Anna in Texas by José Enrique de la Peña
Alamo Sourcebook, 1836: A Comprehensive Guide to the Battle of the Alamo and the Texas Revolution by Tim J. Todish and Terry S. Todish

The Alamo Story: From Early History to Current Conflicts
by J. Edmondson
Alamo Traces: New Evidence and New Conclusions
by Thomas Lindley
The Alamo, San Antonio, Texas

Sir Henry Morgan:
Buccaneer

Henry Morgan's life is simply an astonishing story. The history of Spanish colonies isn't taught in American or British schools, but Morgan was a pirate at a time when Britain had barely a foothold in the Caribbean Sea. Spain was the great power in those waters, with wealthy ports and cities in a vast bowl from Mexico to Venezuela and the Caribbean islands. Even today those countries have Spanish as their first language. Morgan's combination of ruthlessness, leadership, and seamanship would make him the terror of the West Indies and strike fear into Spanish settlements.

He was born in Glamorganshire, Wales, in 1635. At that time, his family worked as soldiers of fortune under foreign flags and achieved high rank in Holland, Flanders, and Germany. They also fought on both sides of the English civil war. Henry Morgan's father, Thomas, took the parliamentary side and reached the rank of major general under Oliver Cromwell.

Given the turbulence of the times, it is perhaps not too surprising that few records survive of Henry Morgan's childhood. At the age of twenty, he traveled as an indentured servant to Barbados. He said later that he left school early and was "more used to the pike than the book." It has been suggested that the young Welshman was kidnapped and sold as a white slave. In his latter, respectable days, he sued anyone who made this claim, but such events were not uncommon and the exact truth is now hidden in history. Another story is that he sailed as a junior officer on an expedition to the West Indies by Oliver Cromwell.

During the English civil war, the West Indies were the scene of battles between Cromwell's parliamentary forces and the Spaniards.

Cromwell hated the Spanish for their Catholicism and said in Parliament: "Abroad, our great enemy is the Spaniard."

Jamaica was seized from Spain, and in the chaos and lawlessness of war, the region became infamous for pirate ships and for privateers, who were exactly the same but sailed with the approval of their

governments. Tortuga, a small island off Hispaniola (modern Haiti), was a particular stronghold.

When Charles II was restored to the throne in 1660, the king of Spain petitioned to have Jamaica returned to Spanish rule. More than 2,500 acres of the island were producing valuable crops at that time, with huge potential for expansion and profits. Charles II refused and Parliament approved the decision. A new governor and legislative council were appointed in Jamaica, along with judges and courts. The colony settled down and immigrants began to arrive from Barbados, Bermuda, and even America. Virgin land was offered to them, and a number of young men made their way to the West Indies, seeking to make their fortune.

It is in that context, in 1659, that Henry Morgan became captain of a privateer at the age of twenty-four. He had taken part in several raiding voyages, but instead of squandering his share of the booty, he lived simply and saved his money until he could buy a small ship of his own.

The government in England was desperate to keep hold of the threatened Caribbean ports and not too worried about who fought for them. It suited British interests to have a raiding fleet in the area, though each ship acted alone and profit was always the first motive. A report on the fledgling colony stated: "We had then about fourteen or fifteen sail of Privateers, few of which take orders but from stronger Men of War."

From raids, slavery, and plantation crops, Jamaica quickly became a wealthy colony. From 1662 to 1688, exports doubled to more than four million pounds' worth of goods. One law passed by Parliament said that produce from all English colonies could only be transported on English ships. It meant that every colony brought a trading fleet into existence and eventually led to Britain's domination of the seas.

Thousands of miles from Europe, a smaller war was fought between Britain, Holland, and Spain for command of Caribbean waters. New men were clearly needed, and Charles II sent Henry Morgan's uncle, Edward Morgan, as senior military officer. From his years as a soldier of fortune, Edward Morgan knew the Dutch well and spoke the language. It must have been a surprise to Henry to have his uncle come out and take such a powerful position. The king made Thomas Modyford the governor and the ultimate power in Jamaica.

Modyford's first proclamation as governor was that all hostilities with Spain were to cease. In theory, all the privateers should have returned to port and been paid off. Predictably, however, they turned a blind eye to the order, Henry Morgan among them. Attacks on rich

Spanish fleets continued, and King Charles II wrote to Modyford to complain about it.

Shortly after Henry's uncle arrived, one of the privateers turned pirate, raiding English shipping as well. Under Modyford's orders, the ship was captured and the crew hanged on the docks of Port Royal in Jamaica. An example had been made, but the governor's ability to stop the privateers was limited and they carried on with their "prize taking" of foreign ships.

As the war with Holland intensified, battles took place in the East and West Indies, the Mediterranean, Africa, and North America. In England, Parliament voted £2.5 million to equip the Royal Navy for the fight. The commercial future of the world was at stake, and they were determined that Britain control the seas and trade. The privateer fleet was still terrorizing Jamaican waters, and rather than try to hunt them down, they offered them letters of marque—official recognition and powers to attack Dutch ships on behalf of the British Crown. The alternative was to see them go over to the French colony on Tortuga, whereby Charles II would lose all control.

The privateer captains accepted the letters of marque, and Colonel Edward Morgan led them in an expedition to seize Dutch islands in the West Indies. A fleet of ten "reformed privateers" left Jamaica, well armed and manned. Henry Morgan was captain of one of them and already becoming known as a good man in a fight.

Colonel Edward Morgan was old and overweight. After landing on the island of Saint Eustatius, he pursued enemy soldiers on a hot day, then had a heart attack and died. His privateer captains were not the sort to return home at this setback and they went on to take the island and one other from Dutch control, gathering Spanish plunder at the same time. More than three hundred Dutch settlers were deported, but his regular soldiers had to come back to Jamaica when the privateers went off to Central America in search of more prizes.

To explain how they had managed to sack Spanish settlements as far away as Nicaragua, Captains Jackman, Henry Morgan, and John Morris claimed not to have heard that war with Spain had ended. It was hardly necessary. Anti-Spanish feeling was still running high in official quarters, and they were in no danger of being seized as pirates.

In 1666, Modyford and his council granted Morgan and the other privateer captains new letters of marque against the Spanish. The official record gives one reason: "It is the only means to keep the buccaneers on Hispaniola, Tortuga, and Cuba from being enemies and infesting the plantations." Modyford may not have liked the idea of employing what was effectively his own pirate fleet, but he felt he had no choice. The privateers would defend the wealth of Jamaica if they had an interest in it and a safe port there. At the same time, the French governor on Tortuga was doing his best to bribe the privateer fleet to sail for him. It was a dangerous game, with both sides trying to feed the wolves.

By then, Henry Morgan was thirty years old and well known as a successful and wealthy captain. His uncle had left a number of children in Jamaica, and Henry Morgan didn't abandon them. Far from it. The exact date is not known, but he married his first cousin Mary and spent a couple of quiet years on Jamaica, enjoying married life. Two of her sisters married officers on the council, and so the Morgan family achieved considerable influence in a very short time.

Officially sanctioned attacks on Spanish settlements and forts continued, the combination of huge wealth and poor defenses a tempting prize for fortune hunters. Privateers raided Costa Rica and Cuba as well as small islands. The Spanish attacked settlements and islands themselves, on one occasion massacring a British garrison of seventy men after they had surrendered. Some of the survivors were tortured, then sent to work in mines on the mainland. It was an unofficial war but as ruthless as any other kind. It is always tempting to take the Hollywood view of piracy as somehow romantic, with swarthy men walking the plank and crying "Yo ho ho!" to one another, but the reality was brutal and settlements that fell to privateers or pirates suffered torture and murders before being burned to the ground.

In 1667, Holland agreed to peace with England, and Spain renewed a peace that had never really happened in the Caribbean. British power in the West Indies remained fragile, and in 1668, the Admiralty finally sent a formidable twenty-six-gun frigate, HMS *Oxford,* to the area.

Henry Morgan had been made colonel and given command of the militia in Port Royal, Jamaica. Before the *Oxford* arrived, he took a raiding expedition of ten ships to a wealthy Spanish town in Cuba. He and his men landed on March 30 and fought off an attack by Spanish militia before storming the town and stealing everything they could lay hands on. He then accepted a ransom of a thousand head of cattle in exchange for not setting the town on fire.

Other raids on Cuban towns and ports followed, often against much larger forces. However, as Morgan said: "The fewer we are, the better shares we shall have in the spoils." It's not quite an Agincourt speech, but he and his men caused havoc on Spanish settlements, removing anything of silver and gold from cities and churches. His crews ran wild in the sacking of towns, and only the payment of large ransoms would send Morgan away. By the time he returned to Jamaica, he had a hold full of Spanish gold.

Morgan welcomed the arrival of the *Oxford* as the most powerful ship in those waters. The Spanish had warships, but they were slow and heavy in comparison. He made immediate plans for an attack on Cartagena, the strongest fortress on the coast of what is Colombia today.

Disaster struck. The *Oxford*'s magazine exploded while Morgan was on deck. Five captains who had sat on one side of a table were killed in the explosion, while Morgan and the rest were thrown clear and survived. His choice of chair had saved his life, though he lost a quarter of his men.

Without the *Oxford,* Morgan was forced to give up the idea of attacking Cartagena. Instead, he gathered the privateers off the eastern coast of Hispaniola. Fiercely independent, some preferred to sail alone, so Morgan went without them and attacked Spanish ports in Venezuela. In 1669 he sacked the city of Maracaibo and went on to the settlement of Gibraltar on Lake Maracaibo. His men tortured the city elders there until they revealed where their treasures were hidden. Morgan was not present at the time, but his name was further blackened with the Spanish as a result. The Spanish citizens of Gibraltar agreed on a ransom to Morgan's captains but could not raise all of it, so some of them were sold as slaves to make up the deficit.

It was not all raids on towns and villages. When Morgan encountered a small fleet of three Spanish warships, he and his captains captured one, sank another, and watched the crew burn the third rather than let him have it. That single raid brought more than thirty thousand pounds back to Jamaica, a vast sum for the times. In port, Morgan's men taunted the captains who had not sailed with him and flaunted their sudden riches.

With new wealth, Morgan turned his hand to owning a plantation. He leased a tract of 836 acres, still known as Morgan's Valley today, from the governor. He might have settled down, but in 1670, Spain renewed hostilities in the West Indies, capturing ships and ravaging British settlements in Bermuda and the Bahamas. In response, the governor of Jamaica appointed Morgan to command all warships in Jamaican waters. His fame, experience, and ruthlessness made him the obvious choice. At age thirty-five, Morgan was an admiral and in his prime.

With unlimited funds, Morgan equipped a fleet at Port Royal for an attack on Panama, another Spanish territory. He crewed them with six hundred men, of the rough sort he knew best. The red-coat uniforms of Cromwell's army still struck fear into Spaniards, so Morgan arranged for his men to wear them.

In England, negotiations for peace with Spain were under way and Governor Modyford had orders to cease all operations against the Spanish. He made the instructions clear to Morgan, and the admiral replied that he would observe them except for landing on Spanish coasts to replenish water and supplies. Morgan also added the caveat that he would of course respond if attacked, or to relieve a British settlement. With those somewhat dubious assurances, Morgan sailed in August 1670.

He sent one ship, the *Dolphin,* to the coast of Cuba, to gather intelligence on Spanish forces in those waters. The rest of his squadron anchored around Hispaniola, gathering fresh meat and water while he waited for other privateers who had promised to join him. Three French captains came from Tortuga to aid him against the Spanish and of course share the spoils. Morgan was a charismatic "pirate's pirate," and national interest came second to the opportunity to sail with him.

The captain of the *Dolphin* met a Spanish ship in a bay off Cuba, and though the crew were outgunned, they attacked. The Spanish panicked, their captain was killed, and many jumped overboard. In the Spanish captain's cabin, Morgan's men found letters of marque from Panama, giving the Spanish authority to raid British ships and towns.

Governor Modyford sent five more privateer ships to join Morgan as they came back from taking the island of Grenada. By then he had the most powerful fleet of privateers ever assembled in the Caribbean. It was a chance to strike a crushing blow against Spanish power.

Morgan interrogated the prisoners taken by the *Dolphin* and learned that Cartagena and Panama were poorly defended. He allowed his captains the final choice, and they decided on Panama as the target. They set sail in December 1670, a fleet of some thirty-six ships and eighteen hundred men, including two or three hundred French. As it happened, peace with Spain had finally been agreed, but it took months for the news to reach the Caribbean and Morgan was not told by the time he set off.

His first stop was at Old Providence, to the north of Panama. It was a well-fortified Spanish island, but with a small garrison. Morgan landed a thousand men, and the Spanish abandoned their gun battery. With Morgan's men pursuing them, they retreated to a smaller island only linked to Providence by a drawbridge. From there, they accepted Morgan's request to surrender peacefully, accompanied as it was by a threat of slaughter if they didn't.

The president of Panama, Don Juan Pérez de Guzmán, had been told that Morgan's fleet was on the way. On the north coast, he reinforced his garrisons with men and supplies of gunpowder, convinced that the English force could not break his defenses. His confidence was understandable. To reach Panama City on the south coast of the isthmus, Morgan's men would have to cross land that would one day become the site of the Panama Canal. It was dense jungle all the way, complete with deadly snakes and spiders as well as aggressive native tribes.

The jewel of Panama's fortifications was the fortress of San Lorenzo de Chagres, built on a sheer cliff and, at that time, filled with three hundred soldiers and native Indian bowmen. In addition, it had heavy artillery guns with which to hammer enemy ships. One of Morgan's captains, Joseph Bradley, came as close as he dared to survey the fort and decided it could only be taken from the land side. Bradley landed along the coast with 480 men and marched to a ravine leading to the rear of the fort. The drawbridge that was usually there had vanished. Spanish troops opened fire from the fort as Bradley looked into the ravine.

His men retreated out of range but were shamed in doing so. "Thoughts of disgrace and being reproached by our Friends on board" spurred Bradley's small force into a slow descent into the ravine. They endured enemy fire the whole way until they climbed the fortress side and attacked the main gate. Bradley himself was shot in the attempt, his legs badly crushed by a cannonball. The first assault was driven back, but his men were undeterred and returned again and again, firing their muskets and throwing primitive grenades at the walls. At least one of those began a fire in the fort that took hold quickly. Wooden palisades burned to the ground, making a breach. Bradley's best marksmen then came forward and fired at anyone trying to quench the flames.

The Spanish garrison held their ground until Bradley sent a storming party armed with cutlasses and muskets. They forced their way in and the Spanish soldiers fled, leaving only the commandant, who continued to fight until he was shot. The fort was theirs. Bradley died of his wounds along with two officers and many of his men, but a crucial defense had been taken from Panama. Morgan flew the flag of England from the battlements of the fortress when he arrived in January 1671. He was only thirty-five miles from the fabled wealth of Panama City, though as yet he had no idea of the hostile nature of the terrain in between.

In January he and his men went inland by river until it became too shallow even for canoes. Morgan disembarked with the plan of marching across the isthmus for twenty-four miles through "wild woods where there was no path." He took twelve hundred men with him, armed with just cutlasses and two muskets each. He was always a lucky man, and his good fortune continued as Spanish garrisons inland set fire to their own positions and abandoned them, believing he was coming with a much larger force.

It was hard going, as every step had to be cut in dense jungle. Morgan had a group of thirty men whose sole task was to hack through the vegetation. As workers on the canal would suffer in the nineteenth century, so his men were tormented by ticks and mosquitoes and terrified by poisonous spiders and snakes, all the while laboring in humid, stifling heat. Some of them grew sick and others fell in exhaustion and had to be sent back. By the sixth day, they had run out of food and were starving. They found some fruit and a planted field of maize, which they devoured like locusts before moving on.

On January 16 they were attacked by natives. The sight of half-naked tribesmen appearing and vanishing around them caused great fear in the ranks, but they fought them off, losing some thirty men in the process.

The next day they came across a village in the wilderness and found it burning. Morgan's men discovered jars of wine in the ruined houses and drank themselves sick. Around the same time, one of them was carried off as a prisoner and Morgan gave orders that any foraging party should be at least a hundred strong.

Ten days after leaving the fortress of Chagres, Morgan climbed a hill and saw the towers of Panama City in the distance. His men had survived the jungle, the attacks, and the heat. Even better, they came across a herd of cattle and shot enough to fill their bellies properly for the first time in days.

In the city, the Spanish were furious that Morgan's force had come so close. Yet they knew as well as anyone what Morgan's men had suffered to make the trip and fancied that their Spanish gentlemen would have no difficulty in bloodying their cavalry swords on a ragged group of exhausted, half-starved sailors.

As the sun rose, the cream of Spanish nobility rode to Morgan's camp, brandishing their swords and shouting elaborate and colorful insults. That task complete, they then rode away and Morgan ate breakfast with his men.

The Spanish had almost double Morgan's numbers, but his sailors were hard-bitten pirates, well used to hand-to-hand fighting. Morgan made a stern speech to them, ordering each man to make two pistols ready but not to fire until he did, or he would shoot them himself.

When his ragged crew formed up, the Spanish cavalry charged them with great excitement and war cries. Morgan waited until the enemy were almost on top of them before he fired both his pistols. The volley that followed completely destroyed the Spanish attack. The survivors fled in panic, and Morgan's men pursued them ruthlessly, for three miles, killing hundreds.

Morgan's men then entered Panama City and set fire to a great deal of it, burning the wooden houses to the ground. He sent another party to seize the ships in the city docks.

At that time, Panama City was a center of Spanish trade. Wealth mined in appalling conditions by slaves in Peru passed through the city, and rich families had collections of gold and silver plates. They had removed some of it by sea when Morgan was still far off, but most of it was recovered when one of Morgan's captains, Robert Searle, captured a Spanish ship in the port and used it to hunt fleeing vessels. Searle missed the best prize of them all, a galleon stuffed with jewels and gold, when his men became drunk on wine they found. However, they captured another ship with twenty thousand pieces of gold on board. Exact estimates are difficult, as Morgan was required to pay a percentage to his superiors in Jamaica, so he was never likely to declare all of it.

Morgan stayed in the battered city for twenty days, removing everything of value and taking three thousand hostages for ransom. His men tortured some to find the location of their treasures, and Morgan was later criticized, though his officers were adamant that he was not responsible for the worst excesses of his men.

In February he and his men began the march back to Chagres. On the way he searched his prisoners and men for hidden loot. He even took his men's muskets apart to check that they had not stuffed jewels into the barrels. This engendered much ill feeling toward him, but Morgan was not a man to let that sort of thing trouble him.

When they returned to Chagres, Morgan announced to his men that the final division of spoils was only twenty pounds a head. Many of them were furious, and he lost a number of loyal captains. He returned to Jamaica with only eight ships but almost all of the plunder. In all, he brought back some £237,000 in gold as well as silk, silver plate, jewels, and lace to a similar value. In today's terms, that would be more than £100 million. It was Morgan's greatest success, but his troubles were just beginning.

As news spread of the attack on Panama, Governor Modyford found himself facing serious difficulties. The sack of the city had taken place during peace with Spain, and the Spanish court made angry demands for punishment of those involved. A new governor, Thomas Lynch, was appointed, and when he arrived in Jamaica, he moved quickly. Modyford was invited on board Lynch's ship and then told he was a prisoner and would be sent home in disgrace. Lynch also began to gather information on Henry Morgan and looked over the records of all the ships involved in the sack of Panama. At the same time he began to get reports of Spanish attacks on British territories in reprisal. He was in the same position as Modyford had been. Lynch had absolute authority in Jamaica but needed force and ships to impose it. Worse, war with Holland looked likely once again, and Lynch had to try to appease the Spanish. He had enough cause to arrest Morgan but resisted for a time, worried that such an act would send the privateers sailing away to Tortuga.

In London there were mixed feelings about the attack on Panama. Spain was an ancient enemy, and as one royal councillor said: "Such an action had not been done since the famous Drake."

Modyford was imprisoned in the Tower of London, where he remained for two years before being released. He would later return to Jamaica, where he would become chief justice.

In 1672, Morgan was finally taken "as his Majesty's prisoner." He

sailed home in the frigate *Welcome,* accompanied by another privateer captain who had already been sentenced to death for piracy. His
hopes depended on being able to convince the king that he had not
known of the peace with Spain when he set sail.

He need not have worried. At home, his explanation was accepted
and it was not long before he was advising the king. War with the
Dutch broke out in 1672, and Morgan put forward plans to fortify
Jamaica. In 1674 he was appointed deputy governor.

When Governor Lynch heard of Morgan's easy treatment, he was
considerably vexed. His own commission as military commander in
Jamaica was revoked, and to his fury, Morgan was granted the same
powers and knighted. The war with the Dutch came to an abrupt end
in 1674, and in 1675 Morgan left England for Jamaica once more in
triumph. Modyford returned at around the same time, and they met
with great pleasure in their old haunt.

At the first meeting of the council, Morgan had the document re-
voking Lynch's powers read aloud in Lynch's presence. He enjoyed
confounding the man who had imprisoned Modyford and himself.
He also appointed himself as part of a committee to audit Lynch's
handling of the stores and munitions on Jamaica. Carelessly, he had
made himself a dangerous enemy.

Morgan's position as a wolf in the sheepfold of power was always
going to be difficult. When the new governor, Lord Vaughan, ordered
him to punish privateer captains, Morgan chose to advise his old
friends how to escape. He also used the governor's authority and name
freely in letters to privateers, telling them to regard Jamaica as a safe
port. When one of the letters turned up, Lord Vaughan brought charges
against Morgan and Modyford.

In Lynch, Lord Vaughan found a stalwart supporter. Lynch described Morgan as a man of "violent humours" and alleged that Morgan had challenged two other members of the Jamaica council to
duels. Slowly, the atmosphere of the council became poisoned, with
many accusations of theft, piracy, and corruption, until Lord Vaughan
finally dissolved it.

In England, the charges Vaughan had made against Morgan and

Modyford dragged through hearings with the Lords of Trade. Eventually, they decided the job was clearly too much for Lord Vaughan. He was recalled after just two years in Jamaica and replaced by the Earl of Carlisle. At the same time, Henry Morgan was confirmed in his post as deputy governor to the incoming earl and as commander in chief of all military forces.

Morgan did not sit idle waiting for the Earl of Carlisle. As soon as Vaughan set sail, he ordered new fortifications and increased the guns defending the port from sixty to more than a hundred. He received news of war with France and doubled the guard on Port Royal against possible attacks. His fabled luck struck again with news that the flagship of a French war fleet had run aground on its way to the Caribbean. When its captain had fired guns in a distress signal, the other ships thought it was a command to come closer and ran aground on the same rocks. The French lost ten ships in the chaos, and their threat was severely diminished in the Caribbean.

When Lord Carlisle arrived, he was very pleased with the fortified port and praised Morgan in letters home. His relationship with Morgan would always be cordial, though it was not always so with the council. Still, it was a happy time for Henry Morgan, until Lord Carlisle finally left the post in 1680.

Spanish ships continued to attack anything flying an English flag and were themselves attacked by privateers. Panama was even assaulted once more by captains who had been on the original journey with Morgan. Pirates infested Caribbean waters, beyond anyone's control. Morgan captured some of his old allies when they turned pirate but tried to prevent them being executed. Their death warrant was confirmed in London by a privy council growing increasingly wary of the powers being exercised in Jamaica. They lost faith that Morgan was sufficiently ruthless with the pirates, and to Morgan's horror, they appointed none other than Thomas Lynch as the new governor in Jamaica. Restored to power, the man Morgan had once humiliated would be a thorn in his side.

When Lynch returned to Jamaica in 1682, Morgan was forced to surrender his offices, which he did with strained good humor. He was still a member of the Jamaica council, but Lynch made it clear that he regarded him as a ruffian and a rogue, without a redeeming feature.

Lynch's chance came when a brawl in Port Royal was referred to Morgan. Lynch ordered a full investigation and found that Morgan's account of the brawl differed from others. It was a small thing, but Lynch leaped on it, making an official complaint that Morgan was not fit for his duties. Lynch managed to have Morgan dismissed from the council in 1683. The governor's version of events reached London first, and the dismissal was confirmed by the Lords of Trade.

Morgan tried to fight the decision, but his petition fell on deaf ears in London and he retired to his estates in Jamaica, putting on a great deal of weight and drinking himself insensible. Thomas Lynch did not have much time to enjoy his triumph, however. In that hot climate, death was always close, and he succumbed to fevers in 1684.

Morgan was not left in peace for long. A colorful account of his career was published in a Dutch book, *The American Sea-Rovers*. Morgan successfully sued the publisher for libel, but the book made him famous as a bloodthirsty pirate.

Charles II died in 1685, and with that, much of the force behind Morgan's disgrace dwindled. A new governor reversed Morgan's ban from the council and restored him to public favor. Yet Morgan's health had suffered, and at fifty-three, he was old before his time. He died on August 25, 1688, leaving the bulk of his vast estates to his beloved wife, Mary. He is buried in Port Royal, Jamaica, though his grave was later obliterated and lost in the earthquake of 1692. Even the earth couldn't hold him.

Though he died without sons of his own, he left part of his fortune to his brother-in-law Robert Bindloss, and his heirs, on the condition that they took the name Morgan. One of those renamed heirs became attorney general and another crown solicitor for Jamaica. Henry Morgan would have loved to see that.

After Morgan's death, it was said of him: "He showed the world that he was qualified to govern as well as fight, and that in all stations of life he was a great man." His talent for organizing the collection of rugged individuals that were the Jamaica privateers was extraordinary, his charisma beyond dispute. Henry Morgan was a knight and a politician, a ruffian and a pirate. He dragged himself up from humble beginnings to become one of the most powerful and respected men in the Caribbean. He was without doubt a ruthless devil when he needed to be. However, it is worth pointing out that empires are never built by vicars. They are built by men like Henry Morgan.

Recommended
The Life of Sir Henry Morgan by E. A. Cruikshank
Admiral Sir Henry Morgan: King of the Buccaneers
by Terry Breverton

Lawrence of Arabia

All men dream, but not equally. Those who dream by night in the dusty recesses of their minds wake in the day to find that it was a vanity. But the dreamers of the day are dangerous men, for they may act their dreams with open eyes to make it possible. This, I did. —T. E. Lawrence

Thomas Edward Lawrence was a soldier, archaeologist, writer, intelligence officer, and international negotiator. During his life he was known variously as "Emir Dynamite," the last great crusader, the most interesting Briton alive, "el Lawrence," "the Uncrowned King of Arabia," and, simply, "Lurens." He was enigmatic, asexual, masochistic, retiring, exhibitionistic, difficult, and charming—an extremely complex man whose life and personality still hold mystery today.

Born in 1888, he was the second of five illegitimate sons of Thomas Chapman and nursery governess Sarah Junner. Chapman gave most of his money to his wife and children, eloped with Sarah, and changed their names to Lawrence. From then on, he and Sarah lived as husband and wife. Chapman inherited a baronetcy in 1914; officially he was Sir Thomas, but he never used the title. He died in the influenza epidemic of 1919, and Sarah went to China with Lawrence's missionary brother, Montague. By then, the name of Lawrence was already world-famous through his exploits in Arabia.

After winning a scholarship to Jesus College, Oxford, Lawrence refused to play organized sports there. Instead, he walked, ran, cycled, and swam. He became an excellent pistol shot and joined the Officers' Training Corps. He was quietly rebellious, independent, and physically tough. Several times he broke through the winter ice to swim the Cherwell River and was famous as one of the illegal night climbers on the university roofs. To complete his history degree he spent a summer walking and camel riding eleven hundred miles through Syria, studying the old Crusader castles.

He divided the next four years of his life between Oxford and the ancient biblical city of Carchemish, excavating with archaeologist Leonard Woolley. Lawrence took to wearing around his waist the Arabian red tasseled belt of the permanent bachelor. There he and the famous Arabian scholar Gertrude Bell met for the first time, though they were not taken with each other. Their love and concern for Arabia and its peoples grew separately.

During those years of archaeological digs, academic reports, and theses for Oxford University, Lawrence learned to speak the Arabic of the bazaars as well as to read and write basic script. From 1300, the Middle East had been part of the Ottoman Empire, the realm of the Turks stretching from Europe to the Persian Gulf, and so Lawrence learned also the ways of the Turks. He was not impressed. He and his Syrian friend Daouhm were arrested and beaten by the Turks in 1912 as suspected deserters from the Turkish army.

When the First World War began in August 1914, Turkey entered in November as an ally of Germany and the Austro-Hungarian Empire. Twenty-six-year-old Lawrence was posted to Cairo as an intelligence officer in the small British army holding the vital Suez Canal. He was made lieutenant and his work involved drawing and correcting maps of the Middle East. As his Oxford lecturers had before, High Command found him difficult.

The Arab Revolt began on June 6, 1916, when Princes Faisal and Ali of southern Arabia attempted to take the holy city of Medina. They were defeated by heavy Turkish artillery fire. In punishment for the attack, the Turkish commander ordered that all Arabs living in Awali be massacred. Those dead and alive were thrown onto their burning homes.

In Mecca on June 10, Faisal's father, Sharif Husayn Ibn 'Ali, fired from his window to signal the official revolt. The Turks, also Muslim, attempted a worldwide jihad to include Britain, France, and Russia, but Husayn refused to sanction this and instead wanted the Turks out of Arabia. Husayn supported Great Britain—but not France—and Britain in turn supported the Arab Revolt against their common enemy, the Turks. In June three British ships steamed into Jeddah on the Red Sea with food, three thousand rifles, and ammunition. In July, the Turks garrisoning at Mecca were defeated, the first victory of the desert revolt.

Britain's intelligence chief and instigator and supporter of the Arab Revolt was Ronald Storrs, and on his visits to Jeddah and Hamra he took Lawrence. They met all of Husayn's sons and agreed that the most likely to succeed in coordinating an Arab regular force were Faisal and Abdullah. Lawrence became the first British officer Husayn allowed to visit the fighting tribes. He met Prince Faisal so many times that Faisal asked him to wear Arab dress to be less conspicuous. Faisal provided him with the white robes of a Hashemite prince, and the legend of "Lawrence of Arabia" began.

In late 1916, Lawrence was appointed military adviser to the Arab Revolt with orders to report and liaise whenever necessary between Arabia and Cairo. He wrote: "The position I have is a queer one. I do not suppose any Englishman before ever had such a place." Faisal presented Lawrence with a British rifle captured by the Turks at Gallipoli, an earlier Turkish gift to Faisal. It was a gesture of friendship, humor, and trust.

Supplies from Britain were trickling through, and it was time for Faisal's regulars and

Lawrence's irregulars to campaign. Yenbo on the Red Sea was saved from a Turkish night attack almost without a shot being fired—the only land approach was lit by Royal Navy searchlights, and the Turks retreated. That success was followed by a joint advance by land and sea on Wejh. In January 1917 Wejh fell to the Royal Navy and Arab regulars as Lawrence and Faisal approached by camel over land. The only Red Sea port then left to the Turks was Aqaba. In the east the British liberated Baghdad in March.

Lawrence initiated guerrilla attacks on the north-south railway from Damascus to Medina, a tactic continued throughout the war by Arab irregulars trained by British explosives experts. The wrecks of the engines are there today, lying on their rusted sides in the desert. Harassing rather than decisive, those attacks kept the Arab Revolt active and were ideal for mobile irregulars. That June, Lawrence trekked some 560 miles by camel through enemy Syria, converting tribes to the revolt, patching up tribal feuds and religious differences, and assuring them of British support if they fought.

Back in the south again, Lawrence, the formidable Auda abu Tayi of the Howeitat tribe, and some thirty-five others quietly left Wejh. They rode a circular route, skirting the great Nefud Desert and crossing a plateau to arrive at the valleys behind Aqaba. On their camels were weapons and gold to raise the local tribes.

The Turkish forts forming the inland defensive line were taken one by one. In one charge to cut off a Turkish retreat, Lawrence excitedly fired his revolver and killed his own camel. On July 6, Aqaba was liberated by Lawrence's irregulars.

Lawrence crossed the Sinai Desert by camel to take the news to Cairo, and a week later a British ship arrived at Aqaba with food and gold. Rifles, mortars, machine guns, and explosives followed. The revolt was going well, the Turks were being stretched, and at headquarters, General Allenby took command for the British advance northward. Yet there were failures among the successes. The Turks were tough soldiers and able to survive on poor rations and in the most hostile of terrains. It was apparent that the liberation of Arabia would be hard-fought.

Deserts are not only rock, sand, and sun; they are also hills, mountains, valleys, and snow. The desert war for Lawrence and his Arab irregulars continued through the winter. They campaigned in rain and mud, forced their unwilling camels through snowdrifts, and scaled ice-covered hills in sandals and bare feet. There were many bitter moments. Of a badly wounded friend, Lawrence wrote: "We could not leave him where he was, to the Turks, because we had seen them burn alive our hapless wounded. For this reason we were all agreed, before action, to finish off one another, if badly hurt; but I had never thought it might fall to me to kill Farraj."

Deep in Turkish territory lay Dara'a, a vital railway junction where the line from the coast joined the north-south line. In the rainy November of 1917, Lawrence, dressed as an Arab, entered the town to study the layout for a future attack. According to his book *Seven Pillars of Wisdom,* he was captured and viciously beaten by Turkish soldiers before he could escape. For many years this episode has been questioned by historians; Lawrence did not report his capture at the time, and the exact details cannot be known. Possibly, it was an echo of his beating in 1912 with Daouhm. Lawrence was certainly under considerable strain for a long period. He suffered regularly from dysentery and fevers, yet continued to make many long and important camel journeys through the deserts.

For some time the Turks had offered a reward of twenty thousand pounds for Lawrence's head, and after early 1917 he usually traveled with an Arab bodyguard. There were still many tribes who worked for the enemy, and perhaps half in the revolt were fighting for British gold as much as a free Arabia. Lawrence, Faisal, Auda, and other leaders had to be careful; seven centuries of Turkish rule could not be changed overnight.

In December 1917 the British army liberated Jerusalem. Allenby, with Lawrence walking behind him, became the first non-Muslim leader since 1187 to enter Jerusalem when he passed through the Jaffa Gate on foot. With the Turkish withdrawal from Medina, the three holy cities of Mecca, Medina, and Jerusalem were free. Damascus, the spiritual capital of Arabia, where lies the tomb of Saladin, awaited.

The new year began well when Lawrence's irregulars fought their only formal battle against the Turkish army. The strange Englishman who spoke and dressed as an Arab was a talisman to the independent tribesmen; they chanted "Lurens! Lurens!" when he gathered them at At-Tafilah. In a classic military action of pretended retreat and then encirclement, Lawrence routed an enemy column; 300 Turks were killed and 250 taken prisoner. There were reverses elsewhere through Turkish counterattacks, and that Easter many British resources were diverted to halt a new German offensive in France.

Faisal's Arab regulars became the desert right flank of Allenby's final advance north in the summer of 1918. The prize: Damascus. In September, one thousand of Lawrence's irregulars, supported by Indian, Gurkha, and Egyptian units, took Dara'a.

During the Turkish retreat north, the villagers of Tafas, including twenty children and forty women, were massacred by a Turkish brigade. In vengeful fury, Lawrence's irregulars fell on the Turks and slaughtered most of them. The Arabs usually took prisoners and handed them to the British, but the butchery at Tafas was too much for them. Witnesses reported that Lawrence tried to stop the killing but with only small success.

By September 29 the armies were in the hills overlooking Damascus. Arab irregulars and the Australian Light Horse entered the city before dawn on the thirtieth, followed by Lawrence later that day. By the time Allenby arrived in October, Lawrence's irregulars and Faisal's regulars controlled Damascus and had created an Arab council to administer the city. That had been Lawrence's promise to Faisal, and he had fulfilled it. Lawrence also removed the bronze wreath that the German kaiser had added to the tomb of Saladin. To Arabs, the wreath was a desecration, with its German imperial crown and German and Turkish script. Lawrence wanted this symbol of dominion over Arabia removed before Faisal arrived. It is now in the Imperial War Museum in London.

General Allenby and Prince Faisal met for the first time in Damascus, with Lawrence as interpreter. Following his instructions from London, Allenby informed Faisal that all Syria except Lebanon was to be his, but under "the security of France" and with a French liaison officer. Faisal replied that he would not accept French security or a French liaison officer, nor would he recognize French authority over Syria and Lebanon. The Arabs did not trust the French at all. Faisal wanted complete independence for Arabia, if necessary secured by Britain but by no other country.

Before the fighting was even over, the politicians had moved in; British and French governments had reached an agreement to divide northern Arabia. Lawrence and Faisal had known of the discussions, but neither could believe such an agreement would actually happen. Lawrence refused to work with any French liaison officer. Instead, he asked Allenby for leave in Britain. Two of his brothers had been killed fighting on the western front, and he was very tired. He also realized that the next round would be fought at the peace conference, and he wanted to be there.

He returned to Britain in October 1918, a colonel with a Distinguished Service Order, Companion of the Order of the Bath, and a recommendation by Allenby for a knighthood. At a private investiture at Buckingham Palace, Lawrence politely refused the knighthood from King George V and informed the king: "Your cabinet is an awful set of crooks." He advised His Majesty that the British government was about to betray the Arabs and that he, Lawrence, would be supporting Prince Faisal, not His Majesty's government. Now one of the most famous figures of the war, he angered many with his refusal of a knighthood, however honorable his reasons. There was certainly some of Lawrence's peculiar masochism in the refusal, yet he was correct that the future of Arabia was in the hands of bureaucrats who cared little for its people.

At the peace conference in Paris, Lawrence, Gertrude Bell, and others supported Arab independence. Against French wishes, Prince Faisal was also there representing Sharif Husayn, but they were outmaneuvered by clever politicians. France was given a mandate for Lebanon, and in November 1919 the British army was withdrawn from Syria. The French invaded Syria in the spring of 1920.

It was as if the Arabs had never fought, as if the British army had fought so that France could take over part of the Ottoman Empire. There had been a small French unit fighting under Allenby in the liberation of Arabia, but they were irrelevant to the outcome. The Middle East was immediately destabilized, and violence flared.

Winston Churchill, appointed colonial secretary, called a conference at Cairo in 1921 to sort out the mess. He appointed Lawrence Britain's "Adviser on Arab Affairs"; Gertrude Bell and Ronald Storrs were also there. Many problems were solved by the conference, but several remained, particularly that of the French in Syria and the warring tribes of Arabia. The tribes had fought one another even while they fought the Turks during the revolt, and now they continued under different banners of tribe and religion. For Britain, it meant another war in Syria, when French forces joined the Nazis in the Second World War.

When the dust had settled, a John Ross applied to join the RAF in 1922 as an aircraftman. He was refused but returned with a letter from the Air Ministry stating who he was and that he should be admitted. The accepting officer was W. E. Johns, author of the Biggles novels, and Ross was T. E. Lawrence. It was typical of that oddly quixotic, romantic man to use a false name. After all, Lawrence itself was an alias chosen by his father. The fiction also protected Lawrence from the press, who hounded him long after he had left public life. He was accepted into the RAF, the authorities believing that he wanted material for a book.

"Honestly, I couldn't tell you why I joined up," Lawrence wrote to author and friend Robert Graves. He admitted that he didn't understand many of the decisions he made.

He served in the ranks of the RAF, then the army under the name of Shaw, then the RAF again for almost the rest of his life. While there he completed, published, and revised his great work, *Seven Pillars of Wisdom,* which Churchill called "one of the greatest books I have ever read." Of his two other books, *Revolt in the Desert* is a précis of *Seven Pillars,* while *The Mint* is about his life as an RAF recruit. Lawrence continued to live his double existence, serving humbly in the ranks but at the same time moving in the circles of power of his famous friends— Robert Graves, Sir Winston Churchill, King Faisal, George Bernard Shaw, Nancy Astor, Sir Edward Elgar, and others.

His enlistment in the RAF ended in 1935, and Lawrence retired to his Dorsetshire cottage, Clouds Hill. He wrote: "My losing the RAF numbs me so I haven't much feeling to spare for a while. In fact I find myself wishing all the time that my own curtain would fall. It seems as if I had finished now." His great friend King Faisal had already "finished," dead at only fifty.

On May 13, returning on his 1,000-cc Brough motorbike to Clouds Hill from the Bovington village post office, Lawrence swerved on the brow of a hill to avoid two boys riding bicycles. He clipped the back wheel of one, crashed, and flew over the handlebars. He hit the road headfirst, cracked his skull, and died six days later without regaining consciousness.

T. E. Lawrence is buried in the Moreton Church graveyard in Dorset. Ronald Storrs, Sir Winston Churchill, and many other friends attended his simple funeral. King George V sent a message to Lawrence's only surviving brother, saying, "Your brother's name will live in history." A memorial service was held at Saint Paul's Cathedral, where there is a small bust of Lawrence, while in the simple church of Saint Martin in Wareham, Dorset, there is a striking stone effigy of Lawrence in the Arab robes of a Hashemite prince.

There are few famous heroes of the First World War, but Lawrence of Arabia was certainly one. Like Richard Burton before him, he was a man in love with exoticism, and mysterious ancient Arabia captured his imagination. British archives released in the 1960s and 1970s confirmed the importance of Lawrence's work in Arabia. If anything, his *Seven Pillars of Wisdom* underplays his contribution to the Arab Revolt. Lawrence was one of the few who saw the future in independent Arab nations. He was an outsider, a romantic dreamer in many ways, yet a man who could see beyond the details to the great sweep of history.

Recommended
Seven Pillars of Wisdom by T. E. Lawrence
Lawrence: The Uncrowned King of Arabia by Michael Asher
Film: *Lawrence of Arabia,* directed by David Lean. There are inaccuracies, but it captures brilliantly the Arab Revolt and the enigma of Lawrence
Clouds Hill Cottage, National Trust, Dorset, U.K.

Florence Nightingale

Victorian soldiers such as Charles Napier and Garnet Wolseley risked their lives for their country—and personal glory. Their courage in the face of enemy fire is made greater when you consider the rudimentary state of medicine and surgery at the time.

Battlefield hospitals were brutal in the first half of the nineteenth century. Surgeons did not wash their hands and operated in blood- and pus-stained clothes. If a knife or sponge was dropped, it was merely dipped in bloody water before being used again. Ether, an early anesthetic, wasn't used in surgery until 1842. Opium and chloroform were both known, but neither was in common use. Even London hospitals were places of squalor. They had no lavatories, just chamber pots under the beds. The windows were boarded up, as fresh air was believed to bring illness.

It would not be until the late 1860s that Joseph Lister cut the rate of deaths from postoperative infection by making his surgeons wash their hands. He also used a spray of carbolic acid to kill germs, even though at that time they could not be seen with the rudimentary microscopes.

Antibiotics were also unknown until the twentieth century and not mass-produced until after World War II. Up to that point, fever and infection were treated with cold cloths, sulphur or sulphurous acid, mustard on the skin, and occasionally mustard-and-salt enemas.

As a result, even light wounds could rot and corrupt a limb. Amputation was extremely common, and surgeons competed for speed with a saw, trying to remove and seal the limb before the patient died from blood loss. The patient would then be very fortunate not to get one of the "surgical fevers"—pyemia or gangrene, which killed almost half of those who had lived through surgery.

In short, it was a different, harder world, where even measles and croup killed tens of thousands of children and a wounded soldier needed more than luck to survive. Being wounded meant certain agony, likely infection, and a good chance of dying in a dirty barracks hospital.

Florence Nightingale was born on May 12, 1820. Her parents were wealthy and their honeymoon in Italy lasted for four years. She was named after her Italian birthplace, an innovation at the time. They returned home to a new and very grand house in Hampshire. Florence and her elder sister, Parthenope, were taught by a governess before their father took it upon himself to teach them Latin, Greek, French, Italian, German, history, and philosophy. From the start, Florence found the lessons easier than her sister did.

When she was sixteen, Florence's life changed. She always kept private notes of her thoughts and experiences, and on one of them she wrote: "On February 7th 1837, God spoke to me and called me to his service." Always a woman with an intense inner world, she would later record that she had heard voices at four times in her life.

She could not act on it immediately. Her mother was intent on launching her daughters into London society, but the house needed to be renovated first, so in September 1837 the Nightingales departed for the Continent while the work was done. Florence loved the experience. She danced at balls and visited romantic Italian cities. When the family returned to England in 1839, her mother arranged to have the girls presented to Queen Victoria, who was just a year older than Florence. Florence's mother was pleased that her intelligent daughter had become such a beautiful and demure young lady. Clearly marriage would soon follow, and Florence could live properly and have daughters of her own.

Instead, Nightingale threw herself into the study of mathematics. Her mother was appalled, of course. Young men were not likely to pursue a "mathematical girl."

In the 1840s there was great poverty in England, in both the slums of the major cities and the countryside, where a single bad crop could mean starvation. The Nightingales spent their summers in a second home in Derbyshire, and there she met some of the poorest laborers. In a first sign of what would become her life's work, she went out of her way to take them food and clothes, even medicine when she could get it. There was no system of benefits for the poor at that time. If a working man fell ill or was injured, his family went hungry until he recovered or died.

Nightingale also nursed an orphaned baby and her own grandmother. She had found her purpose, her vocation, at last, and she refused an offer of marriage to pursue it. She wanted proper training in a London hospital, but that was unheard of for a young woman of her social class.

In 1845, Dr. Fowler of Salisbury Infirmary visited her parents. Taking the opportunity, Nightingale asked him to train her as a nurse. It was the first her parents had heard of her ambition, and they were outraged. In embarrassment at the storm his visit had brought, the doctor left without agreeing to her request.

Nightingale was an unmarried daughter with no rights over her own life. Her mother forced her to continue with social engagements, and her less intelligent sister never lost a chance to show her jealous resentment. Nightingale did her best to study on her own, visiting foreign hospitals when she traveled and reading anything medical that she could find. She made a point of stopping at the Kaiserswerth hospital in Germany on one trip and found the nurses there similar to nuns in their outlook and vocation, even their dress.

Nightingale was thirty-two before her career finally began. A wealthy friend of hers, Elizabeth Herbert, put her name forward for a position running a new nursing home opening in London—the Establishment for Gentlewomen during Illness. As Nightingale wrote in her private letters, it was the second time she heard a voice instructing her. She accepted the position despite the dismay of her family.

From the start, Nightingale introduced changes that were remarkable for the day. She insisted on clean rooms and sheets and that her patients be warm and well fed. She even put flowers in the nursing home. At the same time she collected statistical information, always looking for ways to improve the care of patients.

She was fearless in the face of both authority and disease, even to the point of taking over a ward in a London hospital during a cholera epidemic. In just a year she made her nursing home unique for its gentle care.

In 1854, Nightingale's life changed again. In March the Crimean War broke out between Britain and Russia. Conditions on the Crimean Peninsula were appalling, and disease and exposure were taking as many lives as the actual fighting. Cholera was a particular killer, though at that time no one understood how it was spread. After the battle of Alma, wounded men were laid on filthy straw without opium or chloroform or even splints for broken bones.

In the primitive troop hospital at Scutari (now Üsküdar) in Turkey, the main building was filled with a thousand sick or wounded men. When news came of another thousand on their way, the senior medical officer converted an artillery barracks to hold them. Dirty and bare, with no beds, kitchen, or medical supplies, it was little more than a huge hall in which to put the dying. Delirious soldiers lay in their own filth, untended and unable even to get a drink of water in oppressive heat. The stench of rotting flesh, the screaming and misery, can only be imagined.

The Times brought the situation to the eyes of the public, shaming the minister for war, Sidney Herbert. Good nurses were desperately needed, and he knew Nightingale through his wife and liked her. He wrote her an impassioned letter, offering to pay for her to go to Scutari with a group of nurses. For the third time in her life, Nightingale heard a voice telling her to go.

With the official position of superintendent of the Female Nursing Establishment of the English Hospitals in Turkey, Nightingale was instantly famous. No woman had ever held such a post before, and her mother and sister were finally able to put aside their grievances and be proud of her. Nightingale scoured London for the best nurses to take to Turkey; she preferred solid, doughty old ladies to young ones. She

was later to
regret the weight of some of
them when a bed collapsed. Twenty-four
nuns joined the party and accepted Nightingale's authority, bringing the total to thirty-
eight. They all had to be trained to Nightingale's
standards.

In October 1854 the nurses left England for
Paris to buy medical supplies. News had spread of their mission, and
they were welcomed and well treated by French locals before moving
on to the great port of Marseilles. Nightingale oversaw the purchases of
everything she thought she might need before they sailed on October
27 to Malta and then Constantinople, now known as Istanbul.

By November, after terrible gales, they reached Constantinople.
The British ambassador sent Lord Napier to greet Nightingale and
he was much taken with the handsome and dedicated woman who
was still exhausted from seasickness. However, she could not rest.
The battle of Balaklava had been fought, and the hospital was expecting a new rush of casualties at any moment.

The first sight of the hospital at Scutari was not impressive. Nightingale was used to dirt in hospitals, but she was not prepared to find

thousands of dying men, most of whom had diarrhea. What drains existed were blocked, and the smell of the hospital reached right out to sea. Nightingale later wrote that it should have had "Abandon Hope All Ye Who Enter Here" written above its gate. Her most famous work had begun.

One of the reasons for the appalling state of the hospital was the lifeless hand of British bureaucracy. Even a request for a new shirt might be passed along to a dozen different officials, then lost or forgotten. Her foresight in buying her own supplies was rewarded. The doctors in Scutari had no medicine, dressings, or bandages. Amputation was the main treatment of wounds, and the mortality rate for such butcher's work was incredibly high.

Even so, her first reception was not a pleasant experience. Apart from the sounds and smells of the hospital, the doctors were hostile to the idea of a group of women interfering in their work. They gave Florence and her group of thirty-eight nurses just six small rooms, one of which had a body in it. The following morning the doctors made it clear that they would not allow women on the wards. Nightingale said nothing and put her nurses to work preparing and sorting the supplies she had brought.

On November 5 the battle of Inkerman took place and winter came in a sudden cold blast. Thousands more wounded began to arrive at the already overcrowded hospital. The doctors were overwhelmed and asked Nightingale if she would assist. It is a testament to her character that she made nothing of the small victory, just gathered her nurses and made her first tour of the hospital. "I have seen hell," she said later.

She had funds, both from Sidney Herbert's government purse and a collection organized by *The Times* itself from its readers. She sent to Constantinople for whatever was needed, from operating tables to soap, clothes, food, and bedpans. In the meantime, she set about cleaning the filthy rooms. Two hundred men were hired to unblock the drains. Women were engaged to scrub and scour the floors, while Nightingale set the soldiers' wives to washing clothes and linen. She believed that a clean hospital was a healthy one, though this was not at all common practice, either in Turkey or England.

As the hospital began to lose its worst grime, Nightingale had the nurses begin their work. At last there were medicines and dressings for the wounded. She also understood the importance of small things that the army would never have considered. She bought a screen to give privacy during operations, then held the hand of soldiers as they tried to bear amputation without anesthetic. She made a rule for her nurses that none of the soldiers should die alone. She worked as hard as anyone, staying up for twenty-four hours at a time to tend the men. She also wrote letters home for dying men who could not write.

Despite everything, the death toll went on rising. As well as a new outbreak of cholera, the men suffered from scurvy, a disease brought on by the soldiers' diet of biscuit and pork, without any vegetables. Even those with minor wounds were dying, and Nightingale became convinced the water supply was to blame. She set her workmen to dig up the pipes, and they discovered the dead body of a horse that had been washed into an inlet. All the water in the hospital had run past that diseased flesh. Years later, it was discovered that the Scutari hospital was built on an ancient cesspit, which meant that human waste seeped into the water supply. Florence Nightingale could never have made it completely safe without burning it down and starting again.

Even so, little by little, Nightingale turned Scutari from hell on earth into a quiet, clean hospital. Each night she would make a last tour of the wards, in a black dress and shawl and carrying a small lamp to guide her steps. It was during his time that she became known as "the Lady with the Lamp."

Before she slept for a few hours, she wrote to Sidney Herbert in London, telling him everything she had done and all that still needed doing. She urged him to keep a better record of the wounded and dying, believing that statistics would aid future generations in fighting the same diseases. In this too she was ahead of her time.

Some of her letters were passed to Queen Victoria, who was shocked by the descriptions of such suffering. The queen wrote a reply, saying:

"I wish Miss Nightingale and the ladies would tell these poor noble, wounded and sick men that no one takes a warmer interest, or feels more for their suffering, or admires their courage and heroism more than their queen." The words were read to the men and then pinned to a wall of the hospital. No previous monarch had written such a personal message to soldiers.

By 1855, Scutari had become the best army hospital available to British troops anywhere. However, there were two others on the Crimean Peninsula, and Nightingale saw it as her duty to visit them and assess conditions. She traveled to Balaklava and found them in the sort of state she had seen on her first visit to Scutari. She began another plan of attack, but without warning, exhaustion overcame her. She fainted and was found to be burning with a fever. Her best nurses came out to tend her, but for two weeks she was close to death. Soldiers in Scutari wept when they heard of her illness.

She recovered but had lost a great deal of her vitality and become very thin and worn. Though she was able to return to Scutari, her health was extremely fragile and she wasn't able to go to battle with obstinate doctors as she had before. The soldiers showed their appreciation at her safe return, and that sustained her over difficult months.

The Treaty of Paris was signed in March and came into effect a month later, ending the Crimean War. Almost without exception, it had been badly conceived and badly led. The cost in lives was cruelly high, and in England the public found little to celebrate. "The Charge of the Light Brigade" by Lord Tennyson became famous, but no one wrote stirring poems about hospitals.

Gradually, the soldiers in the Crimea returned home, though Nightingale stayed until the last one had gone. As the hospital emptied, it still seemed full of ghosts. "Oh my poor men," she wrote, "I am a bad mother to come home and leave you in Crimean graves."

Death was often on her mind, perhaps because of her close association with it in the Crimea. Only a year later, she gave instructions to her sister, Parthenope, that she should be buried in the Crimea— "absurd as I know it to be. For they are not there." She would not get her wish.

In England, many survivors described Nightingale's kindness, and her fame as the Lady with the Lamp grew steadily. Soldiers contributed a day's pay for her to set up a training school for nurses. Pamphlets about her time in Scutari were printed. In London, Madame Tussaud created a waxwork of Nightingale ministering to the wounded. Finally, Queen Victoria sent her a brooch that her consort Prince Albert had designed. It had the words: BLESSED ARE THE MERCIFUL around the edge. Huge public receptions were planned, and Nightingale's sister and mother were in their element, overcome with the prospect of honors for the family.

Nightingale herself was appalled at the idea. She avoided the regimental bands and crowds by traveling under the name Miss Smith. She came home alone to the house in Derbyshire and walked from the station. Her mother's housekeeper saw her coming down the road and rushed out in tears, but otherwise it was a remarkable and modest evasion of fame.

At home Nightingale ignored the letters and invitations that came in, telling her sister she could open them if she wished. Instead, she threw herself into work, constantly writing letters. One of her

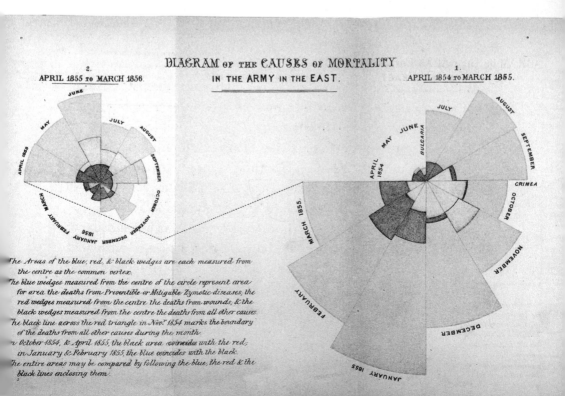

contributions to the public debate was a pamphlet, *Mortality in the British Army,* that presented statistical information with a modified form of pie chart. She followed it with other publications and visited Queen Victoria to put forth her case. The two women were of a similar age and mind. They worked closely together to create a royal commission on the health of the army, with Sidney Herbert as chairman.

At the same time, Nightingale's own health grew worse. She took rooms in London to work but fell ill with fevers, almost certainly the aftermath of her exposure in the Crimea. She drove herself on regardless.

In 1858, Sidney Herbert's health also deteriorated, crushed as he was by overwork. Nightingale was confined to her room with illness, but she was indomitable and forced him to continue his labors on the commission. At times they bickered like an old married couple, but there was great mutual respect and liking between them and Herbert's wife, Elizabeth, encouraged the friendship.

In 1859 another royal commission was set up to investigate the health of the army in India. Sidney Herbert was made chairman, adding immensely to his workload. Unable to refuse important tasks, he was also made minister for war by a new government.

When the Crimean commission reported, Nightingale had the outcome she desired. It would create a new army medical school and reform medical provision down to the design of drains. Yet the conclusions had to be implemented, and the War Office was mired in tortuous bureaucracy. Even with Sidney Herbert at its head, the attempt to reform the dusty halls of power was almost impossible.

Nightingale wrote that her aim was "to simplify procedure, to abolish divided responsibility, to define clearly the duties of each head of department and of each class of office; to hold heads responsible for their respective departments." Those words are as insightful and valuable today as they were then and all the more remarkable for it.

Sidney Herbert finally collapsed in 1861. As he died, he murmured: "Poor Florence. Our joint work unfinished." His statue stands today outside the War Office in London. He need not have worried: the army reforms went ahead. Barracks were redesigned, food improved, and army nurses trained to a higher standard. Death rates dropped around the world as a direct result of Florence Nightingale's and Sidney Herbert's work.

Nightingale was hit hard by the death of her friend. For the fourth time in her life, she heard a voice crying out at the loss. She worked harder if anything, despite poor health. With her duties on the commission, she had been unable to oversee the Nightingale Training School set up with pay from Crimean soldiers. As a result, standards had dropped. Though she was bedridden, Nightingale took over this last task and devoted herself to it. She was back in her element and the work made her happy. She put on weight for the first time in years, and her letters grew milder in comparison with the stern missives she had sent to those in power. The Nightingale School still exists and trains nurses today.

Though she had expected death for years, it was slow in coming. Queen Victoria died in 1901, and her successor, Edward VII, awarded Nightingale the Order of Merit for her life's work. She was the first woman to receive the honor. Nightingale died at last in 1910, at the age of ninety.

It is impossible to guess how many lives were saved or how much suffering eased because of Florence Nightingale. She made nursing a professional occupation for the first time. She opened women's medical schools and trained Linda Richards, who went on to establish nursing schools in America and Japan. She fought against the stifling attitudes and prejudices of her day, forcing new thinking in old halls of power. She won her battles, and her life stands as an example of what a single individual can do with sufficient determination, faith, and spirit.

Recommended
Florence Nightingale by Cecil Woodham-Smith

Flight 93

For they have sown the wind, and they shall reap the whirlwind. —Hosea 8:7

On a morning flight from New York (Newark) to San Francisco, everything was normal. Captain Jason Dahl and First Officer LeRoy Homer ran through their preflight check in the cockpit. The plane, a Boeing 757, was less than half full, with only thirty-seven passengers and five flight attendants. Flight 93 had been delayed by twenty-five minutes on the ground by heavy airport traffic, but they took off at 8:42 A.M. The weather was good, and the first forty-six minutes of the flight had been completely routine.

Four men of Middle Eastern descent sat in different rows of the first-class section, as close to the cockpit as they could get. Just before

9:28 A.M., all four took out strips of red cloth and tied them firmly around their heads.

September 11, 2001, is one date that will never be forgotten. On that early morning with blue skies, four planes were hijacked in American airspace by Islamic terrorists and used as missiles against vital targets. At 8:46 A.M., American Airlines Flight 11 struck the North Tower of the World Trade Center in New York. Between five thousand and ten thousand people were in each tower. Only the early hour prevented a much worse disaster, as many thousands more were on their way to work in the towers.

As well as the passengers of Flight 11, hundreds were killed in the North Tower as the plane slammed through steel and glass at hundreds of miles per hour. No one above the impact point survived. Below it, around seventy-two people were killed and four thousand successfully evacuated.

As black smoke and roaring flames erupted from the impact site, media crews believed at first that they were witnessing the aftermath of a horrific accident. Even so, two F-15 fighter jets were scrambled from Cape Cod. The pilots left their afterburners on and went flat-out, breaking the speed of sound to get to New York.

They were still minutes away at 9:03 A.M., when a second plane, United Airlines Flight 175, was deliberately piloted into the South Tower. For the first time in history, the Federal Aviation Administration ordered all flights across the country to land.

Even from the distance of almost a decade later, the shock of those images remains vivid. The Western world watched in horror as trapped men and women jumped to their deaths from windows rather than be engulfed in spreading flames. Emergency services entered both towers and saved hundreds if not thousands of lives.

At 9:50 A.M. the South Tower suddenly collapsed, killing those left inside, including police, medics, and fire department rescuers. At 10:28, as America reeled in shock and the images were beamed around the world, the North Tower fell.

That morning 2,749 people from all walks of life—young and old, male and female—died in the Twin Towers. Yet in the minutes before they fell, Flights 77 and 93 were still in the air and heading toward their targets.

By the time Flights 11 and 175 hit the World Trade Center, the hijackers on Flight 93 had not yet taken over the aircraft. At 9:24 A.M., Captain Jason Dahl received an emergency warning sent to all planes in the air, telling him to beware of "cockpit intrusion" and that two planes had struck the towers. Dahl asked for the extraordinary message to be confirmed. In the first-class seats behind him, the four hijackers were tying their red cloths as bandannas, readying themselves for their appalling mission. Thus prepared, they drew box-cutter knives and took over the front section of the plane. The flight record shows that Flight 93 dropped seven hundred feet in just a few seconds as they struggled with the pilot and first officer for control.

In panic, a passenger named Thomas Burnett called his wife. She contacted the FBI, and when he called a second time, she told him about the attacks in New York. It would be confirmed by other passengers as they called their loved ones, but it was that vital piece of information that made a difference to the outcome.

Planes had been hijacked before and passengers had been killed, but for the individual passenger there had always been a good chance of surviving the ordeal. The hijackers' demands would be met or not met, the plane might be stormed, casualties might occur, but the event need not be a death sentence. But almost from the first frightening moments, the passengers on Flight 93 understood that they would *not* survive if they did nothing. The news spread quickly among them. They knew the fate of two other morning planes roaring into downtown Manhattan.

There are gaps in the record of Flight 93. Some of the passengers left recorded messages, but most of the information comes from those they phoned throughout thirty-five minutes of flight. Their intent was not to leave a historical record. Many of them were simply calling to say good-bye to their husbands, their wives, their parents and children. As a result, some details will always be sketchy. We do not know how the terrorists gained access to the cockpit after the warning message had been sent, or the fate of the pilots. It seems probable that they were killed quickly, as one of the four Islamic men taking over the plane, Ziad Samir Jarrah, had trained as a pilot.

They claimed to have a bomb and guns. They certainly had utility knives and used them to terrify the passengers and herd them to the back of the plane. Ziad Jarrah, by then in the cockpit, tried to speak directly to the passengers. He told them the plane had been hijacked and that they were to sit still. It was a vital part of the plan that the passengers be controlled through fear, and he went on to say that the demands had been met and the plane was heading back to the airport. Jarrah pressed the wrong button and made part of his announcement over open air, stunning the air-traffic controllers.

At 9:35, as if to confirm his words, Jarrah turned the plane in a great sweep back toward the east—but not on the same track. The passengers did not know it then, but they were heading to Washington, D.C. One of the flight attendants managed to get through to a United Airlines call center and confirmed that the plane had been hijacked.

At 9:37, American Airlines Flight 77 crashed into the Pentagon at more than five hundred miles per hour, the third catastrophic impact of the day. Everyone on board and many more in the building were killed instantly. On Flight 93, other passengers were making calls to their families. Mark Bingham called his mother; Jeremy Glick called his wife; Lauren Grandcolas her husband.

The news of that third, terrible blow spread among the huddled group in the rear of the plane. It became clear that the hijackers were not returning to an airport. Like the three other planes, they were heading toward another target—perhaps Capitol Hill, perhaps the White House, even then being evacuated. We will never know the target with any certainty. At 9:45 Thomas Burnett called his wife again and told her that he and some others were making a plan to retake the plane.

At 9:53, passenger Linda Gronlund got through to her sister and confirmed that the passengers knew about the attacks on the World

Trade Center and the Pentagon. Neither tower had fallen at that point, but the first three attacks were complete.

The passengers in the planes that hit the towers could not have known that the hijackers were on a suicide mission. The passengers on Flight 77 didn't learn of the concerted attacks on the towers until around 9:26, just minutes before they hit the Pentagon.

On Flight 93 the passengers had those events to harden their resolve. Their flight had taken off late, which meant that they were the only ones in the air who had time to learn of the unfolding disaster and act on the information. Even so, only thirty-five minutes passed from the moment their plane was hijacked to the end.

Seven different callers told their loved ones that they were going to try to retake the cockpit. They could not fly the plane themselves, but that was a problem for afterward. They had realized by then that the plane would be used as a missile, killing hundreds more than were on board.

Few of the passengers could have expected to survive the assault on the cockpit. Though they must have hoped, they believed the hijackers had a bomb and would be likely to detonate it in desperation. No trace of explosive material was found at any of the crash sites, and it is likely that the bombs were fake, but the men and women on Flight 93

could not have known that. One phone call from the plane described them voting, making a show of hands about rushing the cockpit.

At 9:57 the assault began. Their voices, as well as the panic of the hijackers, can be heard on the recovered cockpit voice recorder. Ziad Jarrah began to roll the plane to throw the passengers off their feet. He told his companion in the cockpit to block the door as best he could, then began moving the aircraft in a violent pitching motion. Outside the cockpit, yells and thumps and the smashing of crockery can be heard.

Jarrah said: "Is that it? Shall we finish it off?"

His companion replied: "No, not yet. When they all come, we finish it off." It was 10:00.

The attack on the cockpit door continued, and one of the passengers shouted, ". . . in the cockpit. If we don't we'll all die . . ."

Another voice yelled, "Roll it," referring perhaps to a heavy trolley they were using as a battering ram against the door.

Once more Jarrah asked his companion if he should put the plane down. It is clear that the passengers were almost in. At 10:02 a hijacker called for Jarrah to "put the plane in" and shouted that Allah was great.

Flight 93 flipped over onto its back and struck farmland in Shanksville, Pennsylvania, at around 580 miles per hour. Of the four planes used as weapons, it was the only one that failed to reach its target and only then because of the wild courage of the men and women inside. It is no exaggeration to say that they gave their lives to save the lives of others.

The passengers were unarmed and unsuspecting men and women. There had never been such a concerted attack in the United States. Yet in just thirty-five minutes, they went from stunned shock to grim determination. They said their good-byes to those they loved and forced that plane to the ground.

There were many heroes made that

day, such as the emergency workers who entered the burning towers again and again to rescue dazed and injured survivors. There were also the passengers of Flight 93. There were few moments of light on such a dark day, and it is for that reason that so many have found the story inspiring. It is poignant to think that it could easily have been any one of us on that plane, suddenly wrenched out of normal life and faced with terror, anger, and ultimate consequences.

As a result of the events of 9/11, thousands more died in Afghanistan as the perpetrators were sought and their leaders punished. In 2009, at the time of this writing, that conflict continues.

Recommended
Among the Heroes: United Flight 93 and the Passengers and Crew Who Fought Back by Jere Longman
Film: *Flight 93*, directed by Peter Markle

Winston Churchill

The lecturer tonight is Mr. Winston Churchill. By his father, he is an Englishman, by his mother an American. Behold the perfect man!
                                                        —Mark Twain

Churchill is one name that has not been forgotten. With men like Marlborough and Wellington, he stands atop a pantheon of British, commonwealth, and empire heroes, and rarely a year goes by without a new book or television special on his life. For that reason, he nearly didn't make it into this book. Yet how can any list of heroes be complete without him? Long before he was prime minister, he had an extraordinary life, as a soldier, politician, and writer. As a young man he rode in one of Britain's last cavalry charges with a sword, and later he saw a nuclear bomb explode. There have been few lives in history to witness such changes. As important, he has come to represent a sense of stubborn Britishness, of indomitability and courage. His wit and intelligence were famous in his own lifetime, and when he died, the U.S. ambassador said that he was "the greatest apostle of freedom of the twentieth century. Foremost in courage, many-sided in genius."

Churchill witnessed the end of the British Empire, seeing it battered and broken in a fight to the death against Nazi Germany. That final struggle justified the centuries of empire, so that when the time came, there were men who could come home to fight: from Canada, Australia, New Zealand, America, India, Africa, and anywhere else that felt kin to the mother country. As a result of that relationship and shared history, Hitler's Reich and his grandiose dreams died with him.

Winston Churchill was born prematurely in a bedroom at Blenheim Palace on November 30, 1874. By the time he was six, the Anglo-Zulu War was being fought, and young Winston was thrilled to hear stories of the battle of Rorke's Drift. He made assegai spears out of fern stems and stalked the countryside with them.

He was a naughty child at school and earned numerous canings for his misdemeanors. He stole sugar from the school pantry and, when he was punished, destroyed the headmaster's hat in revenge. He bore a grudge against that head for many years, and when he was fully grown, he returned to the school with the intention of birching the headmaster in front of the boys. To his disappointment, the man had died long before.

At thirteen, he went to Harrow School. His prodigious memory showed itself when he won the Headmaster's Prize for memorizing *twelve hundred* lines of Macaulay's *Lays of Ancient Rome*. He was never particularly skillful on the sports field, but he devoured books, soaking up information at a terrific rate and creating the beginnings of an extraordinary general knowledge. At home he played with his vast collection of toy soldiers. When his father asked him if he wanted to join the army, Winston was overjoyed. It was many years before he discovered that his father had believed him unsuitable for anything else.

At Harrow he learned to box and fence, winning the public schools fencing championship of 1892. With his father's colleagues often in attendance at home, young Winston took a keen interest in politics from an early age. His views were Conservative, and he enjoyed lively debates, often taking the time to sit in the gallery at the House of Commons. When one of his father's friends learned that Winston had heard a speech he had made, he asked the boy what he had thought. With characteristic bluntness, Winston replied: "I concluded from it, sir, that the Ship of State is struggling in heavy seas."

He left Harrow and scraped into the Royal Military Academy at Sandhurst, where he appears to have matured almost overnight. He delighted in all things military and threw himself into learning everything he could. At the same time, his father became seriously ill. Winston and his brother John met him for the last time a month before his death in 1895.

In spring, Churchill became a subaltern in the Fourth Hussars. He was eager to see active service and used his leave to persuade a newspaper to appoint him to report on a revolt against Spanish rule in Cuba. Before he left home, Churchill gave a dinner party for those "who are yet under twenty-one years of age, but who in twenty years, will control the destinies of the British Empire." He might have meant the other diners; he certainly meant himself.

In Cuba, Churchill saw his first fighting and took part in repulsing Cuban rebels, writing about his experiences in letters to the newspaper, for which he was paid five pounds each. For his service, the Spanish authorities awarded him the Order of Military Merit, first class. In 1896, as his leave ended, he returned to his own regiment and was sent to India on a tour of duty.

British India was a strange place in those long-ago days. Churchill was introduced to the parades, the heat, polo, and boredom. It was a far-from-exciting life, and it wore on him. At only twenty-one, he wanted to see action and perhaps earn some of the glory his ancestors had won for themselves.

In 1897, when a British garrison was besieged in Afghanistan, Churchill volunteered to join punitive expeditions against the Mohmand tribes of Bajaur. He found little excitement until he joined a squadron of Bengal

Lancers and fought with them against the tribesmen. Churchill was mentioned in dispatches for his courage, though he was officially a noncombatant. When his leave expired, he had to return to India, where he wrote a book on the campaign.

He was regarded by his superiors as a young man in a hurry, a "medal-snatcher" and a nuisance. Churchill tried to find action on every leave or returned home to apply influence with those who could send him to conflicts. He was balked by Lord Kitchener, who disliked his brash self-confidence and refused to allow Churchill to take part in an expedition in Egypt against Arab forces. Kitchener's powers in Egypt did not extend to the Twenty-first Lancers, however, and Churchill managed to persuade General Evelyn Wood VC to send him out to them with the condition that if he was killed, he would pay his own funeral expenses. He became a correspondent for the *Morning Post* before he went to Cairo.

Kitchener was disgusted that the young soldier had come despite his wishes and put Churchill in charge of lame horses, following the main force as they trekked into the Sudan. However, it would be Churchill who spotted the army of sixty thousand Arab Dervishes when he rode out to reconnoiter an area. He galloped back to tell Kitchener.

The main charge of what would become known as the battle of Omdurman occurred later in the day, when four hundred Lancers, Churchill among them, attacked a vastly superior force. They crashed through the enemy, and Churchill emerged unscathed from his first major battle. He then turned back to rescue fallen men.

He returned to England as a successful author and journalist, though that reputation had only come about from his desire to see battle. In 1898 he also expressed the ambition to follow his father in a political career. At the same time, the *Daily Mail* published a piece on him as one of the most promising young men of the day. With surprisingly accurate foresight, the war correspondent wrote: "There will hardly be room for him in Parliament at thirty or in England at forty."

However, before he began his political career, Churchill returned to India to take part in the regimental polo tournament. His team won and he scored three of the goals, despite his right shoulder being torn from an old injury. With that done, he resigned his commission and completed his book on the Kitchener campaign, *The River War.*

In June 1899, Churchill launched his first campaign for Parliament, representing for Oldham. His speeches against his opponents had the wit and verve that would become his hallmark. When his opponent, Mr. Runciman, mentioned disdainfully that he had not been a swashbuckler as Churchill had, Churchill replied: "The difference between Mr. Runciman and the Lancashire Fusiliers is that, while they were fighting at Omdurman for their country, he was fighting at Gravesend for himself. And another difference between them is that, while the Fusiliers were gaining a victory, Mr. Runciman at Gravesend was being defeated."

Nonetheless, Mr. Runciman won the election, though Churchill was not particularly disheartened. The Boer War had broken out in South Africa, and he arranged to act as a war correspondent once more, traveling to Cape Town in the autumn of 1899. It would be the scene of some of his greatest adventures.

The city of Ladysmith was under siege by the Boers when Churchill joined other war correspondents and the main army. He met an old friend near the city and was invited to join a regular patrol that used an armored train to survive the Boer snipers. The train was ambushed when Boers opened up on it with two field pieces and a Maxim machine gun. The driver put on full speed, and the train struck a rock the Boers had laid on the tracks. The engine was in the middle of the train, with cars before and behind. In the impact, the front three cars were derailed and overturned. Churchill climbed out of the wreckage as the Boers opened fire on the helpless train. He ran to inspect the damage and found the driver about to run for it. As the man had already been shot, Churchill assured him "No man is hit twice on the same day" and steadied his nerves.

Churchill then ran back to report that the train could be saved if the front cars were dragged out of the way by the engine. He took command of the entire operation, with bullets whistling around him. Under his orders, the driver uncoupled the rear cars and then dragged free the one blocking the line ahead. Churchill called for volunteers as the Boer fire increased and nine men helped him shove the car off the rails. The car jammed while still on the line, and Churchill told the driver to ram it clear. By that time, the Boers had brought up their heavy guns and shells were bursting against the side of the train. In a final surge of power, the wrecked train car crunched aside.

Churchill ordered the men to push the rear trucks up to the engine, but the storm of Boer fire made it impossible. In the end, they brought their wounded onto the engine itself and Churchill told the driver to get clear, riding with him before jumping off and running back.

It was too late to save the other men. The Boers had forced them to surrender. As he lay watching, Churchill himself was captured by a Boer horseman and made a prisoner.

One of the wounded men later wrote to his mother: "If it hadn't been for Churchill, not one of us would have escaped." It was also said that if Churchill had been a regular soldier, he would have received the Victoria Cross.

Interestingly, when Churchill later met the prime minister of South Africa, General Botha, Churchill told him the story. Botha replied: "So you were the man? I was the Boer on the horse."

Churchill was held in Pretoria, with sixty other British prisoners. His captivity was not particularly harsh, and he was able to read and plan an escape. Two separate plans were abandoned, and on the third attempt, Churchill climbed onto the top of the prison wall and had to wait in agonized silence while guards walked just feet away. His companions had a compass, maps, and food, while Churchill had just four bars of chocolate in his pocket. He waited until one of them shouted a mixture of English and Latin, letting him know that the guards were watching and they could not follow. He was on his own. He could have gone back and waited for a better chance, but that was not in his character. He climbed down the outer wall and strolled past the sentry, who assumed he had every right to be there. Churchill was in Pretoria and free, but in enemy territory and unable to speak a word of Dutch.

He found the railway tracks and in darkness waited at a curve in the line where trains would slow, then jumped aboard an open car as it passed. He jumped off before dawn and began life as a hunted fugitive.

Wanted posters went up all over South Africa, and Boer newspapers were full of the escape. Meanwhile, Churchill hid by day and walked the train tracks at night, heading to the neutral frontier with Portuguese territory. For weeks he lived on whatever he could find or steal, almost starving to death. In desperation, he knocked on the door of a lonely house and, by incredible good fortune, found it owned by an Englishman, Mr. Howard.

Howard said later: "I never saw a man with the grit that Churchill has. He simply fears nothing."

Howard and a friend gave Churchill food and a revolver and hid him in a local mine for a time before finally smuggling him onto another train, under a tarpaulin. When Churchill saw that he had passed the frontier at last, he threw off the tarpaulin, stood up, fired his pistol, and shouted: "I'm free! I'm Winston bloody Churchill and I'm free!"

Of this part of his life, he said later: "I should not have been caught. But if I had not been caught, I could not have escaped and my imprisonment and escape provided me with materials for lectures and a book which brought me in enough money to get into Parliament in 1900."

His second attempt to become a Conservative MP was a success, and he made his maiden speech in 1901. It was not long before he fell out with his party and "crossed the floor" of Parliament to join the Liberals in 1904. A year later, he was appointed to government office as undersecretary for the colonies. He was promoted to the cabinet in 1908 under Prime Minister Asquith.

From the beginning, Churchill was fast on his feet in debate. He was often witty and, with his extraordinary memory, always able to answer any question with authority. In Asquith's government, he brought in laws forbidding boys under fourteen from working in mines and with David Lloyd George, then chancellor of the exchequer, created the National Insurance scheme. He was promoted again in 1910, to the Home Office, one of the most powerful positions in government. His self-confidence and energy seemed limitless. He said once that he felt "as if I could lift the whole world on my shoulders."

In 1911, Churchill became first lord of the Admiralty and did vital work refitting an obsolete navy to answer the threat of Germany in World War I. He supported the creation of new battlecruisers and submarines as well as founding the Royal Naval Air Service. In that same year, he was involved in the famous Sidney Street siege, which involved a group of armed anarchists determined to fight to the death against police in London's East End. Policemen had already been shot and killed by the time Churchill was informed. He went to the scene and authorized the deployment of Scots Guards and *a field gun* to support the police. One bullet passed through his hat while he observed. Before the big gun arrived, the building was on fire and Churchill forbade the fire department to enter the building. The authorities waited for the gang to come out through the flames, but they stayed and died inside.

Churchill's handling of the armed gang was controversial but did little to damage his reputation as a man of action as well as politics. His calm demeanor under fire was reported across the country. After the siege, a colleague inquired: "What the hell have you been doing now, Winston?" He replied: "Now, Charlie, don't be cross. It was such fun!"

When World War I broke out in 1914, Churchill had brought the fleet to full war footing. He did well in organizing the relief of the Falkland Islands from a German naval squadron. However, when an assault on the Dardanelles failed, Churchill was made the scapegoat and left the Admiralty. In self-imposed exile, he traveled to the trenches of Flanders and commanded the Sixth Battalion of the Royal Scots Fusiliers. In 1917 he was asked to return and became minister for munitions, then secretary of state for war and air.

After the First World War, Lloyd George was the Liberal prime minister. In 1921 he arranged to meet Sinn Féin president Eamon De Valera to discuss Irish independence from Britain. Northern Ireland wanted to remain British and later fought with the rest of the United Kingdom in World War II.

De Valera suspected the eventual deal would not reflect well on him and sent Irish Republican Army Commander Michael Collins to negotiate on his behalf. Lloyd George and Churchill, two of the most cunning and intelligent men in politics, brokered the deal. Collins was out of his depth from the beginning. The partition between northern and southern Ireland was confirmed and Ireland given dominion status. Collins had signed his own death warrant. He was later killed by Irish nationalists, while the "old fox," De Valera, went on to be president of Ireland.

Lloyd George's coalition government collapsed in 1922, leaving Churchill without office or a seat in Parliament. Undeterred, he rejoined the Conservative Party in 1924 and became chancellor of the exchequer under Stanley Baldwin. He presented five budgets as chancellor up to 1929, when another general election brought Labour to power.

That was the beginning of a very low period in Churchill's life. Over the next decade he was almost completely alone in warning of the dangers of Hitler's Germany. His belief that Britain was unprepared for the inevitable conflict flew in the face of government opinion, and he was considered an excitable warmonger. Still, he remained at the center of power and in 1936 helped draft the abdication speech of King Edward VIII.

In 1938, Prime Minister Neville Chamberlain famously returned from meeting Hitler in Munich with the promise that he had delivered "peace in our time." When war broke out in 1939, Churchill returned to the Admiralty and the ships at sea signaled "Winston's back." Chamberlain resigned and Churchill formed a coalition government in May 1940 to lead Britain in the war against Nazi Germany. His first speech as prime minister would include one of his most famous statements: "I have nothing to offer but blood, toil, tears, and sweat."

Bearing in mind his previous association with Ireland, it is interesting to note that during World War II, Churchill offered to give up British rule of Northern Ireland if the Irish would allow his ships and subs to use their ports. De Valera refused the offer, believing at the time that Germany would win.

The first years of the war were brutal for British forces. Churchill made his feelings clear when he said: "What is our policy? I will say: To wage war, by sea, land and air, with all our might and with all the strength that God can give us. . . . What is our aim? I can answer in one word: victory—victory at all costs, victory in spite of all terror, victory, however long and hard the road may be; for without victory, there is no survival."

Throughout 1940, German armies seemed unstoppable. France fell incredibly quickly, prompting Churchill to comment: "The Battle of France is over. I expect the Battle of Britain is about to begin."

Holland and Belgium fell to Hitler's invasion forces, and only by extraordinary exertions had the British Expeditionary Force been rescued from Dunkirk. Churchill uttered what may be his most famous words then: "We shall defend our island, whatever the cost may be, we shall fight on the beaches, we shall fight on the landing grounds, we shall fight in the fields and in the streets, we shall fight in the hills; we shall never surrender."

The battle of Britain secured air superiority in 1940, but it was almost the only moment of hope in the first disastrous years. Churchill held the nation together when all looked dark, but it was more than inspired oratory. He traveled all over the country to lift the spirits of the beleaguered people. At the same time, he was the overall commander of British Empire forces and took an interest in every tiny detail.

In 1941, Germany invaded Russia and Japan attacked America. Churchill had his grand alliance that would defeat Hitler and the beginning of the special relationship with America that survives today.

The fighting was brutal, and British possessions Hong Kong, Singapore, and Burma were lost to the Japanese. Churchill organized massive bombing raids against Germany in retaliation for the Blitz on London. At the same time, in North Africa, he removed men from command until he found one who could bring victory against Rommel's Afrika Korps: General Montgomery.

After the vital battle of El Alamein in North Africa, Churchill said: "Now this is not the end. It is not even the beginning of the end. But it is, perhaps, the end of the beginning."

Churchill met Stalin and Roosevelt in a "Three Power" conference in 1943. The tide of the war was turning, and Allied forces entered Rome in 1944, hoisting the first U.K. flag over an enemy capital. That flag was given to Churchill and hangs from a beam at his home in Kent.

The invasion of Europe from Britain in the Normandy landings was the beginning of the end for Nazi Germany. Every foot had to be taken back by force, and the death toll for Allied armies was huge. In support, Stalin overran eastern Germany and eastern Europe, creating what would become the Soviet bloc of countries for the next forty years.

Mussolini was executed by his own people in April 1945, and Hitler committed suicide in his bunker two days later. German troops throughout Europe surrendered on May 7, 1945. The following day Churchill, acclaimed as the architect of the great victory, joined the royal family on the balcony at Buckingham Palace.

Britain had endured years of war and come close to the brink of utter annihilation as a nation. At the same time, immense social forces were at work, and after the victory the voters were desperate for change. In the general election of 1945, Churchill's war government was thrown out and Labour came in.

Churchill took the defeat in the polls badly at first, but he was seventy-one years old and needed a rest. As well as painting, horse riding, and writing, he enjoyed building brick walls, finding the work peaceful. In the Commons, he warned of an "iron curtain" descending between the western and eastern Europe. As with Hitler's Germany, Churchill was one of the few with the vision to see the danger of a new and aggressive Soviet Union.

In 1951 the Conservative Party was returned to power. Labour had endured a tempestuous term, nationalizing industries and continuing food rationing long after the need for it had passed. As prime minister for the second time, Churchill enjoyed a rise in national prosperity. Queen Elizabeth II was crowned in 1953, and the country began to leave the dark years of the war behind.

Shortly afterward, Churchill's health deteriorated. He suffered a serious stroke and, though he recovered, decided to resign in 1955. The queen offered to make him a duke for his service, but he preferred to remain in the Commons until the end. After retirement, honors flooded in, including a Nobel Prize and honorary citizenship of the United States in 1963. He spent his final years in peace, in the south of France as well as England.

Winston Churchill died in his London home in 1965, so far from the years of his birth that it is easy to forget he was a Victorian and saw the end of the empire. At the express wish of the queen, he was accorded the honor of a lying-in-state and a state funeral, before being buried at Bladon, near Blenheim.

In all of British history, there are few lives that accomplished so much. He supported the morale of British people through the darkest years and defined the nation's spirit in his speeches and books as he crossed from the Victorian empire to the twentieth century.

I now put Churchill, with all his idiosyncrasies, his indulgences, his occasional childishness, but also his genius, his te-

nacity and his persistent ability, right or wrong, successful or unsuccessful, to be larger than life, as the greatest human being ever to occupy 10 Downing Street. —Roy Jenkins

Recommended
Winston Churchill by C. Bechhofer Roberts
Sir Winston Churchill: A Memorial, edited by Frederick Towers
The Wit of Winston Churchill by Geoffrey Willans and Charles Roetter
A History of the English-Speaking Peoples by Winston Churchill

The Gurkhas

The Almighty created in the Gurkha an ideal infantryman, indeed an ideal Rifleman, brave, tough, patient, adaptable, skilled in fieldcraft, intensely proud of his military record and unswerving loyalty. Add to this his honesty in word and deed, his parade perfection, and his unquenchable cheerfulness, then service with the Gurkhas is for any soldier an immense satisfaction.
—Field Marshal William Slim

The father of the authors of this book flew in Bomber Command during World War II and later in the Fleet Air Arm. One of his jobs was training parachutists, and he tells a story of a group of Gurkhas, fresh to England from Nepal to begin their training. The Gurkha soldiers spoke no English, and their senior officer only understood a few words. After a final lecture, they were taken up in a plane for the first practice drop. Even at that late stage, the RAF crew weren't at all sure the soldiers had understood what was going on. One of them went back to the waiting Gurkhas and tried to explain once more.

"We are rising to an altitude of five hundred feet," he said, "at which point, a green light will come on and you and your men will jump." He mimed jumping.

The Gurkha officer looked worried but went back to his men to explain. When he returned, he said: "Five hundred feet is too high. We are willing to try three hundred feet."

The RAF officer went pale. "You don't understand," he said. "At three hundred, your parachute will barely have time to open. You'll hit the ground like a sack of potatoes."

The Gurkha officer beamed at him and went to tell the men. They all beamed as well. They hadn't realized they would be allowed to use the parachutes at that stage of the training.

Now that story must surely seem apocryphal, but it was told at the time and it demonstrates how the British armed forces saw the regiments from Nepal—keen, tough, uncomplaining, and unbelievably courageous. They have always been held in the highest regard, a respect they have earned time and time again in their history.

The Gurkhas have been part of the British army for almost two hundred years, beginning in 1816 when the British East India Company signed the peace treaty of Sugauli with Nepal, which allowed them to recruit local men. Gurkhas had fought them to a bloody standstill on a number of occasions, and the company was very keen to have such a martial race on its side. Lieutenant Frederick Young was one of those fighting the Gurkhas in 1815. His troops ran away, and only he refused to run as he was surrounded. The Gurkhas admired his courage and told him: "We could serve under men like you." He is known as the father of the Brigade of Gurkhas. He later recruited three thousand of them and became the commander of a battalion, later named the Second King Edward VII's Own Gurkha Rifles. They still serve today as part of the Royal Gurkha Rifles.

Gurkhas are small men, drawn from a rugged and inhospitable land, the sort of herdsmen who must once have formed the backbone of Genghis Khan's armies. They are famous for carrying the kukri, a curved knife that, once drawn, must be blooded before it can be sheathed.

Along with the Sikhs, Nepalese Gurkhas remained loyal to Britain during the Indian Mutiny and have fought for Britain in every major conflict since then, winning thirteen Victoria Crosses in the process. The British officers who commanded them won another thirteen. It is part of the legend of the Gurkhas that their officers have to be as enduring and self-reliant as the men themselves, or they don't get to command.

They have seen service in Burma, Afghanistan, the northeast and northwest frontiers of India, Malta, Cyprus, China, and Tibet. At the beginning of World War I, the king of Nepal placed the entire Nepalese army at the disposal of the British Crown. More than a hundred thousand young Nepalese men fought in France and Flanders, Mesopotamia (Iraq), Persia (Iran), Egypt, Gallipoli, Palestine, and Salonika. Twenty thousand of them were killed or injured, an almost unimaginable loss to a nation with a population of just four million. In 1915 they captured and held heights at Gallipoli, some of the worst fighting in the war. It is interesting to note that when Australian infantry battalions made a suicidal charge into Turkish and German machine-gun positions, taking them after fierce fighting, they were nicknamed "the White Gurkhas" by their allies afterward.

In World War II there were 112,000 Gurkhas in the British military, serving as rifle regiments, special forces, and parachutists. In 1940, the bleakest part of the war for Britain, permission was sought to recruit another twenty battalions to match the first twenty. The Nepalese prime minister agreed, saying: "Does a friend desert a friend in time of need? If you win, we win with you. If you lose, we lose with you." Once again, the whole Nepalese army was placed under the disposal of the British Crown. They fought in all theaters of operation, from North Africa to Italy and finally Burma, where they repelled a massive Japanese invasion from Thailand.

As infantry, they have a reputation for incredible toughness, but it is not a historical footnote. In 2006, in Afghanistan, just forty Gurkhas held a police station against massed attacks by Taliban fighters over ten days. One of them, Rifleman Nabin Rai, was hit in the face by a rifle bullet but refused to leave his post. When he was dazed by another round that struck his helmet, he had a cigarette to recover, then returned to his position. The Taliban attackers eventually left to seek out an easier target, leaving a hundred of their dead behind. The Gurkhas had suffered three wounds and lost no one.

Their history abounds with such examples, including the true story from 1931 of a mule kicking a Gurkha in the head with an iron-shod hoof. He wore a sticking plaster over the gash, while the mule went lame. Another tale, from World War II, involved Havildar Manbahadur being shot through the spleen, then gashed in the head by a Japanese officer. Left for dead, he walked sixty miles to catch up to his unit. Medical orderlies told him he should have died from his wounds, but he just grinned and asked to rejoin his men.

In 1943, having understood that a soldier must never lose his weapon, one Gurkha had to be rescued by Brigadier Mark Teversham after sinking to the bottom of a river. The weight of his gun was holding him underwater, but he would not let go of it. Their reputation for stoicism and macabre humor only grew in that time.

Against the Japanese, the Gurkhas earned a reputation as relentless and skilled hand-to-hand fighters. They cleared machine-gun positions by approaching under heavy fire and then leaped among the enemy, wielding their kukris' blades with terrible efficiency. The Japanese developed a grudging respect for the fearsome little men. The British commander in Burma, Field Marshal Slim, told with relish a story of a Japanese officer who challenged a Gurkha to a duel with blades alone. The Japanese officer lunged with his sword, and the Gurkha swayed away from it, untouched. The Gurkha then stepped in close and swung his kukri.

"You missed as well," the officer said.

The Gurkha replied: "Wait till you sneeze and see what happens."

In June 1944 in Burma, a Gurkha unit was faced with Japanese tanks and unable to move forward. Bhutanese rifleman Ganju Lama went on his own with an antitank gun. Although he was shot three times and his left wrist was broken, he used the gun to destroy two tanks, then stood up with bullets whipping around him and used grenades to kill the other tank crews. Only when the way was clear for his unit to move forward did he allow his terrible wounds to be dressed. He won the Victoria Cross for that action, yet it is only one story of hundreds that go some way to explain the enormous affection and respect the Gurkhas have earned for themselves.

After Indian independence in 1947, there were ten Gurkha regiments in the army of British India. Four of them transferred to the British army as a brigade: the Second King Edward VII's Own Gurkha Rifles (the Sirmoor Rifles), the Sixth Gurkha Rifles (later Queen Elizabeth's Own), the Seventh Gurkha Rifles (later the Duke of Edinburgh's Own), and the Tenth Gurkha Rifles (later Princess Mary's Own). They would play a vital role in the Malayan emergency (1948–60) and the Brunei revolt (1962–6). They also took part in the defense of Cyprus in 1974 after a Turkish invasion and as a garrison in Belize in 1978.

In the battle for the Falkland Islands in 1982, the Gurkhas were involved in the final assault to liberate Port Stanley from Argentinian troops. They were particularly feared by the Argentinian soldiers, whose own propaganda had led them to believe the Gurkhas were savages who killed their own wounded, slit Argentinian throats, and sometimes even ate the enemy.

While the Second Scots Guards took Mount Tumbledown and the Second Para took Wireless Ridge, the Gurkhas' objective was the key position of Mount William. To the north of Tumbledown, there was a minefield the Gurkhas could either go around or feel their way through.

At dawn they chose to go through. They came under artillery fire but didn't falter as fourteen were wounded.

Meanwhile, some three hundred Argentinians were retreating before the Scots Guards when they ran into an advance Gurkha patrol. They immediately turned about and surrendered to the guards.

The main force of Argentinians on Mount William then saw that they were faced by the Gurkhas. They left their positions, threw away their rifles, and bolted for Port Stanley. The Gurkhas were bitterly disappointed to take Mount William without resistance.

"They knew we were coming and they feared us," said Lieutenant Colonel David Morgan, then commander of the Gurkha Rifles. "Of course, I think they had every ground to fear us." The Argentinian lines of defense were broken wide open.

Gurkha regiments also served in Iraq and Afghanistan at the beginning of the twenty-first century. Despite their history, they are in every way modern riflemen, but they maintain an age-old spirit and discipline. They see courage as the greatest aim and honor in life and regard those of their number who have won the Victoria Cross as an elite group of Nepalese national heroes. Every young man who joins the regiments today cherishes the idea that he may one day be part of that small, valiant number.

One problem faced by Gurkhas from World War II is that they did not qualify for a pension unless they had served a full fifteen years. Those who had fought in Malaya, Borneo, and Brunei were sent home with just a small gratuity in 1967–71 as the overall numbers were reduced. More than ten thousand of those who returned to Nepal after risking their lives for Britain are still alive today and depend on the work of charities such as the Gurkha Welfare Trust for support.

In a landmark ruling in September 2008 the British High Court ruled that Gurkha soldiers who retired before 1997 should have the right to live in Britain. That was a huge step forward for a group that has rarely been rewarded as it deserves. Even so, after many decades of being forbidden the right or the pension to live in Britain, a large number will prefer to spend their final years in Nepal, where the continuing work of British charities is vital.

Recommended
The Gurkhas by Byron Farwell
Supreme Courage: Heroic Stories from 150 Years of the Victoria Cross by General Sir Peter de la Billière
Journeys Hazardous: Gurkha Clandestine Operations: Borneo 1965 by Christopher Bullock
The Gurkha Museum, Winchester, U.K.

Horatio Nelson:
The Immortal Memory

The 29th of September, 1758: the Wife of the Rector of Burnham Thorpe Parish, of a Son.

All Saints' Church, Burnham Thorpe, Norfolk, is today much as it was in 1758 when a son of the rector and his wife was baptized and christened. The most notable additions to this quiet Anglican church since that christening are the wooden lectern and rood, carved from the original oak of HMS *Victory*. For the boy born that autumn was Horatio Nelson, destined to become the most famous naval commander in the world—with his and *Victory*'s name forever joined.

Beneath the flat skies of East Anglia, Horatio lived an ordinary boyhood. Although the family was educated, they were not wealthy. He attended local schools, went hunting for birds' nests, and pilfered apples and pears from orchards with his friends. His mother died when he was nine years old, and it was through her family that there was a connection with the sea—Captain Maurice Suckling, an uncle serving in the Royal Navy. Horatio asked his father for permission to join his uncle in a ship being commissioned for possible war with Spain over the Falkland Islands. It was agreed. In January 1771, aged twelve years and three months, Horatio Nelson joined his first ship, the sixty-four-gun *Raisonnable,* at Chatham Naval Dockyard, Kent.

Across the dock from the *Raisonnable* was the new first-rate *Victory,* a one-hundred-gun ship of the line launched in 1765 but held in reserve. There's no doubt that Midshipman Nelson noticed her. It's likely he boarded and looked her over, for she was a most impressive ship: two thousand English oak trees had been used to build her.

Five months later, Spain withdrew her claim to the Falklands and Captain Suckling and Nelson transferred to the seventy-four-gun *Triumph*. Suckling arranged for his nephew to ship for a year to the West Indies in a merchant vessel. Most seamen in the Royal Navy of that era spent time in the merchant service; it was the best training in seamanship available. One such officer, James Cook, had returned from a voyage around the world that July, and all Britain was talking about him.

A year after his return, Nelson joined an Arctic expedition seeking the Northeast Passage through the ice around the top of Russia to the Pacific. At fourteen, he wangled a berth in the bomb ketch *Carcass* as coxswain, a petty officer in charge of one of the small boats. Icebound one polar night, Nelson left the ship on foot to hunt polar bear across the sea ice. He wanted to send his father a white bearskin for his hearth, but the bear escaped when Nelson's musket misfired. Nelson himself escaped the enraged bear only after *Carcass* fired a cannon to frighten it off. Heavy ice turned the expedition back north of Norway.

At the end of 1773, Midshipman Nelson joined HMS *Seahorse*, a twenty-gun frigate in a squadron sailing to the East. He served on the *Seahorse* for two years, visiting Africa, India, and the Spice Islands before he contracted malaria and almost died. Semi-paralyzed, Nelson was invalided home but was to suffer from the aftereffects for the rest of his life. Yet only a few days after his return, five days before his eighteenth birthday in 1776, Nelson was appointed acting lieutenant to the sixty-four-gun *Worcester,* escorting convoys to Gibraltar and elsewhere. The following year, having served the required minimum six years aboard ship, he passed his lieutenant's examination.

The bitter American War of Independence was then being fought, and Nelson was posted to the West Indies station in the frigate *Lowestoffe*. In her he obtained his first command, the captured American schooner *Little Lucy*. A year later he was promoted to first lieutenant on the flagship HMS *Bristol*. In December 1778 he was promoted again, to be master and commander of the brig *Badger*, his second command. Only six months later, of just twenty years of age, Horatio Nelson was posted captain. That same year, in the far Pacific, Captain Cook was killed.

Although Nelson was "known" at the Admiralty through his uncle, promotion on the West Indies station was due to the fact he was keen, imaginative, and good at almost everything he did. Most superior officers appreciated his talents, most contemporaries enjoyed his company, and most seamen liked him and worked willingly for him because he looked after them—their health, their conditions, and their few comforts.

On being appointed to the twenty-gun frigate *Hinchinbrooke,* replacing a captain killed in action, Nelson wrote: "I got my rank by a shot killing a Post-Captain, and I most sincerely hope I shall, when I go, go out of the World the same way."

He contracted yellow fever during a combined naval and army assault up the shallows and swamps of the San Juan River on the Spanish Main. His efforts were the main reason the expedition finally succeeded in capturing Fort San Juan, but in 1780 he had to be invalided home. By the spring of 1781 he'd recovered, to be appointed captain of the frigate *Albemarle* for convoy work into the Baltic and to Canada. In 1783 a treaty with the colonial Britons was signed by which the independent United States of America was created. The *Albemarle* and many other vessels returned home and were paid off, and Nelson took leave to visit France.

Before he himself was paid off the active list, Nelson served once more on the West Indies station, from 1784 to 1787. He incurred the displeasure of British planters and traders for enforcing the new trading laws with America, and the displeasure of his king, George III, for associating with his womanizing sailor son, Prince William. On the Isle of Nevis in March 1787, Nelson married "Fanny" Nisbet, a widow with one son. Prince William gave away the bride.

In his career to that point, Nelson had accumulated some very talented friends and admirers, both senior and junior to him—Admirals Parker, Hood, and Jervis; Captains Cornwallis and Ball; Lieutenants Collingwood, Troubridge, Saumarez, Berry, and Hardy.

During the twenty-two years of French wars, these men became household names in the long fight for freedom from tyranny.

Yet in 1787, Horatio Nelson was "on the beach," a captain without a ship, living on half pay in the Burnham Thorpe parsonage with his wife, stepson, and father. He was twenty-nine years old. He was also beginning to go blind, from a then untreatable disease of the conjunctiva spreading slowly across each eye.

Nelson remained on half pay for five years, concerning himself with the conditions of farm laborers and campaigning for improvements. He thought he might never go to sea again, but in 1792 revolutionary France declared war on Austria, Sardinia, and Prussia and invaded the Austrian Netherlands. Despite Britain's neutrality in continental politics, the die was cast in early 1793, when French batteries fired upon HMS *Childers* without warning or provocation. Nelson was appointed captain of HMS *Agamemnon*.

The British government still refused to respond, but on February 1 France declared war on Britain and Holland. Thus began a world war that was fought from Ireland to Russia, from Norway to South Africa, in North and South America, in India and in Southeast Asia, and across almost every sea in the world. France further inflicted on the world a gunnery corporal named Napoléon Bonaparte, the man responsible for the greatest destruction in Europe until the rise to power of Adolf Hitler. During the war against French oppression Nelson grew to despise Bonaparte.

Ship of the line *Agamemnon* was a sixty-four-gun vessel from Hampshire, strongly built yet fast, maneuverable, and with a crew mostly of volunteers. She was Nelson's favorite command. Soon after joining, he was offered the command of a seventy-four-gun ship. He declined. In a fleet under the command of Admiral Hood in HMS *Victory*, Nelson sailed for Gibraltar and the Mediterranean.

Nelson and the *Agamemnon* were deployed continuously for three years throughout the western Mediterranean. During the capture of Corsica, Nelson received a severe wound to his right eye from a stone chip, leaving it virtually useless. However, he never wore an eye patch; it was over his weakening left eye that he occasionally wore an eyeshade to protect it from glare. At sea he usually wore a green shade beneath his cocked hat to protect both eyes. The Trafalgar Square statue depicts him accurately with no eye patch.

In the *Agamemnon* Nelson hoisted his commodore's pennant, fought a series of successful actions against the French and the Spanish, and wrote a brief autobiography, *Sketch of My Life*. A weather-beaten *Agamemnon* was sent home for a refit in 1796, and Nelson transferred his commodore's flag to HMS *Captain*. In February 1797 came the first great sea battle of the war—and of Nelson's career. It was named the battle of Cape Saint Vincent, fought in the waters off southwest Portugal.

On the morning of Valentine's Day, a Spanish fleet of twenty-seven ships of the line—the 130-gun four-deck *Santissima Trinidad*, six 112-gun ships, two 80s, and eighteen 74s—was intercepted on its passage to the English Channel by Admiral Sir John Jervis. Jervis's fleet comprised only fifteen ships of the line, including the 100-gun *Victory* and *Britannia*, three 98s, one 90, eight 74s, and one 64. As the enemy vessels gradually emerged from a bank of fog, Captain Calder in the *Victory* counted them for his admiral: "There are eight sail of the line, Sir John." "There are twenty sail of the line, Sir John." "There are twenty-five sail of the line, Sir John." "There are twenty-seven sail of the line, Sir John."

"Enough, sir. No more of that!" Jervis thundered. "If there are fifty sail, I will go through them!"

Go through them he did. The *Culloden* led the British fleet and opened fire at 11:30 A.M., splitting the Spanish line in two. The majority of Spanish vessels on the right altered course to the north, engaging the British sailing on the opposite course. Jervis ordered his captains to tack in succession to pursue the main body and to prevent the gap being closed by the eight Spanish ships on the left. Broadside after broadside drove those ships out of the battle.

Close to the rear of the British line in the north, Nelson saw that the majority of Spanish ships were attempting to escape. Disobeying orders, he hauled the 74-gun *Captain* out of the line and engaged the 130-gun *Santissima Trinidad*, the largest warship in the world.

Collingwood followed Nelson in the *Excellent*. With Troubridge in the *Culloden*, Frederick in the *Blenheim*, and Rear Admiral William Parker in the *Prince George* arriving from the south, a fierce battle within a battle took place as those five British ships attempted to stop the Spanish fleet from escaping.

All the vessels suffered heavy damage. At one stage the *Captain* was fighting five ships at once, and Nelson was wounded in the stomach by a flying splinter of wood. Then the Spanish first-rates *San Jose* and *San Nicolas* ran onto each other and were locked together. Nelson saw his chance. He steered the *Captain* onto the the *San Nicolas*. "Calling for the boarders, I ordered them to board," he wrote later.

From the *Captain*, Nelson led the British marines and seamen onto the 80-gun *San Nicolas* and captured her. Seeing no reason to stop, he then led them onto the 112-gun *San Jose* and captured her, too. On the quarterdeck of the *San Jose* he received the sword of the dying Spanish admiral and handed it to bargeman William Fearney, who "placed it, with the greatest sang-froid, under his arm." Pursuing the Spanish fleet, the *Victory* passed by and her crew lined the rails and cheered the amazing sight of the three ships all now flying Royal Navy ensigns. This unique action of boarding one enemy ship via another was referred to as "Nelson's patent bridge for boarding first-rates."

Although his understanding of tactics was supreme, he had taken an enormous risk, disobeying both Jervis's order of battle and Admiralty Fighting Instructions. Jervis had told him to use his initiative, but it might have been a court-martial offense. Instead, after the battle, Jervis welcomed him to the deck of the *Victory* with open arms. The last shots were fired at 5 P.M., and the Spanish retreated into Cadiz. They had lost four ships and three thousand men killed, wounded, or captured; the British lost no ships but seventy-three killed and four hundred wounded. Jervis was created Earl Saint Vincent, Nelson made a Knight of the Bath and, unknown to the fleet, was already promoted to rear admiral, though the news didn't arrive until April. He was just thirty-eight years old.

Elsewhere, there was mutiny in the Channel Fleet. The cause was partly due to ill treatment by a few captains but primarily to the government not paying the seamen. One of those vessels, the *Theseus,* was ordered to Jervis's fleet. Jervis transferred Rear Admiral Nelson, Captain Miller, and a handful of former *Agamemnon* seamen to her.

The *Theseus* was under-provisioned, lacked most of her military stores, had never seen action, and her seamen were still mutinous. It's indicative of Nelson's leadership and care for his men that within one month a note was left on the quarter-deck. It read: "Success attend Admiral Nelson, God bless Captain Miller, we thank them for the officers they have placed over us. We are happy and comfortable and will shed every drop of blood in our veins to support them, and the name of *Theseus* shall be immortalised as high as Captain's. Ship's Company." It was all part of what came to be called the "Nelson touch."

A month later Nelson experienced his greatest defeat. He devised and led an attempt to capture the port of Tenerife in the Canary Islands and a Spanish treasure galleon lying there. He was soundly beaten. He lost a quarter of the landing force—250 men killed or wounded—as well as his right arm. It was shattered by grapeshot and amputated below the shoulder. There was no anesthetic in those days, only the surgeon's saw, a leather pad to bite upon, and rum or opium afterward. The next day, using his left hand, he wrote a request for sick leave. Nelson was sent home to convalesce, the first time he'd been in England for more than four years.

At that stage of his life Horatio Nelson had seen action against the French and Spanish more than 120 times. He'd become the man we recognize from the portraits: slightly built, five feet six inches tall, white-haired, sightless in his right eye, impaired in his left, one-armed, with his decorations worn proudly upon his blue uniform coat. Behind this public image, he sometimes wore, for fun, a diamond wind-up clock in his cocked hat. He famously suffered from seasickness as well as the continuing effects of malaria and yellow fever, and the splinter wound to his stomach caused him great distress. He was in almost constant pain. Yet the three greatest achievements of his career, three of the most important naval battles of all time, were yet to come.

On March 29, 1798, Nelson hoisted his flag as rear admiral of the Blue—the Blue Ensign—on the *Vanguard* at Portsmouth. Through the Royal Navy, Britain was taking the offensive. Under overall command of Earl Saint Vincent, a fleet was sent back to the Mediterranean to wrest control from the French. Intelligence reports had indicated that Bonaparte was about to make a major attack there—perhaps Greece, perhaps Constantinople, perhaps Egypt—then move on India. It was a pivotal moment in world history.

Admiral of the French fleet transporting Bonaparte and his thirty-thousand-strong Army of the East was François Brueys, a very capable tactician. Skillfully, he avoided the hunting British squadrons and landed Bonaparte in Egypt. Alexandria fell by July 2, and leaving his fleet in Aboukir Bay by the estuary of the Nile River, Bonaparte marched on Cairo. That city fell on July 24, and Bonaparte declared himself a Muslim. In France he had declared himself an atheist revolutionary; during his invasion of the Italian principalities and Rome he'd become a devout Catholic.

Although the fall of Egypt was not known to Nelson, he was certain that Bonaparte was somewhere in the east and continued searching. On August 1, 1798, the lookout of HMS *Zealous* reported the topmasts of the French fleet in Aboukir Bay. Brueys had anchored hard up against sandbanks along the western side of the bay to force any attacking ships to approach from the east. He'd also landed guns on Aboukir Island at the head of the bay. Accordingly, Brueys had the majority of his men manning all the guns on the eastern, starboard, side of his ships. It was a tactical position of great strength. Nelson summoned his captains to the *Vanguard*.

In the anchorage were more than twenty-two French warships;

thirteen ships of the line comprising the 120-gun flagship *L'Orient*, three 80s, and nine 74s, as well as four large frigates, two brigs, three bomb ketches, and several gunboats. Approaching from the sea, the sun about to set, were fifteen British warships, comprising thirteen 74s, one 50, and a brig.

Brueys did not expect Nelson to attack that evening—in the dark, in an uncharted bay, in shallow water, outnumbered and outgunned. However, at 5:30 P.M. Nelson signaled his fleet: "Form line of battle as most convenient." The 74s swept past Aboukir Island into the darkening bay.

Almost immediately, the *Culloden* went aground to become a helpless spectator of the battle. Brueys now had 250 more guns than Nelson. As the remaining twelve British 74s reached the head of the French line, they split into two divisions; six and the 50 taking positions along the eastern side of the French fleet as expected, while the other six proceeded along the western side—between the French and the sandbanks. Nelson had told his captains: "Where there is room for a French 74 at single anchor to swing, there is room for a British 74 to attack." There was. The first shot was fired at 6:28 P.M.

Despite his careful preparations, Brueys's ships were attacked on both sides. Nelson leapfrogged his ships along the enemy line, sweeping the ships from port and starboard with broadside after terrible broadside, destroying or capturing one ship after another. The *Conquérant* surrendered after twelve minutes. By 8 P.M., four more had surrendered. Nelson was once again wounded, cut to the bone above his left, good eye. Bleeding heavily and severely concussed, he was carried below to the surgeon and the horrors of the cockpit.

In *L'Orient*, Brueys was also injured, both his legs cut off below the knee by shot. The French ships surrendered or fought on until they were incapable, mastless hulks. After intense gunnery from HMS *Bellerophon*, *Swiftsure*, and *Alexander*, *L'Orient* caught fire. Brueys was dead. In the *Vanguard*, Nelson insisted on being helped back to the quarterdeck.

The fire spread in the enormous French flagship until the flames illuminated the battle like a giant candle. It was soon evident that there could be only one outcome. Nelson and the captains of nearby British ships lowered their boats to rescue the French seamen leaping into the dark waters. Shortly after 10 P.M. the fierce blaze reached the magazine.

The mighty *L'Orient* disintegrated in a shattering explosion that was heard thirteen miles away in Alexandria. Flying debris set the *Swiftsure* and the *Alexander* briefly alight. All ships stopped firing for about twelve minutes, in awe at the destruction. With *L'Orient* went gold plate and bullion looted by Bonaparte from Malta. Only seventy of her crew were found by the British boats.

The great battle resumed, continuing through the warm night. The perspiring crews, stripped to the waist with handkerchiefs bound over their ears, worked their guns continuously. The tongues of flame illuminated the darkness like a series of paintings. By midmorning, eleven French ships of the line had been captured or destroyed, the two that escaped being captured shortly afterward. Two frigates were also destroyed. It's estimated that 1,700 French seamen lost their lives, 1,500 were wounded, and 3,000 taken prisoner. Not one British ship was lost, although 218 men were killed and 678 wounded.

The battle of the Nile is the most comprehensive naval victory ever achieved, and its effects were immense and far-reaching. The Royal Navy had taken control of the Mediterranean. Bonaparte and his Army of the East were isolated, and the Egyptians and Arabs willingly turned against him. Eventually, Bonaparte abandoned his army and fled back to France in a fast frigate, a Muslim no longer. A force from India under General Abercrombie later disposed of this army. In thanks to Nelson and Abercrombie for their liberation from the French, Mohammad Ali, the viceroy of Egypt, presented to Britain Cleopatra's Needle, from 1500 B.C. It stands today on the Victoria Embankment in London.

Other countries saw that the French could be defeated, inspiring Austria and the Italian states to resume the struggle. Although there would be a further seventeen years of warfare, Nelson and the navy had shown that victory was possible.

Overnight, Nelson became a hero to Britain and Europe. He was created Baron of the Nile and of Burnham Thorpe, a wonderfully unlikely combination of place-names.

Nelson's private life also changed. In Naples, he began the affair that lasted the rest of his life—with Emma Hamilton, wife of British ambassador William Hamilton, Nelson's friend. The affair caused society outrage, yet the three lived much of their lives together and remained steadfast friends until their deaths. With Emma, Nelson had his only child, Horatia.

In 1801, a "treaty of armed neutrality" among several Baltic Sea nations led by Russia had closed the Baltic trade to Britain. The trade in timber, flax, tar, and other supplies was vital for the navy to continue the fight against Bonaparte. Russia seized three hundred British merchant ships, while Denmark closed all her ports. The treaty was effectively an alliance with France. Britain sent a fleet to the Baltic under Admiral Hyde Parker with Nelson, now vice admiral, second in command.

Negotiations between Parker and the Danish court failed in March, and an attack on Copenhagen began. The Danes had protected their port capital by anchoring their ships in an unbroken line of floating batteries and gunboats between the city and the Oresund Strait, which led out to sea. There would be no British attack to both sides of their fleet here. The channel markers had also been removed, yet Nelson had a plan.

The Danes expected the British to attack from the north, the main channel into Copenhagen, whereas Nelson planned to sail a division of ships through a narrow channel outside and attack from the south. Admiral Parker's division would still attack through the main channel from the north to engage the formidable guns of Fort Trekroner.

Nelson shifted his flag to the 74-gun *Elephant* for the battle. In all, the Danish had 380 guns, the British 400, but the Danish had immense superiority in the caliber—the size—of their guns. In addition, Fort Trekroner, the ships, floating batteries, and gunboats were continually replenished with fresh men and ammunition from Copenhagen. Nelson relied upon the superior rate of fire of his seamen to counter these disadvantages.

On the morning of April 2, Nelson sailed ten 74s, one 54, and one 50 to the southern and central Danish defenses. Positioned behind the *Elephant* in the 54-gun *Glatton* was Captain Bligh of the *Bounty* mutiny. Seven bomb ketches firing mortars were anchored beyond the *Elephant*.

Battle commenced at 10:05 A.M. but Nelson's plan had to be changed immediately. Parker could not bring his ships down from the north because of a dead foul wind, while three of Nelson's 74s went aground in the unmarked channel and were out of the battle. Nelson now had only seven 74s and fewer guns to attack the Danes. He sent five frigates to the north to prevent any Danish ships from coming south against him.

In the chill Baltic spring, the great guns thundered outside Copenhagen, the Danish putting up a strong resistance. Firing continued uninterrupted until 1 P.M., when Admiral Parker sent his famous signal of recall.

In fact Parker was not retreating; he was shouldering the blame for what he thought might become a defeat. Both Danes and Britons were suffering heavy losses in what was simply a slugging match, for no further maneuvering was possible in the confined waters. By his signal, Parker gave Nelson the opportunity to withdraw under his commander's orders if he wished.

Nelson said to the captain of the *Elephant*: "You know, Foley, I have only one eye—I have a right to be blind sometimes." Then he put his telescope to his blind right eye and exclaimed: "I really do not see the signal!" The expression "turning a blind eye" entered the language.

Gradually the fire from the Danish ships and batteries slackened. The flagship *Dannebrog* caught fire, struck her colors, and drifted out of control. Like *L'Orient,* she blew up, but British boats were prevented from rescuing her crew because of fire from the Danish shore batteries. By 2:30 P.M. the Danish firing had almost stopped. Nelson offered a truce, which at just after 4 P.M. was accepted, and an armistice was later negotiated. Seventeen Danish ships were captured, burned, or destroyed, with a loss of almost 1,700 men killed or wounded and 3,500 taken prisoner. Yet again Nelson lost not one vessel, although 941 British were killed or wounded.

It was a brutal battle and one that both nations—usually friends and allies—regretted having to fight. It's indicative that only two honors were awarded for the battle of Copenhagen. Nelson was made viscount and his second in command, Rear Admiral Graves, invested with the Order of the Bath. Yet the victory was vital to the progress of the war against France. It kept the Scandinavian countries and Russia neutral, it maintained Britain's Baltic trade, and it affirmed that, although Bonaparte's armies ruled the continent, the Royal Navy controlled the seas. French military dictatorship ended where the sea was deep enough for Britain to float a boat.

The 1802 Peace of Amiens lasted barely a year before Bonaparte broke it. He had used the peace to rebuild his navy, invade Switzerland, the Netherlands, and Elba, and assemble some 7,000 barges to carry the 200,000-strong Grand Army across the English Channel to invade Britain. In May 1803 war resumed.

Nelson hoisted his flag in the refitted *Victory* as Vice Admiral of the Red—the famous red ensign now used by the merchant navy. Saint Vincent was at the Admiralty, Admiral Cornwallis was in charge of the English Channel and Western Approaches, and Nelson was given charge of the Mediterranean.

Despite controlling the seas, Britain remained in a critical situation. A change of wind might blow the Royal Navy blockading fleets away and allow the rebuilt French and Spanish fleets out of port. If they could combine and take control of the English Channel for a single day, Bonaparte might slip his army across and French boots would march up Whitehall.

Cornwallis's brief was to blockade the French fleet in Brest and control the Western Approaches, while Admiral Keith's division held the channel. Nelson's orders were to blockade the French fleet in Toulon. With Saint Vincent at the Admiralty, those four men controlled the destiny of the world. A single mistake, a single error of judgment, would have tipped Europe into a military abyss.

Nelson commanded the *Victory*, nine ships of the line, a frigate, and two sloops. Captain of the *Victory* was Thomas Hardy, Nelson's old friend who'd been present at both the Nile and Copenhagen. For two years the blockades were maintained, two years in which the British fleets were continuously at sea. Such a time at sea without refitting in a dockyard has never been surpassed by any fleet. Those square-rigged sailing ships, constantly patrolling the channel, off Brest, off Cadiz, and in the Mediterranean, were the "wooden walls" of Britain. Nelson never left the *Victory,* though his eyesight deteriorated further and his stomach wound bothered him constantly.

Finally, in April 1805, under the very capable Admiral Villeneuve, the French fleet slipped out of Toulon while the majority of Nelson's ships were taking on water. A great chase ensued—over the western Mediterranean, through the Strait of Gibraltar, across the Atlantic to the West Indies, and back to Ferrol in northern Spain by the end of July. Yet nothing had changed. The French fleet still avoided major action, the French army remained camped by the channel ports, and the invasion barges sat waiting. Nelson was given leave and set foot off the *Victory* for the first time in two years.

At the end of August, Villeneuve slipped his fleet south to Cadiz, where, with Spanish reinforcements, it numbered more than forty ships. Bonaparte ordered him to combine with the fleet in Brest and gain control of the English Channel.

Nelson was recalled from leave. When he rejoined the *Victory* at Portsmouth, a large crowd collected. Some were in tears, some cheered and lifted their children high to see him, others knelt and blessed him as he passed. He said to Hardy: "I had their huzzas before. I have their hearts now." The *Victory* arrived off Cadiz on September 28.

The combined French and Spanish fleets under Villeneuve's command put to sea on October 19 and 20 and assembled south of Cadiz. The British under Nelson lay out of sight, while his inshore frigates relayed the enemy's movements.

During the night, Nelson maneuvered his fleet. At daybreak on the twenty-first they were positioned so that if Villeneuve continued south to Gibraltar, he would have to fight, if Villeneuve sailed northwest to the channel, he would have to fight, and if Villeneuve returned to Cadiz, he would also have to fight. Importantly, Nelson had maintained the commanding, windward position.

As Nelson had predicted, when Villeneuve sighted the twenty-six waiting British ships at dawn he altered course to return to Cadiz. At 5:40 A.M. Nelson signaled his captains: "Form the order of sailing in two columns." This signal was repeated at 6 A.M. so that the captains knew this was also the order of battle.

In the *Victory*, Nelson commanded the northern column of eleven ships of the line, which included the *Temeraire*. Vice Admiral Collingwood, second in command in the *Royal Sovereign*, commanded the southern column of fifteen ships of the line. A latecomer, the 64-gun *Africa*, was ten miles to the northwest, sailing to join Nelson.

His Majesty's ships were *Victory, Royal Sovereign, Britannia, Temeraire, Revenge, Prince, Tonnant, Belle Isle, Mars, Neptune, Spartiate, Defiance, Conqueror, Defense, Colossus, Leviathan, Ajax, Achille, Bellerophon, Minotaur, Orion, Swiftsure, Polyphemus, Agamemnon, Dreadnought, Thunderer,* and *Africa.*

East and downwind of the Royal Navy, the French and Spanish fleet of thirty-three ships of the line sailed northward in a curved formation, roughly two abreast. It included Villeneuve's flagship, the *Bucentaure,* and the largest and second-largest warships in the world, the 130-gun *Santissima Trinidad* and the 112-gun *Santa Ana.* The enemy fleet had superiority by six ships of the line, 474 guns, and 8,124 men. In addition, Villeneuve had seven frigates to Nelson's four.

A total of seventy-one warships, sixty of them ships of the line, slowly converged at the shoals of Cape Trafalgar off Spain on the morning of October 21, 1805—the day ever after known as Trafalgar Day. Although the wind was only light from the west-northwest, drawing the fleets together at just one and a half knots, the swell was gradually increasing, indicating a coming gale. It would blow hard by the end of the day. The British ships—flying the white ensign for easy identification—set all sail, including stunsails, instead of the usual, reduced fighting sails so as to close on the enemy as quickly as possible. In the tense waiting Nelson remarked to his officers: "I'll now amuse the fleet," and so was hoisted the most famous naval signal ever made.

It began as "Nelson confides that every man will do his duty." At the suggestion of another officer Nelson amended it to "England confides that every man will do his duty" (there was a single code flag meaning "England" but not for "Britain" or "Nelson") and, at the suggestion of the flag lieutenant in order to use even fewer flags, it was finally hoisted as "England expects that every man will do his duty." The fleet cheered, although Collingwood said: "I wish Nelson would stop signaling. We all know well enough what we have to do."

The plan of battle, an improvement on the battle of Saint Vincent, was already agreed. Instead of one column, two British columns would break the enemy line from windward, turn port and starboard to lay alongside from leeward, and so prevent the enemy from escaping downwind. It was simple and brilliant. Nelson's last words to his senior officers were: "No captain can do very wrong if he places his ship alongside that of an enemy."

In his diary he wrote the prayer he had composed that morning: "May the Great God, whom I worship, grant to my country and for the benefit of Europe in general a great and glorious victory, and may no misconduct in anyone tarnish it, and may humanity after victory be the predominant feature in the British Fleet. For myself, individually, I commit my life to Him who made me and may His blessing light upon my endeavours for serving my country faithfully. To Him I resign myself and the just cause which is entrusted to me to defend. Amen, amen, amen."

It was Collingwood in the 100-gun *Royal Sovereign* who first came under fire, just before noon, from the 112-gun *Santa Ana*. Minutes later the *Victory,* feinting as though to attack the head of the enemy fleet, came under fire from several ships. Her wheel was destroyed and she had to be steered by emergency tackle from below. The *Royal Sovereign* broke the enemy line astern of the *Santa Ana,* the eighteenth ship, into which Collingwood fired double-shotted broadsides.

Nelson steered the *Victory* back toward the 120-gun *Santissima*

Trinidad and the 80-gun *Bucentaure,* thirteenth in the line. After sustaining twenty minutes of unanswered fire, the *Victory* passed astern of the *Bucentaure* to fire a running port broadside, double-shotted, through Villeneuve's stern windows and the entire length of the vessel. French reports state that twenty guns were destroyed and four hundred men killed or wounded from that first broadside alone.

The *Victory* passed on, turned alongside the *Redoutable,* and fought that ship with her starboard guns while her port guns fought the *Santissima Trinidad.* The *Redoutable* under Captain Lucas was one of the best-manned French ships, and it was hard going for the *Victory*—she was almost boarded—until HMS *Temeraire* approached and fired a series of broadsides into the *Redoutable.* Then the *Fougueux* came to the *Redoutable*'s assistance and the four vessels fought it out for a further three hours. One after another, the British ships broke the line, turned, and engaged one or more enemy ships, until the ships and the sea itself were obscured by greasy cannon smoke.

At about 1:15 P.M., on the quarterdeck of the *Victory,* Nelson was shot. A marksman above in the mizzenmast of the *Redoutable*—her only surviving mast—fired and the musket ball passed through the gold epaulette on Nelson's left shoulder. It broke two ribs, severed a main branch of the pulmonary artery to the heart, and continued on to break two vertebrae. He sank to his knees and then slid to the deck as Hardy went to his assistance. "They have done for me, at last," Nelson said to him. He was carried below to the cockpit—on the way ordering damaged tiller ropes to be repaired—but there was nothing surgeon Beatty could do for him.

Nelson asked for Hardy to come to him, but the fighting was fierce. At 1:45 P.M. Villeneuve surrendered the flagship *Bucentaure* to HMS *Conqueror.* The *Bucentaure* had been dismasted, and her decks and gangways were filled with wreckage and the dead. At 2:15 P.M., the *Santa Ana* struck her colors to the *Royal Sovereign.* It wasn't until the *Fougueux* and the *Redoutable* surrendered to the *Victory* and the *Temeraire* that Hardy could leave the quarterdeck at 2:20 P.M.

"Well, Hardy, how goes the battle?" Nelson asked weakly. "How goes the day with us?" Hardy reported that twelve or fourteen enemy ships were already captured, but another five were bearing down upon the *Victory*. "I hope none of our ships have struck, Hardy?"

"No, my lord," Hardy replied, "there is no fear of that." Hardy shook his friend's hand and returned to the deck.

Some fifty minutes later Hardy returned to the surgeon's cockpit, took and held Nelson's cold hand, and this time was able to congratulate him on a brilliant victory. The Royal Navy had carried the day, again without the loss of a single ship. The news of Nelson's mortal wound was passed only to Collingwood in the *Royal Sovereign*.

"Don't throw me overboard, Hardy," Nelson whispered, and then: "Take care of my dear Lady Hamilton. . . . Kiss me, Hardy." The tall, angular Hardy knelt down and kissed his cheek. Nelson murmured: "Now I am satisfied; thank God, I have done my duty." Hardy stood gazing at his friend for a moment and then knelt again and kissed his admiral's forehead. "Who is that?" asked Nelson. It appears his sight had gone.

"It is Hardy," the captain replied.

"God bless you, Hardy." Then Hardy returned to the quarterdeck.

Nelson lingered a little longer, saying again: "Thank God, I have done my duty." The *Victory*'s logbook records in pencil: "Partial firing continued until 4.30 P.M., when a victory having been reported to the Right Hon. Lord Viscount Nelson, KB, and Commander-in-Chief, he died of his wound."

At 5 P.M. there was a massive explosion. The French *Achille*, dismasted and on fire, had blown up. The tally that day was twenty-eight French and Spanish ships of the line surrendered and one destroyed. Eleven of those surrenders, including the *Santa Ana*, escaped during the gale to reach Cadiz. One was wrecked on the beach, while the remainder were found to be so severely damaged that they never put to sea again. In addition, three more French ships of the line were wrecked in an attempt to retake captured French ships the following day, while the final four ships that escaped to the south were captured fourteen days later.

Ultimately, twenty-six enemy ships were captured or destroyed in the battle of Trafalgar, 5,860 French and Spanish killed or wounded, and 20,000 taken prisoner. No British ship was lost, but 1,600 seamen were killed or wounded. The battle of Trafalgar was Nelson's third total victory.

That night, when the gale lashed the fleets and the British seamen risked their lives to rescue French and Spanish crews from their battered ships, it was observed with dismay that the three admiral's lanterns at the stern of HMS *Victory* were not lit.

Nelson's body was preserved in a cask of brandy and returned to Britain. Battle-hardened, tarred, and pigtailed sailors wept when they learned of his death. One wrote home: "All the men in our ship are such soft toads, they have done nothing but Blast their Eyes and cry ever since he was killed. God bless you! Chaps that fought like the Devil sit down and cry like a wench." Britain mourned.

On January 9, 1806, in the first state funeral for a commoner, Horatio Nelson—in a coffin made of timber from *L'Orient*—was placed in a tomb of black marble in the crypt of Saint Paul's Cathedral, exactly below the center of the dome. He was posthumously created earl. Memorials to Captains Duff of the *Mars* and Cooke of the *Bellerophon,* who also died at Trafalgar, are nearby. So also is the modest tomb of Admiral Collingwood. Succeeding Nelson in the Mediterranean, controlling all the seas and coasts from Gibraltar to Turkey, Collingwood literally worked himself to death only five years later in the cause of freedom.

Nelson and his "band of brothers" gave Britain command of the seas for some 140 years. The famous uniform worn by sailors of the Royal Navy, most commonwealth navies, and copied by almost every other navy in the world remembers Admiral Nelson. The three white stripes around the border of the shoulder flap record the three great victories of the Nile, Copenhagen, and Trafalgar. The black silk neck scarf echoes the mourning bands worn by the seamen who pulled the gun carriage carrying his coffin, from Whitehall steps to the Admiralty and Saint Paul's.

Horatio Nelson's most enduring qualities were his humanity and care of others—the enemy as well as his own men—and a leadership inspired by love rather than dominance. Lord Montgomery of Alamein judged him on all counts to be "supreme among captains of war." In the French language, a sudden decisive blow is called a "coup de Trafalgar." At Trafalgar Day dinners, the toast is a unique silent toast—to "the Immortal Memory."

HMS *Victory* is now preserved in Portsmouth as she fought at Trafalgar and is the honored permanent flagship of the commander in chief of the Naval Home Command. She is the oldest commissioned vessel in the world. Because of battle, decay, and rot from over 250 years, little of the original oak remains today. Yet, in All Saints' Parish Church, Burnham Thorpe, Norfolk, you can touch still the timber that was afloat off Cape Trafalgar on October 21, 1805.

Recommended
The Authentic Narrative of the Death of Lord Nelson
by William Beatty
The Life of Nelson by Robert Southey
Nelson and His Captains by Ludovic Kennedy
Nelson the Commander by Geoffrey Bennett
Trafalgar Square, London
HMS *Victory*, HM Naval Dockyard, Portsmouth, Hampshire, U.K.
The Royal Naval Museum, Portsmouth, Hampshire, U.K.
The National Maritime Museum, Greenwich, London
Chatham Naval Dockyard, Chatham, Kent, U.K.
Saint Paul's Cathedral, London
Guildhall Monument, Guildhall, London
Trafalgar Cemetery, Gibraltar, U.K.

The Marines at Iwo Jima

T he order to land was given at 0630 hours.
At 0902 the first landing craft reached the shore. At 0915 the first enemy mortar rounds crashed into the marines and corpsmen struggling up the steep, soft volcanic-ash beach. In two hours the shoreline was a mass of floundering equipment—jeeps, field guns, tanks, bulldozers, amtracks, and men, hefting their individual eighty-pound loads. The Japanese pounded them with artillery, mortar, and machine guns. It was February 19, 1945. Operation Detachment, the battle for Iwo Jima, had begun.

By February 1945 in World War II, the Allied navies, armies, and air forces were in ascendency over the fascist Axis powers.

In western Europe, American, British, and Canadian armies gathered themselves for the final assault into Nazi Germany and Austria, and in southern Europe they were poised for complete victory. In eastern Europe the Soviet army

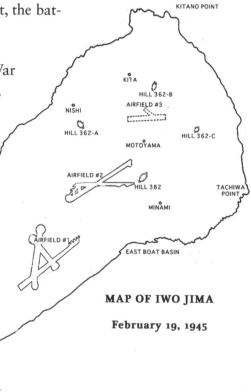

MAP OF IWO JIMA

February 19, 1945

paused outside Dresden before its advance on Berlin. Battles had to be fought and won, but the end of six years of war was at last in sight. In the Far East, though, in the war against Japan, the situation was not so clear-cut.

In Southeast Asia, the British Fourteenth Army under General Slim was fighting steadily southward through the Burmese jungle to liberate Rangoon. In the southwest Pacific, American, Australian, and New Zealand armies under General MacArthur were advancing northward from New Guinea to liberate New Britain and the Philippines, while in the north Pacific, American and Canadian troops were advancing through the Aleutian Islands.

In the tropical central Pacific, however, the going was very tough. After the 1942 stand at Guadalcanal in the Solomon Islands, the U.S. Navy, Marines, and Air Force under Admiral Nimitz had island-hopped westward and northward across the Pacific Ocean. Island by island, atoll by atoll, the Pacific was liberated from Japanese occupation. Now, for the first time, American forces were to invade Japanese territory—the island of Iwo Jima, only 660 miles south of Tokyo. Japanese soldiers had fought fiercely before, but their resistance at Iwo Jima was to be profound. Here was some of the bitterest fighting of the entire war.

Iwo Jima lay halfway between the liberated Mariana Islands to the south and the Japanese mainland to the north. It was strategically important for several reasons. It was the next stage in the island hop to the Japanese mainland and, with Okinawa Island, formed part of the Japanese inner-defense system. This had to be punctured to reach Japan. In addition, Japan had built three airfields on the island, which were needed by the air force for its long-range P-51 Mustang fighters. From these airfields, the British-designed Mustangs would be able to protect the Boeing Superfortress bombers attacking Japan from Guam, Saipan, and Tinian. The Japanese knew the importance of holding Iwo Jima.

"Iwo Jima" means "sulphur island." The island supplied Japanese industry with sulfur, and from its mines and caves, from fissures in the bare volcanic rock itself, sulfur gas constantly seeped into the air.

Shaped like an ice-cream cone and measuring four and a half by two and a half miles, this gray, brown, and black Pacific island is no tropical paradise. At the narrow base of the cone, the southern tip, rises the extinct conical volcano Mount Suribachi. At the broad top of the cone, the northern end, cliffs rise from the sea to a domed plateau. In 1945 there was an almost total lack of vegetation and no water. The Japanese relied upon rainwater collected in cisterns.

Defending Iwo Jima was Lieutenant General Tadamichi Kuribayashi, in command of almost 22,000 soldiers of the Imperial Army. Surviving documents show that Kuribayashi knew that his forces would, eventually, lose to the invading Americans. He'd been told by Japanese High Command to make the island impregnable, for once the Americans attacked, there would be no resupply or reinforcement from Japan. He had a few light tanks—under the command of Lieutenant Colonel Baron Nishi, a gold medal winner at the 1932 Los Angeles Olympic Games—but all his aircraft had been withdrawn for the defense of the mainland. All civilians had been evacuated.

His battle plan, therefore, was for every man to fight to the death. He wanted to cause so many American casualties—ten enemy dead for every Japanese—that an Allied invasion of Japan would be too costly to consider. A negotiated surrender would thus be possible, and the sacred Japanese mainland would remain inviolate.

Kuribayashi pre-ranged and targeted the whole island from numerous concealed artillery, mortar, and rocket positions. The surface was strewn with land mines. The caves and sulfur mines were converted and strengthened into a defensive network of eight hundred concealed pillboxes, artillery emplacements, antiaircraft batteries, mortar posts, and fortified heavy machine-gun nests and rocket bunkers. They were connected by covered trenches and miles and miles of tunnels, some with underground living quarters. One complex was seventy-five feet deep, held two thousand troops, and had a dozen exits. As one marine commented, "The Japanese weren't on Iwo Jima, they were *in* Iwo Jima."

Admiral Spruance of the Fifth Fleet commanded the American invasion force. He'd assembled 450 vessels, 482 landing craft, and 82,000 men in a fleet that took some thirty days sailing to reach Iwo Jima. The expeditionary troops were under overall command of Lieutenant General Smith, USMC, while Major General Harry Schmidt led the invading marines, navy corpsmen, Seabees, and Pioneers. These were a combination of experienced and newly trained servicemen.

Bombing of Iwo Jima had begun in August 1944, but from December to February it was attacked by aircraft and U.S. Navy guns for seventy-two consecutive days. In the final three days, from February 16 to 19, six battleships and five heavy cruisers bombarded Japanese positions with ten thousand shells. Although it was the heaviest naval bombardment of the war, it wasn't enough. The marines had wanted a longer bombardment, yet that wouldn't have been enough either.

The British army discovered at the 1916 battle of the Somme that the heaviest artillery bombardment is not effective against prepared and reinforced underground positions. It's not a pleasant time for the defenders, but they simply snug down until the bombardment stops. At Iwo Jima, American intelligence had also underestimated the strength of the Japanese garrison by about 70 percent. To conquer the island's eight square miles it was expected to take four days, a maximum of a week. But in this individual fight to the death all those calculations had to be discarded.

In their twill uniforms, the Marine Fourth and Fifth Divisions landed on the black, volcanic southeastern beaches of Iwo Jima on February 19, 1945, while the Third Division was held in reserve offshore. Operation Detachment had begun. They found that a beach of volcanic ash and dust doesn't compact under weight and pressure like a sand beach. Movement became two steps forward, one step back as the first wave of men struggled through the ash slurry to reach the initial ridge. From higher ground, Japanese machine-gun fire cut them down in swathes, the survivors pinned behind the ridge.

Below, the beach became clogged with succeeding men and

equipment, while enemy artillery, mortars, and antitank guns "walked" their shells along the numerous targets. If the marines couldn't break out soon, disaster threatened.

With considerable courage and heavy casualties, the "leather-necks" forced themselves over that initial bullet-swept ridge and fought their way through the first Japanese defenses. By the close of the day, thirty thousand men had been successfully landed, a small beachhead had been established, and some marines had actually reached the opposite western shore.

They'd suffered a total of 2,240 casualties, including 501 killed. Two Medals of Honor had already been earned. The ferocious fighting continued throughout the night, but the Japanese refused to be drawn into the open. It was a warning of the battle to come.

By the close of the second day, for a further thousand casualties, the Fifth Division had advanced south and west to isolate Mount Suribachi, while the Fourth had advanced north and west to capture the southernmost airfield. Both advances remained under twenty-four-hour Japanese artillery, mortar, and machine-gun fire.

Offshore, the navy was radioed the coordinates of Japanese positions and pounded them with its heavy guns, while carrier aircraft attacked them with torpedoes, napalm, and rockets. The fleet came under attack just once, on the twenty-first, from suicide kamikaze "divine wind" aircraft from Okinawa. The aircraft carrier *Bismarck Sea* was sunk and the carrier *Saratoga* severely damaged and forced to retire to Pearl Harbor, while *Lunga Point* was damaged but remained operational.

At 550 feet high and with protected gun emplacements, Mount Suribachi in the south was like a medieval fortress. Despite heavy naval and aircraft bombing, its guns continued to wreak havoc on the landing beach and the marine advance. Somehow, Suribachi had to be taken.

On the third day, the Twenty-eighth Regiment of the Fifth Division assaulted the slopes of the heavily defended volcano. After two days of uphill fighting, marines of the Second Battalion at last reached the summit in drizzling rain. Although the mountain wasn't cleared of the enemy, they raised a small Stars and Stripes on a length of broken water pipe. It was 1020 on the morning of February 23.

The flag was seen by the men on the landing beaches. It was seen by the Fourth Division, then fighting for the second airfield. It was seen by the men at sea. They cheered while the ships blew their sirens and horns. Although it was the day when they were expected to have already captured most of Iwo Jima, it was a seminal moment for them all. "We knew then we'd eventually take the island," said James Johnson of the Fourth Division.

Two hours later, while still fighting Japanese snipers for total control of Suribachi, a larger eight-foot flag from a landing craft replaced the first flag. It was this second flag raising that photographer Joe Rosenthal captured in his renowned photograph, instinctively snapping his shutter as he turned around from a discussion.

As the photograph was syndicated overnight across America, the six men who raised that second flag became household names. They were marine privates Harlon Block, Rene Gagnon, Ira Hayes, Franklin Sousley, and Michael Strank and navy corpsman medic John Bradley. The battle on Suribachi continued as Japanese soldiers fought on until killed or sealed in their caves.

"In one cave we counted one hundred and forty-two Japs," said Bradley. "And the flamethrowers did a fine job on top of the mountain. We tried to talk them out. They wouldn't come out, so then we used the flamethrowers as a last resort." This tactic became common throughout the long battle to come.

"It was inhuman," recalled another marine, but tank flamethrowers and portable throwers—shooting jets of napalm—were the only way to defeat soldiers fighting from fortified caves, tunnels, and pillboxes. The enemy was determined to literally fight to the death.

Meanwhile, around the second airfield at the foot of the central plateau, attack after attack by the Twenty-first Regiment and tanks were beaten off by the Japanese defenders. The airfield was ringed by pillboxes, and the Japanese used to advantage their prepared positions as well as the heights overlooking the airfield.

By the twenty-fourth, Major General Schmidt realized that the Japanese defense of Iwo Jima had been vastly underestimated and called for his reserves. The fresh Third Division was sent in between the Fourth and Fifth to attack the Japanese center. On the twenty-seventh the second airfield and the overlooking hills were finally captured, but one company of the Third Division lost three successive commanders in those bloody days. Hill 362 was nicknamed "the Meat Grinder"; more than two hundred marines were killed there in just three hours of fighting.

The battle for Iwo Jima had become a war of attrition. Advancing literally yard by yard, the marines would force the Japanese soldiers from one position only for them to retire to the next prepared defense, so that the whole process had to be repeated over and over again. Even scooping out foxholes was difficult: more than a foot below the surface, the volcanic ash was too hot to stand on in boots, let alone lie down in. Even tanks could only crawl at low speed across the rocky terrain.

Each battalion had its specific navy ship supporting it from the sea, laying down radio-directed artillery support as close as two hundred yards from them. Immediately behind the marines, Seabee bulldozers cleared new dirt roads to bring up tanks, more troops, supplies, and water, and to carry back the dead and wounded. The Pioneers also began clearing and repairing the southern airfield. By March 3, the Fifth Division had reached the third-northernmost airfield on the plateau and placed that under attack.

The battle for Iwo Jima was unique in that everywhere on the island, even in areas supposedly cleared of enemy soldiers, the marines and others were still exposed to Japanese pre-ranged artillery fire as well as surprise attacks. Kuribayashi's battle plan was for many of his soldiers to remain hidden underground as the advance passed over them, then to reappear, *behind* American lines.

For the marines this meant that any movement in front was probably the enemy but might be other marines advancing through the rocks. Movement behind them might be the enemy coming out from hiding to attack. It was nerve-racking. Both Japanese and marine casualties mounted alarmingly.

Everywhere, fighting continued throughout the night. Japanese soldiers used the darkness to infiltrate behind American positions and attack from the rear, so that the nights were lit by innumerable marine parachute flares and star shells. To conserve ammunition, the Japanese often attacked with bayonets and knives, the officers with their wickedly sharp samurai swords. There were also many head wounds from sniper fire. In those days helmets gave protection against glancing bullets and flying shrapnel, but a rifle bullet fired straight into a helmet often went through.

The first emergency landing on Iwo Jima was made on March 4. A B-29 bomber damaged during a raid over Japan and unable to reach the Mariana Islands landed on the southern airfield. It was serviced and refueled, then took off safely to return to Guam. By then, condensers to make water were operating ashore, and aviation fuel tanks had also been landed and filled. Two days later, the first Mustang fighter squadron arrived.

Slowly but steadily the advance continued northward across the rugged domed plateau. On March 8, despite Lieutenant General Kuribayashi's orders, around a thousand Japanese soldiers launched a counterattack against the Fourth Division. It was a suicide charge. Without artillery or tank support, 650 were killed when they were caught in the open by American field artillery and the attack failed.

By then, all the Japanese tanks had been knocked out and the defenders were running out of essential supplies. In their hot, steamy underground bunkers and caves the soldiers suffered from shortages of ammunition and water and were plagued by flies and cockroaches. They were forced to search the dead on the battlefield for water and to eat insects.

Very, very few surrendered, and the majority of those who did were severely wounded. They fought on, holding each position to the last man. Kuribayashi told them: "I want the surviving officers and men to attack the enemy until the last. You devoted yourself to the emperor. Do not think of yourself. I am always at the head of you all."

Yet the marine advance was irresistible. It pushed the majority of the Japanese into a steadily decreasing perimeter in the northwest of the island, with isolated pockets fighting on elsewhere. Sometimes the Americans and Japanese fought in sea fog, at other times in rain with steam rising from the hot ground, but always there was the thick stench of sulfur.

On March 14 Major General Schmidt was able to order the Fourth Division to commence reembarkation in the transport ships anchored offshore. At 1800 hours on the sixteenth, even while fighting continued, he declared Iwo Jima secured. Japanese High Command had promoted Kuribayashi to full general on the seventh. For them the battle was not over.

Of the Suribachi flag-raising group, only Privates Gagnon and Hayes remained uninjured. Bradley was wounded by mortar fire and evacuated with thousands of others, while Block, Sousley, and Strank were already dead. The first army garrison troops, the 147th Infantry, arrived in the south of the island on the twentieth.

Japanese resistance was considered destroyed on the twenty-fifth. Thirty-five days after the first marine landed on the southeastern beaches, firing sputtered to a halt when the last positions and caves on the northern coast were cleared. Only 216 Japanese had surrendered. Between 1400 and 1500 hours, Iwo Jima gradually fell silent— and the marines found that as disturbing as the battle. The sound of any movement seemed grossly magnified and dangerous in the eerie stillness.

However, this assessment of Japanese resistance was premature. There was one final, surprise, coordinated enemy attack—in the center of the island.

More than 260 soldiers, possibly led by Kuribayashi himself, had overnight slipped down the west coast to the central airfield. There, fighter pilots, Pioneers, and others were bivouacked in tents. At dawn on the twenty-sixth the Japanese charged the camp.

The battle lasted for three hours, the Japanese attacking with grenades, bayonets, and samurai swords. Forty-four airmen and nine Pioneers were killed, with 127 wounded, before the attack was driven off. The last Medal of Honor of Iwo Jima, awarded posthumously, was won there. Two hundred sixty-two Japanese were found dead.

The last marines left Iwo Jima the same day, but the infantry garrison was forced to patrol the island continuously throughout the remainder of March, April, and May. They fought and killed a further 1,602 enemy soldiers and captured 867, while yet more hid still in the tunnels and caves. The last two Japanese soldiers did not surrender until 1949, more than four years after the end of the war.

A total of 6,821 American servicemen were killed and 19,217 wounded in the battle for Iwo Jima. Of those killed, 5,885 were marines, as were 17,272 of those wounded. It was the corps' highest casualty count of all its battles. It was also the battle where twenty-nine Medals of Honor were awarded—seven to corpsmen and twenty-two to marines—its highest medal count.

Of those medals, seven were posthumously awarded to marines throwing themselves onto enemy grenades to save their comrades. Such actions of self-sacrifice can only be instinctive, created by a strong esprit de corps. It was why Admiral Nimitz said of Iwo Jima, "Uncommon valor was a common virtue."

Of the Japanese army, 1,083 were captured, and more than 20,000 killed. The exact number of dead is not known; thousands are sealed forever in their tunnels and caves. The body of General Tadamichi Kuribayashi has never been found.

Marines who survived the battle said that you could always identify an Iwo Jima veteran. It was by the scars and gouges on their elbows and knees, from crawling over the volcanic rock of the island.

The three survivors of the flag-raising photograph—Bradley, Gagnon, and Hayes—were flown to the United States to tour the country to raise war bonds. It was a tremendous shock to them, to be fighting in a bitter battle one day and the next to be conducting public relations in a land at peace. They didn't enjoy it. In one city, Hayes, a Pima Native American from Arizona, was refused service because he was "an Indian." It was all too much. He asked to be, and was, sent back to his unit in the Pacific.

Two memorials copying the Mount Suribachi photograph have been made. The first, a stone statue, stands in the Marine Corps headquarters at Quantico, Virginia. The corps is unique among U.S. Armed Forces because it was first formed before the United States of America itself was created. Derived from the Royal Marines—the very first Sea Service Regiment of 1664—the U.S. Marine Corps was raised on November 10, 1775, disbanded in 1783, and re-formed in 1798. The Suribachi statue was unveiled on the corps' 176th anniversary in 1951. Bradley, Gagnon, and Hayes were guests of honor.

The second and larger statue is of bronze. It was approved by Congress as a national memorial to all U.S. military forces and was paid for by public subscription. It is the statue at Arlington National Cemetery, Virginia, unveiled by President Eisenhower in 1954.

From the capture of Iwo Jima to the end of the war in August 1945, it has been calculated that B-29 bombers made 2,251 emergency landings on its airfields. In other words, about thirty thousand airmen were saved from death or injury through being able to land on Iwo Jima rather than crash into the sea. In addition, the dropping of hydrogen bombs on Hiroshima and Nagasaki that August saved the millions of Allied and Japanese lives that an invasion would have incurred.

Iwo Jima was handed back to Japan in 1968, and all over the island are still the ruins and remains of the battle. On the summit of Mount Suribachi are memorials to both the American and Japanese soldiers, the men who fought that epic thirty-six-day battle of 1945.

Recommended
The Ghosts of Iwo Jima by Robert S. Burrell
Flags of Our Fathers by James Bradley with Ron Powers
Film: *Iwo Jima: 36 Days of Hell*
Arlington National Cemetery, Arlington, Virginia

Billy Bishop:
The Courage of the Early Morning

A t 3:57 A.M. on June 2, 1917, a lone Royal Flying Corps fighter took off from the Files-camp airfield near Arras in France. It was still dark, with that hollow predawn cold when the body is at its lowest ebb. The Canadian pilot had pulled his clothes on over the top of his pajamas to keep his bed warmth, drunk a cup of hot tea, and walked out to his Nieuport 17 and waiting mechanic. Soon he was across the front, high above the road to Cambrai.

In June the sun rises early and the first color spread across the World War I battlefields below. At his target airfield near Cambrai there was no activity, so pilot Billy Bishop searched for another target. Near Esnes, twelve miles behind enemy lines, he found an airfield with planes wheeled out for battle: a single two-seater reconnaissance plane and six gray-blue Albatross scouts—enemy fighters. Bishop swooped low at two hundred feet through ground fire, spraying the aircraft below from the Lewis machine gun on his top wing. He saw a mechanic fall.

An Albatross started to take off, so he flew in behind and shot it down sixty feet above the ground, the machine disintegrating as it slid along the grass. Its pilot survived. A second Albatross began its takeoff. Bishop turned tightly, fired but missed. The German pilot swerved away into a tree, tearing off the airplane's right wing. By then, two more Albatrosses had taken off, and Bishop dueled with one while the second watched and waited. He maneuvered in tight turns until he was below the enemy and emptied his gun into the Albatross's engine. The plane fluttered away and crashed near the airfield.

Gripping the stick between his legs, Bishop stood in his cockpit and replaced the empty ammunition drum of the Lewis gun. The fourth Albatross flew in to attack, but Bishop turned the Nieuport head-on toward it and fired the full drum. The German fled and Bishop turned away for home.

Above him at two thousand feet he saw a dawn patrol of Albatrosses. He flew unseen directly below them until he reached the front-line trenches and dived for friendly territory. German pilots rarely pursued across the front, but the guns on the ground fired up at him. Bishop landed back at Filescamp, one hour and forty-three minutes after taking off. His Nieuport had been raked by machine-gun and antiaircraft fire along its lower wings, elevators, and fuselage. Mechanic Sergeant Nicod noted the damage in his report.

Bishop's commanding officer of 60 Squadron, Major Jack Scott, recommended him for the Victoria Cross, Bishop's second recommendation. It was gazetted in August to be Canada's first aerial Victoria Cross. General Trenchard, commanding officer of the RFC (soon after renamed the Royal Air Force), called it "the greatest single show of the war."

Captain William Avery Bishop was already well known along the western front of Belgium and France. By June 1917 he had twenty-one confirmed "victories" against German flyers, making him an ace four times over. He was holder of the Military Cross. Yet in those early years of aerial combat, success was a lottery, determined by the airplane itself as much as by the enemy. Bishop flew first in 21 Squadron, flying the experimental RE7 reconnaissance plane. It was known as "the Suicide Squadron." "The RE7s are nearly as maneuverable as ten-ton trucks," Bishop commented, "but by no means as safe."

At that point, British ace Captain Albert Ball VC of 60 Squadron had the most victories of the 1914–18 war, with forty-four. A victory was given if "an enemy aircraft was seen going down out of control, in flames, to fall apart, driven down or forced to land." It was different from the later battle of Britain, when an aircraft had to be destroyed to claim a "kill."

Bishop learned his tactics from Ball. After Bishop downed his fifth enemy plane to become an official "ace," he painted the front of his engine a bright blue so it would not be mistaken for Ball's red airplane. German flyers called Bishop "the Blue-Nosed Devil." It was Ball who'd first suggested a surprise dawn attack on a German airfield, but he'd been shot down and killed that May. After Ball's death, Bishop was determined to exceed his total.

He was more a lone hunter than one of a team, although he commanded C Flight at Filescamp. With their rare level of skill, Ball and Bishop were two of the very few pilots allowed to hunt alone. Bishop similarly sought the advantage of height, of surprise, of attacking out of the sun and hunting deep behind enemy lines. He was a superb shot, thanks to growing up game shooting in Canada. He had excellent eye-

sight and possessed that three-dimensional aware-ness of airspace vital for a successful fighter pilot. He also made many more flights than most pilots, for he flew both squadron patrols

and alone. It increased his chances of victories. It also increased his chances of being someone else's "victory," but that's war.

April 1917 was known as "Bloody April" in the RFC—the average life span for a pilot was forty-five days, and in Bishop's sector only seventeen days. Flying was increased to support the battle of Arras below, in which the Canadian Corps captured Vimy Ridge. Bishop's squadron suffered particularly badly, for they were opposite the red-painted "Flying Circus" of Baron Manfred von Richthofen, the most successful squadron of the war. Richthofen claimed eighty victories before he was killed in April 1918. Bishop battled with the Circus and, some claim, with Richthofen himself on April 30, although that is doubtful.

During Bloody April, thirteen of the eighteen pilots in 60 Squadron were shot down as well as seven replacement pilots—a 110 percent casualty rate. Yet thirty-five of the enemy were also shot down, twelve of those by Billy Bishop, so April wasn't exactly a honeymoon for German flyers either. It was that May that Major Scott first recommended Bishop for a Victoria Cross, for "prolonged gallantry." He was awarded the Distinguished Service Order instead.

In July the squadron's out-of-date Nieuports were replaced by the excellent SE-5 fighter and

Bishop shot down even more enemy airplanes—two-seater fighters, reconnaissance, single-seat fighters, even German observation balloons—until on the twenty-eighth his SE-5 was hit by the slashing shrapnel of antiaircraft fire. He was still two miles from Filescamp airfield when the spluttering engine caught fire and Bishop crashed into a stand of poplar trees. Wire snapped, wooden struts splintered, canvas wings tore, and Bishop was left hanging upside down in his harness. He passed out. Rain put out the fire, and he was rescued by passing soldiers. Understandably, he was shaken. He wrote home: "I find myself shuddering at chances I didn't think about taking six weeks ago."

Nonetheless, by the time he was given extended leave on September 1, he'd overtaken Ball's total, with fifty victories. He took a steamer to Canada and married his sweetheart, Margaret Burden. Thousands lined the Toronto streets to see Canada's air hero and his bride.

When the United States entered the war in April 1917, Captain Bishop, VC, MC, DSO and bar, was posted to the British War Mission to help America build an air force. While in America, he wrote a quick autobiography, *Winged Warfare,* which more than anything was propaganda for recruiting drives. The truth was embellished and the preface baldly stated that the book would provide "inspiration to every young man in the army 'wings' or who contemplates an army career." Bishop said later: "It turns my stomach."

It wasn't until March 1918 that Bishop was posted back to Britain. He was immediately promoted to major and given command of the new RAF's 85 Squadron at Hounslow, near Heathrow. He was given a relatively free hand in the selection of pilots, and more than two hundred volunteered to join him. There were Australians, British, Canadians, South Africans, New Zealanders, and even the first Americans. In May, flying SE-5a scouts, one of the best airplanes of the entire war, the squadron flew to Petite-Synthe near Dunkirk for operations over Flanders. They were known as "the Flying Foxes."

On May 27 Bishop shot down a two-seater over Passchendaele and on the twenty-eighth two Albatross fighters over Ypres. His phenomenal—and deadly—marksmanship continued until June 17, when his squadron was operating from Saint-Omer. He was advised that he'd been posted to Britain to help create a Canadian flying corps, and he had to leave his squadron by noon of the nineteenth. "I've never been so furious in my life," he wrote to his wife. "It makes me livid with rage to be pulled away just as things are getting started."

However, the Canadian government was worried about him. With the best airplanes and better tactics, the RAF commanded the air over the battlefronts, yet it was feared that, like his mentor Albert Ball, Bishop would be killed. He was more important to the war effort alive than with a few more victories and dead.

On the morning of the nineteenth Billy Bishop flew his last patrol. "One last look at the war," he described it. He intercepted a flight of German Pfalz fighters and in a ferocious fifteen minutes of flying was credited with three more victories, although he claimed five.

In August he was awarded the RAF's new Distinguished Flying Cross in recognition of his recent twenty-five victories in just twelve days of combat. Two days later he was promoted to lieutenant colonel and appointed "Officer Commanding-designate of the Canadian Air Force." In all, he was credited with seventy-two airplane victories and two observation balloons, making him the greatest ace of the RAF and one of the few great aces to survive the war.

Billy and Margaret Bishop's postwar years were up and down. They moved to England in 1921, had three children, and ran a successful business until bankrupted by the stock-market crash of 1929. Returning to Canada, Bishop was appointed honorary group captain in the Royal Canadian Air Force and, eventually, honorary air marshal.

During World War II, Air Marshal Bishop helped expand the Royal Canadian Air Force. He was also instrumental in creating the Commonwealth Air Training Plan, in which thousands of flyers from the commonwealth and empire were trained in the peaceful airspaces of Canada. He had the pleasure of presenting his own son, Arthur, with his pilot's wings. Arthur Bishop flew Spitfires during the battle of Britain to become one of "the Few," and one of the few of "the Few" to survive that war.

In 1942, after the United States entered the war, Billy Bishop appeared in a Hollywood propaganda film, *Captains of the Clouds,* and so became one of the rare actors actually to play himself. More important, King George VI made Bishop a Companion of the Order of the Bath in the Birthday Honours List of 1944, while at home he was awarded the Canadian Efficiency Decoration. After the war, he wrote another book, *Winged Peace.* That book and Bishop himself helped the formation of the International Civil Aviation Organization. Bishop retired in 1952 at the age of fifty-eight, to die in his sleep in September 1956.

Billy Bishop's honor seemed safe. He'd played his part in two world wars, defeating, respectively, militarism and fascism. Many books were written about him, including one by his son, and there is even a play, *Billy Bishop Goes to War.* Yet it seems nothing is sacred. In 1982 a "documentary" film was released by the National Film Board of Canada called *The Kid Who Couldn't Miss.* It caused controversy throughout Canada and led to a senate inquiry.

Through the use of fictional "interviews" with people long dead, played by actors giving fictional replies, Bishop's whole World War I record was questioned—in particular, the dawn attack of June 2, 1917. The film alleges that Bishop lied about this attack. As his Victoria Cross is, so far, the only VC awarded for a specific action not officially witnessed, Bishop was an easy target for defamation. The accusations of lying were built around the argument that (1) there are no German records of an attack on Estourmel; (2) a Nieuport 17 could not have flown that distance and remained in the air for that time; (3) the damage to the Nieuport was self-inflicted by Bishop; (4) Bishop landed in Allied territory and used the plane's machine gun to make that damage; and (5) Bishop then hid the machine gun.

It's the classic defamation of a hero. He's dead, the witnesses are dead, most of the records are destroyed or lost, and the event took place in another era with different standards of honesty. Yet with Billy Bishop, fortunately there is evidence to refute the defamation.

According to Bishop's own combat report, written that 1917 morning, his attack was against an airfield at "either Esnes or Awoingt"—not Estourmel, as the film claims. Bishop wasn't sure which, for both were temporary airfields, both were four miles from Estourmel, and Bishop was fighting a war, not making a documentary. That first and second of June there were six Albatrosses on a temporary airfield at Esnes, during a German squadron transfer to the British front. It's not surprising that no German report survives, because squadron transfer reports were not required. The squadron diary where it might have been mentioned was destroyed by British bombing during World War II. The confusion with Estourmel actually comes from a mistake in Bishop's son's book of 1965.

The flight described in Bishop's combat report that lasted one hour and forty-three minutes was within the capabilities and range of a Nieuport 17. The damage report by mechanic Sergeant Nicod recorded "both machine-gun and heavier anti-aircraft damage." How can a pilot fake antiaircraft damage to the underside of his wings? Further, the Nieuport 17s were renowned for structural weaknesses in their wing struts; Bishop's squadron had already lost five from this dangerous fault. It defies argument that an ace with twenty-one victories would land his aircraft, remove his machine gun from the top wing, and shoot his already weak wing structures.

In addition, it was impossible for the pilot to leave the cockpit of a Nieuport 17 with the engine turning. With no hand or wheel brake and a high-revving rotary engine, the plane would motor away from him. A pilot had to switch off the engine—but the plane had no self-starter. A second person had to swing the propeller, with the pilot in the cockpit, to restart the engine. As to the alleged hidden machine gun, why would Bishop hide it, whatever the circumstances? His combat report does not mention a lost Lewis gun, and the weekly squadron reports record no lost or jettisoned Lewis at all for June. Again, the origin is in Bishop's son's book, written from memory nine years after his father died.

Finally, Bishop's attack was corroborated by British balloon observer Louis Weirter, twelve miles away at the British front line.

Visibility was good that midsummer dawn, and from four thousand feet, equipped with military field glasses, Weirter would have clearly seen a single-fighter attack at Esnes—as he reported. From that height he would have seen clearly thirty miles away.

For confirmation of Bishop's other victories, because he fought deep behind enemy lines, it's no surprise that witnesses to some were hard to find. Yet in fact Bishop had a very high confirmation rate by witnesses, second only to James McCudden of those pilots given commissions to hunt alone.

In Berlin in 1928, Billy Bishop became the only Allied fighter pilot to be inducted into the German Aces Association of the First World War. They had no doubt about the Blue-Nosed Devil from Owen Sound, Ontario, Canada.

Let's leave Bishop's honor to the 1956 obituary by the Montreal *Gazette:*

Death came to Air Marshal Billy Bishop in the early morning. He died at the chill hour before the coming of the dawn—an hour when he must often have been making ready for his solitary flights. Perhaps, if he had had his choice, this would be the hour he would have preferred. For he had that courage which Napoléon Bonaparte once said was the rarest—the courage of the early morning.

Recommended
Over the Front by Philip Markham, vol. 10, no. 3
The Courage of the Early Morning by Arthur Bishop
The Billy Bishop Museum, Owen Sound, Ontario, Canada
The Royal Air Force Museum, Hendon, Middlesex, U.K.

Bletchley Park and the First Computers

[Cryptanalysts were] the geese who laid the golden eggs and never cackled. —Winston Churchill

In the north Buckinghamshire countryside lies a sprawling country house built in Elizabethan, Jacobean, Georgian, and Victorian styles, two stories high with a small central tower and battlement. It's set in a Domesday estate of 480 acres and is listed by English Heritage. It's called Bletchley Park.

In early 1939 the Secret Intelligence Service took over Bletchley Park for its Government Code and Cipher School (GC&CS). After the success of Room 40, the Admiralty's intelligence arm during World War I, the government appreciated the vital role intelligence could play. Nowadays the Government Communications Headquarters (GCHQ), as GC&CS was renamed following World War II, is located in Cheltenham, Gloucestershire. It is without doubt the most successful secret service in the world, if only for what its men and women achieved in Bletchley Park from 1939 to 1945.

Bletchley Park is where the codes of the German Enigma machines were broken, as well as Japanese military and diplomatic codes, and where the world's first electronic computer was invented to break Hitler's top-secret codes. The computer age began at Bletchley Park, Buckinghamshire.

The "golden eggs" to which Churchill referred were the intelligence intercepts Bletchley produced, and the 7,500 women and 2,500 men who worked there were the "geese." Not one word was spoken about their role until the information was declassified in the mid-1970s— the geese never cackled. That thirty years of silence is significant in another way. The vast majority of men and women at Bletchley were not silver-haired professors; most of the code breakers were under thirty. Many were under twenty and a few were straight from school. It was young brains that did the job, assisted by daring raids in the field by other young brains.

By 1939 there was already a history of GC&CS success. Intercepts and code breaks of Russian signals between the wars had uncovered attempts to sow a Communist revolution in Britain—funding left-wing newspapers, the British Communist Party, union unrest, and strikes.

From the efforts particularly of John Tiltman, Hugh Foss, and Australian Eric Nave, GC&CS also broke Japanese codes regularly, beginning in the 1920s. American intelligence didn't make its first Japanese code break until 1940. However, the surprise 1941 attack on Malaya and Pearl Harbor was *not* uncovered. The 1941 German attack on Russia was uncovered by Bletchley; Churchill warned Russia but was not believed.

By 1940, GC&CS was breaking twenty-six diplomatic codes of both enemy and neutral countries. The Americans were then working only four countries. Later GC&CS gave almost all its keys, ciphers, code breaks, and equipment to American intelligence for it to catch up.

The greatest challenge that would face the Bletchley Park code breakers was the German Enigma machine. Resembling a typewriter, it had the advantage of being able to encode messages at typing speed. These machines were a vital part of Germany's war effort and were used by all its armed forces and diplomatic networks. Britain's Polish allies copied the first Enigma machine in 1939 and passed it to GC&CS. When Poland fell in

1939, Polish cryptanalysts fled to France, and when France fell they fled to Britain. Polish intelligence made the first Enigma code break in January 1940, while GC&CS made the second, in February.

There are three parts to a coded message: the plain language, the key to the code used, and the resulting encoded message. Any two parts are required to uncover the third. To operate an Enigma machine, the code designated that day was entered in the code board to prime the machine. For example, the letter *A* became *P, B* became *Q, C* became *R,* and so on. The plain-language message was then typed, and the machine automatically substituted letter for letter. The coded message was then passed by the machine through three separate rotors, each set to one of twenty-six alphabetical positions according to that day's code. That encoded the message three more times. A reflector rotor then "reflected" the message back in the opposite direction, so that the message was encoded another three times. That produced an almost random encoded message with nearly three million combinations. The coded message was then transmitted.

At the receiving end, the coded message was typed into an identical Enigma machine set to that day's code and the plain-language message was revealed, letter by letter. The one weakness of the Enigma machine, not realized by German cryptanalysts, was that it was not 100 percent random. Crucially, *A* could not be encoded as *A, B* could not be *B.* This gave the brains at Bletchley Park the tiny window they needed in order to, slowly, break each day's code.

To speed decoding, the brilliant Cambridge mathematician Alan Turing invented an electromechanical machine utilizing banks and banks of rotors and code boards into which an intercepted coded message was entered. It was called a Bombe, after an earlier but different Polish machine.

The Bombe was not a computer; that came later. Turing's Bombe worked by eliminating every wrong decode for a message to leave only the few possible correct codes. Those were then entered by hand and tested, and the correct code for the day was uncovered. A Bombe was then programmed with that code and every message in that particular Enigma network could be decoded.

There were different Enigma networks for Germany and for Italy, for the army, navy, U-boats, and air force, for High Command, for field units, for the Gestapo, embassies overseas, German spies in Britain, and so on. There was network after network, each using different types of Enigmas—100,000 of them—and different codes.

Thousands of radio operators throughout Britain, the empire, and the commonwealth monitored enemy radio frequencies to intercept the messages. Those intercepts were passed to huts built on the grounds of Bletchley Park. There, teams of women and men decoded their particular network. Cross-feeding of information among sections was carried out by the head of each team. In the early part of the war there were not enough Bombes to handle the number of intercepts. When America entered the war in December 1941, Bletchley Park sent a Bombe to American intelligence for it to copy.

Inevitably, the Germans increased the complexity of their codes and improved the Enigma machines. Very early, a plug board like an old-fashioned telephone exchange was added, increasing possible codes to 159 trillion—159,000,000,000,000. Improved rotors were introduced, rotor wiring was changed, and when a fourth rotor was added to naval Enigmas (increasing decoding possibilities to 26×159 trillion), it almost won the war for the Nazis. Until a break-in could be found, Bletchley was working blind. It was then that the men in the field played their part.

Captures of code books and pieces of equipment took place throughout the war, unknown to Germany. Rotors 6 and 7 were captured from the submarine *U-33,* and code books were recovered from patrol boat *Schiff 26* in 1940. In 1941, Enigma parts and a key list were taken from the trawler *Krebs* during the brilliant Lofoten Islands commando raid, and the surrender of the *U-570* yielded the lid from the new four-rotor naval Enigma. Australian soldiers captured Japanese code books in New Guinea in 1943.

The most vital and famous capture was of the weather and convoy code books for the naval four-rotor Engima from the *U-559* in the Mediterranean. Lieutenant Fasson and Able Seaman Grazier of HMS *Petard* descended into the sinking U-boat on October 30, 1942, to recover the books. With sixteen-year-old Tommy Brown, they passed out code papers as the water poured into the sinking submarine. Brown escaped, but both Fasson and Grazier drowned as they tried to salvage the new Enigma machine itself. They did not give their lives in vain. That code-book capture gave Bletchley Park the break-in to the four-rotor naval code known as Shark.

Before that capture, GC&CS had broken Shark only three times. It caused the crisis in the battle of the Atlantic, when merchant-ship sinkings by U-boats reached their peak and it was thought the United Kingdom might be blockaded into defeat. In the first half of 1942, U-boats sank more than three million tons of shipping, carrying vital men, food, fuel, and military supplies. With the breaking of Shark that December, intelligence flowed again to the Admiralty, ship sinkings decreased, and U-boat sinkings increased.

Of the 1.5 million naval Enigma signals intercepted, 1.1 million were successfully decoded at Bletchley Park. How that intelligence was used required very careful decisions. Often, intelligence was not acted upon, for to have done so would have alerted the enemy that its codes were being broken.

One success in March 1941 was by Dillwyn Knox's women, decoding a message from Italian naval Enigma. The intelligence forewarned the Royal Navy, so that Admiral Cunningham's ships sailed from Egypt to surprise and defeat an Italian fleet at the battle of Matapan. Italian ships never put to sea again during the whole war. Believing its Enigma codes unbreakable, Germany accused Italy of harboring a traitor, but it was Dilly Knox's crew at Bletchley.

Intelligence is a game of bluff, counter-bluff, and apparently unrelated events. For example, RAF Bomber Command dropped mines into various continental sea lanes, apparently to disrupt enemy shipping. In fact, it was not primarily to sink enemy vessels but to generate enemy signals. The coded signals announcing that the sea lanes had been cleared were intercepted and passed to Bletchley. Knowing roughly what those signals concerned allowed code breakers to decode them, then use the decodes as "cribs" to break more important messages and ciphers.

Similarly, Nazi spies in Britain and Ireland were captured or "turned" without the Germans realizing. Carefully compiled accurate but not vital information was sent to German intelligence as if from these agents. The coded responses were intercepted and passed to Bletchley, where another crib was obtained.

Some codes were unbreakable. Pike German naval code was never broken, and Staff only once. Of Hitler's three Fish codes, Thrasher was never broken, Sturgeon was solved but was mostly duplicated by other signals, while Tunny was solved and exploited without German knowledge. Tunny was used mostly for top-secret messages between Hitler and German High Command.

The absolute brilliance of the women and men at Bletchley Park is demonstrated there, because a Tunny machine was never captured, never photographed, never even seen. Nevertheless, purely from intercepted signals, the brains in Hut 11 worked out that it was a teleprinter, that it used strings of characters from different combinations of five positive and negative dots and crosses, that the machine used twelve wheels to create the code, and so on.

John Tiltman and Bill Tutte first worked on Tunny in 1941, beginning a two-year-long analysis of the code. Alan Turing joined Hut 11 in the summer of 1942, specifically to help with the complex maths needed to break the Tunny wheel patterns. He invented a solely mathematical solution called the Turingery. The breaking of Tunny remains still the greatest cryptanalysis ever achieved by any intelligence service, but to take advantage of the break-in, a computer was needed to decode the signals quickly enough for the intelligence to be used.

Another amazing Cambridge mathematician, Max Newman, joined Hut

11 in November 1942. Initially he devised a photoelectric machine using mechanical relays and valve counters. It compared fast-moving teleprinter tapes of Tunny signals against a decoding tape. It was built in Hut 11 by Post Office engineers. It looked physically impossible, like an iron bedstead on end, an inventor's dream, and so was named the Heath Robinson, after the British artist known for his drawings of ingeniously complicated contraptions. Most important, Newman's machine brought Newman and Post Office engineer Tommy Flowers together. The result was the world's first electronic computer.

A computer is simply a piece of equipment—mainframe, Palm Pilot, desktop, laptop, pocket calculator, or calculating machine—capable of following the instructions and completing the calculations that a human being can do, only quicker. The first modern computers or calculating machines were built by the Third Earl of Stanhope in about 1777, but development was slow.

In 1935, Alan Turing devised the vital breakthrough of controlling a machine with a program stored in the machine's own memory. He was just twenty-three years old. He turned the concept into a practical design he called the Universal Turing Machine. At that time calculating machines were electromechanical—they used electrically operated on-off switches called relays. Turing himself built a small electromechanical binary multiplier. Several such computers were built, but they were slow and they were not electronic. The development of electronic valves for radio and radar—in turn replaced by diode and transistor technology—opened the door to electronic computers.

Tommy Flowers realized that electronic valves were reliable enough to be used as on-off electronic switches and would be hundreds of times faster than mechanical relays. Using those concepts, he invented the world's first electronic telephone exchange, operating in Britain in 1939.

Max Newman had his Heath Robinson photoelectric machine up and running in June 1943. It operated at 1,000 to

2,000 characters per second. Flowers was unimpressed. He said electronic-valve equipment would be four times as fast. Perhaps understandably, the powers at Bletchley thought it would take too long to make and would be less reliable. Flowers went ahead regardless and built his concept at Dollis Hill in London. Working flat out, Flowers's team had it completed and operating by December 1943. It was called Colossus, the first electronic digital computer in the world. It went online at Bletchley Park in February 1944 to decode Tunny signals.

Colossus used 1,600 electronic valves, operated at 5,000 characters per second, weighed a ton, and was the size of a small cupboard. It was a semi-programmable as opposed to a stored-program computer. A basic Pentium 2 laptop today has the same power as that first computer. Flowers's much-improved Colossus II was brought online in May 1944, shortly before D-day. It used 2,400 valves and operated at 25,000 characters per second.

German High Command Tunny signals were decoded regularly and speedily by Colossus. Almost the entire German battle order in France was revealed at Bletchley before the D-day invasion. As a result, Bletchley Park was involved in the deception called Operation Fortitude, where the Nazis were deceived into believing the invasion would be at Calais, not Normandy. In addition, a thirty-two-page report sent by the Japanese military attaché in Berlin was decoded by the Japanese section at Bletchley, filling important gaps in the German battle plan. A late change of German positions in Normandy was also decoded by Colossus, which stopped U.S. paratroopers from landing in the middle of a German division.

Two vital items of military intelligence were not decoded because they were, unfortunately, never sent. The first was the position of the Twenty-first Panzer (tank) Division. That division attacked the left wing of the British landings at Sword Beach and prevented them from taking Caen that June 6, 1944. As a result, the British and Canadian armies were forced into a slow and brutal battle for Caen lasting almost two months. It was the bloodiest fighting in western Europe, with 66,000 German and 80,000 British and Canadian casualties.

The second item never sent was the position of the German 352 Division. They were near Omaha Beach and hammered the U.S. Army in its landings on June 6. From those two gaps in intelligence it can be seen that, without the code breakers of Bletchley Park, the invasion might well have failed.

Message decoding at Bletchley reached a peak of eighteen thousand a day shortly after D-day, then gradually decreased. After D-day, German High Command changed its Tunny codes every day, so that by the end of the war nine Colossus computers were online in Hut 11.

After the war, Max Newman and Alan Turing left the GC&CS and began their own separate projects to design and construct the first stored-program computer. Their designs were both based upon Turing's groundbreaking 1937 paper "On Computable Numbers."

Turing designed his stored-program computer in 1945, using his earlier universal Turing machine. He completed the technical report— "Proposed Electronic Calculator"—by the end of the year, the first complete specification for an electronic stored-program digital computer. Its high-speed memory was equal to the chip memory of the early Macintosh computers of the 1980s. However, Turing had problems with production and soon was eighteen months behind schedule. Newman, meanwhile, wrote his own logico-mathematical design for a stored-program computer. He invited the brilliant electrical engineers Frederick Williams and Thomas Kilburn to join him.

Newman's team produced the world's first stored-program electronic computer in 1948. It was called the Manchester Baby and incorporated the first high-speed random access memory (RAM), called the Williams Tube. The Manchester Baby ran its first program on June 21. So far ahead in production was Newman's team that Turing joined them that year.

With Turing on board, a redesigned input and programming system was built for the Manchester Baby, including a programming manual. That improved computer was called the Manchester Mark I. The Mark I became the first computer mass-produced for public sale.

Very soon Turing was using the Mark I to model biological growth—what we now call artificial life. By 1950, Turing was already devising how to program a computer to think. A fragile genius of the first order, he had always been a shy and retiring man. He committed suicide in 1954 by eating an apple laced with cyanide. He was just forty-one years old.

All the messages decoded at Bletchley came under the general heading of signals intelligence, or "SIGINT." However, there were other people working at Bletchley Park. Sigint people referred to them as "the other side."

The other side specialized in human intelligence—"HUMINT." None of the Sigint people knew what Human Intelligence was, nor what the "other side" did. Even today they don't know, for Humint has not been declassified. There are secrets still to come from Bletchley Park.

Recommended
British Intelligence in the Second World War by F. H. Hinsley, vols. 1 and 2
Codebreakers: The Inside Story of Bletchley Park, edited by F. H. Hinsley and Alan Stripp
The Emperor's Codes: Bletchley Park and the Breaking of Japan's Secret Ciphers by Michael Smith
Action This Day, edited by Michael Smith and Ralph Erskine
Bletchley Park Trust, Bletchley Park, Buckinghamshire, U.K.

William Bligh's Boat Voyage

In 1789, the twenty-ninth year of the reign of His Most Gracious Majesty, King George III, occurred the most famous naval mutiny of all time: the mutiny on the *Bounty*.

At dawn on April 28, Lieutenant William Bligh and eighteen crew were cast adrift in the *Bounty*'s twenty-three-foot open launch. Bligh had been obliged to order some of them out for safety, and four loyal seamen remained behind with the mutineers. Even then, the launch rode only seven inches above the surface of the sea.

In 1787 the Admiralty had appointed Lieutenant Bligh commander of the *Bounty*, to be addressed as Captain on board. His orders were to sail to Otaheite (Tahiti), there to collect breadfruit plants as a crop to feed plantation slaves. Bligh's experiences with Captain Cook and his previous visit to Otaheite made him the obvious choice.

Bligh was allowed to choose the master's mate from the many who applied. He chose his friend Fletcher Christian, who had sailed with him twice before. The Admiralty saddled Bligh with a drunken surgeon, Thomas Huggan, though fortunately Sir Joseph Banks found Bligh an assistant surgeon, Thomas Ledward. The Admiralty would not promote Bligh to captain, would not appoint any commissioned officers, and would not give him marines. Cook had considered commissioned officers and marines essential for discipline in his three voyages to the Pacific, and Bligh agreed. There the Admiralty made a bad decision; Bligh knew the South Seas, the Admiralty did not.

Knowing that the *Bounty*'s voyage would take two years, Bligh divided her crew into three watches instead of two. With two watches, watch keepers work four hours on, four hours off. It's a tiring system. With three watches they work four on and eight off. The advantage of the latter is the opportunity for decent sleep. In a long voyage this is invaluable. Bligh promoted Fryer, Peckover, and twenty-three-year-old Manxman Fletcher Christian as watch leaders. There was also another Manxman on the *Bounty,* the fourteen-year-old unqualified midshipman Peter Heywood, distantly related to Christian. Through Bligh's Manx wife, the Heywood family had requested a berth for Peter.

One of the first signs of a troubled voyage came from carpenter Purcell, who was insubordinate at Cape Town. He refused to obey an order from Bligh and an order from the master, and when they reached Otaheite, he refused another order from his captain. Bligh was enraged by this disobedience. Under the Twenty-second Article of War, Bligh could have hanged or flogged Purcell for the offenses. He did neither. In fact, he ordered only seven floggings in sixteen months, fewer than the great and beloved Nelson, fewer even than the humane Cook. Seven floggings a month was not unusual in those times.

Bligh knew the temptations of Otaheite from his voyage with Cook. The women were bare-breasted, their skins a smooth brown. They were attractive and sensual, and they bathed every day. They had no inhibiting morals. The climate was languid, the lush greens of the hills contrasting pleasantly with the blue tropical sea. The food was plentiful and the Tahitians friendly. They did practice human sacrifice, they did use infanticide to control their island population, and some of their rituals involved sexual intercourse. It was a heady, seductive mix, very different from the grim streets of Georgian Britain. Cook had experienced desertion there on every voyage, with the deserters recaptured and flogged.

With no officers and no marines, Bligh knew it would be impossible to stop his men from going ashore. With the permission of King Tynah, he worked a rotating system where some crew maintained the *Bounty* while others lived ashore to tend the breadfruit nursery.

In five months on the island, only three men deserted, and they were recaptured. They'd stolen a ship's boat, arms, and ammunition while the mate of the watch, Thomas Hayward, was asleep on duty. Bligh disrated Hayward, placed him in irons for four weeks, and flogged the deserters. Desertion on a foreign station was a hanging offense.

At the time, an exasperated Bligh wrote: "Such neglectful and worthiless petty Officers I believe never was in a ship as are in this—No orders for a few hours together are Obeyed by them, and their conduct in general is so bad, that no confidence or trust can be reposed in them—in short, they have drove me to everything but Corporal punishment, and that must follow if they do not improve." Yet only one more man was flogged, for "neglect of duty." This, perhaps, was Bligh's problem: he was too humane for his time.

As well as the *Bounty*'s log and Bligh's journal, there is another day-to-day account: the journal of boatswain's mate Morrison, a mutineer. It was recovered in Otaheite. It agrees with Bligh's journal in every detail and includes the list of possible deserters. There is no recording of cruelty, excessive flogging, gagging, inhumanity, excessive duties, or extra punishments by Bligh. In the journal of mutineer Peter Heywood there is also no mention of cruelty, excessive floggings, or punishment by his captain. In the notes written by John Adams in Fletcher Christian's Bible after the mutiny, there is no mention of cruelty by Bligh.

After five months at Otaheite, the *Bounty* prepared for sea with breadfruit plants in pots around the quarterdeck. There had been minor incidents with the islanders, mostly the breaking of "tabu," but the most unsavory involved the master. Fryer had sex with a woman but did not give her the agreed piece of cloth. Bligh apologized to the woman and ordered Fryer to give her the cloth. Like Fryer, Bligh was a married man, but like Cook, he remained celibate.

Surgeon Huggan drank himself to death on Otaheite from his own private supplies. He kept notes of the patients he'd treated, including those for venereal disease. Among them were Christian and Heywood.

The *Bounty* departed Otaheite on April 4, bound for the West Indies. Bligh stopped at Anamooka island on the twenty-fifth for fruit and water. There he became angry with the crew for letting islanders steal their tools and brandished a pistol at McCoy for not paying attention. Bligh's temper was well known. Cook had a temper, too, but the anger of a captain is not cause to mutiny.

At sea, someone on Christian's watch stole coconuts from the supply stowed on deck. Stealing coconuts may appear petty, but one of the codes of behavior on board ship is to not steal anything. A ship is a small community and possessions cannot be locked away. In the navy it's a criminal offense.

After the theft, Bligh called Christian "a damned hound" and the men of Christian's watch "scoundrels." He might have flogged them. Many captains in 1789 would have flogged a thief without a second thought.

That evening Bligh invited Christian to dinner in the cabin. The incident had obviously not been important to Bligh, but Christian refused, saying he was unwell. Purcell, Morrison, and Lebogue all reported that Christian drank heavily that night.

After dinner in the *Bounty,* Bligh slept, leaving his door open as usual. Shortly before dawn, he was shaken awake by Christian, with a cutlass in his hand. Behind him, carrying loaded muskets and bayonets, were Churchill, Mills, and Burkitt. They tied the captain's hands behind him and pushed him out on deck in his nightshirt.

Christian ordered boatswain Cole to lower the launch. Heywood assisted, and those of the crew who refused to join the mutiny were called on deck and told off into the boat. The sea was very calm. As daylight came, Christian ordered a dram of rum for each mutineer to steady them through the confusion. Bligh's clerk, Samuel, managed to take a quadrant, compass, and the journal into the launch but was warned by Christian "on pain of death" to leave charts, surveys, sextant, chronometer, and navigation tables.

When Bligh had to order some men back to the *Bounty* from the overladen launch, Fryer was told he'd be shot if he returned. Bligh asked Christian if this treatment was the "proper return for his friendship," and Christian answered: "That, Captain Bligh, that is the thing; I am in hell—I am in hell!" In the last moments, with Heywood standing by Christian, Bligh called again for Christian to come to his senses, begging him to reconsider. According to Bligh, Christian replied: "I am in hell," while Morrison recorded: "I have been in hell this fortnight passed and am determined to bear it no longer." It was three weeks since they'd left Otaheite.

Bligh and the launch crew were all aware that midshipmen Peter Heywood, Stewart, and Young were among the mutineers. Morrison recorded that it was Stewart who first suggested that Christian take the ship. Christian said: "Come, Captain Bligh, your officers and men are now in the boat, and you must go with them; if you attempt to make the least resistance you will be instantly put to death."

As the launch veered astern of the ship, the mutineers jeered and threw breadfruit plants from the quarterdeck. The *Bounty* sailed slowly to the west-northwest, although Bligh assumed correctly that it was a false course and the mutineers would eventually return to Otaheite.

At the time of the mutiny the *Bounty*'s crew numbered forty-three. Twenty-two remained loyal to their captain. As the launch and the *Bounty* parted company, those forced to remain called down to Bligh for him to remember that they were loyal.

"Never fear, my lads," he said. "I'll do you justice if ever I reach England!"

In fact, Bligh had greater worries on his mind. He was in the middle of the South Pacific Ocean in an overloaded boat, with no charts, no surveys, no sextant, no guns, no stores, and small odds of surviving. So began the greatest open-boat voyage in history.

As the *Bounty* sailed away, the launch crew also knew their chances were virtually nil. Certainly they could sail for an island where they could rot until disease, starvation, or the islanders killed them. That is what the mutineers expected them to do. They'd thrown into the launch cutlasses and food and water to last for five days. However, William Bligh wanted more than mere survival. He was determined to get his men home.

First he sailed thirty miles to Tofua, in the Friendly Islands (Tonga). There they took on water and food—coconuts, breadfruit, and fish. Yet there had been changes since Bligh had visited the island with Captain Cook. This time the sailors would not be welcomed by the islanders.

On Tofua, Bligh heard a sound he dreaded, the loud clacking to-gether of stones. He knew it as a call to arms for the warlike island-ers. His men had refilled the water barrel and found food, but now it was time to leave. As Bligh and Purcell walked down the beach to the launch, the islanders crowded around and stones began to fly. One hit Bligh's shoulder and drew blood, but he staggered through the shallows to the launch, Purcell ahead of him. Quartermaster Norton leaped into the water with a cutlass, to cut the mooring line.

Purcell and Bligh clambered aboard, but Norton was still cutting the line when a flying stone knocked him down. The islanders beat him to death in the warm, shallow water. With no pistols, there was nothing the men in the launch could do but watch in horror. Bligh himself cut the mooring, and the islanders pitched stones at the launch as they rowed away. They were followed by war canoes until Bligh and others threw their blue uniform jackets into the water to divert them.

At sea once more, Bligh called his men to order. He knew the Pacific as well as any navigator alive. He had sailed it for four years, two of those with his mentor, James Cook. To the west, a new colony was being settled in New South Wales, yet there was no guarantee that the colonists had reached Botany Bay or even survived. However, there was an established settlement to the northwest in Dutch Timor. Bligh had not been there, but two others in the launch had: botanist Nelson and gunner Peckover, who'd also sailed with Cook. Bligh had spent days poring over Cook's charts, and he remembered Timor's approximate latitude and longitude. He thought it was within reach. Either way, it was better than rotting on an is-land.

He discussed the navigation with the master, the gunner, and the boatswain. With tight rations, they had food and water for six weeks—at one ounce of bread and a quarter-pint of water per man per day, supplemented by scraps of meat and occa-sional teaspoons of rum. Bligh spoke to all the men, wanting their views—indeed, their approval—for the voyage. They gave it and Bligh pointed the launch at Timor, 3,500 nautical miles away.

During the great voyage, Bligh recorded the names of the mutineers in his log, as well as those of the loyal men he'd been forced to leave behind: Joseph Coleman, Charles Norman, Thomas McIntosh, and Michael Byrne, the half-blind fiddler. He knew he must stand by those men, if he ever reached home.

The *Bounty*'s launch had seats for ten, so it was extremely crowded for eighteen. Bligh divided his crew into two watches under the master and gunner. Those two, the boatswain Cole and Bligh himself, would steer. Everyone else would rotate their position to ease their cramped and aching joints, while two men could lie outstretched on the bottom boards. The launch was a sailing lugger with six oars. It was a sound boat, but it wasn't designed for a 3,500-mile ocean voyage.

Bligh was also concerned about the crew themselves. There were only two malcontents, but two might have been enough to destroy them all. One was master and second in command of the *Bounty*, John Fryer, who had been shown in the previous sixteen months to have limited abilities. He was disliked by the crew, and even the mutineers had refused to have him. The second malcontent was carpenter William Purcell. Most ships have a "sea-lawyer," and in the *Bounty* it was Purcell. He was insubordinate, argumentative, and asserted his "rights" at every opportunity, spreading discontent in the crew. Yet when invited to stay in the *Bounty* he'd replied: "I'm not staying with a pack of mutineers," and entered the launch with his tools.

The remaining fifteen admired and liked their captain. They were William Peckover, William Cole, Thomas Ledward, David Nelson, William Elphinston, Thomas Hayward, John Hallett, Peter Linkletter, Lawrence Lebogue, John Smith, Thomas Hall, George Simpson, Robert Lamb, John Samuel, and twelve-year-old Robert Tinkler.

For his part, Bligh had lost his ship to mutiny, an almost unheard-of event. What was he thinking as he stared at his overcrowded command? Somehow he had to navigate his loyal men to safety, in a small boat on a vast ocean.

The next morning a gale overtook the launch, increasing to storm force and soaking them all. They bailed water continuously as they ran before heavy seas. It was a foretaste of the weeks to come, although bad weather helped them to survive. It was the southern winter, and the voyage was beset by fogs, rain, and cold nights. Yet they didn't suffer greatly from thirst because of the rain and suffered little from sunburn or heat or the madness that comes with those. You can last for a month without food as long as you have water. The damp and cold, the cramps from lack of movement—those were their greatest hardships. At times they craved tropical heat. The teaspoon of rum in the morning became a necessity rather than a luxury.

Back in the *Bounty,* there was a surfeit of rum. The mutineers were Edward Young, Peter Heywood, George Stewart, Isaac Martin, Charles Churchill, John Mills, James Morrison, Thomas Burkitt, Matthew Quintal, John Sumner, John Millward, William McCoy, Henry Hillbrant, William Muspratt, John Adams, John Williams, Thomas Ellison, Richard Skinner, Matthew Thompson, and William Brown, led by master's mate Fletcher Christian.

Fletcher Christian: the most famous name of them all. It was his third voyage with Bligh. They had met first on HMS *Cambridge,* on which Bligh was fifth lieutenant and Christian a volunteer seaman. Christian was a Manxman and Bligh was then living on the Isle of Man. Bligh later sailed as captain on merchant ships for four years, and in 1786 Christian applied to sail with him as midshipman on the *Britannia*. All berths were taken, so he volunteered as seaman and was accepted. Nevertheless, Captain Bligh and First Mate Lamb instructed and taught Christian as an officer and to navigate.

Bligh sailed through the Cannibal Isles (Fiji) without stopping. Tales of brutality were legend in the area, and he would not risk another attack. Two canoes chased them and they rowed desperately to escape. While they threaded their way through the islands, the first white men to sail those waters, Bligh surveyed, named, and charted positions using quadrant and watch. "Boat Passage" still marks the reef through which the *Bounty*'s launch entered the Fijis.

Succeeding days passed slowly, with incessant bailing, increasing hunger, and more aches and cramps than it seemed possible to bear. On May 12, Bligh observed: "At length the day came and showed to me a miserable set of beings, full of wants, without anything to relieve them. Some complained of great pain in their bowels, and everyone of having almost lost the use of his limbs. What sleep we got was no ways refreshing, as we were covered with sea and rain." Botanist Nelson was already weakening.

Bligh discovered the Banks Islands, north of the cannibalistic New Hebrides (now known as Vanuatu). He sketched them, charted their positions, and named them after Sir Joseph Banks. He sailed west toward the Great Barrier Reef and the north of New Holland, as Australia was then known. He wrote on the twenty-third: "The misery we suffered this night exceeded the preceding. The sea flew over us with great force, and kept us bailing with horror and anxiety. At dawn of day I found everyone in a most distressed condition, and I began to fear that another such night would put an end to the lives of several. I served an allowance of two spoonfuls of rum."

Bligh was forced to reduce rations further. They now received, twice a day, 1/25th of a pound of bread plus the usual quarter-pint of water and any food they might catch. Several seabirds blundered into the sails, and this raw flesh—including eyes, claws, intestines, and stomach contents—restored a little interest in the weakening men. In navy fashion, the portions were offered by "Who shall have this?" while a man with his back turned called a name.

On the night of May 28, Fryer heard the breakers of the Great Barrier Reef. In daylight, Bligh navigated through a gap in the reefs and they were inside, in relatively protected water, with slight damage only to the rudder. The following day they stopped at an island. It was their first time out of the cramped launch in four weeks. They stumbled onto the sandy beach. Some collapsed, some fainted, others rested on their knees or staggered a few steps before falling. For two days they rested on the island Bligh named Restoration, eating oysters, hearts of cabbage palm, some berries that Nelson thought edible, and fern roots. When they weren't suffering from stomach cramps, they stretched out on the ground to sleep.

In the meantime, Purcell had repaired the rudder. Bligh put to sea hurriedly when a large party of naked Aborigines assembled on the mainland. They carried spears and shouted at the castaways. No one knew whether they were friendly or threatening, so wearily they sailed on, northwestward, inside the reefs. Bligh decided to stop again soon after, for Nelson's health had worsened and others were visibly weakening.

He beached the launch again on Sunday Island, where Nelson, Ledward, and Lebogue crawled up the sand and collapsed. The others argued bitterly about who was to forage for food. "I'm as good a man as you are!" Purcell argued with Bligh. They shouted at each other and Bligh flourished a cutlass. Why not after five weeks cooped up together in a twenty-three-foot boat? Bligh faithfully recorded this incident in his log. The amazing thing is that no one came to blows.

After two days recuperating on Sunday Island, Bligh sailed north to Cape York and on June 3 turned west through Endeavour Strait on a course for Dutch Timor—all from his memory of Cook's charts. In open seas again, they resumed bailing the launch. By then, the weather was hot, but they had enough water to continue the quarter-pint a day.

They caught a fish, their first, but the part given Bligh by "Who shall have this?" made him violently ill. He vomited again and again over the side of the boat, his head burning hot. When he'd stopped retching, he looked at the others, who very worriedly stared at him. Their legs were swollen, their joints bruised, their skin ulcerated. He said how sorry he was that they were all so ill. Boatswain Cole replied: "I really think, sir, that you look worse than anyone in the boat." There was actual laughter.

Bligh's entry for June 12, 1789, reads: "At three in the morning, with an excess of joy, we discovered Timor bearing from WSW to WNW, and I hauled on a wind to the NNE till daylight."

At dawn the launch was six miles offshore, so Bligh steered southwest along the coast through yet another gale. He wrote: "It appeared scarce credible to ourselves that in an open boat, and so poorly provided, we should have been able to reach the coast of Timor after leaving Tofoa, having in that time run, by our log, a distance of 3618 miles; and that notwithstanding our extreme distress, no one should have perished in the voyage."

The eighteen men spent one more night at sea, and the *Bounty*'s launch arrived at the town of Coupang (Kupang) on Timor the following morning. It was Sunday, June 14, 1789, forty-seven days after they were cast adrift in the South Pacific, 3,670 miles away.

Although himself sick with fever, the Dutch governor of Timor met Bligh and expressed his sympathy at the mutiny, incredulity at the voyage of the launch, and amazement that only the one man had died. A Dutch surgeon treated their sores, ulcers, cuts, and swellings, and they were given the only uninhabited house in Coupang in which to recuperate. Bligh ordered Fryer to give his bed to Nelson, who was still desperately ill. Bligh was determined to report the mutiny as soon as possible, but he had to wait for a ship to take him home.

Bligh wrote to his wife from Coupang, seven weeks after the mutiny: "Besides this young villain [Christian] see young Heywood, one of the ringleaders, and besides him see Stewart joined with him. . . . I have now reason to curse the day I ever knew Christian or a Heywood or indeed a Manks man."

Nelson succumbed to the fever, which also killed the Dutch governor. He died on July 20, mourned by Bligh as a friend and as the only non-naval witness to the mutiny. After transport by ship to Batavia (Jakarta), all the castaways came down with fever, Hall the next to die. Bligh had brought his crew through an incredible voyage only to see them perish ashore. The first ship departing Batavia had only three berths. Bligh had to take one, but who else? He chose Samuel and Smith, ex-*Britannia* men, knowing the choice might condemn others to death.

It was so. Within a fortnight, Elphinston and Linkletter died. Lamb died during the voyage home, while Ledward's ship disappeared. Bligh had brought seventeen men safely over 3,670 miles, yet only eleven reached Britain. He, Samuel, and Smith arrived in Portsmouth on March 14, 1790.

In October, after the surviving launch crew returned, Lieutenant Bligh was court-martialed at Portsmouth for the loss of his ship. He was honorably acquitted. Purcell was court-martialed for refusing to obey orders and insubordination. He was found guilty and reprimanded.

William Bligh became a national hero for his brilliant navigation and command of that amazing open-boat voyage, the greatest ever completed. He was promoted to captain at last.

Many years passed before the fate of the mutineers was known. Bligh thought he had heard them cry "Huzza for Otaheite!" Morrison wrote that they were keen to return to Otaheite, where "they might get weomen without force."

The *Bounty* had sailed first to Toobouai (Tubuai) Island, 350 miles south of Otaheite, arriving there on May 24, 1789. They stayed a week there before sailing to Otaheite for livestock—and women. Lies were told to deceive King Tynah, and in June the *Bounty* left with livestock, nine women, eight men, seven boys, and one girl. The mutineers lived for three months on Toobouai, fighting among themselves and fighting the islanders. In one battle, sixty-six islanders were killed. It was not the life of ease the mutineers had desired, and in September the different factions agreed to return to Otaheite.

In the *Bounty*'s final visit to Otaheite, Christian stayed aboard. The four loyal men, most of the Tahitians, and twelve mutineers went ashore, while other island women came aboard in welcome. According to Tahitian woman Teehuteatuaonoa (known as Jenny), who escaped from Pitcairn Island in 1817, all but three of seventeen Tahitian women were kidnapped by Christian when he cut the *Bounty*'s anchor cable and sailed from Otaheite. Those kidnappings are confirmed in the Pitcairn journal of Midshipman Young.

In January 1790, after four months searching for a hideaway, Christian located Pitcairn Island, marked on the charts as "position doubtful." The ship was stripped of valuables—including the chronometer and Christian's Bible—and then burned. There would be no going back, no change of mind.

The twelve mutineers left at Otaheite included Heywood, Stewart, Churchill, and Morrison. Churchill was murdered by messmate Thompson, who was in turn sacrificed by the Tahitians to their gods as a punishment.

A year later, in 1791, Captain Edwards in the frigate *Pandora* apprehended those fourteen who remained at Otaheite. Assisting the search for the mutineers were Hayward and Hallett of the *Bounty*'s launch. Edwards locked loyal men and mutineers alike in a wooden cage on the *Pandora*'s quarterdeck so that there could be no subversion of his crew. There was no sign of the others, and after three months of searching, he set sail for Britain. It was to be a troubled journey.

In August 1791 the *Pandora* ran aground on the Great Barrier Reef and sank. Thirty-one crew and four of the mutineers drowned. Captain Edwards and ninety-eight survivors sailed four boats eleven hundred miles to Coupang, the second open-boat voyage to Timor for Hayward and Hallett. From there, they were repatriated via Batavia and Cape Town.

Meanwhile, the Admiralty had appointed Bligh captain to the frigate *Providence,* and with the brig *Assistant,* he was sent to Otaheite to complete his original task of transplanting breadfruit to the West Indies. On that occasion, the Admiralty appointed commissioned officers and marines. Interestingly, four *Bounty* crew—Peckover, Lebogue, Smith, and Samuel—volunteered to sail with Bligh. He took all except Peckover. Bligh stated he didn't want to sail with any *Bounty* warrant officer ever again.

In April 1792 they arrived at Otaheite, where Bligh was welcomed by King Tynah. He met Heywood's Tahitian wife and the children of other mutineers. Disagreeable changes in Tahitian life were noted by Bligh and others—particularly swearing—the effects of the mutineers having lived there for more than a year.

At Portsmouth the surviving ten of the *Bounty*'s recaptured crew were court-martialed for mutiny in September 1792. The four loyal men—Coleman, Norman, McIntosh, and Byrne—were honorably acquitted. Bligh, as he had promised, had registered their innocence with the Admiralty.

Peter Heywood, Morrison, Burkitt, Muspratt, Millward, and Ellison were all found guilty and sentenced to death. Muspratt was discharged on a legal technicality and pardoned. Heywood was given a royal pardon, possibly because he was young, but probably because of his family's naval connections. Morrison was pardoned because he had not actively supported the mutiny. Three were hanged.

Far away, on Pitcairn Island, the murders began. Williams's wife died, and he demanded one of the Tahitians' wives instead. The Tahitian men were furious. They rebelled and in one day murdered Williams, Christian, Mills, Martin, and Brown. They then fought one another, and the survivors of those murders were murdered in turn by the four surviving mutineers and their Tahitian wives. McCoy committed suicide. In 1799, Quintal was murdered by Young and Adams, and Young died of asthma in 1800, leaving Adams the sole survivor.

Fletcher Christian was identified by both loyal and mutinous crew as leader of the mutiny. Peter Heywood had been tried and found guilty of mutiny. Despite his later pardon, not one loyal man or mutineer had said Heywood was not part of the mutiny. As a result, the only avenue for the Christian and Heywood families to salvage their reputations was to find an acceptable reason for the mutiny. The only way to do that was to blame the *Bounty*'s captain. So began the slander of William Bligh.

In a letter dated November 5, 1792, the pardoned Peter Heywood wrote to the Christians and offered to provide evidence of "false reports of slander" against Christian by one whose "ill report is his greatest praise" (Bligh). The vilification of Bligh began, with inventions of floggings, gagging, maltreatment, and sadistic cruelty.

Morrison's journal was rewritten to include accounts of cruelty, though Sir Joseph Banks stopped its publication. The Christians arranged a private "inquiry" into the mutiny by their friends, then published its "verdict" as well as a fictional appendix to the courts-martial, containing inventions of cruelty by Bligh. They altered dates, names, sequences, and facts to support the lies. When Bligh returned home, he rebutted the "appendix" but ignored most of the libelous stories about him. Some of his shipmates would not.

One, who had been with Bligh and Christian on the *Britannia*, wrote: "When we got to sea and I saw your partiality for the young man, I gave him every advice and information in my power. Though he went about every point of duty with a degree of indifference that to me was truly unpleasant; but you were blind to his faults. . . . In the Appendix it is said that Mr. Fletcher Christian had no attachment among the women of Otaheite; if that was the case he must have been much altered since he was with you in *Britannia,* he was then one of the most foolish young men I ever knew in regard to the sex."

If Christian had no attachment with the women of Otaheite, how did he contract venereal disease? Before Otaheite, Bligh had his surgeons inspect the men of the *Bounty* for VD and found none. Before the mutiny, Bligh reported that Christian's hands were sweating badly and affected everything he touched. Heywood's family admitted that Christian "was a man of violent temper," and Rosalind Young, mutineer descendant, wrote in her 1890 history that on Pitcairn, Christian was "a violent man."

In all the accounts written before, during, and immediately after the mutiny, in all the evidence given at all the courts-martial, there is not *one* accusation of ill treatment by Bligh and not one allegation that the mutiny was caused by cruelty. All those came later, via the Christian and Heywood families. If a reason for the mutiny must be found, it lies in the simple words of the last survivor, Adams, who said: "We only wanted to return to our loved ones on Otaheite."

William Bligh died as Vice Admiral of the Blue in 1817, having served with distinction at the battles of Camperdown (1797) and Copenhagen (1801), where he was personally commended by Admiral Nelson. In 1805 he was appointed governor of the colony of New South Wales, with specific instructions to stop the illegal rum trade in Sydney. Unfortunately, it was the New South Wales Corps under his command that organized most of the trade. The corps refused Bligh's orders, and he was faced with another rebellion. He was completely exonerated, and the officers and colonists concerned were punished.

In 1825, after both Bligh and Sir Joseph Banks had died, Peter Heywood published *Biography of Peter Heywood, Esq.* It was based upon Morrison's rewritten journal, bought from Morrison by Heywood's family. It's this biography and Morrison's doctored journal that is the source of the films, stage shows, and books portraying Bligh as an evil sadist. Some fifty films have been made about Bligh's "cruelty" causing the mutiny.

The tragedy of the Christian-Heywood slander is that it destroyed the recognition and fame due to Admiral Bligh for his command of the 3,670-mile voyage in the *Bounty*'s launch. Like his mentor, Captain Cook, he was a brilliant navigator, a brilliant seaman, a brilliant surveyor, and a humane man. The honor owed him for that voyage is long overdue. Simply, it is the greatest open-boat voyage of all time.

Recommended
A Voyage to the South Seas by William Bligh
Mutiny of the Bounty *and Story of Pitcairn Island 1790–1894*
by Rosalind Amelia Young
The Voyage of the Bounty's *Launch as Related in William Bligh's*
Despatch to the Admiralty with the Journal of John Fryer
by William Bligh and John Fryer
The Bounty by Caroline Alexander
Bounty replica, Hong Kong

Apollo 11: Landing on the Moon

The conquest of space began in October 1957, with the launch of the Soviet satellite *Sputnik 1*. It completed an orbit in ninety-six minutes at a speed of around seventeen miles per hour. In addition, it sent back information on the earth's upper atmosphere. It was a stunning achievement, and for a time the USSR threatened to have a man in space before America had launched its first satellite.

Sputnik 2 launched barely a month later, carrying the first living creature in space, a dog named Laika. There was no capacity for returning Laika to earth, and temperature and humidity increased steadily as the satellite completed its orbits. By the fourth orbit, Laika was dead; the craft burned up in the atmosphere five months later.

America's first response was a U.S. Navy satellite. In front of an audience of millions, it flamed out on the launching pad. The army took over and successfully launched a small satellite named *Explorer 1* in January 1958. It discovered the Van Allen belts, bands of radiation that surround the earth. The "space race" had begun, and *Sputnik 3* launched as early as May 1958. It was a hundred times heavier than *Explorer 1,* and the Soviets were clearly ahead.

The National Aeronautics and Space Administration (NASA) was created as a single-purpose organization in 1958. There would be no more interservice rivalry. NASA's mission was to take on the Soviet programs and beat them. By early 1959, one-man capsules were being designed and seven astronauts were chosen. At the same time satellite launches continued, so that by 1960 America had launched eighteen and all three *Sputnik*s had been destroyed as their orbits degraded and they reentered atmosphere. For a short window of time, space was solely American. But the Soviet launches had stopped for a reason. They had set their sights on the moon.

The moon travels in an ellipse around the earth, and the distance between them varies from around 225,000 miles to over 250,000. America's first attempts to reach it showed the magnitude of the task. In August 1958, *Able 1* blew up while still in earth's atmosphere. In October, *Pioneer 1* reached a third of the way to the moon before falling back and burning up. The sheer pace of these launches seems incredible even today. The Sputnik program had rocked America. National pride was at stake, and it took another dent when the Russians successfully launched *Lunik 1* in January 1959. It reached within 5,000 miles of the moon.

The U.S. *Pioneer 4* was more successful, but then the stakes were raised again. In September 1959 the Soviet *Lunik 2* sent back photographs of the hidden side of the moon. Only a month later, *Lunik 3* successfully crash-landed on the surface, another astonishing first.

In 1960 the Apollo program was conceived with the intention of landing a man on the moon and successfully returning to earth. At the same time, the Soviet Union was training twelve cosmonauts in the race to be first. President Kennedy in America and President Khrushchev in the USSR were both committed to the task. There were no constraints on budget, only on time.

Both countries had shown that they could physically reach the moon. The two main problems remaining were engineering a "soft landing" on the surface and the even more dangerous reentry to the earth's atmosphere. Depending on where you're standing, the earth spins at around a thousand miles per hour. The friction involved in reentering that atmosphere is immense and leads to temperatures of 2,700° F, just under the melting temperature of iron. It was an era of startlingly new and astonishing challenges for mankind.

Yury Gagarin was a Russian air force pilot who had retrained as a cosmonaut. On April 12, 1961, he reached space in a Vostok three-stage launch rocket. With parachutes, he and his capsule landed separately but safely in Russian farmland. As he walked across the fields in his orange jumpsuit, a little girl asked him if he had come from space. "I certainly have," he replied, smiling.

When he heard, the delighted Soviet premier Khrushchev said publicly: "Let the capitalist countries *try* to catch up."

Less than a month later, Alan Shepard was the first American in space, reaching a height of 116 miles before returning. He too landed safely, and on May 25, President Kennedy gave what may be his most famous speech, saying: "I believe that this nation should commit itself to achieving the goal, before this decade is out, of landing a man on the moon and returning him safely to earth." Never before or since has a president staked his nation's pride on so clear an objective. The Soviet Union had put the first man in space. Now it was the moon or bust.

In February 1962, American John Glenn completed successful orbits in his *Friendship 7* capsule. In the same year Soviet cosmonauts spent four days in space before returning. The Apollo program kicked into high gear with a two-module spacecraft system, consisting of a command/service model that could orbit around the moon and a lunar module that could land on the surface. A three-man crew was necessary, as two men would descend to the surface and one man remain behind in the command module.

America launched a series of Gemini test flights, so named because it held two astronauts. The Soviet Union responded in 1963 by putting the first woman in space, Valentina Tereshkova. It was another propaganda triumph for the Soviet regime.

Space was there for the taking, and both countries launched probes to other planets as well as weather and observation satellites. In 1963, America announced a new three-man team of astronauts: Neil Armstrong, Edwin "Buzz" Aldrin, and Michael Collins. They would become the most famous men on earth. In 1964, America sent back television pictures of the hard landing of *Ranger 7* on the moon and the first television pictures of Mars. A year later a cosmonaut completed the first space walk, leaving his launch vehicle in orbit. The space age had truly begun.

In 1967 disasters struck both the American and Soviet programs.

Three astronauts died in a fire as they rehearsed an Apollo mission at Cape Kennedy. A Russian cosmonaut was killed when his capsule parachute failed, and in early 1968, Yury Gagarin died when his plane crashed.

The Apollo tests went on, sending back television pictures of the maneuvers in earth orbit. The *Apollo 7* mission proved that the command-capsule sequence with three men could work. On Christmas Day 1968, the *Apollo 8* crew of Frank Borman, James Lovell, and William Anders flew around the moon and returned to earth. They were the first men to see the moon up close. Frank Borman said that it was beautiful but hostile. The end of the decade was looming, and President Kennedy's promise had not yet been fulfilled. But reentry had been conquered. Only the soft landing on the moon remained.

The *Apollo 9* mission tested the docking and separation of the lunar lander in orbit, and *Apollo 10* reached the moon once more, testing the entire system in lunar orbit and looking for suitable landing sites. The team of Thomas Stafford, Eugene Cernan, and John Young had prepared the way for the final assault on the moon.

In just *twelve years,* humankind had gone from a successful satellite launch to a manned attempt at a moon landing. To put it another way, in barely sixty years, we had gone from the first crude airplanes to the moon. *Apollo 11* was ready to launch.

At sunrise on July 16, 1969, Neil Armstrong and Michael Collins took their seats in *Apollo 11,* above the immense *Saturn V* rocket that would blast them out of the atmosphere. Buzz Aldrin was the last to board, but he had trained endlessly for the task ahead and was quietly confident.

To reach "escape velocity" and leave the gravity well of earth, the *Saturn V* rocket had to accelerate up to 24,200 miles per hour, around 7 miles per second. It is of course possible to leave earth more slowly, but only at the expense of vast amounts of fuel.

In the case of *Apollo 11,* it was similar to sitting on top of an enormous bomb. Even so, Aldrin later described the initial acceleration as so gentle that he had to check the instruments to know they were moving. They had all been in space before, on Gemini missions, but it is difficult to imagine the excitement they must have felt.

Apollo 11 reached earth's orbit in just twelve minutes. It completed one and a half orbits before a secondary engine fired and catapulted them toward the moon.

All three men looked out of the window as they left, watching the blue-green planet shrink to the size of a coin. The journey to the moon would take four days, so they ate and slept and checked the instruments, waiting for the chance to make history.

After traveling 238,587 miles, they established an orbit around the moon on July 19. Thirty orbits followed before *Apollo 11* separated into two parts: *Columbia,* which would remain in orbit with Michael Collins, and *Eagle,* the four-legged lunar lander that would take Armstrong and Aldrin to the surface. It was an incredibly light, fragile vehicle. Aldrin said he could have pushed a pencil through its walls.

The computer had selected a landing site, but as the two men approached the surface, they realized it was too rocky. Neil Armstrong took manual control of *Eagle,* guiding it with small puffs of propellant. Aldrin called out the height from the ground as they came down as gently as possible. By the time they landed, they had only fifty seconds of fuel to spare, but they were down safely. The two men grinned at each other.

The first words spoken on the moon were actually by Buzz Aldrin, while still in the lander. He was confirming technical data with Armstrong and said: "Contact light! Okay—engine stop. ACA—out of detent." After that Armstrong said the more famous words: "Houston, Tranquility Base here. The *Eagle* has landed." They rested and ate a meal, then began to put on their space suits to go outside.

One lesser-known fact is that Aldrin was an elder of the Webster Presbyterian Church, and he also took communion, the first ever religious service off-planet. The chalice he used is still used to commemorate the event each year.

Neil Armstrong climbed out first, activating the cameras as he did so. He clambered down the ladder and landed gently in the one-sixth gravity of the moon. Famously, he said: "That's one small step for . . . man, one giant leap for mankind." Aldrin then climbed down to join him on the surface.

There is no color on the moon. Aldrin described it as "magnificent desolation." The landscape is gray and white, and without an atmosphere, the sky is as black as the darkest night on earth. In the distance, they could see earth hanging in the sky. For the first time in human existence, a man standing on another world could look at the home of Einstein, Galileo, Newton, and every other man and woman who had ever lived.

With cameras sending a broadcast back to earth, Aldrin planted the Stars and Stripes and saluted. They went on to deploy an array of scientific equipment, collect forty-eight pounds of rocks, and leave a plaque with these words: HERE MEN FROM THE PLANET EARTH FIRST SET FOOT ON THE MOON JULY 1969 A.D. WE CAME IN PEACE FOR ALL MANKIND. It has two images of earth and the signatures of the astronauts and the president, Richard Nixon. In addition, they left a silicon disk with etched messages from former presidents Eisenhower, Kennedy, and Johnson, as well as Nixon and other world leaders.

In all, they spent just over two and a half hours on the surface before returning to the *Eagle* to rest and prepare for takeoff and docking with the orbiter. Reentry and the splashdown in the Pacific went without a hitch on July 24, and the astronauts were honored around the world.

Since that extraordinary event, nine other men have visited the moon. We did not find precious metals or even the remnants of civilization there, as many had hoped, but if there is ever to be a launching pad for further manned exploration, the moon is the obvious choice. We will go back.

Recommended
The Invasion of the Moon 1969: The Story of Apollo 11
by Peter Ryan
Apollo 11: *The NASA Mission Reports* by Buzz Aldrin and Robert Goodwin, vols. 1 and 2

Arthur Wellesley,
Duke of Wellington

No collection of heroes could be complete without the man known as "the Iron Duke." There are few for whom becoming prime minister of England is only a small part of their life and honors. Winston Churchill was one of those, Arthur Wellesley certainly another.

He never lost a major battle and is famous as the man who stopped Napoléon on land, as Nelson stopped him at sea. It is no exaggeration to say that without the military talent of this particular man, Britain would not have remained a free nation. Interestingly, the pantheon of British, commonwealth, and empire heroes has as its brightest stars not those who conquered but those who resisted dictators and oppression.

Arthur Wesley (originally "Wesley" until the family adopted the earlier spelling of "Wellesley") was born in 1769 to a Protestant family in Ireland. In the same year a boy was born in Corsica who would go on to be Emperor Napoléon Bonaparte.

Arthur Wesley's father was the Earl of Mornington and owned land in Ireland, so that young Arthur was born with the title "the Honorable." Regarding his Irishness, he later said famously that being born in a stable does not make one a horse.

His earliest years were spent in Dublin before his family moved to London. His father died in 1781, and his older brother Richard inherited the title. Arthur attended Eton in the same year. However, his family lacked financial security and he left after only a short time. His mother then moved to Brussels.

In those days, the army was not regarded as a suitable career for noble sons, in part because of its use as a police force at times of national unrest. Even so, Arthur was sent to be trained at the Royal

Academy of Equitation in France. He learned basic French as well as becoming a decent hand at the violin before returning to England in 1786.

His brother wrote to the lord lieutenant of Ireland to secure a commission for Arthur, and he was gazetted as ensign, joining the Seventy-third Highland Regiment of Foot. His brother's support aided his rise, and a year later Arthur Wesley was promoted to lieutenant in the Seventy-sixth Regiment, then transferred to the Forty-first, which was on its way to Ireland.

In Ireland, Wesley also tried his hand at politics for the first time. He spoke well at public meetings and was elected to the Irish House of Commons as MP for Trim. Around the same time, he met Kitty Pakenham, the daughter of the Earl of Longford. However, when he asked formally for her hand in marriage, her family refused. In great distress, Wesley burned his violins and never played again.

With that defeat behind him, Arthur borrowed money from his brother and purchased the ranks of major, then lieutenant colonel, commanding the Thirty-third Regiment. In later years, when men such as Garnet Wolseley were reforming the system that allowed men to purchase commissions, it became generally accepted that the practice had allowed great incompetence and corruption. That may be true, but it also gave us the man who would become the Duke of Wellington.

In 1794, the Thirty-third was sent to Flanders to resist a French invasion. There Wesley was promoted to command a brigade of three battalions and saw his first major military action at Breda in September. He and his men stopped a French column with steady fire from their flintlocks.

In 1795, faced with overwhelming French forces, the army was evacuated in chaos and Wesley saw firsthand the incompetence of senior officers. The experience taught him a great deal and stood him in good stead years later. He suffered with illness caused by damp and a frozen winter and had a good idea of the horror and misery that was a part of the soldier's life.

In 1796, at the age of twenty-seven, Wesley traveled as colonel of the Thirty-third to India, leaving behind a troubled Ireland that would erupt into violent rebellion just two years later. In the same year, Napoléon married his mistress, Josephine, and took command of the armies of Italy.

The India of that time was experiencing the last great days of John Company before it was taken over by the Crown. The British East India Company was in almost sole control of the subcontinent, and there were still fortunes to be made when Wesley landed at Calcutta in 1797. France, Holland, and Spain had all declared war on Britain, and advancement could be quick for a competent young officer. It could not have hurt that his brother Richard was being sent as governor general of British India. It was his brother who changed the spelling of the family name back to a much older form. Young Arthur accepted the change readily enough and used "Wellesley" first in a letter announcing the arrival of his brother in India. Another brother, Henry, also came as Richard's private secretary.

Arthur Wellesley went with the Thirty-third to Madras in 1798, a harsh sea journey during which fifteen of his men died from fevers brought on by bad water supplies. He joined the staff of General Harris for a time, handing command of the Thirty-third to Major John Shee. By December 1798, Wellesley was in command of a mixed force of British and Indian units intent on battle with the forces of Tipu Sultan, known as "the Tiger of Mysore." As an open ally of France, Tipu Sultan was seen as a potential threat.

With his men, Wellesley traveled to the sultan's fortress of Seringapatam. Another large force under Harris moved up from the east, while a smaller one marched from the Malabar coast.

On March 10, 1799, Tipu Sultan's cavalry attacked the rear guard. Wellesley led the counterattack and saw them off without major losses. In another attack, the Thirty-third routed the enemy with bayonet charges. Tipu withdrew to the fortress.

Wellseley took part in a night attack on an outlying village, but it was chaotic in the darkness and the Thirty-third was beaten back by Tipu's rocket teams and musket fire. Wellesley was hit in the knee by a spent musket ball, though not seriously wounded. He took the position easily enough the following day but said later that he had learned "never to attack an enemy who is prepared and strongly posted, and whose posts have not been reconnoitered by daylight."

Seringapatam fell after British guns made a breach in the walls. Tipu Sultan was killed in the fighting that followed, his body found by Wellesley himself. He returned to his camp, bathed, and slept. Overall command was not his, and he could do nothing while British soldiers looted and gutted the fortress.

The following morning Wellesley was appointed governor of Seringapatam. He strode back in, hanged four soldiers, and flogged many others to suppress the orgy of looting and destruction. He was paid four thousand pounds as prize money for his part and offered to pay his brother Richard back for the loan to purchase a commission. His proud brother refused the offer. Despite recurring sickness, Wellesley completed his duties as governor. He was promoted to major general shortly afterward.

In 1802 he was ordered to battle against the Maratha Confederacy, a number of Hindu principalities united in opposition to British power in India. Arthur Wellesley planned the campaign in great detail, which was already a habit of his but unusual for the time. In 1803 he took around 15,000 of his own men and 9,000 Indian troops six hundred miles to a Maratha fort. He had decided that a long defensive war was impossible, so moved quickly and boldly. His men took the defended local town in less than an hour.

As one of the Maratha officers said: "The English are a strange people, and their general a wonderful man. They came here in the morning, looked at the Pettah wall, walked over it, killed the garrison and returned to breakfast! What can withstand them?" The fort itself surrendered only days later.

The brilliantly fought battle of Assaye followed on September 23. Wellesley's men were outnumbered seven to one, but he was still intent on quick victory as the only possible plan. Under heavy cannon fire, his army had to cross the Kaitna River, then attack a vastly larger force. He briefed his officers in person once they were across the river, impressing them with his calm demeanor as shot whistled on all sides. The Seventy-eighth Highlanders were the first to meet the Maratha infantry. Wellington had his horse killed under him and calmly mounted another. It was a chaotic scene, and Wellesley's regiments were battered by cavalry as they advanced and eventually routed the enemy. Wellesley lost 1,584 men killed or wounded, while the Marathas lost around 6,000 as well as all their guns. It had been a costly victory, and Wellesley said later that it was "the bloodiest for the numbers that I ever saw."

Other battles followed, and in December, Wellesley took the key fortress of Gawilghur, a loss that was the final straw for the Maratha forces. They sued for peace, giving up disputed territories and disbanding their men.

Wellesley was made a Knight of the Bath in 1804 and had amassed a personal fortune of some £42,000. He applied for leave to return home in 1805. On the way, his ship stopped briefly at the island of Saint Helena, which would one day be the final prison of Napoléon Bonaparte. In India he had learned his trade, from the need for personal fitness and moderation to the logistical importance of planning a campaign down to the vital supplies of food, water, and ammunition.

In England, an expeditionary force was being prepared to fight against Napoléon. Wellesley was keen to command it and traveled to the Colonial Office on Downing Street to put his case to Lord Castlereagh. In the outer office he waited for a time with an admiral named Horatio Nelson. Wellesley recognized him, but at first Nelson did not know the general fresh from India. When Nelson found out who he was, they talked for some time and Wellington said later that he'd never had a conversation that interested him more. The following day, Nelson joined HMS *Victory* and went out to the battle of Trafalgar and his death.

While Napoléon was winning the battle of Austerlitz, perhaps his greatest victory, Arthur Wellesley was given a brigade at Hastings in England, a long way from the action he desired. There he offered marriage to Kitty Pakenham for a second time. He was no longer a penniless young man without a future, and in November 1805 she agreed to marry him. He also returned to the political debates of the day. He was elected as MP for Rye in 1806 and used his position to support his brother when Richard was accused of wasting public money in India.

Wellesley married Kitty Pakenham in April 1806, though with an extraordinary lack of grace, he muttered to a friend that "she has grown ugly, by Jove!" It was not to be a happy marriage and may have come about in part because of the obligation and challenge he felt after the first proposal was turned down. After a brief honeymoon, he returned to his brigade.

In 1807, Wellesley was given command against the Danes. In what is known as the second battle of Copenhagen, he bombarded the Danish capital until they surrendered. The British aim of securing Danish ships for their own fleet was accomplished. More important, it denied those ships to the Napoleonic fleet. Wellesley was promoted to lieutenant general.

In 1808, he prepared to take command of an army heading to defend allied Portugal. His years there in what would become known as the Peninsular War would secure his fame and Napoléon Bonaparte's eventual downfall.

At that time, Spain had deserted its alliance with France and was using guerrilla tactics against French forces there. Britain was keen to support any European nation willing to fight Napoléon. Wellesley had a small army of around fifteen thousand, and his first action was to march from Mondego Bay on the west coast, to join up with sixteen hundred Portuguese soldiers. He faced two active French armies in Portugal as he pushed on south to Lisbon, the capital.

He reached Óbidos by August 1808 and climbed a church tower to view a French army only miles away. The following day he attacked. The French army under Delaborde was forced into a fighting withdrawal. Though it was not a rout, it was an auspicious beginning, and reinforcements arrived for Wellesley, so that he had around seventeen thousand men.

The battle of Vimeiro followed on August 21. Wellesley's forces met two large French columns. His riflemen engaged them as they approached, killing many before the enemy was close enough for his artillery to fire one round from cannon. The French column then met a British line and was hammered by concentrated musket volleys. The French broke quickly and the rifle regiments ran out again to shoot them as they left the field. Wellesley used the new shrapnel ordnance to great effect against the massed French forces, though he felt his cavalry could have done better, having lost their heads and many lives by galloping wildly after the fleeing French. In all his career, he preferred infantry to cavalrymen, whom he regarded as having very little common sense.

The battle was over by noon, and shortly afterward senior British officers agreed the Convention of Cintra, a French request to evacuate peacefully from Portugal. Wellesley was among those who imposed very generous terms and allowed the French to take even looted supplies with them. It took the rest of the summer to organize and would later be ridiculed at home. He was summoned back to Britain for an inquiry, leaving Sir John Moore in command of the force in Portugal.

Wellesley was eventually cleared in the inquiry, but by then, Sir John Moore had been killed in the famous retreat to Corunna and successful evacuation from Spain. It was around that time that Wellington visited his bootmaker in London to commission a pair of calfskin boots that would resist being waterlogged. Though they were not made of rubber until the 1850s, the Wellington boot became extremely popular in his lifetime and remains so today.

In 1809 Wellesley returned to Portugal in overall command. By then, French marshal Soult had overrun much of Portugal and two veteran French armies were in almost complete control. Wellesley had around 20,000 under his command. He made a lightning march north to Oporto, but Soult was too experienced to be trapped in the city and had destroyed bridges across the Douro River. Wellesley was forced to rely on barges to get slowly across, but there was no help for it. His army retook the city of Oporto and forced Soult's men out, killing or wounding 4,000 in the process.

Moving east into Spain, Wellesley was not impressed by his Spanish allies, though they brought around 20,000 men to join him. With reinforcements, Wellesley had 55,000 to move against the French under Marshal Victor and Napoléon's brother Joseph. However, when he approached the area and looked for the Spanish, there was no sign of them. His messenger was told that the Spanish were too tired to fight that hot day, and the French escaped the trap.

The French attacked first at the battle of Talavera in Spain toward the end of July 1809. Their skirmishers very nearly captured or killed Wellesley as he observed the distant French forces with a telescope. He reached his horse and managed to escape, with shots fired after him. His Spanish allies had assembled for the battle and fired a volley at the French. To Wellesley's astonishment, around two thousand Spaniards "were frightened only at the noise of their own fire" and ran away.

As night fell, Wellesley rode across to investigate some firing and was again almost killed by French skirmishers. In pitch-darkness, he was dragged from his horse and his aide was shot dead. He managed to regain his saddle and returned to his lines, shaken but unhurt.

The following morning the French bombardment began and

Wellesley ordered his men to lie down on the far slope of a small hill while the riflemen engaged the French skirmishers. This "reverse slope defense," using the lie of the land to protect his men, was one of his favorite tactics. The French columns advanced confidently into the gun smoke, expecting the British forces to be smashed and reeling. Wellesley's men rose to fire point-blank volleys. They drove the French back, and once again the wide British line, where all the guns could bear, broke the French column, a hallmark of the Peninsular War. Even so, the fighting was brutal and often came down to hand-to-hand and bayonet charges.

Wellesley saw a large French force of infantry coming to a breach in his lines and sent a single battalion to stop them with more of the devastating volleys. His talent was in his coolness, and he never lost the overall sense of a battle, even when the shot was flying around him and men just paces away were being killed.

That night, Joseph Bonaparte withdrew the surviving French forces in defeat. For that victory and others, Wellesley was later made Viscount Wellington of Talavera.

In 1810, Marshal Masséna was ordered to retake Portugal with an army of 138,000 men. Wellington moved to block the French advance into the country, while Portuguese irregulars attacked the French wherever possible. He also ordered the creation of the famous lines of Torres Vedras—a system of fortified positions to protect Lisbon that stretched right across part of southern Portugal. At that time, before the trenches of World War I, it was one of the most efficient and impressive fortification lines ever created. On his orders, 108 forts, 151 redoubts, and more than 1,000 heavy artillery pieces formed the lines, with almost 70,000 men in place to defend them.

A brief battle was fought at Bussaco, where the French lost more than 4,500 men to Wellington's 1,252. Even so, Wellington justified the immense expense and labor that had gone into the lines when he was forced to retreat to them against overwhelming numbers. Behind him, he used a "scorched earth" policy, his men stripping the land of anything that might feed the French soldiers coming south. It was successful. The French began to starve, and Marshal Masséna had to leave for Spain to resupply his army. In all, Masséna lost some 30,000 men over that winter. In 1811 he returned to Portugal and attempted to relieve the fortress city of Almeida on the eastern border with Spain.

The war continued with Wellington defending Almeida, while part of his force under Beresford besieged the French-held fortress of Badajoz in the south. Marshal Masséna launched a massive attack on Almeida to relieve it but could not break Wellington's forces.

At Badajoz, without Wellington's watchful presence, things were much worse. The siege of the fortress had begun in May 1811, though its massive and ancient walls proved resistant to the guns. Marshal Soult arrived to relieve Badajoz and fought a fixed battle after pinning the British forces down. For once, the Spanish allies held their ground long enough for reinforcements to arrive during vicious fighting. Even then British forces were almost cut to pieces in French cavalry charges. A rainstorm had soaked the gunpowder in their flintlocks, and for a time they were almost overrun. Galbraith Lowry Cole brought up his Fourth Division, and they moved forward slowly against the French, hammering them with volleys.

The battle of Albuera was over before Wellington arrived, despite him having killed two horses riding to reach his men. It was a slender victory for the British forces, though it cost them 6,000 dead. Famously, when Wellington visited the field hospital, he told the wounded men that he was sorry to see so many of them there. One replied: "If you had commanded us, my lord, there wouldn't be so many of us here."

At that time, French armies were always in range and poised to retake Portugal. Wellington's forces began to besiege Ciudad Rodrigro, a fortified town across the Spanish border. Like Badajoz, it guarded one of the two main routes into Portugal from Spain.

Artillery made a breach in the walls of Ciudad Rodrigro, and the assault on the town took place on January 18, 1812, against ferocious French resistance. After their surrender, Wellington went south and took Badajoz at last, after a month of siege and heavy bombardment. It is said that he broke down at the sight of the British dead in the breaches there, weeping in front of his men for the only time. The Spanish made Wellington a Duke of Ciudad Rodrigro for his part in the defense of their nation.

The year 1812 would also see the battle of Salamanca in Spain, when Wellington's Anglo-Portuguese force routed a French army of around 50,000. It was a triumph of maneuver as well as force. Wellington was watching the French positions when he saw a weakness in their lines as they moved. He shouted: "By God, that will do!" before ordering the attack.

The defeated French marshal said that Wellington had maneuvered his men "like Frederick the Great." The road to Madrid was open, and that battle, as no other, established Wellington as the most able general Britain could field, though his greatest victory was still to come.

A new allied offensive in 1813 included the battle of Vitoria, where Wellington beat the army of Joseph Bonaparte. Seeing his men loot abandoned wagons after that battle, Wellington made one of his most famous comments: "We have in the service the scum of the earth as common soldiers."

By 1814, French forces had been forced to withdraw from Spain and Portugal and Wellington had crossed the Pyrenees to invade France, his men the first foreign troops to enter the country at the beginning of Napoléon's downfall. Napoléon's armies were in disarray.

The self-titled French emperor abdicated in 1814 and was exiled to the island of Elba. Before Wellington returned to England, he published a final word to his army, in which he wrote: "The Commander of the Forces, being upon the point of returning to England, again takes this opportunity of congratulating the army upon the recent events which have restored peace to their country and the world."

He was made a duke by a grateful nation, the highest order of nobility, to add to his previous titles of viscount, earl, and field marshal, among many others. The tyranny of France over Europe had been broken, and peace was possible at last.

Wellington visited Paris for a time, where he met the abolitionist Thomas Clarkson. Clarkson found him well informed. Wellington had previously promised Wilberforce that he would do everything in his power to help abolish slavery. Wellington was in fact balked in this desire by those who had made fortunes from the trade. It would be many years before slavery was eventually abolished across the empire.

Wellington attended the peace negotiations for the Treaty of Vienna in January 1815. It was still going on when he heard the news that shook Europe. Napoléon had escaped.

In March, with the help of a French ship, Napoléon Bonaparte set foot in France once more. On news of his return, King Louis XVIII of France sent a regiment to intercept him before he could reach Paris. Famously, Napoléon threw open his coat to reveal his military decorations and said: "Let him who has the heart kill his emperor!" Instead, they cheered him and followed him back to Paris. The Hundred Days' War began as he gathered 118,000 regular soldiers, 300,000 conscripts, and another 100,000 support personnel. Finally, he had the veteran Army of the North around Paris—another 124,000 men.

Against him, Wellington had an Anglo-Dutch and Hanoverian force of 92,000 in Flanders and a Prussian army of 124,000 under Marshal Blücher. The Austrians had 210,000 men and an army of 75,000 more stationed in Italy. There was also a Russian army in the east of 167,000 mobilizing to march against this threat of another reign of terror. The stakes had never been higher, and only Napoléon could have tried to win against such odds. He might even have been successful if the commander facing him had not been the Duke of Wellington. Before Wellington left Vienna, Tsar Nicholas of Russia laid a hand on his shoulder and said to him: "It is for you to save the world again."

Napoléon's only hope was to try to crush the armies against him one by one rather than allowing them to join forces. No one else could have done it, but he was a superb military tactician and, like Wellington, always kept a clear sense of the vast tapestry of units that made up a campaign area. His armies moved quickly into Belgium, but Wellington was also on the move and his allied force stopped one of Napoléon's marshals at Quatre Bras, south of Brussels. As a result, the beleaguered Prussian forces were preserved after losing a battle at Ligny, where the French failed to follow up for lack of support.

Wellington moved his forces to the south, taking command of the ridge Mont-Saint-Jean near a village named Waterloo. That night, June 17, it rained in torrents.

The Prussian general, Blücher, had given his promise to Wellington that he would support and reinforce his men. His deputy, Gneisenau, was convinced that Wellington would be quickly routed by the French army and wanted to leave the area. Though Blücher was seventy-two years old and already wounded in previous fighting, he held to his word.

On June 18, 1815, the French bombardment began. Napoléon had a force of around 74,000 compared with Wellington's 67,000. His guns, known as his *belles filles* or "beautiful daughters," hammered the allied force before his veteran troops marched forward to take the British-held ridge. They endured artillery fire themselves but climbed the ridge in the teeth of it, fighting with bayonets and rifles against Wellington's men. The Earl of Uxbridge then smashed them with a cavalry charge over the ridge.

Napoléon was by then aware of the approach of the Prussian forces under Blücher. He sent almost his entire reserve force of nearly fifteen thousand infantry and cavalry to hold that flank, keeping back only his elite soldiers, the Imperial Guard. They had never been defeated in battle, and their reputation made them a feared force on any European battlefield. It was a vital decision. Delaying the main attack on Wellington to repel the Prussians may well have lost Napoléon the battle.

At the same time, Marshal Ney tried to break the British center with cavalry alone. Wellington responded with small square formations that were weak against infantry but almost impossible for a cavalry charge to shatter. Horses will not leap into a solid mass of men with bayonets.

One British captain later recalled the French horse as an "overwhelming, long moving line, which, ever advancing, glittered like a stormy wave of the sea when it catches the sunlight. On they came until they got near enough, whilst the very earth seemed to vibrate beneath the thundering tramp of the mounted host. One might suppose that nothing could have resisted the shock of this terrible moving mass."

Massed artillery and musket fire poured into the French cavalry as they came close, driving them back again and again as the light faded. It was around that time that the Earl of Uxbridge had his leg smashed by grapeshot as he sat in the saddle by Wellington.

"By God, sir, I've lost my leg!" he said in surprise.

"By God, sir," Wellington replied. "So you have."

Marshal Ney gave up his attempt to attack with cavalry alone and ordered French guns to fire grapeshot into the British squares, some of

whom were beginning to run out of ammunition. The carnage was terrible and the British forces wavered. Napoléon saw the moment, felt victory in his grasp. His main reserves were still embroiled in battle against the Prussians on the flank. Yet his Imperial Guard had not fought that day, and they were fresh and straining at the leash. He sent them in at last, to break the British center.

Their morale was high as they marched in three columns through a storm of skirmisher and canister fire. One of the columns smashed a British force of grenadiers, and then their own flank came under fire and they were charged down and routed. Another Imperial Guard column marched toward British Guard regiments under Colonel Maitland. They were lying on the ground to survive French artillery attacks. When Wellington saw the Imperial Guard closing on their position, he roared: "Up Guards and at 'em!"

The British Guards met the French with massed volley fire and a bayonet charge. With the Fifty-second Light Infantry, who wheeled in line to attack their broken flank, the Imperial Guards and Napoléon's last hope were smashed and broken. Famously, their bearskin hats were taken by the victorious regiments and are still worn by British Guards today. As the French soldiers ran in shock and terror, they shouted *"La Garde recule!"*—the Guard retreats.

The Prussians attacked once more, coordinating with Wellington's own counterattack. The French army collapsed and Napoléon withdrew from the battlefield, returning to Paris where he would be forced to abdicate again and surrender. It had been his greatest gamble, and Wellington later said of Waterloo that it had indeed been a "close-run thing."

Napoléon was taken to the island of Saint Helena off the coast of West Africa, one of the most isolated British possessions in the world. He died there six years later, in 1821.

Waterloo was Wellington's last battle, as well as his finest hour. He spent some time in Paris before finally coming home. In England he was lionized as he returned to his career in politics. He also enjoyed hunting and shooting, though he was a terrible shot and managed on different occasions to hit a dog, a gamekeeper, and an old lady as she did her washing.

Wellington represented Britain at an international congress in Verona in 1822 and took on various roles, such as Master General of the Ordnance, so was still connected to the military. He was part deafened from being too close to guns being tested, and he never recovered from the treatment, which involved a caustic solution being poured into his affected ear. He traveled to Vienna and Russia, where he met the tsar once more.

In 1828, Wellington became prime minister and held his first cabinet meeting at his home, Apsley House in London. Interestingly, he had a statue of Napoléon at the bottom of the stairs there, where it remains today. Wellington used to hang his hat on it.

He found the idea of a cabinet somewhat trying, saying, "I give them my orders and they stay to discuss them!" By then, he was close to sixty years old and had lost much of his youthful energy. Even so, he forced through a bill on Catholic emancipation, in the face of much opposition. The English people were still very wary of giving Catholics any rights whatsoever, and mobs threw stones at Wellington's home, smashing the windows. He ordered iron plates to be put in place and carried on. For this action, rather than any military success, he became known as "the Iron Duke."

When the Earl of Winchilsea said that Wellington planned to infringe liberties and introduce "popery into every department of the state," Wellington demanded satisfaction in a duel, which took place in March 1829. In the end, both men fired deliberately wide and the earl apologized to Wellington. At that time, dueling was illegal, and it was an extraordinary thing for a prime minister, even one with Wellington's history, to undertake.

The bill was passed and a reluctant king gave it royal assent. Wellington went on to assist in the creation of the Metropolitan Police in 1829. The continuation of that work would fall to his successor, Robert Peel, whose policemen were known as "bobbies" or "peelers," nicknames that endure today.

Wellington retired from political life in 1846. As Lord Warden of the Cinque Ports, he spent part of his final years at Walmer Castle and died there in 1852 at the age of eighty-three. He was given a state funeral and finally interred in Saint Paul's Cathedral, where his tomb lies in the room next to that of Admiral Nelson.

Britain has since survived perhaps even darker moments and greater dangers than Napoleonic ambition, so that it is difficult to imagine the threat of foreign tyranny in those times. There is even a tendency to romanticize Napoléon in a way that Hitler has never been. Yet Napoléon wanted nothing less than the complete subjugation and destruction of British freedoms. Nelson stopped him at sea and Wellington stopped him on land. That is Wellington's enduring legacy, far more than any marble tomb in London.

Recommended
Wellington: The Iron Duke by Richard Holmes
Saint Paul's Cathedral, London

Alcock and Brown:
Transatlantic, Nonstop

When the First World War ended, the new world of aviation turned its attention from military to peaceful challenges. Flying an airplane in those glorious, dangerous, pioneering years meant sitting in a wooden cockpit open to the elements, with a wooden propeller in front and the wind roaring too loudly for speech. Both pilot and passenger were burned by the sun and soaked by the rain. Airplanes were called flying machines, stringbags, and birdcages, with fragile wings of wood and canvas. It was the closest thing possible to being a bird.

When the *Daily Mail* offered a prize of ten thousand pounds for the first nonstop flight across the Atlantic Ocean by an airplane, "from any point in the United States, Canada or Newfoundland to any point in Great Britain or Ireland, in 72 consecutive hours," there was much shaking of wise heads.

The traditional first aeronautical challenge, the English Channel, had fallen as much earlier as 1785. In an Anglo-French effort by Jean-Pierre Blanchard and Dr. John Jeffries, a hydrogen balloon flew from Dover to Calais, but only by throwing all nonessentials out of the wicker basket—including Monsieur Blanchard's breeches. Being British and realizing that the first crossing was also the first international flight, Dr. Jeffries retained his breeches.

It was 124 years before an airplane crossed the channel. In a tiny 25-horsepower, home-built monoplane, Frenchman Louis Blériot flew from Les Baraques to Dover in 1909 to claim a *Daily Mail* prize of one thousand pounds. He very nearly crashed as he landed on the white cliffs, proving Australian flyer Charles Kingsford Smith's observation "Flying is easy. It's landing that's difficult."

Dover to Calais is twenty-three miles, yet only ten years later the talk was of crossing the Atlantic Ocean nonstop: 1,880 miles at its narrowest. The *Daily Mail* first offered the prize before the war as an incentive to aviation, but with the advances made in airplanes—in particular by Britain and Germany—such a flight had entered the realms of the barely possible.

By April Fools' Day 1919, six contenders announced that they would attempt the crossing that year. There were five Brits and one Swede, but almost immediately Swede Hugo Sundstedt crashed his biplane during a test flight in America.

Major John Wood was the first to fly, on April 18. He took off from Eastchurch, on the Isle of Sheppey in Kent, and flew westward across Britain in a two-seater seaplane named the *Shamrock*. Slung between the floats was a massive extra fuel tank. Twenty-two miles west of Wales, his engine seized and he was forced down into the Irish Sea. He and his navigator were picked up by a passing ship. Wood's enterprise embraced the prewar spirit of aviation—adventurous, against the odds, glorious, and extremely dangerous. Disappointed, the flying major declared, "The Atlantic flight is pipped!"

The remaining four transported their planes by ship to Newfoundland to fly west to east with the prevailing winds to reach Britain or Ireland. The intrepid flyers, engineers, and riggers assembled at Saint John's, capital of Newfoundland, in early May 1919. The four teams were experienced aircraft manufacturers: Sopwith, Martinsyde, Handley-Page, and Vickers, proud names in the history of aviation.

Sopwith Aviation Company chose for its pilot Harry Hawker, a lean Australian and the company's chief test pilot. His navigator was Lieutenant Commander Kenneth "Mac" Grieve, Royal Navy. For the attempt, Sopwith chose its new biplane called Atlantic. It was powered by a single Rolls-Royce Eagle Mark VIII engine. At that time it was the most powerful air engine in the world. In the Atlantic, it produced a speed of 100 knots and a range of 3,000 nautical miles. After takeoff Hawker could ditch the Atlantic's undercarriage in the sea to give an extra 7 knots of speed. Every knot might be needed. Hawker made two 900-mile test flights of the Atlantic in Britain, and the team was the favorite to succeed. As Hawker Company, Sopwith later produced the superb Hurricane fighter.

Martinsyde Aircraft Company also chose a small airplane. Its Raymor, a two-seater biplane, was powered by a single Rolls-Royce Falcon engine. Cruising speed was 110 knots with a range of 2,750 nautical miles, making the Raymor the fastest entrant. Its pilot was Freddie Raynham, age twenty-six. Raynham's navigator was Captain C. W. Fairfax "Fax" Morgan, a Royal Navy flyer. During the war he'd been shot down over France and used an artificial cork leg as a result. Fax was a descendant of the buccaneer Sir Henry Morgan. The Raymor was named after its pilot and navigator.

Handley-Page Transport, Ltd., then produced the largest airplane in the world, the V/1500 bomber, and selected a three-man crew for its attempt. Overall commander was fifty-five-year-old Admiral Mark Kerr with a Handley-Page pilot and navigator. The V/1500 was powered by four Rolls-Royce Eagle Mark VIIIs. The fuselage of the V/1500 was even large enough to have an enclosed cabin. Handley-Page later produced the *Victor* nuclear-strike bomber.

Vickers, Ltd., the last entrant, chose twenty-six-year-old Captain John "Jackie" Alcock, DSO, as pilot and Lieutenant

Arthur "Teddie" Brown as navigator. Alcock was born in Manchester and Brown in Glasgow. They were both ex-RAF flyers, and both had been brought down during the war. Brown had a lame left leg to remind him of his crash. He was engaged but delayed the wedding when offered the position as navigator.

Vickers chose its Vimy bomber for the Atlantic attempt, an aircraft named after the battle of Vimy Ridge. The Vimy was the second-largest aircraft in the world, 43½ feet long with a wingspan of 68 feet. A good-looking biplane—and good-looking airplanes are usually good-flying airplanes—it was powered by two Rolls-Royce Eagle Mark VIII engines. With its bomb racks and gunner's equipment removed and two extra gas tanks filled into the fuselage, the Vimy had a cruising speed of 90 knots with a range of 2,800 nautical miles. Vickers later produced the brilliant Supermarine Spitfire fighter.

The strong naval presence may seem odd now, but in 1919 the majority of air navigators were seamen. Both flyers and sailors navigate using the heavens and land features. Both use rudders, both use port and starboard, both use cockpits and cabins, and so on. The different airflows above and below a wing that "lifts" a plane into the air are exactly the same as the airflows in front and behind a sail that "draw" a vessel through the water.

The four planes had at least 1,880 nautical miles to fly—by a long, long way the greatest distance ever attempted—yet the biggest obstacle to success was the Atlantic weather. It was unpredictable, unknown, and dangerous, with no weather ships and no weather satellites; conditions could change in moments. Gales and wind shear can blow an aircraft miles off course. Clouds and fog can blind and disorientate pilot and navigator. Ice can form on wings, destroying the lift of the machine, and in those days, instruments and engines often packed up in such extreme conditions.

In their favor was the west-to-east prevailing wind, so that even if they met contrary winds within a weather system, the system itself usually moved east. Yet even prevailing winds sometimes don't blow, and weather systems don't always follow the rules laid down by meteorologists.

"It's a piece of cake!" said Jackie Alcock after a test flight in England. "All we have to do is keep the engines going and we'll be home for tea."

Fields long and flat enough for aircraft to take off from were rare in rugged Newfoundland. Sopwith and Martinsyde were first to arrive and found meadows suitable for their small aircraft—just. Handley-Page located fields sixty miles from Saint John's at Harbour Grace and spent a month clearing and joining them together. Vickers took down hedges, dismantled walls, felled trees, rolled boulders, filled ditches, and even removed a stone dyke to create a five-hundred-yard airfield close to Saint John's.

Every Newfoundlander knew what was at stake, of course. Willingly, they helped the four teams prepare. Alcock christened Vickers's airfield Lester's Field, after the drayman who hauled the crated aircraft from the dockside. To ease the hard labor new words were added to a local folk song:

> Oh, lay hold Jackie Alcock, lay hold Teddie Brown,
> Lay hold of the cordage and dig into the ground.
> Lay hold of the bowline and pull all you can,
> The Vimy will fly afore the Handley-Page can.

However, it was Sopwith's Atlantic that first left Newfoundland, on the afternoon of May 18. That morning Hawker described the weather as "not yet favourable, but possible," and began to fill his fuel tanks. Raynham made the same optimistic forecast and fueled Martinsyde's Raymor. The V/1500 was not yet assembled, while Vickers still awaited its aircraft's arrival.

At noon, Hawker and Grieve decided they'd fly and informed the other teams. In a gentleman's agreement it had been decided that each team would let the other know its plans. At 3:40 Hawker called cheerily from the cockpit: "Tell Raynham I'll greet him at Brooklands," and sent the Atlantic swaying across the soggy field. After three hundred yards the wheels lifted, then cleared a row of trees. The airplane was off.

Harry Hawker and Mac Grieve circled once above Martinsyde's

field alongside Lake Quidi Vidi to wave, crossed the coast, jettisoned the Atlantic's undercarriage, and headed for the British Isles. In six minutes they were out of sight in the Atlantic murk.

Two hours later, the faster Raymor, was ready and about two thousand Newfoundlanders had gathered to watch the takeoff. Freddie Raynham and Fax Morgan waved. Raynham opened the throttle and began the Raymor's run across Quidi Vidi field into a crosswind. There is less lift from a crosswind than from a headwind. After three hundred yards, the Raymor's wheels left the ground and she rose about ten feet—and obstinately stayed there, drifting slightly sideways. The Raymor dropped to the ground, the undercarriage collapsed, the propeller dug into the turf, and she crashed. Raynham was not seriously injured and crawled from the cockpit with a bang to his head, but Fax had to be lifted out and taken to the hospital. He was told he'd lose an eye.

Alcock and Brown visited Martinsyde's flyers in the hospital that evening. Raynham offered them the Quidi Vidi field so that they could assemble the Vimy for test flights while Lester's Field was completed. Meanwhile, no radio message had been received from the Atlantic. In itself this was of no concern, for 1919 was also the pioneering age of radio; they frequently stopped working.

When the Atlantic's maximum flying time of twenty-two hours was reached the next afternoon, there was still no word from Britain or any ship. It was evident that the aircraft was down somewhere in the Atlantic Ocean.

The dismantled Vimy arrived at Saint John's Harbor on May 26—the day after good news had arrived by telegram. Hawker and Grieve had been picked up from the Atlantic Ocean by a Danish steamer and reached Scotland on the twenty-fifth. The Atlantic's radio had broken immediately after takeoff. The weather had worsened with heavy rain squalls, and after four hours the engine began to overheat. The problem was a blockage in the cooling system. By repeatedly switching off the engine, diving, then switching on again, Harry Hawker had partially cleared the blockages. They'd continued until dawn on the nineteenth, but it was clear the engine was not going to take the aircraft to Britain. With a gale approaching, Hawker and Grieve had searched for a ship and ditched the Atlantic alongside it. Half an hour later the gale came through.

In Newfoundland, the Vimy was assembled in record time, working in the open through rain and snow. Only two weeks after arriving, the aircraft made its first test flight from the Quidi Vidi field. The same day, the V/1500 made its first test flight from Harbour Grace. On June 8 Alcock and Brown flew the Vimy in its second test flight to Lester's Field.

At Quidi Vidi, engineers and riggers were also repairing the Raymor and a navigator was found to replace Fax Morgan. Raynham was trying for another attempt. The V/1500 made her second test flight but also encountered engine-cooling problems. It was a toss-up which of the three aircraft would depart next.

Alcock drained the cooling systems of the two Vimy engines, boiled the water twice, and filtered it to remove any matter that might block circulation. He thought that the sediment in the Newfoundland water might have caused the Atlantic and V/1500 cooling problems. The weather closed in again with successive gales before clearing on the morning of the thirteenth.

Alcock made another decision at Lester's Field, possibly taking a leaf from the Atlantic's book. He removed the Vimy's nosewheel in order to reduce drag. The nosewheel was there only for landing, to stop the plane from pitching forward should the undercarriage snag in grass. The Vimy normally rested and landed on the four wheels of the main undercarriage beneath the wings and a small tail wheel. Without a nosewheel Alcock would have to ensure he made a decent three-point touchdown when he landed.

Riggers and engineers worked throughout the day and night, and by the morning of the fourteenth the Vimy was refueled and ready to fly. Stowed on board were 197 letters, potentially the first transatlantic airmail. Alcock and Brown spoke together briefly and decided to fly. They sent a message to the V/1500 at Harbour Grace and a telegram to Vickers. The *Daily Mail* sent a telegram to London. Raynham came to see them off.

Early that afternoon, with the Rolls-Royce engines running smoothly, the Vimy jolted across Lester's Field and gathered speed, heading slightly uphill into a west wind. The picnicking Newfoundlander crowd watched interestedly then anxiously: 100 yards, 150 yards, the tail lifted, 200 yards, 300 yards, 400 yards. Only 100 yards of field remained.

Brown wrote later: "We were almost at the end of the ground tether allowed us." He glanced at Alcock. "The perspiration of acute anxiety was running down his face." The distance between success and disaster would be just feet. The watching Raynham knew how Alcock would be at the controls, the throttles wide open, gently coaxing the machine up.

The jolting stopped as the undercarriage finally left the ground, the four wheels skimming the grass. Alcock eased back the stick a touch—only a touch—or the aircraft would stall and crash. Brown held his breath as they reached the end of the field. The Vimy rose, cleared a stone dyke, then the first trees, then disappeared behind rising ground 300 yards away. The crowd gasped and began running toward the hidden ground. The Saint John's doctor ran with them.

Then the big Vimy reappeared beyond the crest in a shallow climb, rising slowly into the gray sky. Brown waved his arm above the cockpit; Alcock concentrated on his airspeed. At 1:42 P.M. on Saturday, June 14, 1919, they were off.

Alcock gained height, then banked the Vimy in a gentle turn to the east to fly over Saint John's Harbor, where ships' whistles blew farewell. At 1,200 feet, Brown took a departure position from the Newfoundland coast and sent a radio message: "All well and started." They flew out over the Atlantic Ocean, and thirty minutes of steady climbing took them to 5,000 feet.

In the previous attempts to fly the Atlantic nonstop, one airplane had ditched in the Irish Sea, one had ditched in the Atlantic Ocean, and one had crashed on takeoff, but no one had been killed. Now the fourth was finally airborne, the first of the heavies.

Looking from their windy cockpit to the north, to port, Alcock saw icebergs on the horizon; beyond was Greenland and the Arctic.

Ahead there was only ocean until Europe, sixteen to twenty hours away. To the south, to starboard, there was also nothing but ocean. Behind and diminishing rapidly was North America.

At 5 P.M. they passed over sea fog below and the ocean disappeared. Clouds gathered above and the sun disappeared, then the fog reached up to them and everything disappeared—no clouds, no horizon, nothing. Alcock steered his compass course, holding the bubble in the turn-and-bank indicator central to keep the wings level and checking the altimeter to keep the nose level. He flew "blind" for more than an hour.

The small propeller of the radio generator sheared off in the slipstream, and their communications were finished. Suddenly, the starboard engine clattered. The two men looked to their right in alarm.

"A chunk of exhaust pipe had split away and was quivering before the rush of air like a reed in an organ pipe," wrote Brown. "It became first red then white-hot and, softened by the heat, it gradually crumpled up. Finally it was blown away." The clattering stopped.

They dined on sandwiches and coffee, Brown feeding Alcock, who kept one hand lightly around the control stick. When darkness fell, Brown wanted an accurate position, so Alcock took the Vimy above the clouds at 6,000 feet. It was cold up there, and Brown's fingers were numb as he took star sights of Polaris and Vega at 10 P.M., using an artificial horizon fixed to his sextant. He calculated their position while Alcock came down to a lesser cold at 4,000 feet.

After eight hours' flying they had covered 850 nautical miles, a speed over the ground of 106¼ knots. A light tailwind and less drag without the nose wheel had given them a greater speed than expected. They were almost halfway across the Atlantic Ocean.

Flying through cold, misty moonlight, the aircraft skimmed across the top of the clouds. Beneath them were silvery gray valleys, above the distant starred heavens. Brown found an aura of unreality about the flight. He recorded in the logbook: "The distorted ball of a moon, the weird half-light, the monstrous cloud shapes, the fog, the misty indefiniteness of space, the changeless drone, drone, drone of the motors." On they flew, growing stiff and numb on the wooden bench seat. "I looked toward Brown and saw that he was singing," Alcock said later, "but I couldn't understand a word!"

Behind them the moon set, and ahead, perhaps above Ireland and Britain, came the first suggestion of the pale dawn. Suddenly, a massive cloud towered in the darkness ahead, silhouetted for the first time against the eastern sky. There was no way around: they flew straight in. It was 3 A.M. on the fifteenth.

Inside the black cloud a storm was raging. The temperature plunged, the air heaved and roared about them, and the Vimy shook and twisted in violent wind and rain.

"The aircraft swung, flew amok and began to perform circus tricks," Brown said. "Until we should see either the horizon or the sky or the sea and thus restore our sense of the horizontal, we could tell only by the instruments what was happening."

The bubble in the turn-and-bank indicator had disappeared, giving no indication of how level the wings were. The airspeed indicator had jammed at ninety knots, while the roar of the storm masked the roar of the engines. Only the altimeter registered, just under four thousand feet. The aircraft pitched and tossed like a cork and, with Alcock disorientated in the roaring cloud, flew slower and slower in the darkness.

Without warning, the plane shuddered and stalled. The nose dropped, and immediately the big Vimy slipped into a spinning dive, the most dangerous and deadly condition for any aircraft.

In 1919 a spinning nosedive was called a Parke's dive, because Lieutenant Parke was one of the very few pilots who had managed to fly out of it. Unfortunately, even Parke wasn't sure how he had done it. Once begun, a diving spin more often than not continued down and into the ground—or sea. Early airplanes often disintegrated in a spin, their wings torn off.

The theory is that with enough height, you get out of a spin by putting the stick forward into a steeper dive to regain airspeed and thus lift. Apply rudder opposite to the direction of the spin, then the plane will stop spinning and you can level out. Even in daylight, when you can see the ground and the horizon, it's about the greatest test for any pilot.

In the Vimy's cockpit, inside the cloud, the altimeter reeled away the height down and down. The compass spun continuously, which in reality was the aircraft spinning around the compass, while Alcock tried to fly out of the spin in complete blackness. "How and at what angle we were falling we knew not," wrote Brown. "Jackie tried to centralise [the aircraft] but failed because we had lost all sense of what was central."

Spinning through 3,000 feet, 2,500 feet, 2,000, 1,500, 1,000 feet, the altimeter unwound until Brown could hear, somewhere around them, the hissing and churning of the ocean. He thrust the logbook into his Burberry flying jacket. If they ditched, one of the extra fuel tanks would become their lifeboat, and it was his responsibility to drag it out.

Abruptly, the Vimy dropped out of the bottom of the immense cloud a few hundred feet above the Atlantic Ocean—almost upside down. Alcock saw the luminescence of the wave tops above his head, flipped the aircraft over, kept the nose down, opened the throttles, countered the spin with the rudder, and leveled out fifty feet above the water. The propellers clawed at the air and dragged the aircraft from danger, hauling her slowly away from the sea. Pilot and navigator exchanged glances.

Alcock eased back the stick and set the aircraft climbing between the clouds. They had to get height, away from the turbulent air over the surface of the sea. "The salty taste we noted later on our tongues was foam," Alcock said.

A check of their situation showed that the instruments were registering again. There was no damage to the aircraft, there was still plenty of fuel, and dawn had broken. They needed a position to reset their course since the last 10 P.M. position, another very good reason to climb above the clouds into the sun.

Heavy rain drove into the cockpit, onto their leather helmets, their goggles, and their flying jackets. It drummed upon the canvas of the wings and fuselage. As they gained more and more height, the rain became lighter and changed into snow. At eight thousand feet, still climbing, still in dense gray cloud, the aircraft was coated with snow, which then froze to ice. Alcock kept working the controls to stop permanent icing, rotating the stick and moving the rudder pedals backward and forward. As yet there was no danger to the aerodynamics of the Vimy, but some of the instruments would be affected.

While Alcock kept the plane level, Brown slipped out of his harness. He stepped up onto the seat, clutched a wooden wing strut with one hand, pushed himself out into the slipstream of 100 knots with the other, and knocked away the ice from the instruments. The propeller blades swished nearby. He cleared the air tubes of the speed indicator and the glass faces of the fuel gauges, for once ice formed, the only way to melt it would be to descend again to near sea level.

Four times they completed those maneuvers, until at 11,800 feet they finally broke clear of the cloud. There was the red-yellow morning sun, low in the east. There was no warmth in the rays at that altitude, and with stiff, frozen hands Brown took his sextant shot and calculated their dead-reckoning position, Alcock maintained the hard-won altitude.

Eventually, Brown leaned across the cockpit to Alcock with a new course and a written message: "About eighty miles to the Irish coast!"

The starboard engine backfired. Ice had formed over the air intakes, which Brown had no way of reaching because of the spinning propeller, so Alcock switched the engine off. Closing the throttle of the port engine to idling speed, he put the Vimy into a shallow glide along the new course. At a lower height, the seal of ice would melt and he'd start the engine again.

They were still over the Atlantic, so there was no danger of flying into a mountain, yet no pilot enjoys losing height in cloud. There was the altimeter, but altimeters work according to air pressure, and their instrument had been set sixteen hours ago in Newfoundland. They had no way of knowing how accurate it was.

They leveled out in clear air five hundred feet above the sea, gray and white beneath them. Alcock opened the port throttle for flying speed, then started the starboard engine and opened that throttle too. The Rolls-Royce Eagles roared. All was well, so they stayed just below the cloud, peering through their goggles for the continent of Europe.

They saw first two small, rocky islands in the distance, with a low smudge across the horizon farther on. Twenty minutes later they flew over Eeshal and Turbot Islands. Ten minutes after that, they crossed the west coast of the Emerald Isle. Turning to starboard, they flew south along the desolate coast until Brown identified the tall masts of the British wireless station at Clifden. They'd reached Ireland over Connemara, only ten miles north of the planned route.

"What should we do?" they discussed, shouting and using hand signals.

"We had plenty of fuel, enough to fly on to England," Alcock said later, "but there didn't seem any point." In fact they'd used only two-thirds of their fuel, with enough left to reach France if they'd wished. They cruised above Clifden looking for a suitable landing field. They flew over a long, green field with no trees near the wireless station, and Alcock decided that would do.

On the ground, people had come out to see the flying machine, for it was evident it was going to land. Those by the green field waved at the Vimy. Alcock and Brown saw waving arms, mouths opening and closing. The two flyers grinned from on high and waved back. That was good, an Irish welcome. They could do with a drop.

Alcock completed his circuit, turned into the final upwind leg, and brought the aircraft down for a three-point landing—nose a little higher, tail a little lower than the bottom wings. Without the safeguard of the nosewheel, he concentrated on a good landing. The Vimy touched down, the large wheels of the two undercarriages and the small tail wheel almost at the same time. It was 8:40 A.M. on Sunday, June 15, 1919.

The aircraft bounced over the tufted grass, slowing down, when suddenly the undercarriage wheels dug in, the tail flew up, the nose tipped forward, and they came to a sudden halt. In a land of many bogs they had very carefully selected and landed on one of the flattest. The waving people had actually been waving them away.

The two men clambered out of their cockpit, now at ground level, Brown with a bump to his nose. They pushed their goggles up and grinned tiredly at each other. They had been in the air for sixteen hours and twenty-seven minutes. They had flown 1,890 nautical miles. They had crossed the Atlantic Ocean nonstop.

"What do you think of that for fancy navigation?" navigator asked pilot.

"Very good!" pilot replied. Beside the Vimy, Alcock and Brown shook hands.

Soldiers from the wireless station arrived, feeling that an unidentified aircraft landing near a military installation was possibly in their jurisdiction. "Where're you from?" asked one.

"Saint John's," replied Alcock. No one knew Saint John's. Was that Scotland?

"Newfoundland," Alcock explained. No recognition.

"North America?" he tried.

"Get away!" the soldiers said, laughing, thinking it was a joke. It took a while for the truth to sink in: they'd witnessed the completion of the greatest flight ever made. The flyers' hands were shaken, their backs were slapped, their shoulders gripped, their hands wrung again. "North America, eh?"

In Newfoundland the news of Alcock and Brown's safe arrival on the other side of the Atlantic was greeted with rapture. Lester's Field was indeed the first transatlantic airfield. North America to Europe, nonstop, in sixteen and a half hours.

Telegrams announcing their amazing feat flashed around the world. It was a sensation. In the year 1919, the achievement was almost unbelievable. Only ten years after the first airplane had struggled across the English Channel, Jackie Alcock and Teddie Brown had flown the vast Atlantic Ocean. They'd blazed the trail. Others would surely follow in the years ahead, but they were the first.

They were driven to Dublin, where a telegram from the king awaited them. From Dublin they traveled to Liverpool by ferry, from Liverpool to London by train. Alcock and Brown made a triumphant journey and were fêted wherever they stopped. These were the men who had conquered the Atlantic. Occasionally, Vickers and Rolls-Royce were mentioned.

The Times reported: "In Crewe station there was yet another crowd which insisted on the airmen leaving the train during the halt. Suddenly an Australian soldier called to a porter 'Up with him' and Lieutenant Brown was lifted shoulder-high so that all the people could see and cheer him. Another soldier with assistance hoisted up Captain Alcock."

Waiting crowds in London cheered them through the streets, where they were driven in an open Rolls-Royce limousine. The Royal Aero Club (the Royal Aeronautical Society) honored them with a reception and officially validated the flight. They successfully delivered to the post office the first transatlantic airmail. At a grand luncheon at the Savoy Hotel the minister for war and air, Winston Churchill, presented them with the *Daily Mail* prize of ten thousand pounds, which was shared with the Vickers team.

They were summoned to Windsor Castle. There King George V knighted the two airmen with the same sword with which Queen Elizabeth had knighted Francis Drake in 1581. Alcock and Brown, their surnames forever joined, were national and international heroes.

Significantly, they had flown the Atlantic in a production airplane with production engines. The Vimy hadn't been redesigned for the flight; it was the standard model. The weight reduction achieved by removing the bomb racks and machine guns was replaced by the weight of the extra fuel tanks. It was the thirteenth built, it had cost three thousand pounds, and it had crossed the Atlantic nonstop. There was the future of aviation.

Barely three weeks later, on July 2, airship *R34* of the RAF took off from East Fortune, east of Edinburgh, and flew westward to North America against the prevailing winds. Under the command of Major George H. Scott, *R34* reached New Jersey through terrible weather in a nonstop flight of four and a half days. Airships were new to America, so Major Pritchard parachuted down to organize the landing. *R34* then flew back to Britain to land at Pulham in Norfolk. Major Scott and his crew became the first to fly the Atlantic Ocean east to west nonstop and the first to fly both ways nonstop. Alcock and Brown had certainly started something.

Their 1919 conquest of the Atlantic remains the greatest pioneering flight of all. It was the first nonstop ocean crossing and the first long-distance flight. It encountered bad weather and overcame it. It convinced the skeptics that airplanes were for civilian use as well as for war, and it carried the first oceanic airmail. Intercontinental air travel had begun.

Outside the Queen's Building at Heathrow Airport there is a statue carved in stone of Alcock and Brown. The Vickers Vimy they flew is on permanent display at the Science Museum in London.

In December 1919, Sir Jackie Alcock delivered a Vickers Viking to France. Landing in thick fog, his wing tip snared a tree and he crashed and struck his head. He died a few hours later without regaining consciousness. Sir Teddie Brown married that October, decided he wouldn't fly again, and died in England in 1948.

Recommended
Flying the Atlantic in Sixteen Hours by Sir Arthur Whitten Brown
Our Transatlantic Flight by Sir John Alcock and Sir Arthur Whitten Brown
The Vickers Vimy by Paul St. John Turner
Queen's Building, Heathrow Airport, London
The Science Museum, London

Sir Walter Ralegh
and Sir Francis Drake

The Elizabethan age was a time of extraordinary optimism in England. Queen Elizabeth I's reign lasted from 1558 to 1603, and during that period, the Renaissance flowered in literature, music, art, and exploration. Shakespeare and Marlowe were at the peak of their powers, the wealth of the world was brought home and the bedrock laid for the British Empire. In many ways, it is still considered a golden era.

It was also a time of relative peace when compared with the upheavals of the seventeenth century. The monarch held absolute power, and Parliament did not challenge the divine right to rule. As a queen, Elizabeth was a skillful mistress and dominated the court for decades, surrounding herself with the best men of the age. The great leaps in science that would mark the next three centuries had their beginnings in her reign, but the foundation stone of power and wealth lay with men like Sir Walter Ralegh and Sir Francis Drake, as they discovered new lands and brought riches to England. At the same time, the natural resources of timber, coal, wood, wool, and iron were exploited on a massive scale in the beginnings of what would eventually become the Industrial Revolution.

The great enemy of the period was Spain. By the time Elizabeth reached the throne, the Spanish had established settlements in Central and South America, a cultural influence that continues today in countries as far apart as Mexico, Peru, Argentina, and Nicaragua. Great wealth flowed back to Spain from those colonies, and their ships were dominant in that part of the world. Inevitably, the fleets of England and Spain would come into conflict, for the highest stakes.

Walter Ralegh was born in Devon in 1554. There are few surviving details of his early life before he attended Oriel College, Oxford, at around the age of sixteen. From the first, he was possessed of restless energy and a desire for adventure. He spent only a year at Oxford before joining a unit of mounted volunteers in France, where he fought at the battle of Moncontour in 1569. Returning home, he trained as a lawyer for a time but took no special interest in his studies. He was tall and handsome, with a sharp wit and a furious temper. Around that time, he spent six days in Fleet Prison for a public brawl and on another occasion in a tavern grew so angry with a man that he sealed up his mouth with wax to stop him from talking.

His half-brother, Humphrey Gilbert, was a renowned sailor. When he was granted a patent to mount an expedition to the New World, or the Americas, Ralegh decided to join him. They sailed in November 1578 from Plymouth, with Ralegh in command of one of seven ships.

This first expedition ended in complete failure and would introduce Ralegh to the dangers of Spain. As well as violent squalls, Gilbert's small fleet met a squadron of Spanish warships off the west coast of Africa. They fought and lost, and the battered and damaged ships returned to Plymouth. There was no official war with Spain at the time, but both countries were capable of that sort of action if the odds were right. With sufficient force and enough wealth at stake, there was simply no law at sea. At that time, the Spanish Inquisition was at its most powerful and captured English sailors were sometimes handed over to the torturers as enemies of the pope.

After that chastening experience, Ralegh used Gilbert's connections to secure a commission to put down an uprising in Ireland. Catholicism made Ireland the natural ally of Spain and France, right on the doorstep of Elizabeth's court. It was Ralegh's first opportunity to show his abilities. English forces marched across Ireland, attacking castles and strongholds and massacring garrisons much as Cromwell's men would do in the following century. Ralegh became known as a captain of particular dash and ruthlessness. He took the castle of Lord Roche by talking his way in to discuss peace, then gradually brought more men in as he ate dinner with the host. When he had enough men, he threatened to destroy the castle if Roche refused to surrender. Some sources say Ralegh held a knife to his throat as he made his offer.

A force of a hundred mainly Italian mercenaries authorized by Spain landed to support the rebellion, but they were pinned down on land in the Bay of Smerwick. Ralegh and another captain went in after their surrender and hanged or slaughtered everyone except for twenty officers held for ransom. It is perhaps worth pointing out that it was a perfectly normal action by the standards of the day. The threat of Spanish invasion was a constant danger, and both sides were utterly ruthless in a struggle to the death. Ralegh was unmoved by horrors, though he wrote letters of complaint about the inept decisions of his military superiors. It was an early example of his complete lack of subtlety in political matters. He never learned to guard his tongue.

Ralegh's unit was disbanded in 1581, and he returned to London with a growing reputation for both gallantry and courage. He prepared to meet Queen Elizabeth with great care, spending almost everything he owned on ostentatious clothing. She was extremely taken with the young soldier from Devon. She enjoyed his accent as much as his forceful manner, grand apparel, and good looks. It was not long before he was regularly called to court, and it was around that time that one of the most famous incidents of his life took place.

Elizabeth and Ralegh were walking in Greenwich when they came to a marshy patch of ground. Ralegh whipped off his jeweled cloak and placed it over the wet ground. That act of conspicuous gallantry was completely in character and cannot have failed to impress the queen. It is too cynical to suggest that he saw her simply as a way to gain power and wealth. Elizabeth was in her late forties at the time, and there was genuine affection for her among the dashing young blades of the day. A female monarch was a rarity in England, and her relationship with men at court was often one of adoration, almost reverence. There was also an element of flirtation that would not have gone down well with Henry VIII. Ralegh, for example, was a gifted poet. He scratched a line on a window for Elizabeth to see: "Fain would I climb, yet fear I to fall." With a diamond ring, she added another line: "If thy heart fail thee, climb not at all."

Queen Elizabeth favored Ralegh with a house in the Strand and the right to export woolen cloth, a hugely lucrative license. He had arrived at the highest levels of society and quickly became very wealthy. Like the equally famous Francis Drake, he came from a minor Devon family, but with royal favor, he rose quickly.

Francis Drake was born around 1540, to a very poor family. In later years, the motto on his coat of arms would be *"Sic parvis magna"*— "great things from small beginnings." His sailing career began at the age of fourteen in a merchant ship carrying grain. On that small vessel, he began to learn the skills of navigation that would play such a part in his later life. When the owner of the ship died, he left it to Drake, which shows the respect he had earned in just a few years. Like Ralegh, he was a staunchly Protestant, restless young man, always keeping his eye out for ways to make his fortune.

In 1564 he sold the ship he had inherited to join Captain John Lovell on a trading expedition to Spain. It was his first experience of ocean navigation and his first encounter with the Spanish. In a Spanish port, Drake saw his cargo confiscated. After that, he hated them with a passion.

In 1567, Drake joined his cousin John Hawkins in a fleet sponsored by Queen Elizabeth to capture Spanish treasure ships. Drake and Hawkins sailed to Africa, then the Spanish

Main—the coasts of Central and South America. Storms forced them to make landfall in Mexico, just as the annual Spanish treasure ship was about to set sail. Drake and Hawkins were vulnerable after the storm and needed repairs and supplies. They anchored by a small island, but that night the Spanish struck them in force. English sailors on shore were slaughtered and Spanish ships sailed out to attack Hawkins's battered fleet. Only two of the ten ships—the pair commanded by Hawkins and Drake—escaped. They limped home to Plymouth, and from then on it was a very personal war for both men.

In 1572–3, Drake raided Spanish settlements on the coast of Panama, seeking the gold and silver that came from the slave mines of Peru. In February 1573, he heard of a mountain where it was possible to see the Pacific on one side and the Atlantic on the other. When he reached the top, he was overcome with excitement and made a vow to navigate and explore the new world that had opened up to him. At the same time, he ambushed a Spanish mule train heavy with silver and captured two Spanish ships before returning to Plymouth a very wealthy man. However, Queen Elizabeth could not publicly acknowledge his success while she negotiated with the Spanish king.

By 1577, the talk in London was of finding the fabled Northwest Passage that would allow ships to reach the Pacific without having to go around South America, a lengthy and extremely dangerous journey. Hawkins was one of those who organized an expedition to seek out new territories, and Drake was given command. He met the queen in secret to discuss the plans and understood that Elizabeth wanted revenge on the Spanish king. Drake was certainly the man for that. He sailed with five ships in December of that year and crossed the Atlantic to land on the Brazilian coast. By August, Drake reached the Strait of Magellan, a notoriously difficult passage through the tip of South America. To mark the event, he renamed his ship the *Golden Hind*. It took sixteen days to navigate through the strait. Drake and his crew were the first Englishmen ever to make the trip and reach the Pacific by that route. Storms battered them in the Pacific, driving the ships south and east so that Drake realized he had not crossed a continent, only the southernmost tip of it in modern-day Chile.

With a better idea of the geography, Drake raided Chile and Peru for silver, fresh fruit, and water. At Lima, Peru, he discovered twelve merchant ships and took their cargoes before sailing on a rumor of a treasure ship, the *Cacafuego,* which was heading for Panama. Drake used all his sailing skill to catch the *Cacafuego* and captured her easily, breaking her mast with his third shot. It took *days* to transfer the vast cargo of pearls, jewels, silver, and gold. His ships stuffed with treasure, he set sail for home. He suspected the Magellan Strait would be blockaded by the Spanish, and he ran north, looking for the legendary passage through to the Atlantic.

He landed for a time on the coast of what is now California. Drake named the area New Albion, and while he was there Native Americans crowned him as a king. From there, he sailed west across the largest ocean on earth, looking for a path through to circumnavigate back to England. He reached the Spice Islands (the Moluccas), off Indonesia, then ran aground on a hidden reef and almost lost the *Golden Hind.* The damage was not too great, however, and he made landfall at Java, a thousand miles northwest of Australia. From there he crossed the Indian Ocean, rounded South Africa's Cape of Good Hope, and eventually returned to Plymouth on September 27, 1580, three years after he had set out—making him the first man to return alive from a circumnavigation of the world. Magellan had managed it earlier, but died before reaching home. When he landed in England, Drake asked if the queen still lived.

In that voyage, Drake had demonstrated to the world the new English power on the seas. He was summoned to meet the queen and, like Ralegh, had the sense to take gifts of jewels. She ordered him to bring the *Golden Hind* from Plymouth to London, and she knighted him on the ship's quarterdeck in 1581. Both Ralegh and Drake were high in royal favor, and Elizabeth allowed Drake to remove ten thousand pounds from the treasure before the official tally was taken. The queen used the riches Drake brought back to found what would one day be known as the British East India Company.

At home, Sir Walter Ralegh had become an MP for Devon. He remained a favorite at court, and the the queen also made him Captain of the Yeoman of the Guard, the men responsible for her personal safety. She adored the dashing young courtier and made him a gift of vast estates in Ireland. In his London house, he invited poets and friends such as Christopher Marlowe and Edmund Spenser. At the same time, he prevailed on Elizabeth to grant him a patent to explore the New World and claim territories for her. Drake's success was the talk of the country, and as a fellow Devonian, Ralegh was hungry for similar adventures. It was not enough for him to wear jeweled clothes and have the queen hang on his words. He was too vital and energetic for that sort of life.

Ralegh was no professional sailor, like Drake or Hawkins. In a sense, he was a talented amateur when he sailed with Sir Humphrey Gilbert to America in 1583 in command of five ships. That voyage was a disaster, as four ships were lost and only one managed to make it back to Plymouth. Gilbert's own ship went down in a storm. Ralegh had failed, but he showed his mettle in organizing another expedition the following year. In 1584 he reached America and named an area Virginia after England's virgin queen. It was an inspired name that survives today. Ralegh was knighted on his return, four years after Drake received the same honor.

Ralegh sent colonists out in 1585, but they ran into trouble and had to be rescued by Drake, who was cheerfully raiding Spanish settlements in that part of the world. Drake lent them a ship to get home, and only fifteen men stayed behind to keep the colony alive. All fifteen were murdered by natives by the time Ralegh sent new colonists to relieve them. In that group, the first Christian baby was born in America, a little girl appropriately named Virginia.

The constant war with Spain was intensifying, and Ralegh had enormous trouble getting ships to support his Virginia colony. He sent two ships only to see them turned back by French pirates. He had practically bankrupted himself in the venture and was forced to turn over the queen's patent to a company of London merchants with funds to continue the work. Even then it was a failure. The Native Americans killed everyone there. Later he wrote: "I shall live yet to see it an English nation." He did live to see a permanent English colony established in 1607. His name is remembered there, and in 1792 the seat of government in North Carolina was named Raleigh. As with Shakespeare, his name has always been spelled in different ways.

Though the exact truth cannot be known, Ralegh is often credited with having brought potatoes to England. Tobacco was already known, but with a long silver pipe and gold tobacco box, Ralegh also made smoking fashionable in London. It became a widespread luxury and later a major source of national revenue. He also made fortunes by growing potatoes from the New World on his Irish estates. However, though he made the wealth he wanted, Queen Elizabeth never saw him as a military commander. When the great fleet known as the Spanish Armada sailed to invade England in 1588, Ralegh was not chosen to command.

The Armada was first sighted off Cornwall on July 19. It would have come earlier, but Drake had been sent by the queen to "distress" Spanish shipping and disrupt the invasion plan. He had succeeded brilliantly, destroying or disabling more than thirty ships in Cadiz. He later referred to this as merely "singeing the King of Spain's beard," but it delayed the Armada for a full year. Philip of Spain put a reward on his head of twenty thousand ducats, the equivalent of millions of dollars today.

Famously, Drake was playing bowls with Lord Howard on Plymouth Hoe when the news of the Armada reached them. Tradition has it that Drake replied to the messenger with the words: "There is time to finish the game and beat the Spaniards too." He was correct, in that the tide was against him at that moment and he could not sail for another three hours. By noon the following day, Lord Howard and Drake were out at sea. Howard had the fleet's flagship, the *Ark Royal,* while Drake, as his vice admiral, commanded the *Revenge.* At the start, they had 80 ships against the Spanish force of 127. The Spanish had come in a great crescent down the English Channel and brought more than eighteen thousand men to invade. The stakes were at their highest. Not until Napoléon and Hitler threatened invasions in later centuries would England be in such direct peril again.

Drake and Howard engaged the Armada, alarming the Spanish officers with the agility of their ships. They skirmished with the Spanish for two whole days, preventing a landing. By chance, one enemy ship blew up and caused chaos in the crescent as they dropped sail to pick up casualties. Even so, they reached the Isle of Wight by July 24. The English captains knew those waters better than any others on earth and maneuvered to drive the Spanish onto rocks. The enemy ships barely avoided the trap and tacked toward Calais. By then, every English ship had joined Drake and Howard, so that they had a fleet of 197 under sail. Howard sent fireships among the Spanish, causing some to scatter east into the North Sea without reaching a safe haven in France. At the same time, Drake engaged the Spanish flagship, firing into her.

The Spanish managed to re-form north of Calais, but they were under constant fire and forced to retreat still farther. It was then that a squall hit and blew the fleets away from each other. By then, the Spanish had lost their taste for the fight and intended to head north and around Scotland to make their way home. Drake's captains harried and fought them all the way up the east coast, still fearing a landing in force. He and Howard pursued the Spanish right up to the Firth of Forth before they turned back.

The surviving Spanish fleet limped past Scotland. Many were lost on rocks around the Irish coast in waters they did not know well. Some of them were washed ashore in Ireland and killed on the beaches. Of the 130 ships that had set out, 63 were lost in the attack. Protestant England had been saved from Catholic Spain.

Flushed with success, Drake organized a raiding fleet the following year. It was not successful, however, and he lost his investors, the queen among them, a small fortune. From hero and savior, he saw his star fall quickly and retired to Devon to tend his estates. His last voyage took place in 1595, to the Spanish Main. He raided Panama and other settlements, though he had been so successful in the past that there were few riches to be plundered. There he became ill with dysentery and donned his armor for the last time, determined to die as a soldier. He died on January 28, 1596, at the age of only fifty-five. He was buried at sea. Famously, the drum from his ship was returned to England and remains at Buckland Abbey, his home. It is said that whenever England is in peril, the drum sounds across the land, summoning men in her defense. The Spanish poet and contemporary Juan de Miramontes Zuázola wrote:

> *This realm inconstant, changeable in faith*
> *Has raised a captain whose glittering memory*
> *Will last undimmed through future centuries.*

Ralegh's fall from grace was more tragic. It began in 1587 with the arrival at court of Lord Essex, a youth of such unusually handsome figure that he captured the queen's attention, at Ralegh's expense. Ralegh and Essex quarreled bitterly over the queen's favor, each jealous of the other. After the Armada had been sent home, the two men arranged a duel, but the queen forbade it, rather than lose one or both of her favorite men. Essex used his influence with Queen Elizabeth to have Ralegh sent to his estates in Ireland for a time.

In Ireland, Ralegh wrote poetry with Edmund Spenser, at the same time as that man created his masterwork, *The Faerie Queene*. Both were around thirty-seven and at the peak of their powers. Sadly, only a small part of Ralegh's poetry and prose survives.

Ralegh found favor with Elizabeth for a time in the reflected glory of *The Faerie Queene*'s publication. It also helped that Essex had married without telling Queen Elizabeth, who preferred her handsome admirers to remain single and devoted to her.

However, in 1591, Ralegh made a serious error. He fell in love with one of the queen's maids of honor and married in secret, just as Essex had done. Elizabeth regarded it as a betrayal. She had both husband and wife sent to the Tower of London. By happy chance around this time, an expedition he had organized captured the *Madre de Dios,* the greatest Spanish treasure ship ever taken. Queen Elizabeth took the lion's share of the riches, and Ralegh and his wife were released. A son, also named Walter, was born shortly afterward, in 1594.

Free, Ralegh returned to his life as a privateer for the Crown, mounting an expedition to seek out El Dorado, a legendary place of fabulous wealth somewhere in South America. Ralegh spoke both Spanish and French fluently and spent many months reading everything he could find on the subject. He was granted the right to search for it by Queen Elizabeth and sailed in 1595. He and his crew explored Guiana on the northeast coast of the continent but found no fabled cities. He considered Guiana to be a worthy possession for England even so, but the lack of gold meant his entreaties fell on deaf ears at court. The era of the great English pirates was ending, and the queen herself was aging and growing weary. Ralegh spent fortunes on other expeditions to Guiana, but the queen had other concerns and remained unmoved.

In 1596 a huge fleet of ships was gathered to attack Cadiz in Spain, then one of the richest cities in the world. Ralegh commanded a squadron and was badly wounded in the fighting, so that he had to be carried back to his ship, the *Warspite*. The victory came quickly, and Cadiz was taken and sacked. Unusually for the times, the English crews were forbidden violence, and the Spanish king later commended them for their conduct. Ralegh won great goodwill for his conspicuous bravery, and in 1597 he was allowed at last to return to court.

The next five years were relatively tranquil. Ralegh was back in the queen's favor as well as being wealthy and famous. He still had enemies at court and perhaps relied too heavily on the queen's shadow to protect him. Essex had fallen from her favor to the point of raging arguments and Elizabeth walloping him around the ears. She sent Essex to suppress a rebellion in Ireland, but he negotiated instead of crushing the rebels as Elizabeth wanted. When Essex returned, he was arrested, though she later relented and canceled his trial in 1600.

Essex became an enemy of the queen and conspired to remove her from the throne. Ralegh was one of those who fought against the plot, which involved a few hundred armed men riding through London. Essex had hoped to create a mass rebellion in the English, but they quite liked Elizabeth and merely looked at him in astonishment. Essex was beheaded in 1601, aged only thirty-six.

When Elizabeth died in 1603, James I, king of Scotland, was the next in line for the throne. He was no friend to Sir Walter Ralegh and distrusted anyone who had risen so high under the queen who had executed his mother, Mary, Queen of Scots. He also desired peace with Spain, and Ralegh was the last of the raiding captains known and hated by the Spanish king. King Philip of Spain demanded that Ralegh be executed. To appease him, James convicted Ralegh of treason. Ironically, the charges involved passing information to the king of Spain in return for huge sums of money. That part is almost certainly true and a clear trap laid for Ralegh. He was locked up in the Tower of London for the second time in his life. Abandoned by friends and supporters, Ralegh would remain there for fifteen years. He was allowed to live in a suite of well-appointed rooms but not to leave. Alone, he wrote poetry and books and experimented with chemistry.

Ralegh was allowed out in 1616 at the age of sixty-two on the promise to King James that he would bring back a shipful of gold from Guiana. When the Spanish ambassador heard, he wrote to the king of Spain to advise that all ships travel only in convoy. Such was their alarm at the prospect of Ralegh back on the high seas. Ralegh was aware that he was being used as a pawn, but he had no choice. He remained youthfully optimistic that he could win back his place, fame, and fortune. Sadly, the odds were stacked against him, not least because King James gave all the secret plans to the Spanish ambassador.

The expedition was doomed before it began, though Ralegh reached Guiana and began looking for gold mines. As he searched, Spanish soldiers harassed his men and Ralegh's son was killed in the fighting. No gold was found. Ralegh was distraught and wrote at the time: "What shall become of me now I know not. I am unpardoned in England, and my poor estate consumed."

He wanted to press on, but his men mutinied and deserted him. He returned in only one ship to Plymouth in 1618, ready to face his king. He was put under house arrest shortly afterward. His argument that Guiana was not Spanish territory held no weight with a monarch determined to be rid of him. Ralegh considered escaping to France, but a servant betrayed the plan and Ralegh was taken to the tower for the third time in his life. He was already under sentence of death for his previous conviction of treason, and James merely had to lift the temporary reprieve that had allowed Ralegh his last trip to Guiana.

The king of Spain took a keen interest once more and wrote to James to demand Ralegh's execution. All appeals at home failed, and Ralegh prepared for death with great courage and calm.

On October 29, 1618, Ralegh walked out into the Palace Yard, Westminster, and addressed the gathered crowd. He talked of his innocence and his loyalty to the king, then added: "So I take my leave of you all, making my peace with God. I have a long journey to make, and must bid the company farewell." He was asked if he wanted a blindfold, and he scorned it, saying: "Think you I fear the shadow of the axe, when I fear not the axe itself?" He prayed for a time, and then, when the executioner hesitated, Ralegh snapped: "What dost thou fear? Strike, man, strike!" Moments later, he was dead.

His body was buried in Saint Margaret's Church, Westminster, though his head was embalmed and kept by his wife until her death, when it was finally buried. Ralegh was much loved by the people of England, and his passing caused enormous resentment toward the Stuart dynasty. They had killed the last of the great captains, just to appease Spain. It has been said that Ralegh's execution began the unrest that ended with the execution of Charles I, which took place only a quarter of a mile from the site of Ralegh's final moments.

Ralegh and Drake were opposite sides of the same Elizabethan coin. Ralegh was the gentleman, the diplomat, the dreamer and elegant courtier. The way he was treated by his queen and then his king makes his story one of the great romantic tales of the era. Drake was the rambunctious seaman and privateer. Both were vital to the flowering of Elizabethan England.

Recommended
Sir Francis Drake by George Malcolm Thomson
Sir Walter Raleigh by Philip Magnus

Harry Houdini: Escapologist

In the 1870s, Rabbi Mayer Samuel Weiss traveled from Hungary to America like so many thousands of other immigrants, looking for a better life. It took him two years to earn enough to bring his wife and four sons over as well. One of those sons, Ehrich Weiss, would become the most famous escapologist who ever lived. While Samuel earned two dollars a day as a rabbi in Appleton, Wisconsin, his nine-year-old son renamed himself "Eric the Prince of the Air" and gave acrobatic displays at a traveling circus.

Around that time, an English magician, Dr. Lynn, was on tour in nearby Milwaukee. Rabbi Weiss took Ehrich to the show. The boy was spellbound, but it was not the blinding flash that gave him his life's purpose—that came later.

Neither Rabbi Weiss nor his wife, Cecilia, spoke English, and when the rabbi lost his job, he moved to Milwaukee. He was a scholarly academic but had no talent for earning a living. During the years that followed, the Weiss family knew grinding poverty.

Aged just twelve, Ehrich ran away from home, making one less mouth to feed. With no food or spare clothes, he jumped on a freight train heading to Missouri. His story could well have ended there, but he knocked at a door offering to work for food and was taken in by a Mrs. Hannah Flitcroft. Ehrich stayed all winter in that house, and for the rest of his life he sent gifts to the woman who had shown him such kindness when he was lost and alone.

Ehrich heard that his father had gone to New York for work and followed him east, taking a job as a messenger boy while his father worked as a Hebrew teacher. Together they earned enough to bring the family to them once again.

At his adult height of five feet four inches, Ehrich was a compact, muscular boy when he joined the New York Pastime Athletic Club. Fast and doggedly determined, he won medals for sprints, but he had not yet found his path in life. That came at a bookstall, when he picked up the autobiography of a French magician, Jean-Eugène Robert-Houdin.

"From the moment I began to study the art, he became my guide and hero," he said later. While still in his teens, Ehrich Weiss chose the name of Houdini to honor him, believing that it meant "one like Houdin." In his family he was known as Ehrie, so "Harry" fit easily enough. For his new life, he began to reinvent himself completely, even to the point of increasing his height on promotional posters.

Houdini was fascinated by magic from the beginning and spent every last cent on a collection of books and pamphlets that is still unequaled. He was never taught magic but instead practiced sleight of hand for hours every night while working as a necktie cutter during the day.

With Jacob Hyman, another man from the factory, he put a formal magic act together for the first time. They called themselves the Brothers Houdini, and Harry left his job to make the act work. It didn't. After a short run and small change, Hyman left the act and Houdini brought in his brother Theodore, known as Dash, to be his assistant. They needed tricks and Houdini persuaded Dash to give him his life savings—sixteen dollars. With that, he bought the stock-in-trade of a retiring magician. Among the props was an old and bat-

tered trunk with an escape hatch, and Harry and Dash worked it into the act. Escapology had already captured Harry's interest, and he spent his evenings studying every pair of handcuffs and re-straints he could lay his hands on, looking for weaknesses.

In the act, Dash would bind Houdini with ropes, put him inside a bag and then the trunk, and lock it securely. Dash then closed curtains around it and stepped behind it to count to three. On three, Houdini would throw back the curtain and Dash would be revealed inside the trunk, bound as his brother had been.

The act was not a success at first. Houdini thought it might be the fact that he spoke bad English, with a strong New York accent. He began to work on polishing his grammar and diction as well, moving further away from the Jewish immigrant from Hungary that he had been.

When Harry was eighteen, his father died. Harry knew he had to support his mother and worked even harder to perfect the act. The trunk trick was going over well, and he began to concentrate on escapology and drop some of the usual rabbit-in-hats, card, and coin tricks. He could do all that, but no one could work knots, chains, and handcuffs the way he could.

In 1894, when working the cabaret circuit on a low billing, Houdini met the eighteen-year-old Wilhemina Beatrice Rahner, "Bess." He was just twenty, she eighteen. They married after only three weeks, and he adored her until his death. Her mother was appalled at Bess marrying a Jew and sprinkled holy water around her house whenever he came to visit.

Houdini made Bess his assistant, and Dash struck out on his own. He too had a successful career as a magician, but it is amazing to think that of all of his contemporaries, the name Houdini was the one that everyone came to know. It wasn't the magic that made him, but the physical prowess and incredible showmanship.

Houdini and Bess worked every night, taking any booking they could get, no matter what the billing. A turning point was a week's booking at the Tony Pastor Fourteenth Street theater. Houdini had to borrow a tuxedo for the first night. He called himself "the King of Handcuffs," and the crowd loved the act, but it was a hard business and every break seemed to be followed by the return of poverty. Desperate for work, the Houdinis joined a traveling circus. Harry even made himself up as "Wild Man" for a time, growling at the audience through cage bars—anything to earn a buck and keep body and soul together.

It was around this time that the entire troupe was locked up for performing on a Sunday—forbidden by the laws of the time. When the sheriff had gone, Houdini borrowed a pin from his wife and opened the cell door, letting them all out. It gave him the idea for stunts that would irritate police in a number of countries for years afterward. He also visited an insane asylum and became interested in the possibilities of working with a straitjacket. It suited him perfectly, as escaping from one involved no trick, just strength, dexterity, and practice.

His life at that point was one of traveling around the country to shabby clubs and bars—anywhere that would take his act for a night. At times, he and his wife starved, and at the lowest point, Houdini offered to sell his secrets to a newspaper for twenty dollars—only to be turned down. He began a conjurer's school for a while but earned little from it. Next came a fifteen-week booking with a medicine show in Kansas, and it was there that he met a group of traveling acrobats. Part of their act was throwing their one-year-old son around the stage. Away from the crowds, Houdini caught the toddler when he fell down some stairs.

"That's some buster your kid took," he told the parents. They kept the nickname, and Buster Keaton went on to become a famous silent-film star and director of knockabout comedies.

When the show went bust, Houdini, in desperation, turned to a new act. Spiritualism had become popular all over the country, and as a professional magician, he knew the tricks that mediums would use to fool an audience into thinking they could speak to the dead. Houdini booked a show and visited a local cemetery to take notes from the gravestones. He reduced some of the audience to tears with the extraordinary "accuracy" of his knowledge. He kept the act going for a time but despised himself for making money from the true grief of his audiences. In the end he stopped the performances completely. For the rest of his life, he made it a personal mission to expose the charlatans in the world of Spiritualism, destroying the careers of a number of the more famous ones, who used all his tricks and had none of his scruples.

His career to that point had been hit-and-miss, with nothing to raise him above the hundreds of similar acts traveling the boards in America as the nineteenth century came to an end. In 1898 he realized that publicity was everything. Newspaper headlines would fill the largest halls with audiences. First he tried walking into newspaper offices and challenging them to tie him up or chain him, but the cynical journalists assumed his handcuffs were props and threw him out. Remembering the experience of getting a circus out of jail, he challenged the Chicago police instead, saying that they could use their own cuffs and lock him in a cell. To his delight they agreed, and Chicago newspapers sent reporters to cover the event.

It was barely minutes before Houdini walked out of the cell, but the first attempt was met with indifference. The reporters heard he had visited the cell the day before and assumed he'd made a key from a wax impression. Indignantly, Houdini offered to do it again—this time naked and with his mouth checked and sealed with wax. His clothing was placed in another locked cell. For a second time, he strolled out in just minutes, fully dressed and grinning.

By the time the newspapers were on the stands the following morning, he was famous. Most important, he now had all the ingredients that would make him the best-known escapologist of his generation.

Modern magicians assume he used keys, though he always denied it, or wire to pick the locks if he hadn't. He did apprentice to a locksmith for a time and studied handcuffs until he knew them as well as any man alive. Even so, there were times when it all went wrong. Once during each performance, he would challenge the audience to produce some restraint to test him. In Chicago, a burly policeman produced a set of standard handcuffs. When Houdini went behind a curtain, he found that he could not spring the lock. He came out again and the man triumphantly explained that he had jammed the locks with lead. The great Houdini would have to be sawn out of them. Houdini's defeat made the papers, with gleeful headlines. He was mortified and never again allowed cuffs to go on without examining the workings first.

Once more, the Houdinis were saved from a low point, this time by Martin Beck, a theater manager who saw potential in the act and became a mentor for a time. He offered Houdini regular bookings and the princely sum of sixty dollars a week. That is the equivalent of almost fifteen hundred dollars a week today and shows the extent of Beck's faith in Harry Houdini. It was the first taste of the big time, and Houdini grasped it with both hands. On Beck's advice, he dropped the last of the card tricks and focused his act on three main events. He would swallow needles and thread, then pull the thread back out of his mouth with the needles threaded in a neat line. The trunk trick remained, and he continued with miraculous escapes from chains and ropes. With Bess, he traveled to San Francisco and once again challenged the police.

The San Francisco police were intrigued by a man who thought he could get out of their best cuffs. They strip-searched him before putting on ten pairs of handcuffs and manacles around his ankles. He dropped them all at his feet in just moments. The newspapers reported his triumph, and the chief of police said publicly: "Should Houdini turn out to be a criminal, I would consider him a very dangerous man, and I suggest that the various officers throughout the United States remember his appearance in case of future emergency." You just can't buy that sort of publicity. The Houdinis went on to Los Angeles, where they did it all over again.

Martin Beck advised that Houdini should travel to Europe and make a name for himself there. His advice was farsighted, and the Houdinis went by passenger ship to London on a tour that would make him world-famous. In the American embassy in London, Houdini had to fill out a passport application. He put his birthplace down as Appleton, Wisconsin, and rubbed away another piece of his past.

The tour didn't start well. The manager of the London Alhambra Theatre was skeptical about the grand claims Houdini made and refused to honor the booking. Houdini was furious, and eventually the man agreed that Houdini could go ahead if he could beat the policemen of Scotland Yard. Houdini insisted on going straight to that ancient police station.

The English policemen were amused at the brash American escapologist. They agreed to his challenge and handcuffed him to a pillar
with a few pairs of their handcuffs. With a smile, a senior policeman
pointed out that they weren't "stage handcuffs."

"Here's how we fasten Yankee criminals who come over here and
get into trouble," he said, adding with a chuckle that he'd come back
and set Houdini free in "an hour or two."

As the policeman turned to go, Houdini said, "Wait, I'll go with
you." The handcuffs fell to the floor with a clang, and Houdini
walked out. Magicians still argue about how he managed that. The
story quickly became famous, and Houdini packed London theaters
for six months.

Riding a wave of success, Houdini and Bess
traveled to Germany, where in 1900 he moved on
to the signature escapes that would become his
trademark. The first was in Dresden. In front of a
large crowd, he was manacled and bound. He was
about to be thrown into the river when the local
police stopped what was clearly a murder in
progress. Houdini was forced to move onto a boat
midriver to complete the stunt.

He sank below the surface, and many in the audience
held their breaths with him. One minute went by, then
another. The audience began to pale, realizing they had
witnessed a terrible death.

Then he surfaced, to wild applause and immediate
arrest. He was fined a tiny amount, for publicity that
was priceless. It was not the last time he would run
afoul of the law. In the German city of Cologne,
Houdini was accused of using trick manacles by a policeman named Graff. Houdini's entire career depended
on the fact that he used real police-issue ones, so he
sued. The case came before the highest court in
Germany and a judge who was not at all sure how
to resolve it. In the end, the judge took Houdini into his

office and showed him the safe there. He told Houdini that if he could open the safe, he would go free.

Left alone, Houdini must have had a moment of doubt. He was a genius with locks, but safes were not his specialty. Disaster lay before him. Listlessly, he turned the handle of the safe and the door swung open. It had been left unlocked. The judge was amazed and more headlines followed.

In all, Houdini stayed in Europe for four and a half years. In Holland he had himself strapped to the blade of a windmill. In Moscow he escaped from an "escape-proof" steel prison van. How he did it is still a mystery.

On his return to England, an event occurred that shows why Houdini was more than a man with keys and hidden lock picks. His challenge to the audience was taken up by an English weight lifter named Hodgson. Houdini spotted that the cuffs Hodgson had brought had scratches around the locks. At first Houdini refused, but Hodgson was adamant. He said Houdini claimed he could escape from anything, so he should not back down. The audience agreed, and reluctantly Houdini allowed himself to be chained and bound in a kneeling position. A cabinet was placed around him.

He was in trouble from the beginning. As Houdini had suspected, the locks were all jammed. The orchestra played on while the crowd waited, and waited.

Houdini's arms began to turn blue, and he asked to have the chains loosened and then replaced. Hodgson told him to admit defeat and give in. Houdini glared at him and returned to the cabinet.

It was just under two hours before he came out. He was sweating heavily. His clothes were torn and his arms and wrists were bleeding. He threw the pile of manacles at Hodgson's feet and told him to get out. The crowd went wild.

Before he left Europe, Houdini, aged just twenty-seven, visited the grave of Robert-Houdin in Paris, to pay his respects. Houdin's family spurned his attempt at contact, and he returned to America with his wife. They bought a four-story house in Manhattan, and he put his mother in it. However, Martin Beck's promise that American theaters would clamor for Houdini was not yet coming true. The Houdinis returned to London, where he could earn two thousand dollars a week, the equivalent of forty-five thousand dollars today. Almost all of it went on rare books and tricks, as his personal collection of thousands of volumes grew steadily. He bought entire libraries as easily as single books.

Back in Europe he perfected an escape from a straitjacket while hanging upside down, far above a crowd. We can never know for sure how long it took him, as he had long before realized that an appearance of real struggle made his escapes more of an event. Nothing could look easy, even to the Great Houdini. His fame grew steadily, and he took great pleasure in being too fully booked to accept an offer of five thousand dollars a week from a New York theater. It was clearly time to come home.

All through his career, Houdini was sensitive to the fact that he had to keep the act fresh and come up with greater and more baffling escapes. In Washington, D.C., he had himself locked in the cell that had held Charles Guiteau, the assassin of President Garfield. The lock was a five-tumbler combination and could not be reached from the cell itself. It was a suitable challenge, and Houdini was stripped, searched, and left there, only to walk out moments later. His escape was so quick, in fact, that he spent a little extra time letting the prisoners out and then putting them back into different cells.

In Boston, locked in another police cell, he let the waiting guards and journalists think they had succeeded before he called them from a theater halfway across the city. Around the same time, in 1906, Houdini published the first of his books: *The Right Way to Do Wrong*, which was a study of techniques used by petty criminals. It was so comprehensive that many feared he had written a textbook for thieves and con men. It sold very well, and Houdini began a publication called *Conjurors' Monthly Magazine* and took on a secretary. He also began work on *The Unmasking of Robert-Houdin*—the hero who had fallen from his pedestal for Houdini. The book was published in 1908 to great success.

Meanwhile, his escapes had become ever grander, though he never stopped the challenges that were taken up around the country. He escaped from a huge leather football, an iron boiler, a piano box, a thick sack, tarred ropes, packing cases, and whatever else was brought to his theater performances. Even so, he suspected that his act was becoming stale and worked on a new escape that would set the world on its heels once again.

It involved a milk can just big enough to hold him in the fetal position. It was filled with water and securely riveted together. He was handcuffed and the can secured with six padlocks on the outside. He asked audiences to hold their breath along with him. He had practiced holding his breath in his bath until he could survive for astonishing times, but it added a vital element of tension to the performances. He also had a stagehand ready with an ax to strike off the padlocks. The audience literally held their breath as the seconds ticked agonizingly by—one minute . . . two. . . . At two minutes fifteen seconds, he broke out. It was his greatest triumph, and his fame was renewed. He hardly needed to embellish stories of this sort, but Houdini knew the importance of myth and legend and added details to his achievements, so that a river plunge became a struggle under the ice or a childhood trick became picking up needles with his eyelids while hanging upside down. Not since P. T.

Barnum had a man understood so well that the legend could be bigger than the man. Even so, the man himself was simply extraordinary.

At the height of his fame, he returned with Bess to Europe and adoring audiences. There he fell in love with the new airplanes and bought one for five thousand dollars. From Germany, he took the plane by ship to Australia, where he was welcomed like a returning son. His was not the first flight in Australia. It was probably the second, but the newspaper coverage meant it might as well have been first. Houdini had conquered the air, and his interest in flight waned as quickly as it had struck him.

In 1913, while in Copenhagen, he received a telegram that his mother had died. He was distraught and broke all his contracts to go home. For a long time Houdini was inconsolable and visited her grave constantly. Eventually, he recovered enough to complete his European contracts. While he was there, he bought the secret to walking through a brick wall from the English magician who had created it. By 1914, Houdini was back in New York and performing it for audiences to great acclaim. It was described as "the Wonder of the Age."

World War I broke out that year, and Houdini went to the recruiting offices, though he was forty-three. His offer to fight was refused, and instead he performed for the troops. His legendary generosity involved him doing coin tricks with real gold coins and letting the soldiers keep them. One source estimated that he gave away almost seven thousand dollars this way, a vast sum for the day. He was becoming a statesman for magic, with immense influence, so it is no surprise that he became president of the Society of American Magicians. Years later it came out that he also paid wages to poverty-stricken members from his own pocket.

In 1918 he made an elephant disappear at the New York Hippodrome. But the film business was booming, Buster Keaton was famous, and Houdini turned to the new medium with as much panache as his stage shows. He always played a detective who could escape from anything, and the films were only reasonably successful, though they leave a record of the man that is still available today. He usually did his own stunts, which at least once resulted in him breaking his wrist. He was no longer a young man, but Houdini remained convinced that a life of tough exercise, with no tobacco or alcohol, gave him a sort of perpetual youth. He claimed that he could withstand any blow as long as he tensed his muscles first.

His interest in the film business vanished as quickly as his infatuation with planes. The end of the war, with so many dead, had brought about a resurgence of Spiritualism, and Houdini was appalled at an industry that made money out of the pain of others. He knew all the tricks of course—he had once used them himself. Even so, he understood the desperate need that made people believe. He longed to speak to his mother again and attended dozens of séances in the hope of meeting someone with real talent. He also made a pact with his wife that they would try to reach each other after death. To that end, he gave her two passwords: "Rosabell" and "believe." A true medium would be able to reveal them.

He found no one of real talent, and in anger he set out to debunk the entire industry. On one famous occasion he traveled to see a Cleveland medium, George Renner, who claimed to have spirits speak through a megaphone. In the darkness, Houdini put lampblack on the mouthpiece and when the "spectral voices" had stopped and the lights came up, there was Renner with blackened lips, blissfully unaware that he had been exposed.

To his stage act, Houdini now added a section on Spiritualism, where the audience could see what he did, while the people at the table wore sacks on their heads. It was a success, and in response to his act and his written articles, lawsuits for defamation were brought against him from the prominent Spiritualists of the day—at one point adding up to a million dollars. Houdini engaged his own lawyer and carried on. He never tired of revealing the lies of those who claimed to speak to the dead, read tea leaves, or tell the future from the stars. On astrology, he said: "They cannot tell from a chunk of mud millions of miles away what is going to happen to me." He even proposed a law to have fortune-telling made illegal, but it was rejected.

Using only what he called "natural methods," Houdini proved that the mystical powers claimed by an Indian fakir were false. Like that performer, Houdini had himself sealed into a watertight coffin, then submerged in the swimming pool of New York's Hotel Shelton. Inside he had a telephone in case it went wrong. Doctors estimated that he had enough air for only three to four minutes, but he survived ninety underwater, almost twice what the fakir had managed. Once again, Houdini had shown that "mystical powers" could be equaled or beaten by strength and ingenuity. The Spiritualists hated him.

At the same time, he perfected his masterpiece, which he called the Chinese Water Torture Cell. In it, he was hung upside down underwater, chained, and manacled. Years of physical strain were beginning to have their effects, and it was his most difficult stunt, but he did it over and over again, to delighted audiences. At last, a bone in his ankle snapped and he had to abandon the water torture for a time until it healed.

His act continued despite the injury, and as always, Houdini pushed himself to the limits of endurance, driven by some need to go faster and further than he ever had before. He and Bess took the show to Montreal in 1926. He gave a lecture on the tricks of Spiritualism there, and afterward three young fans came to see him backstage. One of them brought a picture he had drawn of Houdini. Another was a keen amateur boxer.

Resting his broken ankle, Houdini was lying down reading letters when they approached him. The boxer asked if it was true that Houdini could take any punch. Houdini was distracted, but he nodded. Without warning, the young man hit him four times in the abdomen. Houdini bore up well and sent them away with smiles, but he felt terrible pain, which only grew as the hours passed. Regardless, he traveled to Detroit for the next show, arriving with a temperature of 102 degrees. It was 104 by the time the show was due to begin. The water torture was out because of his ankle, but he managed to finish the rest of the show. He was close to collapse, but even then refused to see a doctor. At last, when it was clear he was dying, he was rushed to the hospital. His appendix had been ruptured and peritonitis had set in, the organ rotting inside him. His last words to his brother were "I'm tired of fighting, Dash."

After his death, Bess offered ten thousand dollars to any medium who could reach her husband. She saw hundreds, but not one was able to give her the code words Houdini had arranged. His vast library on magic was given to the Library of Congress.

Through courage, skill, and showmanship, Ehrich Weiss took himself and his family from poverty to riches and fame. Houdini was in every sense the ultimate self-made man.

Recommended
Escape! The Story of the Great Houdini by Sid Fleischman
The Great Houdini by Beryl Williams and Samuel Epstein

Scott of the Antarctic

After Captain Cook's 1774 circumnavigation of Antarctica there had been only the one determined exploration south, despite the continent being first sighted in 1820 by Britons Bransfield and Smith.

James Clark Ross, discoverer of the North Magnetic Pole, sailed south to search for the South Magnetic Pole in his great expedition of 1839–43. He forced his two ships, HMS *Terror* and HMS *Erebus,* through the pack ice south of New Zealand to discover and chart the Ross Sea and the active volcano Mount Erebus, to determine that the Magnetic Pole was inland, and to land on the islands to claim the territory for Britain.

In 1898, the Royal Geographical Society and the Royal Society announced a new scientific expedition to explore Antarctica inland from the Ross Sea. Commander Robert Falcon Scott was appointed leader. Thirty-two-year-old Scott was a modern and innovative officer, carving a promising career for himself in the Royal Navy. He specialized in the new torpedoes, marine electronics, and mines. The Admiralty commented that Scott would be "relinquishing a brilliant Navy career" in commanding the Antarctic expedition, but the First Sea Lord recommended him, and his commanding officer wrote: "He is just the fellow for it, strong, steady, genial, scientific, a good head on his shoulders, and a very good naval officer."

Officers and seamen from Scott's Royal Navy ship volunteered to join him in the new 172-foot *Discovery,* while the balance of the expedition consisted of merchant navy officers, seamen, and scientists. Scott ran the expedition along modified navy lines, and despite recent suggestions, it was completely successful.

Other Antarctic expeditions of the era—led by Amundsen (Norwegian), Shackleton (British), Borchgrevink (Norwegian/British), Gerlache de Gomery (Belgian), Mawson (British/Australian), Drygalski (German), and Nordenskjöld (Swedish)—suffered insurrection, mutiny, shipwreck, and even insanity. Antarctica is perhaps the harshest environment in the world, yet Scott's two explorations, with more than one hundred scientists, officers, seamen, soldiers, sledgers, dog handlers, skiers, and photographers, had not one major problem.

Australian scientist Louis Bernacchi wintered with both Borchgrevink (1899–1900) and Scott (1901–4). He recorded that Scott's broad formality and discipline "helped to preserve an atmosphere of civilised tolerance such as has seldom been found in polar expeditions" and was "of infinite benefit."

As he made his preparations, Scott sailed first to Norway for advice from Fridtjof Nansen, scholar and great Arctic explorer of the time. Nansen had made the first crossing of Greenland by man-hauling his sledge and attempted to reach the North Pole using dogs. He recommended dogs but admitted that over rough ice they were not much use—in those conditions only man-hauling would get you through. Scott and Nansen became good friends, and Scott followed his mentor's advice. His second in command, Lieutenant Armitage, had also made several Arctic sledging trips; he recommended Siberian ponies. Previously, James Clark Ross and Leopold McClintock of the navy had made a 1,175-mile Arctic journey averaging nearly 17 miles per day man-hauling. As no one knew the conditions of inland Antarctica, Scott took dogs, ponies, and motor sledges and used all four methods of sledging.

The *Discovery* left Britain in August 1901, bound for Antarctica. Before he sailed, Scott was made a Member of the Royal Victorian Order by the newly crowned King Edward VII and Cadbury supplied thirty-five hundred pounds of chocolate.

The expedition crossed the Antarctic Circle on January 3 and landed at Cape Adare to inspect Borchgrevink's hut, where Bernacchi had completed the only previous wintering-over in Antarctica. In the *Discovery*, Scott explored the limits of the Ross Sea: eastward he discovered King Edward VII Land, while southward all was bound by the Great Ice Barrier (Ross Ice Shelf).

The ice barrier reaches five hundred feet high from sea level, in massive vertical cliffs of floating ice. It stopped Ross in 1843 and has stopped every ship since. In a natural inlet in the ice at the Bay of Whales, Scott sailed the *Discovery* south for twelve more miles to reach the southernmost water in the world. Beneath twelve-foot cliffs, a landing was made for the first scientific journey inland by Armitage and Bernacchi.

Scott, followed by third mate Ernest Shackleton, made the first Antarctic flights there in February 1902, in a British army hydrogen balloon named *Eva*. They rose to eight hundred feet, tethered by cable in what Scott termed a "very inadequate basket," to take the first aerial photographs of Antarctica. Seals basking on the ice were slaughtered in great numbers. Scott—like Cook before him—ordered their killing for fresh meat, a vital preventative against scurvy. Nowadays, we know a lot about scurvy, but at the beginning of the twentieth century, little more was known than at the time of Cook, in 1770.

Scott established winter quarters at Hut Point on the southern promontory of Ross Island, next to the ice barrier. In two weeks the expedition erected the main thirty-ton hut, two magnetic huts, and kennels for twenty-three huskies (from Nansen's supplier). After landing stores and scientific equipment, sledge-training parties with dogs immediately set out into the white wilderness, and skiing exercises began.

For the skiing, only minimal training was required. Norwegian skis then weighed ten pounds each, and a single pole was used. It took longer to organize the dogs, yet within a month the first dog-sledge expedition set off; within two months they were on the ice barrier, laying stores depots for the following summer's explorations. Scott learned quickly.

After the winter months of total darkness, scientific parties set out in the bitter-cold spring, sledge training continued, and more depots were laid. Navigation was difficult so close to the Magnetic

Pole, so Scott improvised. He invented a shadow scale for navigating by the sun and devised a simple way to calculate the sun's daily declination changes. He also invented tapered sledge runners, a face hood to deflect the wind when sledging, and a trawling net for the marine scientists. Some of his inventions, including the "face funnel," are used today.

For the southern exploration, Scott selected a party of three, which was considered safer than two for crevasse work and emergencies. As well as himself, he chose Dr. Edward Wilson, a physician, scientist, and artist, and Ernest Shackleton. The three men—one Royal Navy, one civilian, one merchant navy—got along well and respected one another.

On November 2, 1902, the southern exploration departed, the first expedition into southern Antarctica. Before them stretched the ice barrier toward the South Pole, 740 miles away. Between lay the last unexplored continent in the world. They set off with twenty-two huskies, their skis and sledges, and a support team led by second mate Michael Barne. After two weeks they were on their own.

They experienced the alarming "barrier shudder," eerie echoing reverberations when suspended ice and snow suddenly collapse underfoot. They were traversing an immense, featureless, white wasteland of ice and could not help but wonder if it was like that all the way to the pole.

By the twenty-fifth, they'd reached 80° south, six hundred miles from the Pole, and individual features were visible in the southwest. Wilson sketched as often as possible. They left a supply depot for their return and continued with lighter sledges. They tried to leave the ice barrier several times, but the dogs could not cross the ice joint—the tumbled ice linking the floating ice to the land ice on their right. They drove the dogs farther south.

On December 19, Wilson killed the first dogs to feed the others, standard Arctic practice. By then the three men were suffering from sunburn, snow blindness, chapped lips, and numerous small ice cuts. On their right they were close to the Transantarctic Mountains, which crossed the island continent to a similar ice barrier (the Ronne Ice Shelf) on the other side. Icy cliffs tinged black and red rose to fourteen thousand feet, and Scott named them the Britannia Range. They crossed a white world of ice and snow no man had traveled before.

For Christmas dinner Shackleton produced a small plum pudding he'd hidden. The twenty-eighth was their provisional turn-back date, but a wide valley led into the mountains to their right. Scott named it Shackleton Inlet and the headland Cape Wilson. All agreed to push on to the southern headland, which revealed a new "coastline" farther south. Wilson sketched the view to 83° south. They attempted to gather rock samples from the mountains but again could not cross the ice joint.

On New Year's Day 1903, the three men and eleven surviving dogs turned back. They were at latitude 82° 11′ south, the farthest south man had ever reached. They'd established that any journey to the South Pole must find a crossing of the ice joint, ascend one of the glaciers tumbling down the Transantarctic Mountains, and then cross whatever lay on the other side.

The three men were within their safety margins with four days of emergency rations remaining, but the dogs were finished. From the fifth, the men were forced to do most of the sledge hauling while the fittest dogs killed the weakest. At their stores depot they killed the last two dogs. Neither Scott, Wilson, nor Shackleton was satisfied with the performance of the huskies.

Shackleton's health broke down, his lungs hemorrhaging on the fifteenth. It was all he could manage to ski as he struggled with a heart and lung problem that would one day kill him. On January 25 they saw the smoke plume from the Erebus volcano a hundred miles away. By February 3 they were back at the original base. All three were exhausted, and Shackleton went to bed in the *Discovery* before dinner. Scott suggested: "I say, Shackles, how would you fancy some sardines on toast?" There was no reply; "Shackles" was asleep. The three men had traveled 960 miles through Antarctica.

The resupply ship *Morning* arrived, and regretfully, Scott sent Shackleton home. After a month's rest and good food he was still seriously ill, and winter in Antarctica was no place to recover. Some historians claim that Scott and Shackleton fell out during the southern exploration. There is no evidence for this. Both men's reports, diaries, and letters record the greatest respect for each other, while other people's diaries, including Dr. Wilson's, record no disagreement. Shackleton welcomed Scott home personally in 1904, and Scott hosted a dinner in Shackleton's honor in 1909. The allegation of a falling-out was made twenty-two years later—after Scott, Shackleton, and Wilson were all dead and could not sue.

After a second winter in Antarctica, five more scientific expeditions were made into the interior. Scott led a three-man expedition over the Transantarctic Mountains at the Ross Sea end and onto the Polar Plateau, nine thousand feet high. Scott, Petty Officer "Taff" Evans, and stoker Bill Lashly reached farthest west on November 30 and saw that the plateau continued west and south as far as the eye could see. As Scott surmised, it continued to the South Pole. During their return, he discovered Antarctica's amazing Dry Valleys. Networks of bare rock valleys free of ice and snow with lakes, melt streams, and floors of fertile alluvial mud, they are the driest places on earth—no rain has fallen there for more than two million years, and nothing grows.

In those 1903 journeys, Scott man-hauled 827 miles in eighty-one days, an average of 10¼ miles per day, including mountain ascents and descents totaling 19,800 feet. The Scott Polar Research Institute of Cambridge reports: "Few dog parties, working under plateau conditions, have ever exceeded Scott's best, when on foot." There was no doubt man-hauling was successful and versatile; it could cross any ice terrain, whereas dogs could not.

Scott's 1901–4 *Discovery* expedition collected such a wealth of scientific data and specimens that the final analyses were not completed until the 1960s. Of the other expeditions to Antarctica at that time, the Swedes had their ship crushed by ice and had to be rescued, the Germans were trapped by ice and went nowhere, and a second British expedition under William Bruce collected valuable scientific data but did not penetrate inland.

The *Discovery* left Hut Point to reach Portsmouth on September 10, 1904. At thirty-six years of age, Robert Scott returned from commanding the most extensive and successful scientific and geographic Antarctic expedition ever mounted. He found himself a national hero and world-famous.

During his leave, Scott became good friends with author James Barrie (*Peter Pan*) and artist Aubrey Beardsley. Through Beardsley, he met and wooed sculptress Kathleen Bruce. The Admiralty, meanwhile, promoted Scott to captain, and he returned to sea in command of the flagship and battleship HMS *Albemarle*. He was the youngest battleship commander in the navy. In September 1908, in the Chapel Royal at Hampton Court Palace, he and Kathleen Bruce were married.

Many from Scott's expedition had caught the polar itch. Scott, Barne, and Shackleton all had Antarctic plans—initially unknown to one another. Barne joined Scott and together they pursued the vital development of motorized sledges. In 1907, Shackleton publicly announced his plans and agreed with Scott that he would make his base on King Edward VII Land, not Ross Island. Shackleton had stamps issued by the New Zealand Post Office with "*King Edward VII Land*" printed on them, but when he arrived there in 1908, he could find nowhere to land.

He inspected the Bay of Whales but discovered that since their balloon flights, massive slabs of the ice barrier had separated or "calved" away. He considered it too unstable and dangerous to camp there. Reluctantly, he sailed west to Ross Island and erected his hut twenty miles north of Hut Point.

Using four ponies and no dogs, Shackleton headed south across the ice barrier at the end of 1908. He discovered a route over the ice joint, ascended the Transantarctic Mountains by the Beardmore Glacier—losing his last pony in a crevasse there—and reached the Polar Plateau. Shackleton, Frank Wild (ex-*Discovery*), Eric Marshall, and Jameson Adams man-hauled with no skis to reach ninety-seven miles from the South Pole before turning back. At the same time, a three-man party under Australian Edgeworth David man-hauled to the South Magnetic Pole and raised the British flag.

Scott officially announced his second scientific and geographic Antarctic expedition on September 13, 1909—the day before Kathleen gave birth to their only child, Peter. The Royal Geographical Society, Nansen, the Admiralty, Barne, Shackleton, and others had known of Scott's plans since 1907. Trials of the first motorized sledge were announced in January 1908, while newspaper reports of Scott's marriage confirmed his plans to go south again. Further motorized-sledge trials took place in Norway in March 1909, with Nansen watching. There was no secret about Scott's plans; his second expedition was known about for years.

In 1907, meanwhile, Norwegian explorer Roald Amundsen had announced his plans for an Arctic voyage, an attempt to be first to the North Pole. However, on September 15, 1909, American Robert Peary announced that he had reached the North Pole, while another American, Frederick Cook, claimed to have reached it in 1908. In secret, four days after Scott's official announcement, Amundsen changed his destination to the South Pole. Only a brother knew. Even his patron Nansen—who lent him his ship *Fram* for the Arctic expedition—was not told. Historians who claim that Amundsen did not know of Scott's expedition are clearly wrong. It was Scott who knew nothing of Amundsen's plans.

French explorer Jean Charcot, also eyeing the Antarctic, stated: "There can be no doubt that the best way to the Pole is by way of the Great Ice Barrier, but this we regard as belonging to the English explorers, and I do not propose to trespass on other people's grounds." When Peary proposed an attempt on the South Pole—from the other side of Antarctica—he actually asked Scott if he had any objections. They met in London and agreed on joint scientific programs. Amundsen himself wrote to Nansen: "It is not my intention to dog the Englishmen's footsteps. They have naturally the first right." Yet that is exactly what he did.

Amundsen lied to Nansen, lied to the Norwegian government who helped finance him, lied to his sponsors, and lied to the press. Scott tried several times to contact Amundsen to arrange Antarctic-to-Arctic scientific programs, so Scott's Norwegian skiing expert Tryggve Gran—recommended by Nansen—arranged a meeting. Scott and Gran traveled to Amundsen's home, but Amundsen did not show up. His secrecy reveals his chicanery.

It was not until Scott and his seventy-strong scientific expedition reached Melbourne in the *Terra Nova* in October 1910 that they received the truth from Amundsen. He telegrammed: BEG LEAVE TO INFORM YOU *FRAM* PROCEEDING ANTARCTIC, AMUNDSEN. He had taken nineteen men, including a party of six champion skiers, and 120 dogs, and said he would be based on the opposite side of Antarctica.

When the news reached Norway, its people became hostile to Amundsen and Nansen remained ominously silent. Amundsen's sponsors asked the government to request more funds from Parliament; the government refused.

Scott reached Ross Island again in January 1911 and established a new camp at Cape Evans, ten miles north of Hut Point. A larger hut was erected, and the huskies, ponies, the first motorized sledges in the world, scientific equipment, and stores were transported ashore. Scott's plans for the next three years were many but simple.

Science was the major purpose of the expedition—the largest ever to Antarctica—and that is how it would continue. Scientific parties set out as planned that summer, including two more wintering-over parties to the north and east. Using dogs and ponies, they laid depots southward across the ice barrier for an exploration to the South Pole the following summer, while Hut Point hut was cleared of ice and used as a forward depot. Scott laid the first Antarctic telephone line between the two huts.

In February, during a voyage to deploy the eastern wintering-over party, the *Terra Nova* discovered Amundsen camped just along the Ross Sea at the Bay of Whales. To his credit, Scott never condemned Amundsen for his subterfuge, even in his private letters. In fact, his instructions to his men were to lend assistance if the Norwegians needed it. Scott knew how unstable the ice barrier at the Bay of Whales was. Amundsen was taking a gamble making a base there.

A Norwegian sailor wrote of their discovery: "Well, if they are planning something bad (we were constantly asking ourselves in what light the Englishmen would view our competition) the [120] dogs will manage to make them turn back. . . . I had better be armed for all eventualities." The Norwegians apparently considered Amundsen's actions so bad that they thought they might be attacked. Tryggve Gran wrote: "I think Amundsen's enterprise falls far short of what a gentleman would permit: there is nothing like it in polar history."

Even at Melbourne, it had been too late for Scott to make a race of it: he had only thirty-three dogs and seventeen Siberian ponies. Scott knew and admitted this. He wrote several times that if Amundsen found a route up the mountains suitable for dogs, he would undoubtedly reach the pole before him. Shackleton, though, had reported the Beardmore—the *only* known route—as unsuitable for dogs.

The irony is that American Frederick Cook had not reached the North Pole and it's probable that Peary hadn't either. After eighty years of doubt, Arctic and Antarctic explorer Wally Herbert, first to cross the whole Arctic via the North Pole, was given access to all Peary's records by the American National Geographic Society. He concluded that Peary was probably thirty to sixty nautical miles west of the pole and knew it. The North Pole had been there for Amundsen to conquer after all.

During the winter of 1911, a dangerous and bitter journey in twenty-four-hour darkness was made from Cape Evans to collect penguin eggs. Dr. Wilson was attempting to establish the mutation of birds from marine to land life by examining penguin embryos. Wilson, Bowers, and Cherry-Garrard completed this harrowing five-week journey. They used themselves as guinea pigs, experimenting with three different rations to find the best for extreme polar conditions, as well as testing improvements in polar equipment and clothing. It's from Scott, not from Amundsen's reindeer skins, that modern polar clothing derives.

With the return of the sun in a cold September, Scott authorized three short scientific journeys. These included a twenty-mile run for airing the dogs to Hut Point and back under Cecil Meares and Demetri Gerof, British and Russian husky experts. Meanwhile, at the Bay of Whales, Amundsen, with six men and his dogs; set out for the South Pole on the eighth.

A week later he returned. Five of his dogs had frozen to death, with the other dogs' paws cut and bleeding from the ice. His men were frostbitten and demoralized. There were accusations of cowardice, and a near mutiny by second in command Johansen. Having failed to learn from Scott's and Shackleton's earlier expeditions, Amundsen had not understood the differences between Antarctic and Arctic weather and snow. He banished Johansen and one other from the polar party and on his later return to Norway publicly humiliated him. Johansen later committed suicide. Amundsen then set out for the pole a second time, on October 19, with four men.

Tryggve Gran, who knew both Scott and Amundsen, was withering in his comparison of the two leaders. "Scott was a man. He would always listen to you. Amundsen would listen to nobody. He was only interested in himself. So Amundsen, as a human being, was not worth much, but Scott was worth a lot." Without doubt, Scott had charisma.

From Cape Evans in October, the two motorized sledges set out hauling supplies for the polar depots. Those sledges were the world's first tracked vehicles—forerunners of the tank as well as the modern polar sledge. They covered fifty-one miles across Ross Island and the ice barrier before breaking down, all that was expected at that first stage of their development. Photographer Herbert Ponting wrote: "To the memory of Scott must therefore be given the honour due to a pioneer of motor traction in the Polar regions, for he used it with a certain measure of success."

Scott's 883-mile polar journey started on November 1 with ten ponies and sledges. He had to reach Shackleton's farthest south earlier than Shackleton, with more food and more fuel, in order to reach the pole and return safely. With Shackleton's willing permission, Scott used his Beardmore Glacier route to the Polar Plateau, the only known route across the ice joint. In comparison, Amundsen took two huge gambles in that he hoped to find another crossing farther east as well as a glacier suitable for dogs.

Despite soft snow, the Siberian ponies averaged twelve miles a day across the ice barrier, the men skiing or walking alongside. The dog teams were the last to leave, for they were the fastest. Closer to the Beardmore, the ponies were killed one by one with a bullet to the head. Their meat was buried for use on the return journey, a precaution against scurvy and food for the dogs. At the foot of the Beardmore, an unseasonal four-day blizzard delayed the expedition.

Farther east and unknown to Scott, Amundsen's good fortune was remarkable. He'd reached the mountains and found a passage across the ice joint. In addition, the glacier before him was not split by crevasses, ice falls, and chasms like the Beardmore—it was suitable for dogs. Near the top, Amundsen killed twenty-two dogs to feed the others.

Scott—who was nothing if not flexible—used his dogs two weeks longer than originally planned, hauling sledges a further forty-five miles up the Beardmore until it was too dangerous to use them more. Many of the roped men fell into hidden crevasses, but if a dog team had gone down, it would have taken its sledge, stores, and, possibly, the driver with it. Meares, Demetri, and their dog sledges returned to Cape Evans.

From then on sledges had to be man-hauled, yet both Scott's and

Shackleton's experiences of the Polar Plateau showed that a good speed could be maintained. Three depots were left up the 136-mile glacier, and the Polar Plateau was reached on December 21. This was a scientific exploration, so the men were surveying, recording, mapping, and writing as they traveled because, in the future, others would follow. Robert Scott had a lot in common with James Cook. Both were Royal Navy, both were great explorers, both were scientists, neither would be unnecessarily rushed, and both looked after their men.

From the plateau, four more men returned, with Scott's instruction to store dog food at One Ton Depot on the ice barrier. Eight men then continued toward the pole. On Christmas Day 1911, they hauled sledges for fifteen miles. Bowers observed: "One gets down to bedrock with everybody, sledging under trying conditions. The character of a man comes out and you see things that were never expected. I think more highly than

ever of our leader." Their average increased to twenty-three miles a day across the plateau and soon they were ahead of Shackleton's time, mostly on skis but walking when it was faster. They were using the polar rations tested in the midwinter journey and found them sufficient, while two more depots were left on the plateau, at 3° and 1.5° degrees latitude from the pole. The two teams celebrated the new year in their tents, drinking tea with chocolate rations and talking until 1 A.M.

On January 4, 1912, Scott announced the final polar party as Edward Wilson (doctor and scientist), Henry "Birdie" Bowers (Royal Indian Marine lieutenant, navigator, and meteorologist), Edgar "Taff" Evans (immensely powerful as well as their sledge and ski repairer), and Lawrence "Titus" Oates (Royal Inniskilling Fusilier also powerfully built). The three returning men were second in command Lieutenant "Teddy" Evans and stoker Bill Lashly, who were the most tired of them all, and Tom Crean. Scott judged Oates only slightly stronger than Crean, his most difficult choice of all.

Much has been written about why Scott took five men rather than four, but there's no evidence that he had originally decided upon four. Four was often the sledging format employed, but not always: three men sledged south in the *Discovery* expedition. There is a sketch made by Wilson at Cape Evans of a five-man team, and it's possible that is what Scott had always planned. A five-man team from the last depot to the pole and back makes a lot of sense. The sledge weight would remain essentially the same but for fuel and a sleeping bag, yet there would be another man hauling. In addition, five men is safest for crossing crevasses.

Scott's last order to Teddy Evans was for the dog teams to meet the five returning men between 83° and 82° south, between the Southern Barrier and Middle Barrier depots, fifty to ninety miles from the Beardmore.

Southward the five sledged. They passed Shackleton's farthest-south point on January 6. At 10,500 feet, they had to cross a sea of difficult fishhook ice waves, or sastrugi, and resorted to walking. They were back on skis by the tenth when the temperature plummeted. By noon of the sixteenth they were approaching the South Pole, a featureless white plain with a long downhill slope. They saw mock suns with long horizontal halos. At around 4 P.M. Bowers saw something ahead—a black speck, perhaps a cairn, perhaps a reflection from the sastrugi.

As they approached, the object grew into a black mark, then larger until they could see that it was a flag and an abandoned campsite. In the disturbed snow they saw sledge, ski, and paw marks. "The Norwegians have forestalled us and are first at the Pole," wrote Scott. "It is a terrible disappointment, and I am very sorry for my loyal companions."

Scott continued, navigating his own path to the southernmost point on earth and checking his position with sun sights. They camped and on January 17 marched outward on different bearings—"the coldest march I ever remembered," wrote Wilson. With the sextants of the time, it was impossible to establish the exact location of the pole. Even the best of them were accurate only to about a quarter of a mile. Compasses were completely useless and spun wildly.

With the final set of sun sights, Scott and his men established their position at latitude 89° 59′ 14″ south, within three-quarters of a mile of the most southerly point on earth. They planted the United Kingdom flag.

Amundsen had been less painstaking with his sun sights. Wilson noted: "From Amundsen's direction of tracks he has probably hit a point about 3 miles off . . . but in any case we are all agreed that he can claim prior right to the Pole itself." In the Norwegian tent were the details and a letter for Scott from Amundsen. He had arrived on December 14, 1911, four weeks and five days before. Scott's scientific exploration had taken twenty days longer to reach the pole than Amundsen's racing expedition, which had left earlier.

"Great God, this is an awful place," Scott famously wrote. It still is.

On the return journey, there was disappointment but no depression, observed Dr. Wilson. However, Scott noted on January 23 that Taff

Evans was not well—"There is no doubt that Evans is a good deal run down"—but no one knew what was wrong with the powerful man. Back across the sastrugi, some skied while others walked, but none slowed the others and they still covered twenty miles on such days. They found all their depots and reached the top of Beardmore with no trouble. They had food and fuel and were on schedule to return to Cape Evans before the end of March, the end of summer.

On February 8 Evans was unable to haul, yet that was not yet alarming. There were good and bad days for all of them, and at the same place in 1909, Shackleton had had to stop hauling. Evans skied behind to resume hauling the following day.

The scientific programs continued. While descending the mountains, Wilson and Bowers uncovered rocks containing fossilized leaves, coal, and other minerals, with important discoveries at Mount Darwin and Mount Buckley cliffs. They collected thirty-five pounds of specimens. These discoveries established that Antarctica was once a warm-climate continent, and the Permian period leaf fossils led to the realization that it was once part of the ancient supercontinent "Gondwana," with Australasia, India, Africa, and South America. Was carrying the thirty-five-pound samples critical? No. Such a small weight did not make any difference. What caused their later problems was something else entirely.

By February 16 the team was approaching the base of the Beardmore when Evans collapsed in the sledge harness. Dr. Wilson described Evans as "sick and giddy and unable to walk even by the sledge on ski, so we camped." Scott recorded: "Evans has nearly broken down in brain we think." Something catastrophic had happened to Evans, but no one knew what it was or how to treat it.

They were ten miles from the next depot. After a short rest, four men hauled the sledge while Evans skied behind as he'd done before. He had troubles with his ski bindings and stopped at least twice to adjust them—a slow and bitterly painful business with sore and frostbitten hands. Gradually, he fell behind the others. At the next halt he was out of sight, so the four immediately went back to him.

Scott wrote: "I was the first to reach the poor man and shocked at his appearance, he was on his knees with clothing disarranged, hands uncovered and frostbitten, and a wild look in his eyes. Asked what was the matter, he replied with a slow speech that he didn't know. . . . He showed every sign of complete collapse." By the time they got him into the tent he was comatose. He died quietly at 12:30 A.M. without regaining consciousness.

There is only guesswork still about Taff Evans's condition. Of the likely causes for his death, Dr. Wilson thought it might have been a brain hemorrhage caused by a fall into a crevasse two weeks before. In his "Message to the Public," Scott put his death as "concussion to the brain." Yet Scott actually recorded the beginning of Evans's deterioration on January 23, before the fall. Wilson makes no mention of scurvy, and he would have known, being familiar with the disease. Scurvy takes three to four months to present itself, and it was only two and a half months since Evans and the others had eaten fresh meat. A recent theory is that Evans was suffering from cerebral edema. This condition of fluid on the brain was unknown in 1912, but it can cause sudden clinical deterioration of the body. It can be caused by infection, a blockage, a fall, even a minor stroke, and can be exacerbated by altitude.

Anti-Scott biographers point to Petty Officer Evans being spiritually alone, cut off by his "social superiors," which hastened his decline. There's no evidence for this; it's mere invention. In fact, Taff Evans was an extrovert. He swapped yarns with Scott, Wilson, and Bowers. He'd sailed with Scott in the navy, sledged with him many times, and cheerfully shared three-man sleeping bags with Scott and others. There was no class divide. Scott was the son of a Plymouth brewer, while Wilson and Bowers chatted with anyone.

A few hours later Scott, Wilson, Bowers, and Oates reached the depot. The next day they crossed the ice joint onto the barrier and reached the first pony camp, where they dug fresh meat out of the ice. They were ten thousand feet lower than the plateau, and the temperature was appreciably warmer. The dog teams should have been approaching from the north, and there was a line of depots all the way to Cape Evans. They had fresh meat, extra rations and fuel, a new sledge left for them, and only four hundred miles of the sixteen-hundred-mile journey remained. They set out and reached the Southern Barrier depot on the twenty-second, to find that some cooking fuel had evaporated from the sealed cans. Away from the mountains, though, their speed increased and they averaged fifteen miles per day.

Without warning, the weather changed. On the twenty-fifth, the temperature dropped to −20° F, on the twenty-seventh it was −30, and by March 2 it had reached a vicious −40, which is the same in both centigrade and Fahrenheit. Yet it wasn't the cold itself that threatened disaster—it was the change the temperature made to the ice and snow underfoot. The surface turned crystalline. This created immense friction, anchoring the sledges to the ice, dragging at the runners like thick mud.

Although Wilson and Bowers still recorded their scientific data, Scott was by then the only one keeping a diary. On March 2 they reached the Middle Barrier depot. Again they found that fuel had evaporated from the sealed cans. The wind was blowing unseasonably into their faces, and Oates's feet were frostbitten: "Titus Oates disclosed his feet, the toes showing very bad indeed, evidently bitten by the late temperatures." He continued hauling with the others.

On the third they traveled ten miles, on the fourth, nine, on the fifth, eight. On March 6 they made only six and a half miles, and Scott recorded that they "feel the cold terribly. The surface . . . is coated with a thin layer of woolly crystals. . . . These are too firmly fixed to be removed by the wind and cause impossible friction on the runners. Amongst ourselves we are unendingly cheerful, but what each man feels in his heart I can only guess."

Elsewhere on the sixth, the *Fram* arrived in Australia and Amundsen telegrammed the world that he was first to the South Pole. Publicly Nansen congratulated Amundsen; in his diary he recorded his disappointment.

In Scott's team, Bowers maintained his meteorological log until March 19, and from this and subsequent weather records it's now understood what happened. Scott planned the polar journey with meteorologist George Simpson, later director of the Meteorological Office of the United Kingdom. Simpson's weather predictions were based upon all known information. Yet 1912 was an abnormal year—a rogue year. In late February and March was the worst weather ever recorded on the ice barrier. Scott experienced temperatures ten to twenty degrees colder than average. The conditions were ferocious, the ice under the sledges like glue. From going very well, suddenly they were in desperate trouble. Where were the dog teams?

Dog food had not been taken to One Ton Depot as ordered. There is no apparent explanation for this. Teddy Evans had passed Scott's second order to Meares and Gerof for the dog teams to meet Scott ninety to fifty miles from Beardmore. By then, though, Evans was near death. He hadn't eaten his meat rations and had contracted scurvy on top of severe exhaustion. Dr. Atkinson assumed command and saved Evans's life, but Scott's orders were not carried out. Meares's father had died in Britain, and Meares left Cape Evans in late February by the resupply voyage of the *Terra Nova,* in which Evans also left.

Only then did Atkinson order Gerof, Cherry-Garrard, and one dog sledge to One Ton Depot. They reached it, a quarter of the way across the barrier, on March 3. More food for the polar party was deposited but still no dog food, and they camped. One hundred three miles south, the exhausted polar party skied toward them.

On the seventh Scott wrote: "We are 16 miles from our depot [Lower Barrier]. We hope against hope that the dogs have been to Mt. Hooper [Lower Barrier]; then we might pull through." They reached the depot on the ninth. There is no diary entry that day.

On the tenth he wrote: "Yesterday we marched up to the depot. . . . Cold comfort. Shortage on our allowance all round. I don't know that anyone is to blame. The dogs which would have been our salvation have evidently failed. Meares had a bad trip home I suppose." As well as fuel evaporation, discovered later to be from faulty can manufacture, there was less food than ordered. Scott reported: "Oates' foot worse. He has rare pluck and must know that he can never get through. He asked Wilson if he had a chance this morning, and of course Bill had to say he didn't know. In point of fact he has none. The weather conditions are awful."

They left Hooper on the tenth, but a blizzard struck after only a few hundred yards and they were forced to camp again. On the eleventh they sledged six miles. All were frostbitten and Oates was near the end, unable by then to use his fingers. Although still hauling, he was slowing the others' progress through the time he took to prepare himself each day.

At One Ton Depot in the same freak weather, Cherry-Garrard was in anguish over what to do. Atkinson had said that if Scott had not arrived at the depot before him, he was to judge what action to take. On the tenth, Cherry-Garrard and Gerof returned to Hut Point and telephoned Atkinson at Cape Evans.

Scott made no entry for the twelfth, but it was probably then that he distributed the opium tablets to Bowers, Oates, and himself, leaving Wilson the morphine. Each man was thus able to make his own decision about his life. On the thirteenth they were blizzard-bound. On the fourteenth they pushed on. It took all morning to prepare Oates, the three cumbersomely dressing him. At noon, in −42° F, they sledged northward a few more miles before the weather deteriorated and they were forced to camp again.

On the morning of March 16, blizzard-bound in their tent, Oates awoke and dragged himself out of his sleeping bag. He said: "I am just going outside and may be some time." Scott wrote: "He went out into the blizzard and we have not seen him since. . . . We knew that poor Oates was walking to his death, but though we tried to dissuade him, we knew it was the act of a brave man and an English gentleman."

Some biographers have belittled Oates's gesture as suicide. Dr. Wilson, a devout Christian and in the tent, wrote to Mrs. Oates: "This is a sad ending to our undertaking. Your son died a very noble death, God knows. I have never seen or heard of such courage as he showed from the first to last with his feet both badly frostbitten—never a word of complaint or of the pain. He was a great example." Oates knew that his frostbite was destroying his companions' chances of survival, that because of his slowness they might never reach the next depot. He also knew that they would not leave him. Twice he asked and twice they refused. Suicide? The Bible states it more clearly: "Greater love hath no man than this, that a man lay down his life for his friends."

The blizzard eased, and the three broke camp and sledged north, still carrying Oates's sleeping bag—in case. On the seventeenth they were blizzard-bound. On the eighteenth they reached fifteen and a half miles from One Ton Depot, just three days away at their improved speed since Oates's leaving. They were eleven miles from One Ton on the nineteenth when another blizzard hit. By then, all of them had severe frostbite, Scott the worst by his own admission. On the twenty-first Wilson and Bowers planned to ski to One Ton and return with fuel and food, but the blizzard made it impossible. They lay inside the frozen tent, battered by the moaning wind.

Scott recorded: "22 and 23. Blizzard bad as ever—Wilson and Bowers unable to start—tomorrow last chance—no fuel and only one or two of food left—must be near the end. Have decided it shall be natural—we shall march for the depot with or without our effects and die in our tracks."

Atkinson and Patrick Keohane reached the barrier from Cape Evans on March 27, searching for their companions. They lasted thirty-five miles in the desperate conditions before turning back.

Scott's last entry was dated March 29. "Since the 21st we have had a continuous gale from W.S.W. and S.W. Every day we have been ready to start for our depot 11 miles away, but outside the door of the tent it remains a scene of whirling drift. I do not think we can hope for any better things now. We shall stick it out to the end, but we are getting weaker, of course, and the end cannot be far. It seems a pity, but I do not think I can write more. R. Scott."

On November 12, a search party led by Atkinson including Gran,

Cherry-Garrard, Gerof, and his dogs reached them. Canadian Charles Wright first saw the tip of the tent poking above a snowdrift. They dug it out and looked inside.

It's probable that forty-three-year-old Scott died last, for the sleeping bags of Wilson and Bowers were tied from the outside, while Scott's was not. Scott's right arm was resting across Wilson, his great friend. Dr. Atkinson certified death from natural causes and recovered the opium and morphine. In their last letters, the three men's thoughts were not of themselves but of their families. Scott's final sentence reads "For God's sake look after our people."

There are always "if onlys," but what killed Scott, Wilson, Bowers and Oates was not "if onlys." It was not because they failed to use dogs and ponies; they used them wherever they could. They also skied wherever they could. It was not because they failed to use accepted Antarctic practices; they established the accepted practices. It was not through missing depots, for they found them all. What killed them was the extraordinary weather.

Scott realized this and blamed no one except himself, for a leader is responsible for everything, even for events beyond his control—as Amundsen and Shackleton are responsible for the deaths in their various expeditions. Scott wrote: "Subsidiary reasons for our failure to return are due to the sickness of different members of the party, but the real thing that has stopped us is the awful weather and unexpected cold towards the end of the journey. The traverse of the Barrier has been quite three times as severe as any experience we had on the summit. There is no accounting for it, but the result has thrown out my calculations."

There is an accounting for it now. From subsequent records and the calculations of meteorologists George Simpson of Britain and Susan Solomon of the United States, it is established that 1912 was a freak weather year.

A cairn of snow was built over the tent and a cross of Tryggve Gran's skis erected on top. He wore Scott's skis back to Cape Evans to ensure that they traveled all the way. Above Hut Point, Scott's men erected a nine-foot-high wooden cross, the ice barrier behind. It's there today. On it is carved IN MEMORIAM, the five names, and the line TO STRIVE, TO SEEK, TO FIND, AND NOT TO YIELD.

It is the last line from Tennyson's poem "Ulysses." They are apt because they are true: the five explorers strove, sought, found, and would not yield, even to circumstances beyond their control.

Evans sledged and skied until he collapsed, struggled forward on his knees until he was unconscious, and died never knowing where his strength had gone. Oates sledged and skied until he saw that his frostbite would slow and kill his comrades, so left to slow them no longer. Scott, Wilson, and Bowers pushed on until constant blizzards made further travel impossible, and died together naturally.

They did not yield.

Recommended
The Voyage of the Discovery by Robert Falcon Scott, vols. 1 and 2
The Worst Journey in the World by Apsley Cherry-Garrard
Diary of the "Terra Nova" Expedition 1910–12 by Dr. Edward Wilson
Scott's Last Expedition (personal journals) by Robert Falcon Scott
The Coldest March: Scott's Fatal Antarctic Expedition by Susan Solomon
Captain Scott by Sir Ranulph Fiennes

The Men of Colditz

There were two qualifications for the Allied soldiers of World War II to be sent to Colditz Castle as prisoners. They had to be officers, and they had to have escaped before. Men who had tunneled out of other prisons, men who had walked out dressed as guards, laborers, and even women were sent to Colditz. In that way, the Germans managed to assemble a group of the most imaginative, determined, and experienced enemy officers in one place. In that context, it is perhaps not so surprising that when the prison was finally liberated by American soldiers in 1945, they found a fully working glider in the attic, ready to go.

The interned soldiers were all Allies, from Poland, Canada, Holland, France, Belgium, Britain, or, toward the end, the United States. However, there was always the chance that one might be a stool pigeon, a man planted by the Germans to spy on the prisoners. Security had to be tight, even among their own men. It is astonishing now to consider that the Colditz prisoners constructed realistic identity papers, uniforms, disguises, a typewriter, keys, and tunnel equipment from the few supplies they had or could steal. Their beds were straw mattresses over boards that found use in shoring up tunnels, false doors, and cupboards and even as carved guns and glider wings. For tunnel lamps, they used candles made from cooking fat in a cigarette tin, with a pajama-cord wick.

Colditz, known to the Germans as Oflag IV-C, had been used in World War I to hold prisoners and is about a thousand years old. One side overlooks a cliff above the Mulde River. To escape Colditz, situated in the heart of the German Reich, one had to cross four hundred miles of hostile territory in any direction. The walls were seven feet thick. But the first escape attempts involved Canadian officers just picking up buckets of whitewash and a long ladder and walking out, pretending to be painters. They were quickly recaptured, then kicked and battered with rifle butts. The stakes were always life and death for those who tried to escape, and despite the schoolboy quality of some of the attempts, it was never a game. In the "Great Escape" from Stalag Luft III in 1944, fifty out of the seventy-six escaping officers were caught and shot.

The garrison at Colditz always outnumbered the prisoners. The entire castle was floodlit at night, and as well as a hundred-foot drop on one side, there was a nine-foot barbed-wire fence, a moat, and a thirteen-foot-high outer wall. The Geneva Convention enforced the humane treatment of prisoners, at least in theory. German officers were interned in England, and there was a joint benefit in avoiding brutal treatment. Food and Red Cross parcels were allowed in at irregular intervals, and the prisoners could send carefully censored letters home. They could buy essential supplies, such as razor blades for shaving, toothpaste, soap, and even musical instruments. They were allowed to cook for themselves on small stoves in the dormitories.

The day began at 7:30 A.M. and was organized into four roll calls in the main courtyard. At first the largest contingents were Polish and British. From those, there were a variety of talents available from the prison population, from lock pickers and forgers to civil engineers. There was a theater in the castle, and the prisoners put on elaborate productions and musicals while in Colditz. One of the posters for a performance was replaced by the following: "For Sunshine Holidays, visit Sunny Colditz, Holiday Hotel. 500 beds, one bath. Cuisine by French chef. Large staff, always attentive and vigilant. Once visited, never left."

Three times a week the prisoners were allowed exercise, from fencing to soccer and boxing. They were even allowed to keep a cat. When it vanished, the prisoners assumed it had gone to find a mate, until its body was discovered wrapped in a parcel in a trash bin. For all the surface gentility of their treatment, savagery was always close by. The last roll call was at 9 P.M., at which point the "night shift" began—the escape committees of Colditz.

In January 1941, a British tunnel plan was put into action with the construction of a sliding box to go under floorboards. The theory was that even if the floorboards were taken up by investigating Germans, the rubble-filled box would look solid enough and hide the tunnel below. It passed inspection shortly after construction, and the guards saw nothing suspicious. However, the tunnel was abandoned as too easy to find. The men involved were locked into their room after some minor offense, and in protest, they unlocked and removed the door from its hinges, carried it around the camp in slow procession, and presented it to the German officers.

Pat Reid, MBE (later MC and author of *The Colditz Story*), spent part of a night in the Colditz brick drains, working to break through a wall. Taking turns with Rupert Barry and Dick Howe, he spent several nights scraping with bits of steel and nails. The underground bricks and cement proved tougher than their improvised tools. Another manhole entrance to the sewers looked more promising, and the men used the canteen as a base, having made a key for the door out of a piece of an iron bed. They made better progress but found the way blocked by thick clay. Reid's next idea was to make a vertical tunnel from the first, so that it would be possible to go some way from the buildings underground before heading for the outer wall.

On a surprise night inspection, the absence of the working tunnelers was discovered and the commandant told the men in the dormitory that they would all be shot. The Germans began tearing up the floor and summoned dogs to search. The dogs found nothing, and Reid had to hang on to a manhole from underneath as guards tried to lift it. He and the others constructed a false wall in the tunnel, hiding their supplies behind it. After that, they returned in darkness to their beds. The Germans were astonished to have them reappear at morning roll call, and the commandant was criticized by his superiors for a false alarm.

After that, the Germans discovered the tunnel location suspiciously quickly, though they did not breach the false wall. The presence of a German spy, or stooge, in their midst had to be considered, and security grew tighter.

The camp population increased in 1941. Around 250 French officers arrived, then 60 Dutch and 2 Yugoslavs. In addition to those, the escape committees now included Irishmen, Canadians, Australians, New Zealanders, Jews, and an Indian doctor. They were united by a common enemy and had to keep one another informed so that one escape attempt did not ruin another.

Some of the British contingent found a guard who was amenable to a trade in contraband goods. They bribed him to look the other way for a crucial ten minutes of sentry duty. Eight Britons and four Poles prepared to use the still-undiscovered first tunnel they had dug in the drains. Cutting a square of earth from below, Reid was the first out into the courtyard, but a floodlight came on instantly. He was surrounded by armed Germans—tipped off by the guard they thought they had bribed to silence.

Other attempts followed. French laborers carried a British officer, Peter Allan, in a straw mattress being taken to soldiers' quarters in a local village. A fluent German-speaker, Allan made it to Vienna and even spent part of the journey with an SS officer who gave him a lift. In Vienna he was refused help by the American consulate, with the United States at that point not in the war. Exhaustion and starvation saw him taken to a local hospital, where he was arrested and sent back to Colditz for solitary confinement.

Around the same time, a French officer, Mairesse-Lebrun, made it to the local station before being apprehended. Mairesse-Lebrun was an athletic and determined escaper, however. In July 1941, during his exercise period, he leaped the outer wire with the help of a friend who made his hands into a stirrup. Mairesse-Lebrun then climbed the wire from the outside and used it to get over the outer wall. He stole a local bicycle and cycled between sixty and a hundred miles a day, posing as an Italian officer. He avoided capture and crossed to Switzerland seven days after his escape. From there he made it to the Pyrenees before he was taken prisoner by the Fascist Spanish and broke his back jumping from a window. Crippled, Mairesse-Lebrun survived the war. His belongings in Colditz were later received at his French home in the parcel he had made and addressed before his escape.

Two Polish officers tried the perilous climb down the outer cliff but were discovered and captured by a German who heard the noise and opened a window right by their rope of tied sheets. In his excitement, he shouted for them to put their hands up, which they couldn't do without letting go of the rope.

Meanwhile, the British prisoners had begun another tunnel. They had homemade compasses, copied maps, rucksacks, and some rare German money, smuggled into the castle with new arrivals. They created civilian clothing by altering RAF uniforms. Twelve men were to escape, but that too failed when the Germans discovered them.

The Dutch contingent was more successful in 1941, managing to smuggle six men over the outer wall and wire in pairs on successive Sundays. Four out of six reached Switzerland safely. The other two were sent back to Colditz.

Winston Churchill's nephew Giles Romilly was sent to Colditz toward the end of 1941. He was closely guarded, though at one point he almost escaped, disguised as a French coal worker unloading supplies. Toward the end of the war, when Germany was losing badly, the *prominente,* or famous prisoners, were moved to a prison camp at Tittmoning, with the intention of using them as hostages. Romilly and two others escaped Tittmoning with the help of Dutchmen he had known in Colditz. One of the three was recaptured, but Romilly eventually made it back to England after the fall of Germany.

By December 1941, the inhabitants of Colditz had managed to get hold of some yeast and began brewing beer from anything organic, sitting on the jars and bottles for hours on end to promote fermentation. After that, they created a still and made "firewater" that the Poles called vodka, of a sort. With Christmas on the way, they had quite a good collection of vintages.

As a trained engineer, Pat Reid had become the official "escape officer" for the British contingent. He noticed that the theater stage overlapped a floor below that led to the German guardhouse. He approached Airey Neave and J. Hyde-Thompson to take part in a new plan. Neave said that only the Dutch could make realistic German uniforms, so two Dutch officers were brought in for the attempt. They made uniform buttons, eagles, and swastikas by pouring molten lead into intricately carved molds, then attached them to adapted Dutch greatcoats, which were similar to the German ones. Leather belts and holsters were cut from linoleum, and they carried well-forged German identity documents.

Reid and a Canadian, Hank Wardle, cut through the ceiling of the room under the stage, camouflaging and repainting a removable hatch with great care. They were experienced lock pickers, and the doors beyond gave them no trouble. It went like a charm. Neave and the Dutchman Tony Luteyn went first, with Hyde-Thompson and the second Dutchman following the next night. As escape officer, Reid could not go himself—his skills were too valuable. The Germans discovered that they were missing four men and began to search the castle.

Neave and Luteyn crossed to Switzerland, making Neave the first Briton to escape from Colditz successfully. He went on to become a Conservative MP in 1953 and later served as a minister in Margaret Thatcher's opposition government. Tragically, after surviving so many perils, he was killed in a car bomb planted by Irish Republicans a few months before the 1979 election. His book describing the Colditz escape, *They Have Their Exits,* is a great read. Hyde-Thompson and his companion were caught and returned to Colditz.

The Germans discovered the stage hatch with the help of a Polish informer whom they controlled by blackmail. The Poles discovered his identity, and their senior officer gave the commandant a day to remove him before they hanged him themselves.

As 1942 crept by, the French contingent worked on a tunnel that had its entrance in the clock tower. They also sent out one Lieutenant

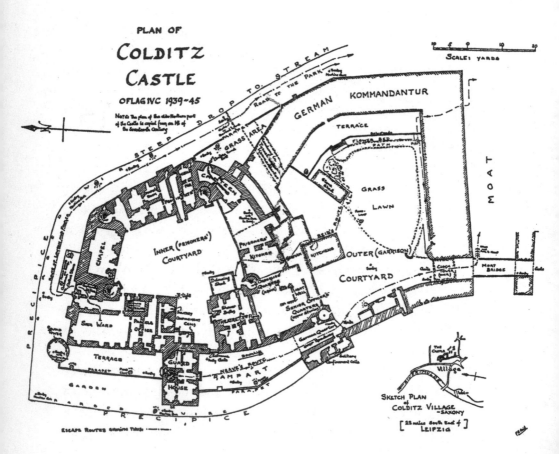

Boulé, dressed as a beautiful blond woman. The disguise was discovered when "she" dropped her watch and a guard returned it. The Dutch tried one large man sitting on the grass, hiding a smaller man beneath his coat while he dug a shallow grave. Dogs found him before he was missed.

By that time, there were sixty British in Colditz. One of the best known, RAF fighter pilot Douglas Bader, arrived during 1942. Morale was dropping with the number of failed attempts and so few successes. Two officers went insane and had to be restrained from committing suicide. Another feigned madness in an attempt to get himself sent to Switzerland. Bader's presence helped morale no end. For a man with artificial legs, he was irrepressible and announced that he was ready to join an escape over the roof of the castle.

Squadron leader Brian Paddon was removed from Colditz around this time to be court-martialed at another prison camp. He escaped his guards and was the second Briton to reach England. Other attempts were less successful, but they went on continuously. Pat Reid planned an escape through the commandant's own office, with the help of a Dutch watchmaker who could get through the more complex locks. Reid began a tunnel under the commandant's desk, working at night. When the time came, eight men assembled in the office and six broke through to a storeroom, leaving Reid and Lieutenant Derek Gill to hide the route. They were all dressed as German soldiers, and their "sergeant" was saluted by the guards as they walked out the following morning. Of the six, four were recaptured, but two made it to Switzerland by September 1942.

Pat Reid's final escape plan came when Dick Howe took over as escape officer and he could make a try for himself. Reid joined Ronnie Littledale, William Stephens, and Hank Wardle in a run over the roofs. Split-second timing was the key as they had only instants to cross a courtyard when the patrolling guard turned. The noise of their run was covered by an orchestra practice, which Douglas Bader conducted. Bader could see the vital sentry, and the plan was for him to stop the music whenever it was safe to run. However, the Germans became suspicious and stopped the practice halfway through. The escapers reached the outer buildings safely but were then unable to go farther when a prepared key failed to open a vital lock. Reid found an unused basement with a very narrow, barred chimney to the outside. To get up it, they had to strip naked, then pass up their kits and re-dress on the other side. They crossed the moat, barbed wire, and outer wall with sheet ropes, then set off in pairs. Reid and Wardle covered the four hundred miles in four days of train journeys and walking. All four made it to Switzerland safely.

In the four years of Colditz's use as a prison camp, more than three hundred escape plans were attempted, and of those, thirty-one ended in a "home run." The German habit of returning escapers to the same place meant that as often as they lost a potential route out, they learned from the experience of those who made it farthest. Vitally, the repeated attempts also tied up German soldiers and resources that would otherwise have been used fighting the Allies.

After fierce fighting, the castle was liberated by American soldiers on April 15, 1945. One of the last British plans was revealed behind a false wall in the attic—a working wooden glider with a wing span of thirty-three feet.

Recommended
The Colditz Story and *The Latter Days at Colditz* by P. R. Reid
Reach for the Sky by Paul Brickhill
They Have Their Exits by Airey Neave

The Unknown Warrior

It is evening on the western front. The year, 1916; halfway through the mud and carnage that is the Great War. An army padre serving in France returns to his billet.

"I came back from the line at dusk. We had just laid to rest the mortal remains of a comrade. I went to a billet in front of Erkingham, near Armentières. At the back of the billet was a small garden, and in the garden, only six paces from the house, there was a grave. At the head of the grave there stood a rough cross of white wood. On the cross was written, in deep black-penciled letters 'An Unknown British Soldier' and in brackets underneath 'of the Black Watch.' It was dusk and no-one was near except some officers of the billet playing cards. I remember how still it was. Even the guns seemed to be resting. How that grave caused me to think."

The Reverend David Railton wrote to the commander in chief of the British Expeditionary Force, Sir Douglas Haig. He proposed that the body of a soldier be removed from the western front to Britain for burial: one soldier to represent all the dead of the British Empire and Commonwealth, to help "ease the pain of father, mother, brother, sister, sweetheart, wife and friend." Understandably, in the middle of a four-year war, there was no reply, but the concept of the Unknown Warrior had begun.

Railton survived the war and in 1919 was appointed vicar of

Saint John the Baptist in Margate, Kent. He left the army with the Military Cross and the memory of that evening in France. He'd thought further that such an unknown soldier should be buried only inside Westminster Abbey, because that great abbey—first dedicated in 1065—was the "Parish Church of the Empire," of a third of the world. In August 1920 he resubmitted the idea to the dean of Westminster, Dr. Herbert Ryle. He in turn approached the king, the prime minister, and the British army, writing: "There are thousands of graves . . . of 'Tommies' who fell at the front—names not known. My idea is that one such body (name not known) should be exhumed and interred in Westminster Abbey, in the nave."

King George V was at first doubtful, suggesting that almost two years after the end of the war such a funeral "now might be regarded as belated." However, he was persuaded that the idea would work, and on October 18, the dean received a letter informing him of His Majesty's approval and of the suggestion that the burial indeed take place on the next Armistice Day, November 11, 1920. From that day BBC radio and newspapers throughout the empire, commonwealth, and the world carried regular reports of the project.

How was the Unknown Warrior to be selected from the more than one and a half million dead British and empire soldiers, sailors, and airmen? How would he reach Westminster Abbey?

The desperately sad process of locating, identifying, transporting to war cemeteries, and reburying the British and empire dead along all battlefronts is carried out by the Imperial War Graves Commission, then under the command of Brigadier General L. J. Wyatt. He gave orders that on November 7, 1920, the bodies of four servicemen be exhumed from the four great British battlefields of the western front; one from the Somme, one from Ypres, one from Arras, and one from the Aisne. Each must be from a grave marked UNKNOWN BRITISH SOLDIER, each must be wearing a British uniform, and all must be placed in identical bags.

Four unknown servicemen were brought that evening by field ambulances to the Saint-Pol headquarters and there taken into the chapel. Each of the ambulance parties left immediately and returned to their base. At midnight Brigadier General Wyatt and Colonel Gell entered the dim, lamp-lit chapel. Wyatt wrote later:

> The four soldiers lay on stretchers, each covered with a Union flag; in front of the altar was the shell of a coffin which had been sent from England to receive the remains. I selected one and, with the assistance of Col. Gell, placed it in the shell and screwed down the lid. The other bodies were removed and reburied in the military cemetery outside my headquarters at St. Pol. I had no idea even of the area from which the body I had selected had come; and no-one else can know it.

Thus the soldier or sailor or airman was selected at random. The name of the man, his age, his regiment, his rank, where he died—all were and shall remain forever unknown.

In Britain, meanwhile, a special coffin was commissioned. It was made of oak from a tree on the grounds of Henry VIII's Hampton Court Palace. Around the coffin were forged wrought-iron bands, and secured to the lid was the sword of a knight of the Crusades, selected by the king from the Tower of London. Carved into the lid was the inscription:

A BRITISH WARRIOR WHO FELL IN THE GREAT WAR 1914–18
FOR KING AND COUNTRY

In Westminster Abbey the nave was prepared. Flagstones were raised and a grave dug in the center of the aisle, in pride of place, directly inside the Great West Door.

A quiet service was held in the Saint-Pol chapel by chaplains from the Church of England, the Nonconformist churches, and the Roman Catholic Church. On November 9, the coffin shell of pine was carried by field ambulance and escort to the Chapelle Ardente in Boulogne, where it was placed inside the oaken coffin brought from

Britain. There the Unknown Warrior rested overnight with an honor guard of British and Dominion soldiers. Brigadier General Wyatt also sent six barrels of earth from the western front with which to cover the coffin in its Westminster grave, so that the Unknown Warrior "should rest in the soil on which so many of our troops gave up their lives."

On the morning of the tenth the coffin was carried to HMS *Verdun,* berthed at Gambetta Quay, for the channel crossing. Lieutenant General Sir George Macdonogh represented the king; Marshal Foch represented the French government.

The procession following the coffin was more than a mile long, made up of French infantry, cavalry, disabled soldiers, and children. More people lined the roadsides to the quay. The destroyer *Verdun,* launched in 1917, was chosen because she was named after the battle of Verdun of 1916.

Halfway across the English Channel, as the *Verdun* entered British waters, six Royal Navy destroyers met and escorted her into Dover. Unbidden, gathering slowly during the day and waiting in silence, thousands of people lined the quaysides of the ancient port. A nineteen-gun salute was fired—a field marshal's salute, the highest military honor—and a band played. The coffin was transferred into the same railway carriage that in 1919 had carried home the body of Edith Cavell, and borne to London.

During the war some 25 million wounded soldiers, sailors, and airmen had passed that way, but the passage of that serviceman was particularly poignant. The *Daily Mail* wrote of the journey through Kent:

> The train thundered through the dark, wet, moonless night. At the platforms by which it rushed could be seen groups of women watching and silent, many dressed in deep mourning. Many an upper window was open and against the golden square of light was silhouetted clear cut and black the head and shoulders of some faithful watcher. . . . In the London suburbs there were scores of homes with back doors flung wide, light flooding out

and in the gardens figures of men, women and children gazing at the great lighted train rushing past.

This serviceman returning might just be their missing serviceman—their brother, father, son, or friend.

The bridges over the line were also packed with silent watchers, the steam and smoke from the engine shrouding them as the marked carriage passed beneath. When the train drew into Victoria Station, more people thronged the platforms and concourses. There the Unknown Warrior remained overnight with an honor guard of the King's Company, Grenadier Guards.

On the morning of November 11, 1920, at 0915, the Unknown Warrior was carried to a gun carriage pulled by six black horses. Draped over his coffin was a very special Union Jack on which were placed a British helmet and sidearms. The flag was the property of the Reverend Railton, and it, too, had seen action. It was the flag that Railton had used as an altar cloth for makeshift services and for the celebration of Holy Communion along the western front.

From Hyde Park, the Royal Artillery fired a nineteen-gun salute. Twelve of the highest-ranking officers—led by Admiral of the Fleet Earl Beatty and Field Marshal Sir Douglas Haig—attended as pallbearers. Following the carriage were the mourners, including four hundred ex-servicemen of all ranks. All that had been arranged.

What had not been arranged—like the men and women on the quayside at Dover and the silent watchers along the railway line—were the thousands and thousands of silent people standing along the curbsides and pavements of London. From Victoria Station up to and along the Mall, through Admiralty Arch and down Whitehall, the mourners watched and paid tribute. One unknown soldier, sailor, or airman returning home at last to represent the million and a half still lying in Belgium, France, Germany, the Middle East, Africa, the

Pacific Islands, in all the seas, and especially the hundreds of thousands with no known grave.

At the newly erected cenotaph—created in the same vein of remembrance as the Unknown Warrior, and meaning literally "empty tomb"—King George V stepped forward and laid his own wreath of roses and bay leaves on the coffin. His handwritten card read: "In proud memory of those warriors who died unknown in the Great War. Unknown and yet well known, as dying and behold they lived. George RI."

There followed a hymn, a simple prayer, and then from Westminster the deep chimes of Big Ben proclaimed 1100 hours; the eleventh hour of the eleventh day of the eleventh month, the moment the Armistice was effective in 1918 to end World War I. On the eleventh chime, the king released the two U.K. flags covering the cenotaph and the tomb was unveiled for the first time. There was a two-minute silence in Whitehall and all across the kingdom—from London to Belfast, Cardiff to Edinburgh, Land's End to John O'Groats. A lone bugler played the forlorn notes of "the Last Post," "calling to them from sad shires."

The procession resumed along the crowded, silent streets of the capital, the king and the Prince of Wales walking behind the Unknown Warrior in his final journey through London and into Westminster Abbey. The congregation of that parish church that day was one thousand widows and mothers of men killed in the war, the nave lined by ninety-six holders of the Victoria Cross. The oaken coffin entered the abbey by the North Door. It was carried by the pallbearers through the quire, along the length of the nave, to the grave immediately inside the Great West Door. The choir sang, "I am the resurrection and the life, saith the Lord." Dean Ryle conducted a simple service.

To the soft singing of the traditional "Lead, Kindly Light" the Unknown Warrior was lowered into his grave, there to lie forever amidst the kings and queens, princes and poets, writers and composers, and other saviors and preservers of freedom.

King George stepped to the grave. From a silver shell he scattered earth from the Flanders battlefields onto the coffin: "Earth to earth, ashes to ashes." The service was completed by the Reveille: the Union Jack from the western front was draped over the pall.

By the time the abbey closed its doors at eleven that night more than forty thousand people had paid their respects to the Unknown Warrior, leaving wreaths, flowers, and single poppies around him and around the four servicemen standing honor guard. Tens of thousands more visited the cenotaph. There, silent lines of men, women, and children wound throughout the misty November night, leaving a sea of wreaths. Two wounded soldiers walked sixty miles to lay wreaths to their comrades. On the morning of the twelfth—unrehearsed—the silent pilgrimage to the warrior in the abbey resumed.

It had been thought to close the grave after three days, but that had to be delayed. A chorister at the service, Reginald Wright, wrote: "A feature that lives vividly in my mind was that, after the service was over, thousands upon thousands of people streamed into the Abbey hour after hour, day after day, and when they got to the grave they cast their red poppies onto it. Gradually, the area became a mass of red poppies."

In the first week, more than 1¼ million people passed the grave of the Unknown Warrior, mourners from the Channel Islands, England, Ireland, the Isle of Man, Scotland, Wales, and countries abroad. A policeman recorded: "One old lady came from the far north of Scotland. She carried a bunch of withered flowers, and told me with tears in her eyes that the flowers came from a little garden which her boy had planted when he was only six."

On November 18 the grave was finally closed and filled with the earth from the battlefields of the western front. A temporary marble slab covered the opening, on which was inscribed A BRITISH WARRIOR WHO FELL IN THE GREAT WAR 1914–18. FOR KING AND COUNTRY. GREATER LOVE HATH NO MAN THAN THIS. Again, the Union Jack covered the tomb. The mourners continued their pilgrimage for almost a year, leaving their flowers and tributes.

For the following Armistice Day, in 1921, David Railton's Union Jack was removed from the tomb and dedicated at the high altar to all those men and women of Great Britain, Ireland, and the Dominions who had died in the Great War. It now hangs permanently in Saint George's Chapel, to the left of the Unknown Warrior. Its removal revealed the permanent tombstone, the stone that lies there today. It is of black marble from Belgium, inscribed with words composed by Dean Ryle set in an inlay of brass from melted-down shell casings. It reads:

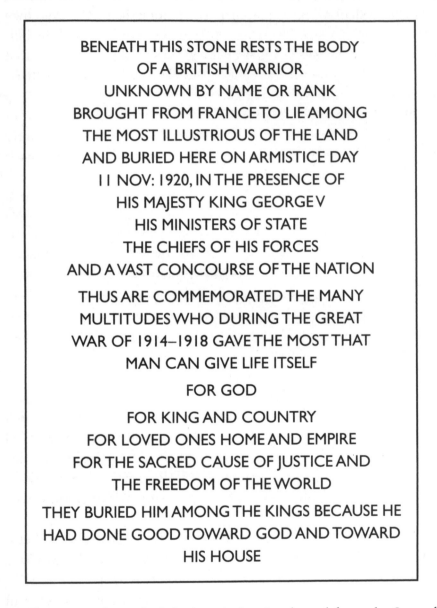

BENEATH THIS STONE RESTS THE BODY
OF A BRITISH WARRIOR
UNKNOWN BY NAME OR RANK
BROUGHT FROM FRANCE TO LIE AMONG
THE MOST ILLUSTRIOUS OF THE LAND
AND BURIED HERE ON ARMISTICE DAY
11 NOV: 1920, IN THE PRESENCE OF
HIS MAJESTY KING GEORGE V
HIS MINISTERS OF STATE
THE CHIEFS OF HIS FORCES
AND A VAST CONCOURSE OF THE NATION

THUS ARE COMMEMORATED THE MANY
MULTITUDES WHO DURING THE GREAT
WAR OF 1914–1918 GAVE THE MOST THAT
MAN CAN GIVE LIFE ITSELF

FOR GOD

FOR KING AND COUNTRY
FOR LOVED ONES HOME AND EMPIRE
FOR THE SACRED CAUSE OF JUSTICE AND
THE FREEDOM OF THE WORLD

THEY BURIED HIM AMONG THE KINGS BECAUSE HE
HAD DONE GOOD TOWARD GOD AND TOWARD
HIS HOUSE

The text at the end of the inscription is adapted from the Second Book of Chronicles, chapter 24, verse 16.

Within the borders of the tombstone are inlaid four other texts: across the top, "The Lord Knoweth Them That Are His"; along the left, "Greater Love Hath No Man Than This"; across the bottom, "In Christ Shall All Be Made Alive"; and along the right, "Unknown and Yet Well Known. Dying and Behold We Live." Around the borders of the grave are banked poppies of red silk, the red poppies that grow in profusion over the British battlefields fought in the defense of Belgium, France, and a free Europe.

Other nations have followed suit with their own Unknown Warrior or Unknown Soldier tombs. France, obviously the first country to be aware of the British intention, copied the concept the same year with a burial at the Arc de Triomphe in Paris.

The United States buried her Unknown Soldier at the Arlington National Cemetery in 1921. That same year, the United States awarded the first Unknown Warrior the Congressional Medal of Honor, while Great Britain awarded his American counterpart the Victoria Cross. On the northeast pillar of Westminster Abbey by the Unknown Warrior hangs the ship's bell of HMS *Verdun;* on the southeast pillar hangs the Congressional Medal of Honor. Australia, Canada, and New Zealand recently have made their own commemorations so that their subjects, too, have in their country an unknown serviceman returned home to represent all those lost abroad.

The tomb of the Unknown Warrior lies in one of the most beautiful buildings in all the world. Above rises a fan tracery of vaulted stone, inspired soaring curves that flow throughout the building to link the intricate roofs of the many chapels into a single harmonious church. The tomb below is purposefully simple, unpretentious, humble, requiring no triumphal arch, no eternal flame, not even a railing.

Yet it is the only grave in the floors of Westminster Abbey that is never walked on—by anyone, at any time, in any service. Coronations, weddings, baptisms, and funerals all proceed around it.

Today the Unknown Warrior has come to represent the dead of all conflicts, of World War I, World War II, those between, and all those after; the men, the women, at home and abroad.

And when we die,
All's over that is ours; and life burns on
Through other lovers, other lips.

—Rupert Brooke

Recommended
The Story of the Unknown Warrior by Michael Gavaghan
The Unknown Warrior and the Field of Remembrance
by James Wilkinson
Westminster Abbey, Westminster, London

Martin Luther King Jr.

Martin Luther King Jr. remains one of the best-known leaders of the American civil rights movement. During his life, he was a charismatic grassroots minister, one of those rare individuals who manage to inspire millions and leave a permanent mark on the world without ever holding high office. He was instrumental in achieving great changes in race relations in America, to the point where his life can be considered the end of one era and the beginning of another.

He was born in 1929 in Atlanta, Georgia, to a middle-class family. His father, Martin Luther King Sr., was a Baptist pastor, and his mother was a schoolteacher who taught her son to read before he went to school. King always had enough to eat and clothes to wear, but it would be a hard world for a boy of his color. For his first few years he played innocently with two white boys living nearby, as unaware of race as any other child of that age. At the age of six, his friends went to a white school, while King went to one for black children. The father of the boys told young Martin that his sons could no longer play with him, as he was "colored."

At home, his parents sat him down and explained some of the history of their people. They told him about slavery and the long struggle for equality before the law. It must have been a momentous day in his young life. Though slavery had ended decades before, segregation was still a common feature of life for blacks in America. As well as the schools, there were separate seats in shops and on buses, separate cinemas, separate churches, even separate drinking fountains. In all ways, black people were treated as second-class citizens or even worse—lynchings were not uncommon in the southern states, and many blacks lived in fear of the late-night knock at the door.

It was not long after that first day of school that Martin was riding in his father's car when he was pulled over by a traffic cop.

"Boy, show me your license!" the man said. Reverend King replied calmly, "Let me make it clear to you that you aren't talking to a boy. If you persist in referring to me as a boy, I will be forced to act as if I don't hear a word you're saying." The policeman booked him for having the nerve to answer back to a white man.

His father had once led a successful protest against pay inequality for black and white teachers in Atlanta. As a Baptist preacher and as a father, he believed strongly that the black population could raise themselves up through education and responsibility. Perhaps because Martin Junior had been fortunate in his own upbringing, he would spend his life seeking those opportunities for all black men and women in America.

When he was fifteen, Martin Luther King used his summer vacation to take two jobs. He worked with the poorest black laborers, loading and unloading freight goods. For a boy with his background, it was a different world—and one where black men were harshly treated and paid less than white men for exactly the same work.

For a time, King felt a great resentment against white people, but his father's faith had taught him that a strong man could turn the other cheek and that enemies should be forgiven. For a time, King wanted to be a lawyer or a doctor, but like his father and grandfather before him, he found that his path lay in helping those around him. When he worked in tobacco fields the following summer, he was asked to lead the prayers for the men. He had a great gift for oratory, and he felt the call to ministry.

At school, King was hardworking and a voracious reader. He jumped two grades and at the age of fifteen enrolled at Morehouse College in Atlanta, then the best theological college for black students in America. In the North, segregation was less obvious and he took part in some interracial discussions. His harsh feelings toward whites were eased during his time there, in part after vacations spent working with white farm laborers.

Like many teenagers, for a time he rebelled against his faith, seeing it as irrelevant to the struggle for equality. He debated the issues with the president of Morehouse and his professor of religion, both of whom saw religion as a vital part of the struggle for rights. Despite his period of doubt, King found his faith refreshed and was ordained as a Baptist minister at the age of just nineteen.

After Morehouse, he went to Crozer Theological Seminary in Pennsylvania, to take a degree in divinity. There, he was able to study the works of some of the great thinkers, from Walter Rauschenbusch and Thoreau to Mahatma Gandhi. King was particularly impressed by Gandhi's ideas on using nonviolent civil disobedience to effect social change. While at Crozer, King made valedictorian and was elected president of his predominantly white class. He graduated in 1951 at the age of twenty-two. Two years later he married Coretta Scott, a graduate student, and moved to Montgomery, Alabama, where King had accepted a position as pastor of the Dexter Avenue Baptist Church. The following year he received his doctorate from Boston University.

King would spend fifteen hours a week preparing his sermons. He knew the role his church could play in the black community and saw no conflict between politics and religion. Martin and Coretta were both passionate about improving civil rights for black people, but they needed a cause to champion, a spark. It was not long in coming.

At the end of 1955, one of the most famous incidents of the civil rights struggle took place in Montgomery. Alabama's segregation laws were then among the strictest in America, and the buses had separate sections for black and white passengers. In the event

that there were too many white passengers, black people were told to get off. Even then, black people were not allowed to sit in the same row with white passengers, so if one white man sat, black men and women had to stand and leave seats empty. There had even been incidents of black passengers being shot by the white drivers if they protested.

Resentment had been growing for some time. Claudette Colvin, a fifteen-year-old girl, was one of the first to make a stand. She was handcuffed and dragged off a bus for refusing to give up her seat. Others had made similar protests, to no avail. There had even been a boycott of the buses in Louisiana, but without strong leadership to organize the black community, it only lasted ten days.

On December 1, Rosa Parks was returning home from work. She was told to give up her seat for a white man, and she refused. She knew she was likely to be mistreated or arrested, but she had a quiet courage and refused to move. She was taken off the bus to jail, and local black ministers, King among them, met to organize a response. He had his cause, and crucially, Rosa Parks was a woman of integrity and good character who could not be easily dismissed or attacked. Despite being only twenty-six, King was quickly elected spokesman of the new Montgomery Improvement Association. He had just minutes to prepare a speech to several thousand black people who had gathered to hear their community leaders.

Speaking with the fluency and force that would become his hallmarks, King held the crowd in the palm of his hand as he told them: "There comes a time when people get tired of being trampled over by the iron feet of oppression." They cheered his oratory, and he made them understand that this was to be a peaceful protest, giving no opportunity for the state to respond with force and greater violence.

Even with the crowd behind him, the demands they made to the bus company were not shocking: the employment of black bus drivers, better manners from white drivers, and first-come-first-serve seating. It was hardly a call to revolution, but the bus company refused every point and the boycott was on.

It was a simple enough idea, that black men and women, who

made up 70 percent of the bus passengers, should walk to work or share the small number of cars available until the bus company agreed to their demands. However, its impact would shake and change the nation.

The volunteers who drove for the car pool, King among them, were harassed and arrested by police from the beginning. King's house was also firebombed, but the nonviolent boycott went on.

In February 1956, with the boycott still in force, a grand jury accused the Montgomery Improvement Association of breaking an antiboycott law. Eighty-nine MIA leaders, including twenty-four ministers, immediately gave themselves up at the local courthouse. The boycott began to attract national media interest, and as spokesman, King was always ready to address the wider audience on justice and equality.

In the end, the boycott lasted 381 days. Eventually, the massive loss of revenue and a decision by the U.S. Supreme Court forced the Montgomery Bus Company to accept integration. Martin Luther King had reached a national and international stage, achieving fame and recognition that he would use to further the cause for the rest of his life.

Shortly afterward, King was one of the founding members of the Southern Christian Leadership Conference (SCLC). The aim of the group was to bring about the national abolition of segregation by nonviolent means. As with Mahatma Gandhi in India, a commitment to nonviolence had given the moral high ground to the Montgomery boycott. The SCLC's well-publicized motto was "Not one hair of one head of one person should be harmed."

As a tactic, it drew the sting from many of their opponents, who would rather have depicted King and his colleagues as dangerous rabble-rousers and a threat to peace and national security. Such avowed aims also brought in funding from the mostly white northern liberal community. Crucially, the SCLC still centered on churches and pastors such as King. Churches were the heart of black communities all over America, places where men and women could congregate and discuss political issues without fear of harassment.

There were obstacles in his way, not least from other organizations such as the National Association for the Advancement of Colored People (NAACP), which preferred to fight battles in the courts and overturn unfair laws rather than organize mass protests. King recruited individual pastors, knowing that through their influence he could reach their congregations as well.

In 1957 the movement to end segregation was gaining pace but against massive opposition. The integration crisis at Little Rock Central High School in Arkansas was internationally publicized. Under federal legislation, schools could not be segregated by race. On the first day of the school year, nine black students, carefully chosen by the school board, showed up to attend the all-white school.

That day the governor of Arkansas, Orval Faubus, chose to send 270 National Guardsmen to the school, where white protesters were lined up to bar the black students. He claimed he called in the guard to prevent the disorder that could follow black students joining a white school, but the guards seemed to think their job was to prevent them entering at all. The nine young students showed up on the second day accompanied by two white and two black ministers, but the guard refused them entry. News cameras captured the scene and the abuse they suffered at the hands of the angry white crowd. When they returned to the school another day, hate mobs showed up ready for violence. President Eisenhower was forced to send eleven hundred paratroopers to restore order, while the black students were smuggled out to safety. It was a deeply shocking event, and Governor Faubus then closed all schools in Little Rock rather than accept desegregation. He was re-elected for four more terms after that, showing the sort of opposition men like Martin Luther King had to overcome just to be accepted as citizens.

In that same year and perhaps influenced by the incidents at Little Rock, the 1957 Civil Rights Act was passed. Its stated aim was to increase black voter registration. At that time, the black population was around 10 percent of the whole and only 20 percent of those were registered voters. Martin Luther King wanted black people to be part of the democratic process. Without voting, he knew change would be even slower and more painful.

The struggle was never going to be easy—not least because only whites could serve on a jury, so it was practically impossible to get a conviction on race-related crimes in some parts of the country.

Nevertheless, King drove himself to exhaustion. Over eleven years, he wrote five books and countless articles, spoke at more than twenty-five hundred public gatherings, and traveled some six million miles. As well as President Eisenhower and Vice President Nixon, he met heads of state in countries as far away as Ghana and India. He was a visible figurehead of the civil rights movement and also the prime target for those who wanted no change at all.

In 1960, King became involved in nonviolent "sit-in" protests, which involved thousands of black students going to restaurants and department stores where black people were usually refused service. Inspired by King's writing on nonviolent protest, they then sat in silence and refused to respond even if struck. Those protests were extremely successful and ended segregation in restaurants, libraries, and other institutions in more than twenty southern cities. King himself took part in a sit-in and was arrested with fifty-one others and jailed.

The judge who heard his case had met King before. He had in fact given King a one-year suspended sentence for driving in Georgia with Alabama plates. That period of probation was still running, and although the charges for the sit-in were dropped, the delighted judge sentenced King to four months of hard labor.

When the news became public, presidential candidate John F. Kennedy called Coretta King and offered to help. His brother Senator Robert Kennedy then called both the governor and the judge and secured King's release on bail. King was more than a little relieved to be out of Georgia State Prison. Both he and his father publicly supported the Kennedy bid for the presidency, and on November 8, 1960, Kennedy won by a margin of only 112,000 votes—out of 69 million votes cast.

Between 1960 and 1963, King was highly active in the civil rights struggle. At one point he was trapped inside a church by a white mob and had to be rescued by the National Guard, while his supporters were beaten up, jailed, and even shot as they tried to carry out nonviolent protests. Again and again, white and black moderates told him that he was going too fast, that they should wait a little longer, but he was impatient for real change.

In 1963 he was arrested and jailed again in Birmingham, Alabama, for taking part in a demonstration against segregation in department stores. At that time, Birmingham was a hotbed of Ku Klux Klan activity and there were many incidents of brutality against black residents, including firebombing their homes. Once again, King put himself in danger. In prison, he wrote his famous "Letter from a Birmingham Jail." It is almost a manifesto for nonviolent protest and a warning to those who chose to ignore the winds of change beginning to sweep the country. More than a million copies were distributed, particularly in the North.

Rather than make King a martyr, on that occasion the judge changed the charge to one of criminal contempt, which meant King left court a free man. He immediately jumped back to the fray. His supporters recruited thousands of black schoolchildren to join the protests, and the media watched in horror as police dogs and fire hoses were turned on the crowds. Not long afterward, President Kennedy made a promise that the issue of race would have no place in American life or law and prepared a new civil rights bill to be submitted to Congress. In January 1963, King was *Time* magazine's Man of the Year, the first black man to be so honored.

At last, King saw the approach of the sort of federal law he had always wanted. He had long said that it might not have been possible to legislate for integration but that it certainly *was* possible to legislate against segregation. Nonetheless, he would not sit back and wait for it to happen. In August 1963 he organized a march on Washington, D.C., of 250,000 men, women, and children, all in support of the new bill. It was on that hot night, by the Lincoln Memorial, that Martin Luther King gave his most famous speech.

"I have a dream that one day on the red hills of Georgia, sons of former slaves and sons of former slaveholders will be able to sit down together at the table of brotherhood." He spoke with all the power of a southern preacher, building to a stirring climax of words and ideas that moved many of those who heard him to tears as he finished, "And when this happens . . . black men and white men, Jews and Gentiles, Protestants and Catholics, will be able to join hands and sing in the words of the old Negro spiritual: 'Free at last. Free at last. Thank God Almighty, we are free at last.'"

In November 1963, President Kennedy was assassinated and the country mourned.

Though it did not go far enough for King, Kennedy's civil rights bill was passed in 1964 under President Johnson. That same year, King received the Nobel Peace Prize and donated the prize money to the civil rights movement.

His work continued, and King broadened his cause to fight against poverty and oppose the Vietnam War. Overall King was arrested around twenty times and assaulted on at least four occasions. It did not stop him. Then, in April 1968, he went to Tennessee to lead a protest march for equal pay for black sanitation workers. There had been always been threats against his life from white extremists—even his plane to Memphis was delayed because of a bomb threat. It was simply part of the landscape in which he had chosen to work.

King was standing on his hotel balcony with friends that night. James Earl Ray, a white man with a string of petty convictions, approached him and shot him once in the head. The killer escaped for a time and was eventually apprehended at Heathrow Airport in London. He would later be sentenced to ninety-nine years in prison, increased to one hundred after an escape attempt.

Martin Luther King didn't live to see the greater part of his work come to fruition. He would never have dared hope that within the lifetime of his supporters, a black man could become president of the United States. Coretta King had died in 2006, but the Reverend Jesse Jackson, who had been with King at that hotel in 1968, wept as the results of the 2008 presidential election were announced.

Recommended
Stride Toward Freedom by Martin Luther King Jr.
A Call to Conscience: The Landmark Speeches of Dr. Martin Luther King, Jr., edited by Claybourne Carson
Martin Luther King Jr. by Vincent P. Franklin

Heroes

When someone rows across the Atlantic, conquers Everest, or runs seven marathons in seven days, he is admired across the world. Our lives are gladdened by the achievement, and we feel that person has done something great. Such people are heroes because they inspire the rest of us, even if it's just for a moment.

Yet there is a second definition of *hero*: one who accomplishes something noble, risking it all in the process. Horatio Nelson may be the best example, as he lost his life defending against a tyranny that would have overrun the world. Most people can see the difference between Nelson and a baseball team winning the World Series.

At no point do those definitions suggest that a hero must be likable. The heroism is in the life, in the achievement across just a short span of years, not in the men or women themselves, and whether they were a good friend, father, or mother. Good men sometimes do bad things, and it is even possible that many great achievements come about because an individual is attempting to atone for some sin, real or imagined, in the past.

When the word is overused, it does reduce its impact, but that is not necessarily a bad thing. We cannot all stand against tyranny, though perhaps more of us should when we encounter its cold hands on a daily basis. Yet if a man is described as a hero for saving a child on a frozen lake, most of us can see that we could be that man. It is heroism within the bounds of possibility.

Being aware that courage is still admired is not a danger to society—far from it. A "have-a-go hero" is a popular phrase for one who risks life and limb to stop a mugging or burglary, or even to have a word with a few kids causing trouble. It is an obvious truth to say there may be risk involved in such an action, but if every good man or woman turned away with eyes downcast, well, that would scorn the memories of Edith Cavell, Robert Scott, and Helen Keller, who would have waded in, eyesight or not.

However we abuse the word, heroism will never be common or easy. The peculiar truth about humanity is that we deal with fear on a daily basis and that it often conquers us. That does not matter as long as we recognize that there are times when we must not "step off the curb" to let someone pass or something terrible happen.

It is true that only a coward can be brave, as a man who feels no fear has conquered nothing. It is also true that when one person speaks up to stop some wrong, others often join in, desperately relieved that, at last, someone said something. It is not easy to be the one to speak up or to step in. If it was, we would not value and admire those who do. One final truth remains beyond the petty irritations of life in which we lose ourselves: all that is necessary for the triumph of evil is for good men to do nothing.

The men and women in this book were sometimes possessed of incredible self-confidence and personal belief. Others doubted their every action to the point where they could hardly act at all. For some, their heroism is contained in a single moment, while others seem to have lived a life that stands out like a thread of gold. It may not be possible to live like Nelson, but we can be inspired by his life and others like it. We can know that in our history is the blood of greatness, and in our culture, for all its flaws and dark misdeeds, there can also be light.

Index

Note: **Bold page locators** indicate chapter entries.

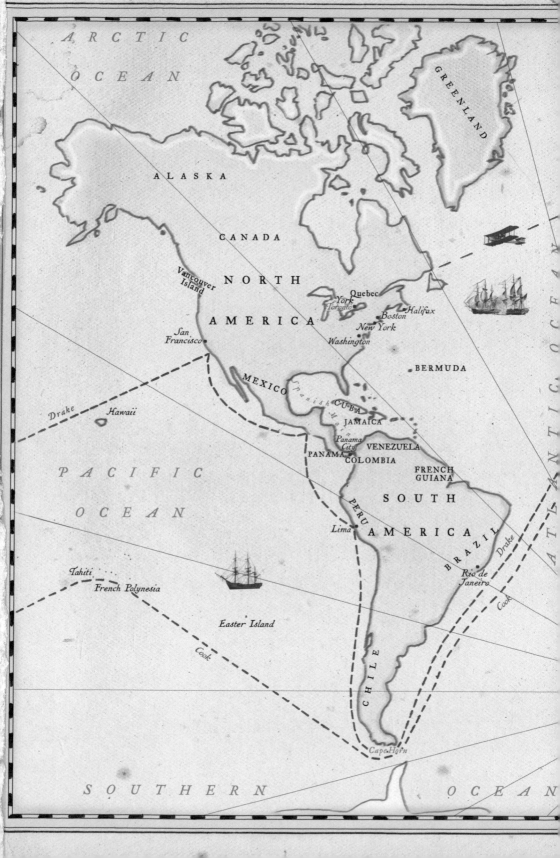

ARCTIC OCEAN

GREENLAND

ALASKA

CANADA

NORTH AMERICA

Vancouver Island

San Francisco

MEXICO

Quebec
York
Toronto
Boston
New York
Washington
Halifax

BERMUDA

Drake

Hawaii

Spanish Main

CUBA
JAMAICA
Panama City
PANAMA
COLOMBIA
VENEZUELA
FRENCH GUIANA

PACIFIC OCEAN

ATLANTIC OCEAN

PERU

Lima

SOUTH AMERICA

BRAZIL

Rio de Janeiro

Drake

Cook

Tahiti
French Polynesia

Easter Island

Cook

CHILE

Cape Horn

SOUTHERN OCEAN

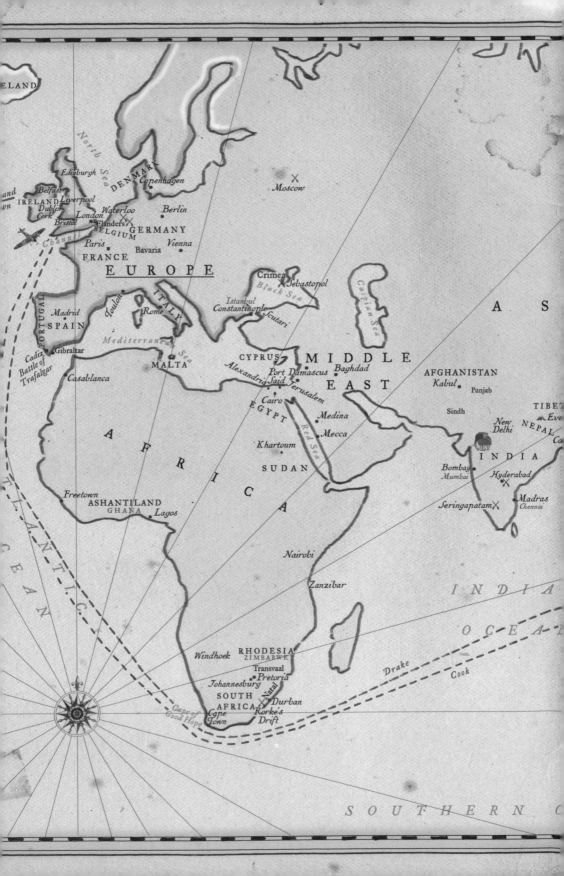